OLD NORSE LITERATURE AND MYTHOLOGY: A SYMPOSIUM

Old Norse Literature and Mythology

A SYMPOSIUM

Edited by Edgar C. Polomé

PUBLISHED FOR THE DEPARTMENT OF GERMANIC LANGUAGES OF THE UNIVERSITY OF TEXAS AT AUSTIN BY THE UNIVERSITY OF TEXAS PRESS, AUSTIN & LONDON

Standard Book Number 292–78386–8
Library of Congress Catalog Card Number 69–19755

Printed by The University of Texas Printing Division, Austin
Bound by Universal Bookbindery, Inc., San Antonio

TO

LEE M. HOLLANDER

AS A TOKEN OF FRIENDSHIP FOR THE MAN

AS WELL AS OF RESPECT FOR THE SCHOLAR

"Happy is he who hath won him
  the love and liking of all;

Happy is he who hath won him
  both winning ways and wisdom."

Hávamál, sts. 8–9, *The Poetic Edda*
Trans. Lee M. Hollander

FOREWORD

THE PAPERS PUBLISHED in this volume were written in honor of Professor Lee M. Hollander. Focusing on Old Norse literature and mythology, they illustrate the various facets of his creative activity in the fields in which he has made his major contributions. But Dr. Hollander is also an indefatigable translator of Scandinavian and German literature. Therefore, the first essay in the series covers the broader subject of the techniques and problems of translation from the Scandinavian.

Five of the papers contained in this volume were first presented orally at the Sixth Germanic Languages Symposium held at The University of Texas at Austin on November 30 and December 1 and 2, 1964. They were read before a large audience of visitors and local participants, who joined with the authors to pay homage to the great scholar. The lively and challenging discussion which followed the readings was thoroughly enjoyed by Dr. Hollander and all the participants. On November 30, the papers by Einar Haugen and Erik Wahlgren were presented, followed by those of Paul Schach, on December 1, and of A. Margaret Arent and E. O. G. Turville-Petre, on December 2. Preprints of the preliminary versions of the papers had been circulated, and distinguished specialists had been invited to take an active part in the ensuing discussion. They included Ernst Alfred Philippson of the University of Illinois, Elmer A. Antonsen of the University of Iowa, and Foster W. Blaisdell, Jr., of Indiana University.

While the papers by Einar Haugen and E. O. G. Turville-Petre are reproduced here with only minor changes, the essays by Erik Wahlgren and Paul Schach were subjected to a very thorough revision and grew into small monographs. Moreover, the titles of two of the essays were slightly modified: Paul Schach's contribution was read under the shorter title of "*Tristrams saga* in Islandic Literature," and E. O. G. Turville-Petre changed the title "Fertility Rites" to "Fertility of Beast and Soil." The contribution of A. Margaret Arent on "Early Germanic Literature as an Amalgam of *Mnemesis* and *Poesis*" was rewritten into a substantial study on "The Heroic Pattern."

Three additional essays are included in the present volume as further marks of respect and consideration for the outstanding scholarship of Dr. Hollander. They deal with subjects that are close to his heart, since they tackle some problems of the interpretation of the *Edda* and of the technique of skaldic poetry.

In presenting the papers of the Symposium and the additional contributions to the scholarly world at large, I hope the outstanding contribution of Lee M. Hollander to Scandinavian studies will be further enhanced by this illustration of the profound impact he has on present-day scholarship. May he continue to influence these studies as fruitfully for many more years!

Edgar C. Polomé

CONTENTS

ILLUSTRATIONS

Following page 132

Permission to reproduce photographs from the following sources is gratefully acknowledged:

Plates 1, 2, 15: Statens Historiska Museet
Plates 3, 4, 19, 26: The Trustees of the British Museum
Plates 5, 6, 7, 8, 11, 12, 13, 14, 22, 23, 24:
K. Hjalmar Stolpe and T. J. Arne. *Graffältet vid Vendel.* Monografiserie, No. 3. Stockholm: Kungl. Vitterhets Historie och Antikvitets Akademien, 1912.
Plates 9, 10, 25:
Greta Arwidsson. *Die Gräberfunde von Valsgärde.* I: *Valsgärde* 6 (Plate 10). II: *Valsgärde* 8 (Plates 9 and 25). In the series *Acta Musei Antiquitatem Septentrionalium, Regiae Universitatis Upsaliensis,* I and IV, ed. Sune Lindqvist. Uppsala Universitets Museum för nordiska fornsaker. Uppsala and Stockholm: Almqvist och Wiksells Botryckeri, A. B.; København: Ejnar Munksgaard; Berlin: W. B. Schwan, G. M. B. H., 1942.
Plate 16:
Sune Lindqvist, "Vendelhjälmarnas ursprung," *Fornvännen,* Årgången 20 (1925). Published by Kungl. Vitterhets Historie och Antikvitets Akademien, Stockholm.
Plates 17, 18, 27:
Karl Hauck, "Alemannische Denkmäler der vorchristlichen Adelskultur," *Zeitschrift für württembergische Landesgeschichte,* Vol. 16. Stuttgart: W. Kohlhammer Verlag, 1957
Plate 21:
Nils Åberg, "Uppsala högars datering," *Fornvännen,* Årgången 42 (1947). Published by Kungl. Vitterhets Historie och Antikvitets Akademien, Stockholm.

OLD NORSE LITERATURE AND
MYTHOLOGY: A SYMPOSIUM

On Translating from the Scandinavian

EINAR HAUGEN

There is a large body of English translations from the Scandinavian languages and a century-old tradition in the field. Yet there has never been a comprehensive study of the problems involved, or even a complete bibliography of such translations. Only in the last few years have partial bibliographies begun appearing.[1] This symposium would seem to be an auspicious occasion to make a few remarks on the subject, in view of Professor Hollander's long activity as a translator, marked most recently by the appearance of his monumental *Heimskringla*.[2] While most of his previous translations have also been from Old Norse–Icelandic, we should not forget that he was the first English translator of Kierkegaard and that he long ago brought out dramatic translations from the Norwegian of Bjørnstjerne Bjørnson, the Danish of Holger Drachmann, and the Modern Icelandic of Indríði Einarsson.[3]

[1] See notes 5 and 7 below.

[2] Snorri Sturluson, *Heimskringla: History of the Kings of Norway,* trans. Lee M. Hollander (Austin, Texas: University of Texas Press, 1964).

[3] *Selections from the Writings of Søren Kierkegaard* (Austin: University of Texas Bulletin No. 2326; reprinted as an Anchor paperback, 1960); Bjørnstjerne Bjørnson, *Beyond Human Power,* in T. H. Dickinson (ed.), *Chief Contemporary Dramatists* (Boston and New York: Houghton Mifflin and Co., 1915), I, 573–597, and "When the New Wine Blooms," *Poet Lore,* XXII (1911), 1–78; Holger Drachmann, "Renaissance, Melodrama," *Poet Lore,* XIX (1908), 369–419; Indríði Einarsson, "Sword and Crozier," *Poet Lore,* XXIII (1912), 225–283.

I

Translators generally have a bad press and are pursued by cheap witticisms, like the Italian one that describes them as traducers (*traditore traduttore*). But the very unity of Western culture depends on translations such as those of the Bible and of the Greek and Roman classics. These have served as models and stimuli of literary endeavor in every Western nation, as far back as the first known literary translation, which according to B. Q. Morgan was the Latin version of Homer's *Iliad* by Livius Andronicus in 250 B.C.[4] The concept of world literature is inconceivable without translations, and the growth of "one world" should bring with it an ever increasing number of them. Perhaps the most useful service bilinguals can perform for their dual language communities is to translate the classics of one for the benefit of the other.

For small countries, like those of Scandinavia, the importance of translation is far greater than for the larger ones. Their literary image abroad is established, if at all, by translations, since few will take the trouble to learn their languages. The Norwegian poet Henrik Wergeland long ago bemoaned the fate of the poet chained to a minor language. Today the Scandinavian countries are overwhelmed by a deluge of foreign books in translation, which tend to drown out the native product. According to the latest volume of the *Index Translationum* (1961), a total of 2,650 books were translated from English into the Scandinavian languages in that year. The heading "Literature" accounted for 1,932 of these (though most of them would not qualify as art); under this same heading there were only 32 translations in the opposite direction, from Scandinavian into English! The disproportion has become so marked that the matter has even reached the attention of the Scandinavian governments. In 1954 the Nordic Council advised its Cultural Commission to study the feasibility of subsidizing a series of Scandinavian classics in English.[5]

[4] *On Translation,* ed. Reuben A. Brower (Cambridge, Massachusetts: Harvard Press, 1959), p. 271 (hereafter abbreviated as *OT*).

[5] *Oversettelse til engelsk av nordisk skjønlitteratur. Innstilling fra Nordisk Kulturkommisjon angående Nordisk Råds Rekommandasjon nr. 2/1954* (Oslo, n.d.), 154 pp. After rejection of a grandiose plan for a five-foot shelf of eighty volumes, a more modest plan was devised for fifteen volumes of twentieth-century classics. This plan was successfully negotiated with the University of Wisconsin Press and is now in

To see the importance for Scandinavia of this and other activities in the field of translation, one need only contemplate the figures on Scandinavian teaching in this country.[6] While a number of institutions teach some Scandinavian language, the roster of our pupils is infinitesimal compared to that of the major languages. For every one who learns to read Ibsen and Strindberg in the original, hundreds are capable of reading Goethe and Racine (whether they eventually do read them or not). In translation, however, some of the Scandinavian classics are read at least as much as those of many larger countries. Courses in Scandinavian literature in translation are a popular part of the curriculum in every Scandinavian department in the country. If only as reading material in these courses, translations are urgently needed. To know the needs in this area one can now turn to the histories of Scandinavian literature published by the American-Scandinavian Foundation in the past few years.[7] These have diligently listed the translations available of all works mentioned, but one need not study the lists long before discovering what huge gaps there are. Many important works are untranslated, or badly translated, or out of print.

One could wish that some foundation with great financial resources would study the problem and provide support for a program of systematic translation. While the American-Scandinavian Foundation has done yeoman service, especially in the field of Old Norse, it is hampered by lack of men and money. It is not easy to find people who can and will perform these difficult and delicate tasks. The rewards are low, both financially and academically. A man like Hollander should have been subsidized for the last thirty years just to give us a complete corpus of Old Icelandic literature, an American Thule Series. He has

process of realization under the title "The Nordic Translation Series" (13 volumes have been published to date). For statistics on translations see *Index Translationum* (Paris, 1932–1940; N.S., UNESCO, 1949 ff.).

[6] As presented in the latest report by Hedin Bronner and Gösta Franzén, *Scandinavian Studies,* XXXIX (1967), 345–367.

[7] Harald Beyer, *A History of Norwegian Literature,* trans. and ed. Einar Haugen (New York: New York University Press, 1956); P. M. Mitchell, *A History of Danish Literature* (New York: American-Scandinavian Foundation, 1957); Stefán Einarsson, *A History of Icelandic Literature* (Baltimore: Johns Hopkins Press, 1957); Alrik Gustafson, *A History of Swedish Literature* (Minneapolis: University of Minnesota Press, 1961). See also Erling Grønland, *Norway in English* (Oslo: Norwegian Universities Press, 1961); Elias Bredsdorff, *Danish Literature in English Translation: A Bibliography* (Copenhagen: Munksgaard, 1950); Nils Afzelius, *Books in English on Sweden* (3rd ed; Stockholm: Swedish Institute, 1951), and *Oversettelse* (see note 5).

gone far in this direction as it is, but no one man can encompass all the tasks that await.[8] Five countries are all pouring out an annual flood of books, many of them well worth translating. Then there is the great treasury of the old literature, locked up in its ancient garb even for the Scandinavians outside of Iceland. The medieval language offers the translators an entirely different set of problems from the modern languages, which have been adjusted to modern culture through a long period of contact marked by extensive translation from the major European languages. For the medieval language, the translator faces many of the same problems that beset the translators of Hebrew, Greek, and Latin classics. It requires true scholarship and deep devotion to produce good English versions of the Eddas and the sagas, not to speak of the tortured skaldic verse.[9]

II

There is an enormous literature on the theory of translation, including some modest essays by American translators from the Scandinavian. The burgeoning interest in machine translation has inspired a great deal of writing in recent years, some of which even throws light on human translation.[10] Two important symposiums, held at Harvard and at The University of Texas, have explored aspects of literary translation, with contributions from a wide variety of scholars and professional translators.[11]

A computer translates like a schoolboy, by matching word to word and applying some simple rules of grammar. Dictionaries and gram-

[8] See Appendix B for translations by Dr. Hollander.

[9] For a discussion of the problem of skaldic translation see Hollander's "The Translation of Skaldic Poetry," *Scandinavian Studies,* XVIII (1945), 233–240, and the commentary by Felix Genzmer, "Ist die Skaldendichtung übersetzbar?" *Journal of English and Germanic Philology,* XLVII (1948), 323–333. This exchange confirms the view that it is easier to translate from Scandinavian into German than into English.

[10] Y. R. Chao, "Translation without Machine," pp. 504–510, and N. D. Andreyev, "Linguistic Aspects of Translation," pp. 625–634, in *Proceedings of the Ninth International Congress of Linguists*, ed. Horace G. Lunt (The Hague: Mouton, 1964); Eugene Nida, "Principles of Translation as Exemplified by Bible Translating" (*OT,* pp. 11–31), and *Bible Translating* (New York: American Bible Society, 1947; rev. ed., 1961).

[11] *OT* (essays delivered at the 1959 Harvard symposium); William Arrowsmith and Robert Shattuck (eds.), *The Craft and Context of Translation* (Austin, Texas: University of Texas Press, 1961, essays delivered at the 1959 University of Texas symposium).

mars were indeed the original mechanical translators. The result is a so-called literal translation, of which the medieval gloss or the schoolboy's crib are the simplest examples.[12] A true bilingual does not match word for word but relives the text in the other language by matching experience to experience.[13] The result is a "free" translation, which may turn into a mere paraphrase of the original, the same "idea" in totally different form. If we regard the literal and the free translation as embodying opposite principles, we may say that *a faithful translation must be both literal and free.* That is, it must convey in the new language both the *content* and the *form* of the message: not only what the original says, but also the way in which it is said.

There is an old saying that "translations are like women, the more beautiful the less faithful."[14] This need not be true, at least for translations, if faithful is distinguished from literal. A literal translation is almost certain to be ugly, since it will violate the accepted usages of the target language. It is a prime demand that a translation should read like an original and stand on its own as a work of art.[15] But, if the means by which it accomplishes this end are totally different from those of the original, an important element of the original has been lost. Shattuck insists that "translation does not consist solely in reducing all foreign works to the limitations of, say, English, but equally in reshaping and enlarging English to reach meanings which it has not yet had to grapple with."[16] The translator's dilemma is thus the problem of how to render both form and content in the new language in such a way that

[12] *International Journal of American Linguistics,* XX (1954): C. F. Hockett, "Translation via Immediate Constituents," pp. 313–315, and C. F. Voegelin, "Multiple Stage Translation," pp. 271–280.

[13] Cf. W. Van Quine: "The bilingual translator works by an intrasubjective communing of a split personality" (*OT,* p. 167); N. D. Andreyev: "Man translates, applying his understanding of the input and the output text; i.e., by correlating the given text and the formed one with his past and present conscious and subconscious perception of reality" (*Proceedings,* ed. Lunt, p. 625).

[14] Benedetto Croce in his *Aesthetic* (trans. Douglas Ainslie [2nd ed.; London: Macmillan and Co., 1922], p. 68) speaks of "faithful ugliness and faithless beauty."

[15] Croce (*ibid.,* p. 73) writes: "The translation called good is an approximation which has original value as a work of art and can stand by itself." Marianne Moore is quoted by Achilles Fang (*OT,* p. 133 n. 1) as saying: "The first requisite of a translation, it seems to me, is that it should not sound like a translation." See also Samuel Butler (*OT,* p. 278) and T. H. Warren (*OT,* p. 277).

[16] Arrowsmith and Shattuck (eds.), *The Craft and Context,* p. 152. Although classical translations may have this effect on the language, the principle can be abused; Samuel Johnson (in the Preface to his *Dictionary*) inveighed against the "corruption" visited upon the English language by translators.

it will have the same effect on its readers as the original had on *its* readers. This demand has been formulated time and again and may be called *the law of comparable effect*.[17] This law raises further questions: what effect does the original have on its readers, and what are the means by which this effect is produced? How can one possibly find comparable means in another language?

Successful translation depends on the translator's ability, first, to interpret the original text correctly and, second, to reproduce his interpretation correctly in another language. The first task is receptive and is akin to that of the literary critic; the second is productive, and akin to that of the original writer. Both are difficult in direct proportion to the inherent difficulties of the original text and the gap in thought and expression between the two languages.

A *correct interpretation* of the original involves a full understanding not only of its content but also of its form. The content may be elusive enough, especially in the case of older cultures. Misinterpretation is possible at every level of language, from the nuances of grammar and syntax to those of lexicon and cultural context. Many a time the translator would like to summon the author from the shades to catechize him on his exact meaning; but even he might be stumped for an answer. Far more difficult is the precise interpretation of form. Here the author would be of little help, unless he were also a highly self-conscious critic of his own work. But any work of art is at least as much a form as it is a content.[18] Form may be a matter of sound structure, a rich interplay of rhyme and rhythm, of assonance and alliteration. It may be manifested in the choice and arrangement of grammatical and syntactic devices. Or it may be expressed in the juxtaposition of words and idioms, subtly woven into patterns of meaning and style.

A *correct reproduction* is hampered by the fact that languages differ both in content and form so that their words need not be identical either in shape or in effect. Every language maps the universe in its own way or even creates its own universe. The content of each language is a reflection of the culture of its speakers, and the translator is driven to

[17] E.g., Edgar Allan Poe in his *Marginalia* of 1844–1849 (*Works* [New York: W. J. Widdleton, 1871], III, 534): "We should so render the original that the version should impress the people for whom it is intended just as the original impresses the people for whom it (the original) is intended."

[18] Cf. Edouard Roditi: "The spirit of poetry resides entirely in its body." *Poetry,* LX [1942], 32–38). Paul Valéry declared accordingly that a poet "is inseparable from the speech of his nation" (*OT,* p. 74).

make comparisons between partly incommensurable cultures. If this is difficult, how much more of a problem it is to find expressions which have a comparable stylistic effect in two different traditions of literary composition. The trap into which many translators fall is that they are deceived by surface similarities of form: they reproduce a meter, a rhyme, an alliteration, a cognate, without considering whether such formal similarities do in fact have a comparable effect. A purely formal fidelity is worse than any infidelity.

Translators, like other people, have in general a much wider passive than active command of the languages they know. They are therefore likely to find the task of interpretation easier than that of reproduction. Yet it is the latter that is most important. For the subtlest understanding of the original is futile unless the product that issues from the translator's pen demonstrates some of the original qualities to the reader of the translation. A tone-deaf translator is bad, but a mute or halting one is worse. This is the weakness of the native speaker of the original language as a translator. The effects of the original may be so desperately clear to him that he is inhibited from even attempting a translation, since no translation can reproduce them for him. If he does attempt it, he may lack completely the skill in production which enables him to find not merely similar, but actually equivalent translations. Productive skill is more likely to be found in the native speaker of the language of translation. What he loses in interpretation may be more than made up for by his skill in production. The danger is only that he will stray so far from his original that he has in effect not reproduced but paraphrased it and thereby created his own original intead of a translation.

III

The Scandinavian languages, being closely cognate with English, are deceptively similar to it in their basic structures. They have the same stress patterns, much the same grammar and syntax, thousands of similar-sounding words, and large areas of common culture. Yet there is a major barrier between the two, which consciously or unconsciously affects the translator from Scandinavian into English. This may briefly be characterized as the Mediterranean element in English. While the Scandinavian languages, aside from Icelandic, also have a great many Greek, Latin, or French words, these have not in the same intimate way entered into the very heart of the language. One simply cannot avoid the Romance-classical vocabulary in an English sentence without conscious circumlocution. Part of the strength of English as an international language is that it is a kind of home-grown Esperanto, a language in which every literate user learns to juggle two basically different systems, the Germanic and the classical, in an intricate and subtly woven pattern. Its literary ideals have been shaped through centuries of intimate association with French and Latin models, which in Scandinavia have usually been filtered through German. It is universally acknowledged that German translations of the Scandinavian are better than those in English; to the extent that this is true, it may be associated with this purely linguistic barrier between Scandinavian and English.

One consequence for the translator is that he will be tempted to imitate in English what he conceives to be an artless simplicity of the original with equally artless cognates and parallel constructions in English. On the other hand he may fail to perceive the subtlety of the original if he is not a native reader. He will then produce what sounds in English like an inarticulate or infantile form of discourse, devoid of sophistication, at best having a certain charm of simplicity. If, on the other hand, he tries to introduce the subtleties that he perceives, he will find that he can do so only by employing the full range of English vocabulary, including the Romance. Thereby he removes a great deal of the particular quality of the original. The English writer William Morris, whose saga translations were celebrated in the nineteenth century, responded to this discrepancy by rejecting the Romance element in its entirety. He reached back into Middle English for an archaic style, in which the use of cognate and frequently obsolete words was a major feature, and the tortured syntax often was drawn right out of the original Norse: "In the autumn at winter-nights was there a blood-offering held at Ladir."[19] But whether in so doing he was producing a comparable effect is questionable, for one can hardly maintain that the sagas were archaic to their first readers in the thirteenth century.

To the modern reader the language of the sagas seems strangely homogeneous; sometimes even monotonous. It has often enough been emphasized that saga style is terse and emotionally restrained, that the dialogue is laconic, and that action predominates over description and reflection. In comparison with other medieval narratives, they stand out by virtue of their oral quality. Specific features that bolster this judg-

[19] William Morris and Eiríkr Magnússon, *Heimskringla, Saga of Hakon the Good* (London: B. Quarich, 1893–1905), Chap. 18.

ment are the short, paratactic sentences, the constant shifting of tense from past to present, the formulaic introductions and conclusions, the dramatic role of dialogue. The further fact that they are all anonymous confirms the feeling that they must be based on a tradition of oral narration. In the last generation, however, more emphasis has been placed, especially by Icelandic scholars, on the sagas as literary texts. The first writers have been rehabilitated as something more than scribes, indeed as authors, each with his own personality revealed through his work.[20]

The very possibility of such a re-evaluation, whether we fully accept it or not, must affect the translator's view of the saga style. Even if the authors were somewhat less individual than is now claimed, no one can remain blind to the extent of stylization that has occurred in the writing down of these fascinating narratives. We need only grant that this is the work of a school of writers to see that the style at its best is something more than a record of contemporary talk. It cannot be equated with our most colloquial form of writing, which contains a large element of the vulgarities and banalities of our civilization. Nor can it be identified with our Latinized historical style. It has been compared to the style of our more realistic novels, but even this fails in the face of its greater concentration and even monotony. No modern style, in fact, precisely corresponds to it. The translator is virtually driven to create, in the translation, a special saga style, which is slanted in one direction or the other by the translator's interpretation of its nature.

IV

The problem has much in common with that which faces translators of the Greek and Roman classics, or for that matter, of the Bible. For such classics of a bygone age there have always been two schools of thought, the *archaizing* and the *modernizing*. In a famous controversy of English literature, F. W. Newman, a translator of the *Iliad* (1856), was taken to task by Matthew Arnold for having improperly archaized Homer.[21] When William Morris first began translating Icelandic sagas in 1868, his view coincided with that of Newman. He saw in the sagas

[20] For a recent survey and discussion see Theodore M. Andersson, *The Problem of Icelandic Saga Origins* (New Haven: Yale University Press, 1964).

[21] Francis William Newman, *The* ILIAD *of Homer Faithfully Translated into Unrhymed English Metre* (London: Walton and Maberly, 1856), Preface, and *Homeric Translation in Theory and Practice* (London and Edinburgh: Williams and Norgate, 1861); Matthew Arnold, "On Translating Homer" (1860), in *Complete Prose Works of Matthew Arnold* (Ann Arbor: University of Michigan Press, 1960), I, 97–216.

a Norse counterpart to Chaucer and Malory, and he wished to reproduce them in English of a corresponding style. As mentioned earlier, he did this by reproducing in the English translation numerous features of the original which violated the norms of contemporary English but which corresponded to those he found in Middle English. He was aided and abetted in this by his collaborator, the Icelander Eiríkr Magnússon, who later defended Morris from the charge leveled against his style by another team of Icelander and Englishman, Vigfusson and Powell.[22] These wrote, in the Introduction to their *Corpvs Poeticvm Boreale:* "There is one grave error into which too many English translators of old Northern and Icelandic writings have fallen, to wit, the affectation of archaisms, and the abuse of archaic, Scottish, pseudo-Middle English words. This abominable fault makes a Saga, for instance, sound unreal, unfamiliar, false; it conceals all diversities of style and tone beneath a fictitious mask of monotonous uniformity, and slurs over the real difficulties by a specious nullity of false phrasing."[23] Two able students of Morris' style, Karl Litzenberg and Karl O. F. Anderson, have been at pains to bolster Magnússon's defense against the charge that Morris wrote "pseudo-Middle English."[24] Litzenberg has shown that most of Morris' archaisms do in fact occur in Middle English authors. Anderson has demonstrated that Morris' share in the work of the two collaborators largely consisted in rewriting Magnússon's fairly straightforward translation into an archaic style modeled on the Old Norse original, a style which gradually became more and more his own style in his original works as well.

Unfortunately neither of these contentions, even if they are accepted, meets the central issue, namely that Morris misinterpreted the style of his original. He was misled by surface similarities into identifying the style of the sagas with one in which modern English had been purged of its French and Latin elements and returned to the pristine purity of the Middle Ages. He did not read his Chaucer and Malory as if he were

[22] For Magnússon's defense see the references in Stefán Einarsson, "Eiríkr Magnússon and His Saga-Translations," *Scandinavian Studies,* XIII (1934), 17–32.

[23] Gubrand Vigfusson and F. York Powell, *Corpvs Poeticvm Boreale* (Oxford: Clarendon Press, 1883), I, cxv.

[24] Karl Litzenberg, "The Diction of William Morris" *Arkiv för Nordisk Filologi,* LIII (1937), 327–363, and *The Victorians and the Vikings: A Bibliographical Essay on Anglo-Norse Literary Relations* (University of Michigan Contributions in Modern Philology, No. 3, 1947), esp. pp. 22–25. Karl O. F. Anderson, "Scandinavian Elements in the Works of William Morris" (Ph.D. dissertation, Harvard, 1940).

their contemporary, but saw them with the eyes of a modern man. Their value to him lay largely in that patina which the changes of language and culture had laid down upon them. It is no accident that he was in the midst of creating his counterpart to the *Canterbury Tales,* entitled *The Earthly Paradise,* when he first encountered the Old Norse sagas. To him the life of the sagas was an earthly paradise, removing him as far as possible from the (to him) distasteful life of contemporary England. His programmatic antagonism to French culture and French loan words, and his desire to restore England to its simple pre-Conquest vigor, colored his view of the style of the sagas, distorting it into something grotesque and wonderful. Kenneth Rexroth probably sums up the modern view of Morris when he describes his work as a "terrible waste—I doubt if Morris' wonderful Saga Library was ever readable by anybody—and there the great sagas are, locked up in that ridiculous language."[25] In passing judgment on Morris, however, we must not forget that Scandinavians had already preceded him in romanticizing the sagas. As early as 1818, Rasmus Rask inveighed against translators who depended on cognates in translating: "It reveals in equal degree a lack of insight into the nature of human language and a lack of taste when some translators from Icelandic regard it as proper to Icelandize as much as possible both in words and phrases, which only serves to make the translation boring and repulsive, while the original may have been attractive and readable."[26]

The reaction against the practice condemned by Rask has gone hand in hand with a more realistic view of the sagas themselves and their style. When the American economist Thorstein Veblen set out to translate the *Laxdœla* (1925), he saw in it no earthly paradise but rather a striking counterpart to the boss politics he had studied in the big cities of America.[27] His style was therefore at the opposite extreme from Morris', simple, bald, and contemporary. The reader is made into a contemporary of the saga and reads it as if it were a tale from his own

[25] Arrowsmith and Shattuck (eds.), *The Craft and Context,* pp. 23–24. In support of the view here advanced on Morris, cf. A. Clutton-Brock, *William Morris: His Work and Influence* (London: Williams and Norgate, 1914), pp. 186–187; William Morris Society, *The Work of William Morris* (London, 1962), p. 8; and Morris, *Collected Works,* (London: Longmans Green, 1913) XVIII, p. xviii.

[26] Rasmus Rask, *Undersøgelse om det gamle Nordiske eller Islandske Sprogs Oprindelse* (Copenhagen: Gyldendal, 1818), p. 38.

[27] *The Laxdæla Saga,* trans. from the Icelandic, with an Introduction, by Thorstein Veblen (New York: B. W. Huebsch, 1925).

day. Since we cannot know precisely how these stories affected their contemporaries, there being no bilinguals to tell us, this view is manifestly a fiction and in its way as misleading as Morris' assumption. Yet it seems to make better sense than Morris' position, if only because we can compare the sagas with other medieval writings, including Chaucer's and Malory's, and find them measurably different. The modern Icelander is the closest thing to a bilingual speaker of Old Norse, though of course even to him the sagas are today in many respects archaic. The translators of the twentieth century have generally taken the modernizing position, for example, George Ainslie Hight, who in 1910 wrote in the Introduction to his *Grettis saga:* "My aim has been to translate in the colloquial language of my own day, eschewing all affectation of poetic diction or mediævalism."[28] E. R. Eddison, who translated *Egil's saga* in 1930, was a belated disciple of Morris, and his "Terminal Essay" on translation has quite rightly been described by Hollander as "pretentious, and for the most part utterly wrong-headed."[29]

Even those who would agree on the wrongheadedness of the archaizers, however, do not always agree on the precise degree of modernity that should be sought. Voices are now being raised to warn against the dangers of triviality and vulgarity. Hedin Bronner has faulted a recent translation of *Njála* for replacing "the terseness, the dignity, the stylistic range between fire and ice" with a "chatty and pedestrian prose."[30] He admits that it "makes good enough reading for those who do not know the sagas," but he misses in it, as also in a recent Norwegian translation,[31] the elevation of style which was part of its charm on his first discovery of the saga. The problem is, of course, that in America and England, as in Scandinavia, tastes are changing. Those who have established for themselves a particular interpretation of saga style will resent any attempt to change this image. The same arguments are con-

[28] *The Saga of Grettir the Strong,* trans. George Ainslie Hight (London: Dent, *Everyman's Library,* 1914), Preface.

[29] *Scandinavian Studies,* XXVI (1954), 126 n. 1; *Egil's Saga,* trans. E. R. Eddison (Cambridge: The University Press, 1930), pp. 229–242: "Terminal Essay: On Some Principles of Translation."

[30] Review of *Njal's Saga,* trans. Magnus Magnusson and Hermann Pálsson (Baltimore: Penguin Classics, 1960), in *American-Scandinavian Review,* L (1962), 317–318.

[31] Hedin Bronner, review of *Islandske Ættesagaer,* ed. Hallvard Lie (Oslo: Aschehoug, 1951–1954), in *Scandinavian Studies,* XXVII (1955), 160–165. For other reviews by Bronner, see *Samtiden,* 1961, pp. 132–136; *Scandinavian Studies,* XXVII (1955), 153–159; and *American-Scandinavian Review,* LII (1964), 459–460.

stantly leveled against new versions of the Bible or of the classics.[32] Any classic is by definition ageless, so that it is at once contemporary and ancient. The problem is to find a style which fulfills the dual requirements set up by Egil E. Johnsen, a Norwegian student of early Snorri translations: "A saga translation should be contemporary, but at the same time give an impression of distance."[33]

V

One of the greatest problems of distortion in translation is the fact that key words in one language may have either no precise equivalent in another or one with a very low frequency. How can one ever render into English the innumerable terms for the craggy, sea-encircled landscape of Norway and Iceland? Saga translations abound in such terms as "skerry," "fell," "tarn," which in English are either archaic or local. When Gunnar of Hlíðarendi looks back at the hillside on which his farmstead is located, and says, "Fǫgur er hlíðin, svá at mér hefir hon aldri jafnfǫgr sýnzk," it is a thrilling moment, even to those other Scandinavians who have to read it in modern translation. "Fager er lien" is as much a part of the Norwegian language as any other literary quotation. But this experience is simply not transferable to English because the language contains no equivalent of a *hlíð* or *li*. If Morris had translated this saga, he would no doubt have written: "Fair is the lea." Bayerschmidt translates, "Fair is the slope," but the word "fair" either means "blond" (as in "fair hair") or suggests Biblical and archaic style, while "slope" merely suggests geography.[34] Magnusson and Pálsson paraphrase and write "How lovely the slopes are," which is more natural English, but still not as impressive as the original.[35] Here I think it has to be granted that anyone who has first met this saga in a Scandinavian language simply cannot hope to get the same impression from a translation. Bronner's acid criticism of the latter version seems to reflect a desire to maintain a degree of archaism in the translation which most modern readers will reject.[36]

While preparing a Norwegian-English dictionary I noticed that

[32] For an entertaining presentation of the modernizer's view see Ronald Knox, *Trials of a Translator* (New York, 1949).

[33] Egil Eiken Johnsen, *Sagaspråk og stil: En undersøkelse av språk og stil i de tre eldste norske sagaoversettelser* (Oslo: Gyldendal Norsk Forlag, 1942), p. 18.

[34] Bayerschmidt and Hollander (trans.), *Njál's Saga,* p. 156.

[35] Magnusson and Pálsson (trans.), *Njal's Saga*, p. 166.

[36] Review of *Njal's Saga, American-Scandinavian Review,* L (1962) 317–318.

some of the most difficult terms to translate were the terms of abuse. Here are three from the same letter: *skrytepave, skrønemaker, skrålhals*. These picturesque terms have in common a structure which is rare in English, and which makes them more comical in effect than the equivalents that were found: "boaster, braggart"; "storyteller, liar"; "loudmouth, vociferous person." The frequency with which this problem arose suggested that Norwegian may have a richer vocabulary than English in this field. Modern Icelandic with its many *mannskratti* compounds is also richly endowed in this respect.[37] In Old Icelandic literature one of the hardest terms of abuse to translate is the word *argr* (or *ragr*), which was applied to men who were held to have some of the attributes of a woman. It is applied to Loki in the mythology because he turned himself into a woman and bore offspring.[38] It is used as a taunt of cowardice, so serious that a man could legally kill another for saying it. It is therefore understandable that Cecil Wood should have used the term "fairy" in translating the taunting by Thorarin of his son Thorstein: "I'd rather have a dead son than a live fairy."[39] If this fails, it is only because the term "fairy" in American usage primarily suggests sexual deviation rather than cowardice. "Sissy" would probably have hit the mark more exactly.

Names are strictly speaking only tags to identify places and people and should therefore not require translation. Yet they are, in fact, shaped by the speakers of each language into a pronounceable and memorable form. Besides, each culture has its own system of naming. For the translator names offer many problems. Scandinavian names, insofar as they are not international (usually Christian) names, often present sequences of sounds or letters that do not come trippingly to the English tongue: Thorbjorn, Ragnhild, Sighvatr. Worse yet, they often fail to reveal the owner's sex and hardly seem like names to those unfamiliar with them. It is not surprising that translators, wherever possible, have substituted closely equivalent English names, for example, "Harold" for *Haraldr* or "Eric" for *Eiríkr*.

In the rendition of Old Norse literature, a much more complex prob-

[37] Cf. Stefán Einarsson, "Compounds of the *Mann-skratti* type," *Studies in Honor of Albert Morey Sturtevant* (Lawrence: University of Kansas Press, 1952), pp. 47–56.

[38] *Lokasenna*, st. 23.

[39] *The Fat Abbot* (Winter, 1960), p. 6; cf. *Scandinavian Studies*, XXXIV (1962) 50 n. 2.

lem of names arises from the culture itself. Family names were nonexistent, and each person had by right only one name. He could be more precisely identified by a nickname or his patronymic (or by his place of origin, like Gunnar of Hlíðarendi). The results can be observed in such well-publicized names as those of Eric the Red *(Eiríkr rauði)* and his son Leif Ericson *(Leifr Eiríksson)*, also known as Leif the Lucky *(hin heppni)*. In our culture, the former type is limited to kings and criminals (Louis the Bald, Jack the Ripper), while the latter misleads journalists into speaking of "Mr. Ericson." The problem in translation is thus not merely one of finding a pronounceable form of the names themselves, according to some consistent principle. It is also one of how to render those names, both of persons and of places, which were so transparent to their users that not translating them would be a genuine loss to the atmosphere of the sagas. *Eiríkr rauði* in an English text would not only be difficult, but also less informative and interesting than "Eric the Red." Place names are often transparent and therefore tempting to the translator. Why should he not translate *Haukdalir* as "Hawkdale" and *Breiðafjǫrðr* as "Broadfjord"? Early translators yielded rather too freely to this temptation, producing such howlers as "Woodcombe" for *Skógahverfi* (Dasent), "Oxwater" for *Øxará* (Dasent), "Thickshaw" for *Þykkvaskógr* (Morris), "Withymire" for *Víðimýrr* (Eddison). In our time a general policy seems to have been adopted, largely along lines proposed by Professor Hollander in 1954.[40] The chief watchdog has been Hedin Bronner, who would prefer not to have place names translated at all.[41] My own view, set forth many years ago in my translation of the Vinland sagas, is that consistency must give way to the needs of the reader.[42] In the framework of our present discussion, I would now rephrase this as follows: names which are only names should be kept intact (aside from appropriate transliteration, which I should prefer to see without the accents of length) since they convey no other information than the identity of the person or place, and to translate them would be overtranslation. But much speaks for the translation, wherever possible, of names

[40] *Scandinavian Studies*, XXVI (1954), 125–129.

[41] *Scandinavian Studies*, XXVII (1955), 156; *American-Scandinavian Review*, L (1962), 317–318. See also Gösta Franzén's remarks in *Modern Philology*, LVIII (1961), 206–207.

[42] Einar Haugen, *Voyages to Vinland* (New York: Alfred A. Knopf, 1942), viii–ix.

that convey (to native speakers) further information about the place or person (e.g., the nicknames, or suffixes like *-dal* and *-á*). Not to do so could be a case of undertranslation, the loss of a vivid resource of the original text.

In this, as in other problems of translation, it is doubtful that general agreement can be reached. In America and England, as in Scandinavia, tastes change, and a style that will appeal to one generation may be intolerable to the next. We can only welcome new attempts to make the sagas and other Scandinavian classics readable in English. We must remember that fidelity does not only mean that a translation shall read like an original, but also that it shall read like an interesting original.

Fact and Fancy in the Vinland Sagas

ERIK WAHLGREN

I

Good fortune, and several branches of scientific learning, are gradually providing striking corroboration of the main indications in ancient Scandinavian records of the first known visits to American shores by Europeans. Zoology, botany, chemistry, and of course archaeology have recently made determinations of note that confirm the Vinland sagas and justify the cautious credence placed in these by several generations of toiling philologists. Without the Icelandic sagas, linguistics and history would have had nothing to labor with. Without humanistic treatises, natural science could not have been brought to bear on the problem in the first place and could scarcely have interpreted the evidence under any circumstances. The historical disciplines organized the problem of Vinland. In their wake, physical and biological science has provided invaluable clues and checks. Inasmuch as the Vinland sagas, and with them the whole question of Vinland, comprise a fabric of interwoven factual and fictional details, literary scholarship must now respond to the combined challenge with the fullest possible measure of elucidation and commentary.

At a time when public attention has been focused on the Vinland voyages through the achievements of modern explorers and archaeologists, linguists and literary scholars have harnessed their esthetic sensibilities and produced excerpts and whole translations of the Vinland sagas that in many cases prove to be compound versions containing, purportedly, the "best features" of the conflicting accounts. This makes for smooth reading—and a host of misapprehensions, the effect of which is then multiplied through the reliance placed upon the blended or conflicting translations by historians, ethnologists, geographers, and students of literature. The sensitive interdependence of different branches of learning is not uniformly appreciated in scientific circles. A monograph on Vinland published for the Bureau of American Ethnology, for example, carries the ominous statement that "the writer is not conversant with the language in which the Sagas were written or the related tongues, but this side of the question has been so carefully covered by others that it is pretty safe to take one's information second-hand."[1] Thus unsuspectingly can conclusions of great moment for science be anchored to the solid bedrock of philological chaos. For the texts of the sagas have indeed been "carefully covered" for three generations now by scholars whose several views are—in total disagreement.

More than twenty years ago, in a work that he hopefully labelled Volume I, Sven B. F. Jansson published a basic study on the manuscript sources that established, in the minds of most scholars, that Haukr lagmaðr had edited and abridged his model for *Eiríks saga rauða* rather than that the author of the *Skálholtsbók* version had digressed in his.[2] Professor Jansson never followed up his initial volume, and despite the editing activities of Storm, Þórðarson, Reeves, Hermannsson, and Strömbäck, the *Hauksbók–Skálholtsbók* tradition has never been fully compared with the variant tradition of *Flateyjarbók*, referred to in this study as *Grœnlendinga saga.* Particularly inasmuch as this version of the Vinland voyages, known in English as the *Saga*

[1] I. R. Swanton, *The Wineland Voyages,* p. 5. Pertinent to this are comments by P. H. Sawyer: "Unfortunately, communication between scholars working with different kinds of evidence has sometimes broken down, not simply because it is difficult to keep up to date, though that is certainly true, but because the nature of the different kinds of evidence, and the limitations which govern its use, are not always properly understood. Historians, for example, do not always recognize how wide is the margin of error in archaeological dating, and archaeologists and numismatists often fail to realize that written sources require quite as much study as their own material. The failure to understand the nature of the evidence can have most serious results." (*The Age of the Vikings,* p. 7). Publication information on the works cited in this article is given in the Selected Bibliography at the end of the article.

[2] Sven B. F. Jansson, *Sagorna om Vinland,* I: *Handskrifterna till Erik den Rödes saga.* Because of its parallel arrangement of texts, this work is indispensable.

of the Greenlanders, has until very recently been the subject of much prejudice as compared with its rival, the *Saga of Erik the Red,* examination and comparison of the two sagas from the point of view of literary theme and motif, as attempted in the present study, should fulfill a useful purpose.[3]

Eiríks saga rauða, which over the years has acquired favored status, speaks of three voyages, whereas *Grœnlendinga saga* deals with no fewer than six expeditions.[4] In both of the sagas initial discovery of the American mainland was through accident; in both sagas mention is made of one totally abortive voyage; both sagas mention Karlsefni and Leif the Lucky. Beyond that, the discrepancies of personnel and detail are considerable. Variant proposed explanations for the inconsistencies have included ignorance, forgetfulness, confusion, derivation, invention, and suppression, with considerations of family pride effectively influencing the two last-named factors. In general, commentators have devoted their energies more to the historical aspects of the Vinland accounts than to their literary qualities, and, in view of the historical controversies involved, that aspect has clearly posed the greater challenge. It should be pointed out that the competing claims of the two main saga traditions have not been settled by the recent archaeological discoveries, by Dr. Helge Ingstad, of what certainly must be an ancient Scandinavian settlement at L'Anse au Meadow, Newfoundland. The conclusive evaluation of those finds for history and literature remains to be given.

To avoid unnecessary explanation and cross-reference, and to facilitate a measure of synoptic recollection of the Vinland voyages in their diverse representations, concentrated *abrégés* of the voyages are given here.[5] *GS* (i.e., the *Flateyjarbók* tradition), despite its having

[3] Attention is called to the Selected Bibliography for a listing of works on this subject.

[4] *Eiríks saga rauða* will hereafter be cited as *ES*; *Grœnlendinga saga* as *GS*.

[5] The lack of uniformity in the various titles attached to these narratives is confusing. *Eiríks saga rauða* is known as the *Saga of Erik the Red,* the *Saga of Thorfinn Karlsefni,* or the *Hauksbók* version (of the Vinland sagas), this last until recently favored by most editors and translators over a variant known as the *Skálholt* version. The rival saga, *Grœnlendinga saga,* or *Saga of the Greenlanders,* has also been known as the *Story* [*þáttr*] *of Erik the Red,* sometimes as the *Story* [*þáttr*] *of the Greenlanders* (unfortunately also the title of the short story about Einarr Sokkason), and as the *Flateyjarbók* version because of its three insertions into that great compilation.

the larger number of voyages, is shorter than *ES* (the *Skálholtsbók-Hauksbók* tradition). *GS* presents its material as follows:

Voyage 1. Bjarni Herjólfsson is the one who discovers the new lands, by accident, in sailing from [Norway and] Iceland to Greenland. Blown off course to the south, he winds up off the coast of North America and then sails toward more northerly latitudes, encountering what one supposes is Labrador and then Baffin Island, the latter recognizable by its glaciers. From here Bjarni manages to make his father's estate at Herjólfsnes at the southern tip of Greenland. The saga states further that Bjarni later makes a voyage to Norway, where he is twitted about his lack of precise knowledge of the lands he once chanced upon.

Voyage 2. After Bjarni's return from Norway, Leifr Eiríksson buys Bjarni's ship and sails to investigate the lands to the west. Though pressed to lead the expedition, Leifr's father, Eiríkr, decides not to do so after falling from his horse while riding to the ship. Leifr's crew of thirty-five men includes a German named Tyrkr. Reversing Bjarni's sailing directions, Leifr finds three lands in succession, which he calls Helluland (Slab Land), Markland (Forest Land), and, upon leaving it, Vínland (Wine Land or Grapevine Land). The grapes have been found and identified by Tyrkr. The men build houses for the winter, the mildness of which convinces them that this would be an excellent place to settle. From solar observations they understand that they are well south of Greenland latitudes. Fish are numerous. In the spring, with a load of timber, they sail back home to Brattahlíð, Eiríkr rauði's estate on Greenland, rescuing on the way a shipwrecked crew of fifteen, headed by Þórir, a Norwegian. For these exploits Leifr receives the epithet *heppni,* "the Lucky." That winter old Eiríkr, Þórir, and many of the latter's crew members die of disease. Þórir's widow Guðríðr survives.

Voyage 3. In one of the immediately following years, Leifr—after thriftily fetching the load of timber abandoned on the reef that had capsized Þórir's ship—lends his ship to his brother Þorvaldr for further explorations. Þorvaldr and his crew of thirty find Leifr's dwellings without trouble and spend a calm winter, living largely on fish. The next spring and summer they devote to exploring. During this they find, on an island, a structure which they conclude is used to store grain. During continued explorations the following summer they suffer a shipwreck and shatter their keel. After constructing a new keel, they raise the old one on a point of land and call it Kjalarnes (Keel's Ness). Shortly thereafter they come upon some natives asleep. This is the Norsemen's first contact with the *skrælingar,* 'wretches,' of the New World. They kill eight of the aborigines and then fall prey to a mysterious drowsiness. Wakened by a mysterious warning voice, the Norsemen are attacked by a multitude of the savages. Only Þorvaldr is wounded.

Knowing that his death impends, Þorvaldr requests that he be buried on a heavily wooded promontory between two fjords, a place that has already appealed to him as a home. His companions do his bidding, and the burial place receives the name Krossanes, after the Christian crosses placed at his head and feet, for the Greenlanders have now been converted to Christianity. After picking up their companions whom they have left to guard their headquarters, the travelers sail back to Leifr on Greenland.

Voyage 4. Leifr's brother Þorsteinn, having meanwhile married Þórir's widow Guðríðr, is anxious to recover Þorvaldr's body, apparently for burial in Christian soil. He sets sail with a crew of twenty-five men and, for some reason, his wife. After being storm-tossed all summer, with no localities indicated, the mariners manage to land at Lýsufjǫrðr in the Western Settlement, that is, the more northerly of the two main Norse establishments on Greenland. Here Þorsteinn dies in an epidemic, after prophesying that the twice-widowed Guðríðr will marry an Icelander and produce a distinguished line of descendants. Supernatural phenomena are reported in connection with Þorsteinn's death.

Voyage 5. Þorsteinn's prophesy is fulfilled with Guðríðr's marriage to a newcomer at Brattahlíð. This is Þorfinnr Þórðarson, usually referred to as Karlsefni (Makings of a Man). Karlsefni is a wealthy trader, who now, by popular request, organizes an attempted settlement of Vínland. He embarks with sixty men, five women, and ample livestock and equipment. After an easy voyage the colonists reach Leifr's houses, which he has indicated that he will lend, but not give, to them. Their first conspicuous source of food is a whale. Game and grapes are found, the cattle thrive and become lively, and the colonists fell timber and dry it. After an uneventful winter, the colony is visited by *skrælingar* who have come to trade their furs. Frightened by Karlsefni's frisky bull, the natives try to crowd into the Norsemen's houses but are kept outside. The Skrælings try to acquire weapons in trade for their furs, but are given milk instead and, seemingly content, "depart with their wares in their stomachs." The prudent Karlsefni now has a stockade built around the settlement. His wife Guðríðr presently gives birth to Snorri, the first white child to be born in America. The Skrælings show up again in the autumn, carrying furs, which they throw over the stockade in return for milk. Rocking her little son, Guðríðr sees a female apparition, who calls herself Guðríðr. At that moment fighting breaks out, inasmuch as one of the whites has slain a Skræling who attempted the theft of a weapon. The Skrælings flee but, as expected, return in force for a third visit. During ensuing military maneuvers in which the Norsemen utilize their dread bull to advantage, the savages are repulsed. A peaceful winter follows, but because of the potential menace of the aborigines, Karlsefni decides that they should return to Greenland. In the spring, therefore, provided with grapevines, grapes and, of course, furs, the colonists sail back home.

Voyage 6. Karlsefni has shared the profits equally with his crew, and the ferment of the profits [and of the grapes?] has worked on men's minds. The same summer that Karlsefni returns from Vínland [?], a ship, owned by Helgi and Finnbogi, Icelanders from the East Firths, arrives at Greenland from Norway. Eiríkr's bastard daughter Freydís comes over from her estate at Garðar the following spring to talk with the two men. She proposes a joint-stock expedition to Vínland, each party to consist of thirty men, women not counted. The expedition is organized and sets out, but the wily Freydís has secretly taken along an extra five men. After the arrival in Vínland, Freydís refuses to honor an agreement whereby Leifr's houses will be shared between the two ships' crews. The brothers and their party consequently erect a dwelling of their own farther inland. Despite efforts at conciliation by Helgi and Finnbogi, Freydís accomplishes the destruction of the brothers and their entire crew, even to the point of slaying the women with her own hand. Thereafter, she threatens her own followers with death if they ever reveal the outrage after their return to Greenland. In the spring Freydís and her party sail back to Eiríksfjǫrðr in the ship formerly owned by the two brothers, bringing an ample supply of Vínland's products with them. Eventually her foul deed becomes known, particularly after her half brother Leifr has three of her crew members tortured into a full revelation of the details. Leifr lacks the heart to punish his unworthy kinswoman as she deserves, but he prophesies that she and her descendants will be shunned forevermore, which prophecy, states the saga, was later fulfilled. Karlsefni in the meantime has been preparing his ship for a voyage to Norway, where he successfully disposes of his cargo and is treated with distinction. He sells his carved *húsasnotra* (gable-carving or carved figurehead at the prow of a ship, probably the latter in this case) to a merchant from Bremen. The piece is carved out of *mǫsurr* (probably a type of maple from the forests of Vínland). Karlsefni and Guðríðr now return to Iceland and settle ultimately at Glaumbœr [the saga's error for Reynines]. After his death Guðríðr makes a pilgrimage to Rome, then builds a church at Glaumbœr, where she ends her days as a nun. Her Vínland-born son, Snorri, is the ancestor of Icelandic bishops.

The so-called *Saga of Erik the Red* records three voyages, for which the first four chapters set the stage by tracing Guðríðr's ancestry, by chronicling Eiríkr rauði's difficulties on Iceland and his exploration and settlement of Greenland, and by describing an incident from Guðríðr's youth (her assistance to Þorbjǫrg lítilvǫlva at a séance), which affords occasion for a favorable prediction by Þorbjǫrg as to Guðríðr's future.

With the assistance of Eiríkr, Guðríðr and her parents settle across the fjord at Stokkanes following their emigration from Iceland to Greenland. Next Leifr Eiríksson and his [older?] brother Þorsteinn, sons of Eiríkr and Þjóðhildr, are introduced (the third brother, Þorvaldr, is mentioned later). The stories of the voyages now follow:

Voyage 1. Leifr sails from Greenland to round out his education in Norway. Detained by bad weather off the Hebrides, he has a love affair there with a highborn woman named Þorgunna, who later bears him a son named Þorgils. The latter is sent by her to Greenland to live with his father, but, says the saga, there was always something uncanny about him. Continuing to Norway, Leifr spends the winter with King Óláfr Tryggvason. On returning to Greenland the following summer, Leifr is commissioned by the proselyting King to preach Christianity to the Greenlanders. During his return trip, Leifr is long at sea and discovers hitherto unsuspected lands, whose location is not even faintly indicated, nor are they named. Their products, however, include wild wheat or rice, or some similar grain, grapevines, and impressive trees, including the maple, samples of all of which are brought along by the voyagers when they finally arrive at Brattahlíð, after rescuing shipwrecked mariners on the way. For his great goodness in introducing Christianity and in saving the shipwrecked men, Leifr becomes known as "the Lucky." Old Eiríkr refuses to accept the new faith, suffering thereby some reduction in his conjugal rights inasmuch as Þjóðhildr builds a chapel in the vicinity and devotes her energies thereafter to religion.

Voyage 2. As a result of Leifr's accidental discovery of lands, a planned exploratory expedition is later got under way, using the ship that Guðríðr's father, Þorbjǫrn Vífilsson, has come to Greenland in. Þorsteinn Eiríksson is in charge, but Eiríkr is invited to join. The expedition consists of twenty men, equipped with weapons and provisions but apparently without domestic animals. Before leaving home Eiríkr hides a chest of gold and silver. Riding down to the ship he is thrown from his pony, suffering broken bones and dislocations. He sends a message to his wife to dig up the treasure, acknowledging that he has been punished for this act of heathen foolishness. [Ambiguous wording in the variant versions makes it unclear whether Eiríkr is foolish enough to set sail after the accident]. The expedition is a fiasco, and after an exhausting summer on stormy seas, during which the weather-beaten men even catch a view of Ireland, they manage to return to Eiríksfjǫrðr with nothing their pains.

Þorsteinn Eiríksson presently marries Guðríðr. The wedding to held at Brattahlíð, after which the young couple move to Lýsufjǫrðr in the Western Settlement, where Þorsteinn owns a farm jointly with another Þorsteinn, who is married to a woman named Sigríðr. That winter the community is struck by a pestilence, during the course of which Þorsteinn Eiríksson dies in a scene that contains supernatural details, including his own post-mortem prophecy about Guðríðr's future. She inherits the property of her father and is received at Brattahlíð, where Eiríkr, still very active, manages her affairs well. Meanwhile, Brattahlíð receives distinguished Icelandic visitors. These are the prosperous merchant, Þorfinnr Þórðarson Karlsefni, from Reynines in Skagafjǫrðr, with Snorri Þorbrandsson of Alptafjǫrðr and a crew of forty, and, at the same time, Bjarni Grímólfsson of Breiðafjǫrðr and Þórhallr Gamlason of Austfjǫrðr, with another forty men. All these people receive hospitality from Eiríkr (aided by a generous contribution of supplies by Karlsefni himself), with the result that the Yule celebrations are extended into a wedding feast for Karlsefni and Guðríðr.

Voyage 3. Renewed discussions of Vínland lead to a mighty expedition in search of it under Karlsefni's leadership. Three ships and 160 men and women set sail. Þorvaldr Eiríksson and Þórhallr veiðimaðr (the Huntsman) are included, the latter being a heathen curmudgeon who has served Eiríkr. Starting from a northerly location [evidently to obtain the fullest strategic advantage of wind and current], they sail before a northerly wind and, with fairly precise specifications of route and geographical features, find a series of places to which they give names: Kjalarnes, Furðustrandir, Straumey, Straumfjǫrðr, Bjarnarey, Helluland, Markland. Vínland they have difficulty in finding, although, anachronistically, a male/female pair of Scots thralls, Haki and Hekja, whom Leifr had received from Óláfr Tryggvason and then given to Karlsefni, return from a three-day expedition on foot with *grapes* and wild wheat. The voyagers spend the winter at Straumfjǫrðr, amply supplied by nature to begin with but in bad shape for food by spring. Þórhallr veiðimaðr disappears and is found on the fourth day, lying on a rock while muttering heathen incantations to the god Þórr, who presently provides the hungry explorers with a whale of unknown species. The cooks prepare its flesh. All who eat of it become ill, but a prayer to the Christian God restores them to health and improves the weather so that edible provisions are found. The explorers have not found Vínland, and disagreements arise as to its location, with the result that Þórhallr with a crew of nine leaves the main expedition and sails northward, after composing poetic jibes on the expedition and its meager results. The prose indicates that Þórhallr plans to seek Vínland to the north, while the verse (second stanza) indicates rather an intention to go back to Greenland. At all events, he and his party fail to make Greenland and ultimately are enslaved in Ireland.

Karlsefni and the others now sail south and find a good location that they call Hóp (Landlocked Bay), with grapes and wild wheat and ample fish. After half a month they are visited by Skrælings in nine skin boats. After a snowless winter, the Skrælings return with furs for trading and receive in turn red cloth strips of ever diminishing width. The bargaining is cut short by the hostility of Karlsefni's bull. The Skrælings run to their boats and disappear, but three weeks later they return in battle array and attack the Norsemen with arrows and even ballistae. The pregnant Freydís distinguishes herself during the mêlée in the famous incident of whetting a sword on her bare breasts, which act throws the Skrælings into a mad rout. The company now decides that life would be hazardous in these parts. A third winter, and various explorations, follow. Þorvaldr Eiríksson is killed by an arrow shot by a uniped. Five Skrælings isolated from their fellows are slaughtered. Two Skræling boys whom the explorers have captured tell the Scandinavians—in Micmac, Icelandic, or Sanskrit—a cock-and-bull story. The would-be colonists return to Brattahlíð.

After a brief, inserted *þáttr* about Bjarni Grímólfsson and his heroic death in the wormy sea, the saga ends with an account of the descendants of Karlsefni and Guðríðr. So far, the Vínland sagas.

II

For a long time now, scholars have been debating certain problems basic to the Vínland discussion. One of these, thanks to recent archaeological achievements, is disposed of—the Vínland sagas need no longer be defended against the charge that they are fables tailored out of whole cloth. But the problem of the location of *Vine*land is still unsolved, although for reasons that involve geography and linguistics the present writer sides with Einar Haugen and others who would place it somewhere in New England. A third problem pertains to the relationships between the two traditions embodied in, respectively, *Grœnlendinga saga* and *Eiríks saga rauða*. A very useful review of the controversy to about 1950 may be found in Valdemar Lendin's article.[6] Since bibliographies of the subject are available, and since many of the works written on the subject are classics in themselves and deserve to be read for the perspective they can give, the present essay will not be padded with a general historical rehash of opinion pro and con. Instead, certain pertinent aspects of recently published scholarly opinion will be examined. Both practical matters and such literary aspects as theme and phraseology will then be touched upon, followed by an examination of the central dispute relating to the word *Vínland*. The balance of this work will then be devoted to the combined topic of relationship be-

[6] "Vinlandsproblemet: En översikt över nyare litteratur rörande källorna," *(Svensk) Historisk Tidskrift*, Andra följden, fjortonde årgången, Häfte 3 (1951), 322–338.

tween the two competing Vínland sagas and the degree to which ascertainable fictional elements appear in each.

We shall here maintain that:

1. The *GS* and the *ES* are related sagas rather than the products of chiefly independent traditions.
2. The *GS* is distinctly the older saga.
3. The *ES* is in large measure an adaptation of the *GS*.
4. The *GS* is the more historical of the two but contains obvious fictions.
5. Despite derivative features the *ES* reveals some genuine historical details.
6. The *GS* may originally have possessed, then lost, some of these same details.
7. The name Vínland is original and genuine, i.e., it is based on an actual discovery of grapes.
8. The Norse settlement recently found on Newfoundland is doubtless authentic but probably is not the "Wineland" of the sagas.

Partly because of blinders imposed by certain misconceptions, and partly for want of systematic comparison between the two sagas, *GS* has been characterized variously as late in composition, imitative of *ES*, influenced by romantic, fictional sagas, and poorly written. Only within very recent years has *GS* begun to come into its own as a bearer of reliable tradition. In 1952 Sigurður Nordal decided that both sagas must have been written at about the same time, but in different parts of the country, and independently.[7] Gwyn Jones inclines to an equitable distribution of authority to the two versions, counterbalancing some of the disfavor with which previous writers have regarded the *Flateyjarbók* accounts. He seems, however, to regard the two sagas as independently based, with *GS* the younger of the two. In his translation of the two sagas, he at times blends the two versions by expanding *GS*

[7] "Sagalitteraturen," *Nordisk kultur,* VIII:B, 180–273. Cf. pp. 248f.:

Endelig skal der om de to sagaer om Vinlandsrejserne, *Eir. s.* og *Grœnl. þ. (Grœnlendinga saga)* bemærkes, at der ikke synes at være nogen særlige grunde til at betragte den sidste som meget yngre (og mere upaalidelig) end den første. Tværtimod er disse to sagaer, der delvis behandler det samme emne, saa *uafhengige* af hinanden, at den naturligste forklaring synes at være, at de er skrevet omtrent samtidig, men i hver sin landsdel. Eir. s. følger den opfattelse, der kan føres tilbage til Gunnlaugr Leifsson og ogsaa er fulgt af Snorri i Heimskringla, at det var Leifr Eiríksson (missionæren!), der havde æren af at opdage Vinland, medens Grœnl. þ. nævner den ellers ukendte Bjarni Herjólfsson i stedet, hvilket trods visse urimelige enkeltheder godt kan være den ældre og mere ægte tradition.

from *ES*, a procedure fatal to all textual criticism. At the same time, Professor Tryggvi J. Oleson finds *GS* more pristine and reliable and thinks, on grounds not spelled out, that it must have been composed early, that is, by 1200.[8]

More decisive are the points of view recently expressed in *Saga-Book of the Viking Society for Northern Research* by two Icelandic scholars, Jón Jóhannesson and Björn Þorsteinsson.[9] Jóhannesson gives excellent evidence for the view that *GS* is more than half a century *older* than *ES* and that nothing indicates that *GS* used written sources, whereas *ES* apparently employed *GS* and repeatedly modified the latter's accounts tendentiously. *ES*, says Jóhannesson, was written later than 1264 since it mentions *Brandr byskup inn fyrri* as distinct from Brandr Jónsson, Bishop of Hólar 1263–1264. This argument is important, though not conclusive, for there is always the possibility of a redactor's alteration. *GS*, says Jóhannesson, must be earlier than once thought. In fact it must be one of the oldest sagas, from the days of Bishop Brandr Sæmundarson (1163–1201). For the saga apparently knows nothing of the later saga of Óláfr Tryggvason by the monk Gunnlaugr Leifsson († 1219), who contaminated all later sources with the notion that King Óláfr (using Leifr Eiríksson as his agent) christianized Greenland along with the other Scandinavian countries whose conversion was credited to his religious zeal.[10] And since the earliest records—antedating Gunnlaugr Leifsson's tendentious fiction—say nothing of

[8] Jones, *The Norse Atlantic Saga: Being the Norse Voyages of Discovery and Settlement to Iceland, Greenland, America*; Oleson, *Early Voyages and Northern Approaches, 1000–1632,* pp. 18–35.

[9] *Saga-Book,* XVI: Part 1, Jóhannesson, "The Date of the Composition of the Saga of the Greenlanders," trans. T. J. Oleson, pp. 54–66; Parts 2–3, Þorsteinsson, "Some Observations on the Discoveries and the Cultural History of the Norsemen," pp. 173–191. Jóhannesson (p. 57) feels that Nordal ("Sagalitteraturen," *Nordisk kultur,* pp. 248–249) should have gone further than his statement that *ES* and *GS* were approximately contemporaneous, but products of different parts of Iceland.

[10] Jóhannesson, "The Date of Composition," *Saga-Book,* pp. 60 ff. Óláfr's christianizing activities on Greenland are not mentioned in Ari's *Íslendingabók. Óláfs saga Tryggvasonar,* in *Heimskringla* (Chaps. 86 and 96), and *Kristni saga* credit Óláfr with this activity. But *Historia Norwegiæ, Ágrip af Noregs konunga sögum,* and *Óláfs saga Tryggvasonar eftir Odd munk Snorrason* all state that Óláfr christianized five countries: Norway, Iceland, Shetland, the Orkneys, and the Faroes. Illogically, the last-named work then lists an uncounted sixth: Greenland! None of these works mentions Leifr. Further confusion of sources is seen in the related poems *Óláfs drápa Tryggvasonar* and *Rekstefja* (by Hallar-Steinn), which substitute Greenland for the Faroes (cf. Finnur Jónsson, *Den norsk-islandske Skjaldedigtning. A. Tekst efter Håndskrifterne,* I. Bind, 575f. and 576, respectively.

this activity in connection with either the King or Leifr Eiríksson, there is no reason to place credence in Leifr's supposed visit to Norway, his return to Greenland as a *missionary,* and his discovery of American shores through *accident* during the home voyage. Many of the peculiarities of *ES* reveal the joint effect of its double source, *GS* on the one hand and the influence of the monk Gunnlaugr on the other. The author of *ES* may, it is true, have had access to some written sources that were older than the *GS* manuscript he used, but the sophisticated and "learned" material in *ES* has no counterpart in *GS*. The two sagas represent different generations, different tastes, and different states of knowledge.

Some of this is enlarged upon by Björn Þorsteinsson, who thinks that our knowledge of the Vinland voyages should be based solely upon *GS*, which was "written before the Fall which the composition of history as entertainment and as propaganda betokened."[11] The author of *ES*, possessing all the geographical sophistication of his age, rationalized the distances and voyages involved in locating Vinland (his major error, concerning the distance from North America to Ireland, resulted from his failure to visualize an increase in the distances between the lines of longitude from north to south!). Artistically superior to his predecessor, the author of *ES* poeticized his narrative, and though he expanded it, he concentrated the story around fewer persons. As a greater master of language, he wrote more flexibly and creatively; and, being particularly interested in Karlsefni and Guðríðr and their descendants, he made them the pivot of the narrative, while supplying Christian edification by crediting Leifr with the missionary achievement not claimed in sources closer to the Greenlanders. At the same time he eliminates the heathen Bjarni Herjólfsson and makes Leifr's discovery of our shores a purely accidental achievement. And finally, in his transformation of Freydís from monster to heroine, he "frees the Brattahlíð clan from a family disgrace."[12] Þorsteinsson does not, however, believe in *Wineland*:

About A.D. 900 Norsemen found the Labrador coast and probably reached a point south of the 50° parallel (i.e., the St. Lawrence estuary or White

[11] Þorsteinsson, "Some Observations," *Saga-Book,* pp. 60 ff. On p. 185 he had already written: "People seem to have been quick to believe stories about Leifr as a missionary, so it was necessary to rewrite the Grænlendinga saga to suit the new wisdom, and to make it pleasanter and more edifying for Christians."

[12] *Ibid.,* p. 186.

Bay in Newfoundland). They saw wide lands, ever more fertile, stretching away to the south and they called this Vínland, either as an advertisement or because a German on board (Tyrkir—probably from Thuringia) thought the land looked like the wine-producing districts of south Germany. The name was enough to cause legends about the isles of bliss to be attached to it.[13]

With this last paragraph Helge Ingstad would doubtless largely agree, for like Sven Söderberg, Fridtjof Nansen, and Väinö Tanner, he has postulated an Old Icelandic *Vinland*, 'meadow land,' rather than *Vínland* (with long vowel), 'wine-land' or 'grapevine land.'[14] To this interpretation Ingstad attributes his success in discovering Norse ruins in what is incontestably an area of meadow, with fine grass for grazing, a matter of great moment for cattle-raising settlers, as nobody will deny. Ingstad, therefore, feels justified in repudiating as apocryphal the whole business of grapes and vines. But, that conclusion is a great *non sequitur*. The evidence indicates that the grapevines were solidly rooted in saga tradition from the beginning. The vines in no way conflict with the discovery of Norse remains in Newfoundland, but comport perfectly with the more southerly additional explorations to which the sagas make allusion and which, even in the absence of such specific reference, would almost certainly have to be posited in the case of men who avowedly had already gone to much trouble to seek out the American coast (not known to them by this name, of course) and were resolved to ascertain its geography, its products, and its suitability for settlement, in the same tradition as that which had already established them in the most favorable areas of Greenland. Good grassland, now, however important to settlers, and despite the scholarly use that

[13] *Ibid.*, p. 187.

[14] Ingstad, "Vinland Ruins Prove Vikings Found the New World," *National Geographic*, CXXVI, No. 5 (November, 1964), 708–734. Söderberg, "Vinland," lecture on this theory at Lund in 1898, developed and printed in *Sydsvenska Dagbladet Snällposten* (Malmö), No. 295 (October 30, 1910). Nansen, *In Northern Mists: Arctic Explorations in Early Times*, trans. Arthur G. Chater, II, 63–65. Tanner, *De gamla nordbornas Helluland, Markland och Vinland. Ett försök att lokalisera Vinlandsresornas huvudetapper i de isländska sagorna* (*Budkavlen*, XX, No. 1 [Åbo, 1941]). Tanner's thesis is negatively reviewed by Sigurður Thorarinsson in "Några reflexioner med anledning av V. Tanners skrift," *Ymer. Tidskrift utgiven av Svenska sällskapet för antropologi och geografi*, LXII, No. 1–2, 39–46. Thorarinsson refers to an article or pamphlet written earlier by W. A. Munn, "Wineland Voyages: Location of Helluland, Markland, and Wineland, from the Icelandic Saga" (St. Johns, Newfoundland, 1914).

Ingstad and Tanner have made of the concept, could not have been quite as spectacular to Icelanders and Greenlanders of that day as we moderns believe. Saga-writers of the later centuries, as well as modern critics, have read into the name Grœnland a certain irony, if not fraud, because the name was assertedly given to the area by Eiríkr rauði as part of his plans for real estate promotion. *Pari passu* with the deterioration of the climate in later centuries, Greenland made a predominantly cold and icy impression upon medieval commentators. That Eiríkr would have wished to portray his discoveries in a favorable light, is obvious. But his description, conceived partly in a spirit of humor, is not dishonest. For in reality the areas on Greenland so wisely chosen by the canny Icelanders for settlement were in summertime green and attractive, with adequate pasturage, and have been described thus by visitors even in our day. A reference by explorer Leifr to green pasturage in his own newly explored territories southwest of Greenland strikes one as anticlimactic. The use of analogy is a natural response in proceeding from a known to an unknown, or to a less well-known, object, quality, or place. The known in this case is that the nomenclature used by Eiríkr for his new colony was the most favorable one that the country legitimately could bear. Eiríkr's son Leifr, investigating and naming yet newer lands with a similar purpose in mind (that of creating a favorable impression in order to induce colonists to take up their abode there) would, other things being equal, have proceeded in exactly the same way. Ignoring for the moment such textual problems as what a saga-writer would have put down generations later, we may assume that the real-life Leifr would not have told fatuous lies about the new land in order to deceive his father, his adventurous brothers whom he encouraged to visit Vínland after him, his neighbors from boyhood on, his brother Þorsteinn's widow, and her distinguished new husband Karlsefni, who subsequently spent a good three years investigating the new lands in the full and reasonable expectation of success, and whose descendants reported the narrative material which forms a large part of the Vínland tradition. We assume that Leifr would have named the land as advantageously and as interestingly as possible. His relatives and colleagues in exploration were themselves men of intelligence. The sarcastic verses on the failure to find grapes (authentic or not), which are attributed to Þórhallr veiðimaðr and are followed by his defection from Karlsefni's expedition, effectively highlight a significant situation: Leifr's descriptions must have carried basic conviction among his contemporaries. The monograph by W. H. Babcock more than half a century ago argued that Leifr's *vínber* must have been grapes and not currants or various other types of berries, several of which grew, and continue to grow, on Greenland itself: "It is not at all believable that men should sail out of one profusion of small fruit into another, like in kind, but inferior and despised at home, and trumpet their experience abroad as something wonderful."[15]

Babcock would locate Leifr's Wineland in southern New England, in New Jersey, or even in the area of Chesapeake Bay. Perhaps a majority of the commentators find southern New England the most likely candidate for this designation, and in view of the probable necessity of connecting the land of grapes with the southern boundary of the salmon that likewise figure in the story, probably the Hudson River, there is good reason for agreeing. It is not the purpose here, however, to attempt precise geographical locations. What does seem conveyed by the sagas is that the Scandinavians got far enough south to sense the apparent endlessness of the American coastline. They spent much time—many months during several different summers—exploring the coast. This implies sailing in and out of inlets, exploring rivers, rounding islands, cautiously tramping inland, climbing elevations, and so on. Their ever-lengthening distance from a trustworthy base, the constant concern for supplies and for winter preparations—for want of which Karlsefni's men once nearly met disaster—would set certain natural limits to their voyaging, even apart from vagaries of wind, precautions as to sandbars and reefs, and the wear and tear on tackle and ships' bottoms. We shall doubtless never know how far south Leifr and/or his contemporaries penetrated, but on purely practical grounds it would be surprising indeed if they had not at least once sailed as far south as present-day Manhattan, though we should hate to think with Tornöe that modern Manhattan actually covers the remains of a Norse colony thus lost forever![16]

On equally practical grounds, consequently, the grapes which are so

[15] Babcock, *Early Norse Visits to North America,* p. 91. See also Thorarinsson, "Några reflexioner," *Ymer.* Of course, the precise descriptions of the saga with respect to the naming operations do not have to be taken at face value since the names may gradually have become attached to the western lands during the protracted discussions (*umrœður*) of them subsequently held on Greenland (see *Íslenzk fornrit,* IV: *Eyrbyggja saga, Grœnlendingasögur,* p. 221 n. 3).

[16] J. Kr. Tornöe, *Early American History: Norsemen Before Columbus,* pp. 100 ff., esp. p. 106.

persistent a feature of the Vínland story, far from being something inherently improbable and derivative, are precisely the most likely features of the entire narrative complex. If anything has impressed itself on all visitors, early or late, to southern New England, it is the prevalence of grapes and grapevines. The vines often range up to six inches in diameter, a circumstance that must have left its mark on visitors from Iceland and Greenland, as well as confused later generations with traditions about "timber" after Vínland again became lost (we sense that whereas Markland remained a precise location to Greenlanders of later centuries, *Vínland* gradually dropped from their expectations.) The grapes themselves, larger and more succulent than any berry that grows in either Iceland or Greenland, would have been a delightful surprise, but scarcely the mysterious product, unidentifiable by the newcomers, that some commentators will make of them. The asserted discovery of the grapes does not, in order for its probability to be established, rest upon our *in toto* acceptance of the precise account given in *GS* about the *suðrmaðr* Tyrkr. Tyrkr was not necessarily *intoxicated* when discovered with the grapes.[17] The saga states merely that he was cheerful, perhaps even exercising his sense of humor by assertedly spoofing his comrades, rolling his eyes, and talking German for a while in order to heighten the effect of his story through the well-known technique of retardation. Or, if Tyrkr is chiefly invented, this heightening of the narrative is part of the art of the *sagnamaðr* himself. There is indeed a distinct possibility that on the score of history Tyrkr is an echo of the "helper" type abounding in various folktales. He is in truth a dispensable figure, one who serves a pleasant narrative purpose but whose absence would in no way diminish the inherent probability of the grapes themselves. One must reject the argument sometimes advanced that our hardy but "primitive" explorers could have known little or nothing about grapes and wine. No staple certainly, wine, acquired through pillage and purchase, had nevertheless been consumed abroad and even imported into Scandinavia for several generations by the time of the Vínland voyages. Men like Eiríkr and his sons, and certainly the mer-

[17] See *GS,* Chap. 4. Holger Arbman is one of those who unnecessarily assume that Tyrkr was drunk (*The Vikings,* p. 113). The dictionaries of Old Icelandic indicate that the word *skapgóðr,* whose neuter form appears here with the dative of the person (*fóstra hans var skapgott*), means "in good spirits." Compare with this such words as *ölr,* 'drunk'; *ölóðr,* 'drunk'; *ölkátr, ölteitr,* and *ölreifr,* 'drunk with ale'; *víndrukkinn* and *vínóðr,* 'wine-drunk.'

chant Karlsefni, were not ignorant and isolated cottagers. One or more of their followers, now lost to history, may even have had some practical knowledge of the rougher methods of wine-making, for which, strictly speaking, nothing more is required than the crushing of the grapes, followed by five or six days of fermentation. The "excellence" of the wine thus produced (see Adam of Bremen) is not to be judged by sensitive modern standards of vintage wine-bibbing. As Babcock remarks, the principal criterion of the Vikings would have been the strength of the intoxication produced.[18]

Tornöe, who thinks that Leifr found grapes in Falmouth and on Martha's Vineyard, writes: "I have made a special study of the wild grapes which still grow in many places in America. . . . Wherever some of the old forests still stand, there are usually many wild grapes growing up along the trees, hanging under the branches, sometimes all the way to the top. These clusters growing on maple, birch, elm, oak, are clusters of grapes, not of berries."[19] I do not know how many "old forests" still stand in New England but I have observed that a similar situation obtains in once cleared areas that now again are covered with forest.

No saga states that these explorers actually did make wine. But they certainly found impressive grape vines and, in proper season, grapes. Thórdarson mentions four wild varieties of grapes, of which the first and second are called "fox grapes and doubtless are the principal kinds found by Leif and Thorfinn."[20] The four kinds are *Vitis labrusca, V. aestivalis, V. cordifolia, V. vulpina.* M. L. Fernald has some strong arguments in favor of *Vaccinium Vitis-Idæa* or cowberry or mountain cranberry.[21] Fernald's philological conceptions are notably weak. In an article on "Philological Aspects of the 'Plants of Wineland the Good'," A. LeRoy Andrews points out that *vín* was an expensive, imported, foreign drink to the Scandinavians, and anything made of native berries would probably not even have been thought of as wine.[22] The Icelandic Annals for 1203 indicate that berry wine was made for the first time in Iceland that year. As for currants (Sw. *vinbär, Ribes rubrum, nigrum,*

[18] *Early Norse Visits,* p. 93.
[19] *Early American History,* p. 70.
[20] Matthías Thórdarson, *The Vinland Voyages,* p. 44.
[21] "Notes on the Plants of Wineland the Good," *Rhodora: Journal of the New England Botanical Club,* XII, No. 134 (February, 1910), 17–38.
[22] *Rhodora: Journal of the New England Botanical Club,* XV, No. 170 (February, 1913), 28–35.

N. *rips,* Da. *ribs.* etc.), the evidence is that their cultivation and use are relatively late.[23]

With respect to Tyrkr's possible unhistoricity (unaccompanied by any corresponding weakening of the purported discovery of grapes in general), one notes the extent to which, in preparation for the narrative of his discovery of grapes, he is characterized in appearance and qualities.[24] In Þórhallr the Huntsman of *ES,* there is a (highly contrasting but similarly detailed) parallel with Tyrkr, one equally consonant with a possibly fictional situation: "Þórhallr was of great size, dark of hue and giant-like; he was rather advanced in age, bad-tempered, taciturn and uncommunicative as a rule, underhanded, but abusive, and ever eager for the worst course. He had had little to do with Christianity since it had come to Greenland. He was little given to friendships, but Eiríkr had long been devoted to him. He was aboard Þorvaldr's ship because he was widely acquainted with the wilderness."[25] Tyrkr and Þórhallr are thus exact opposites in size, character, and degree of loquacity; each is a favorite of a member of the Brattahlíð clan; each has some special capacity to his credit. Each performs, likewise, a peculiar act: Tyrkr rolls his eyes, speaks his foreign tongue, and Þórhallr mutters heathen rigamarole while pinching himself. Each disappears from the party, is searched for, and performs thereafter one additional exploit. But in each of these features, Þórhallr is characterized at greater length and with greater creative skill. *GS* can thus be judged the "giver," *ES* the elaborating receiver, of a "helper" motif. Note the contrasting use of the word *skap,* "disposition," in the two

[23] Elof Hellquist, *Svensk etymologisk ordbok,* Tredje upplagan, Band II: *O:Ö,* p. 1348, s.v. *vinbär.* S. Ö. Bogason, *Ensk-Íslenzk orðabók,* p. 149, s.v. 'currant.' *Vínber* is the ancient and modern Icelandic word for grape. The word for currant is *kúrenna* (*þurkuð smávínber*), *ribsber.*

[24] "Han var brattleitr ok lauseygr, smáskitligr í andliti, lítill vexti, ok vesalligr, en íþróttamaðr á allskonar hagleik." (Tyrkr was prominent of forehead and shifty-eyed, with an insignificant face, of small stature and puny, but expert in every kind of craftsmanship). Arthur Reeves, *The Finding of Wineland the Good: The History of the Icelandic Discovery, Edited and Translated from the Earliest Records,* p. 147 and facsimile facing.

[25] *ES*, Chap. 8: "Þórhallr var mikill vexti, svartr ok þursligr; hann var heldr við aldr, ódæll í skapi, hljóðlyndr, fámálugr hversdagliga, undirfǫrull, ok þó atmælasamr, ok fýstisk jafnan hins verra. Hann hafði lítt við trú blandazk, síðan hon kom á Grœnland. Þórhallr var lítt vinsældum horfinn, en þó hafði Eiríkr lengi tal af honum haldit. Hann var á skipi með þeim Þorvaldi, því at honum var víða kunnigt i óbygðum." This is the *Skálholtsbók* version, quoted from Reeves, *The Finding of Wineland,* p. 133 and facsimile facing.

sagas: *GS* has *skapgott, ES* has *ódæll í skapi,* an interesting case of very probable influence of *GS* upon *ES*, for there are already enough adjectives applied to Þórhallr to make unnecessary any reference to the syllable *skap*. And sure enough, the *Hauksbók* version of *ES* has edited out the telltale phrase in Chapter 8, right in the midst of that part of the *Hauksbók* rendering which received the literary ministrations of Haukr lagmaðr himself.[26]

We are certainly not the first to have noted that each saga has one such character, neither of whom appears in the other saga; that each is dispensable; that the two, in a sense, cancel each other out by the contradictory and yet curiously complementary nature of their exploits. But if Þórhallr is an inverse pendant to Tyrkr, does not this constitute an excellent narrative criterion, not merely for confirming the recent suspicion (on other grounds) that *ES* is younger than the parallel *GS,* but for establishing as well that, instead of being based to any appreciable extent on divergent oral or written tradition of possible equal validity, *ES* is at this point at least a literarily inspired, conscious revision of *GS*? For Karlsefni and his surly follower Þórhallr (the latter known only to *ES*) know that they are expected to find grapevines. This is clearly an item that bulks more largely in their minds than the offhand manner in which the discovery of grapes by Leifr as referred to in *ES* would appear to warrant (see the plot summaries above). Certainties may not be obtained on present evidence, but if probabilities are compared, a Karlsefni disappointed and a Þórhallr angered over the lack of fruited vines not only create, in the artistically sophisticated *ES,* high narrative interest, but are in some measure even dependent upon a rather pointed discovery of grapes by some predecessor. Conversely, the discovery of grapes by Leifr's company is narrated in such detail in the otherwise rather terse *GS* that it could only with much greater difficulty be extrapolated from a thus rather unmotivated story of Þórhallr. Furthermore, the whole concept of Vínland and the urgency of the discovery of grapes become almost meaningless in *ES,* which, despite its artistic skill, is so interested in making Karlsefni the center of interest that his expedition requires four times as much space

[26] There is no indication of the phrase in *Ísl. fornrit,* IV, 222, but Hermannsson (*The Vinland Sagas* [*Islandica,* XXX] p. 20) carries the *Skálholtsbók* variant (his ms B) of this Chapter 8 (not so labeled in *Skálholtsbók*). Gustav Storm's little edition of 1891 (*Eiríks saga rauða* . . .) prints the phrase as does, of course, Sven B. F. Jansson (*Sagorna om Vinland,* p. 61).

as its parallel in *GS,* whereas Leifr's voyage (omitting the Norwegian and Hebridean material) is reduced to about one fifth, with the name Vínland not appearing at all in connection with Leifr's voyage but being first quoted, somewhat without motive, as a proposed goal for Karlsefni. Most commentators agree that the author of *ES* had more knowledge and greater interest where Karlsefni and his clan were concerned.

But *ES* also exhibits derivative details that indicate its dependence upon *GS.* For example, as a substitute for the discarded finding of grapes by Tyrkr *suðrmaðr, ES* introduces a highly fictionalized Gaelic couple, the swift-footed team who in Old Icelandic have been re-Christianized (or reheathenized?) Haki and Hekja.[27] The precious and stylized incident in which they are sent forth and return after three days, the one neatly bearing (a cluster of) grapes, the other a sheaf of self-sown (in *Hauksbók* "newly sown")[28] grain, is a narrative feature that seems inserted once again in answer to some antecedent expectation of just such a discovery. The incident pops up prematurely in the saga, as Þórhallr's spiteful verse about the lack of grapes indicates,[29] and the author may well have intended to order the events differently. But again, dependency upon traditions about Leifr Eiríksson is indicated, inasmuch as the Scots runners have been acquired by Karlsefni from Leifr, who in turn has received them from King Óláfr. Thus, Leifr's reputation and importance have to some extent been preserved

[27] See *Barðar saga Snæfellsáss, Íslendinga sögur,* III, 346, where a male and a female pair of magicians (*sejðmenn*) are sent on a mission to Helluland accompanied by Christian priests! Their names are Kraki and Krekja. For tradition concerning the Scots as fast runners, see the mention of Nagli in *Erybyggja saga,* Chap. 18 (*Ísl. sög.,* III), p. 29: "Álfgeirr fór til vistar í Máhavahlíð til Þórarins svarta ok félagi hans með honum, er Nagli hét, mikill maðr ok fóthvatr. Hann var skozkr at kyni." Álfgeirr and Nagli appear also at the battle of Máhavahlíð; see *Landnámabók* (*Ísl. sög.,* I, 69) and Halldór Hermannsson, *The Problem of Wineland* (*Islandica,* XXV), p. 19 n. 2 and p. 20 n. 1.

[28] The only trace of the grain motif in *GS* is the *kornhjálmr,* which implies a stack of some kind of grain, covered over. This could be either a clever transformation of the theme of grain, or a case of the loss of supporting detail, or a genuine reminiscence.

[29] After six lines of complaint over the fraudulent promise of *drykk inn bazta* (one recalls Adam's or Sveinn Úlfsson's *optimum vinum*), he finishes the stanza:

heldr's svát ek krýp at keldu;
komat vín á grǫn mína.

(instead I must creep to a spring;
wine has not touched my lips.)

in the later saga, while the specific *utilization* of the undoubtedly fictional Haki/Hekja, who are quite unknown to Leifr's saga (*GS*), has been attributed to Karlsefni, chief hero of *ES*. All this seems an eminently reasonable attempt at a toned down rationalization and adaptation of a story about grapes (and wild grain) which the author of *ES* could not in good conscience transfer lock, stock, and barrel to Karlsefni. The opposite hypothesis, namely that the story of Tyrkr is derived from the pale shadow of Haki/Hekja, strains credence.

The foregoing illustrates not merely that Haki and Hekja are derived invention (very few critics will nowadays disagree) but even that the more centrally integrated Tyrkr is also suspect. His role of the traditional "helper" of popular oral fiction is strengthened in *GS* at the point where Leifr and his crew are sailing back to Brattahlíð and Leifr's sharp eyes spy shipwrecked sailors on a reef. When the Greenlanders heave to within shouting distance, is it Leifr, the authoritative skipper, who hails the distressed mariners?[30] No, this action is ascribed to the little man with the foreign accent, Leifr's retainer Tyrkr, somewhat big in the boots, one might thus suppose, now that he has discovered grapes and caused a large country to be named for the viticulture thus enticingly conjured up. But no such motivation is indicated in the saga, which, read in its own terms, ingeniously attempts through this tour de force to persuade us that quaint little Tyrkr, previously portrayed as a family retainer of whom Leifr is very fond, actually is a character of social importance, perhaps first mate aboard ship,[31] and not an ad hoc invention created to account for the finding of the grapes, only to be dropped from the story thereafter.[32] Tyrkr is the only crew

[30] When Þórir identifies himself and asks "*hvert er þitt nafn?*" (Chap. 4) it is, properly enough, Leifr who answers and thereafter conducts the negotiations. The use of Tyrkr's name cannot easily be haplological, for he has not appeared in the saga for twenty-eight lines of ms text (cf. Reeves, *The Finding of Wineland*, pp. 147f. and facsimiles).

[31] The position of first mate would in the sagas ordinarily indicate a person of means and probably co-owner of the ship.

[32] Madelaine R. Brown and Francis P. Magoun argue that Tyrkr was an historical character, perhaps a *Weinkenner* from the Rhine or Moselle districts ("Tyrkir, First German in North America," *Modern Language Notes*, LXI, No. 8 [December, 1946], 547–551). Halldór Hermannsson takes too seriously the designation *fóstri* applied to Tyrkr by Leifr, deeming that in itself an argument against Tyrkr's historicity ("Tyrkir, Leif Erikson's Foster-Father," *Modern Language Notes*, LXIX, No. 6 [June, 1954], 388–393). But the term is surely rhetorical and, as such, no argument in either direction.

member to be mentioned by name under any of the captains mentioned in the rather spare narrative of the first five voyages in *GS* (the remarkable *þáttr* of Freydís is an exception and will be discussed below).

III

To sum it up, this study so far has attempted to confirm the view that *GS* is the older saga and that *ES* not only is materially younger but in some respects represents a rewriting of *GS*. Despite Björn Þorsteinsson, it would be false to assume that we must limit ourselves to *GS* simply because of its greater age and closeness in time to the events narrated.[33] *GS* need not be historical throughout, and *ES* need not at all points be historically inferior to *GS*.[34] Both sagas contain fictions, but the *GS* version, in which Bjarni Herjólfsson stumbles upon the American coast by accident, after which Leifr, later followed by others, carries out systematic explorations, clearly has the greater claim upon our belief. Let us examine that proposition.

Repeated reading of the saga variants leads to the conclusion that Leifr's arrival in the New World was the result of a carefully planned expedition, as told in *Flateyjarbók* (*GS*), rather than a matter of accident, as told in the *Skálholtsbók-Hauksbók* version (*ES*). There are a number of reasons for this view, some circumstantial, some literary. One of the former is family history and the rather unique heritage that Leifr must have received from his father, both genetically and through environment, for Eiríkr's achievements in setting up the Greenland colony on an enduring basis, after careful and persistent exploration, *are* unique. If we should believe anything at all it is that there would have been careful planning and consultation about any voyage that Leifr undertook for the discovery of new lands. Such a voyage, too, would give him scope for careful exploration, collection of products, and the naming of a country after the most interesting, if not the most valuable, of these. If Leifr had stumbled upon our coasts by accident, upon returning to Greenland from a somewhat unlikely apprenticeship with the Norwegian king, it is unlikely that his reputation would have been any greater than that of his prudent countryman Bjarni Herjólfsson, who, following a long voyage in which he ran short of water, was un-

[33] See Þorsteinsson, "Some Observations," p. 191.

[34] See Jóhannesson, "The Date of Composition," p. 65; Nordal, "Sagalitteraturen," p. 249.

certain of his location and fearful as to shoals and unfavorable winds and currents and became increasingly conscious of the shortness of summer. As a matter of fact, since reliable early evidence of that voyage is wanting, a negative consideration may be accorded some weight here, relating to the new involvements, responsibilities, way of life, and ambitions of those who were attempting to establish themselves on the westernmost frontier of Scandinavian civilization. There is considerable doubt that the traditional voyage to Norway which the Family Sagas feature for young Icelanders of good family could play the same role among the Greenlanders. The direct voyages to or from Norway—without stopovers on Iceland—that the sagas seem to suggest for Leifr, Bjarni, and Karlsefni are also probably anachronistic as such for the eleventh century. One sees well enough that narrators of the thirteenth century would not be bothered by such small things.

However, an accidental discovery of the mainland must have been made by somebody, and his response would then have been more in keeping with Bjarni's alleged reaction in the *GS* than with the exploration and gathering of products offhandedly attributed to Leifr in *ES*. But saving only this one accidental skirting voyage by Bjarni (as in *GS*), or alternatively, the combined accidental and exploring journey by Leifr reported in *ES*, all the voyages of exploration claimed in either saga were made from the comparative closeness of Greenland waters. Despite the learned researches of distinguished writers, the correct version of Leifr's voyage must more certainly approximate the reasoned account given in *GS* than the watered-down, illogical, and indeed virtually impossible version of it presented by *ES*. It is remarkable that in *ES* Leifr should be so shadowy as an explorer, whereas the saga is relatively explicit about his romantic affair on the Hebrides. The ironic result of this is that the very saga in which *both* these improbabilities are so incompatibly present has received the most persistent scholarly endorsement over its literary rival, *GS*. Leifr must in reality have made a stay of some length in "Vínland" or whatever, well equipped and with a crew willing and prepared for exactly this type of activity in view of Bjarni's accidental discovery a number of years earlier. By the year 1000 or so, the colony on Greenland would have had fifteen years of maturity, a modest degree of wealth, a good deal of experience of Greenland coastal waters and would have spent many a long winter during which repeated discussion (*umrœður*) would have taken place as to what lands and treasures might be had to the south and west. Leifr, not yet encumbered with the chieftaincy at Brattahlíð, was doubtless ready for some exploit with teeth in it, and surely, in view of the westward orientation of these Icelanders one step removed, he would be more interested in the possibility of a real achievement than a traditional young gentleman's visit to the Norwegian court. Chapter 3 of *GS* states as a matter of fact that Leifr "fór á fund Bjarna Herjólfssonar ok keypti skip at honum" for the voyage to the new countries. In other words, as a young man now ripe for achievement and adventure, Leifr for the first time requires a ship of his own. He has thus not sailed an expedition to Norway, as asserted in the rewritten version found in *ES*. Again, however, there are complications, for readers who rely on translations or even on printed Icelandic texts are likely not to observe that a minimum of fifteen years (and conceivably, though improbably, as many as twenty-eight years) has apparently intervened between the end of Chapter 2 of *GS*, where Bjarni gives up sailing and settles down on his inherited estate at Herjólfsnes, and the puzzling opening statement, seemingly in conflict with it, in Chapter 3: "The next thing to be related is that Bjarni Herjólfsson travelled out of Greenland to visit Earl Eiríkr, and the Earl received him well."[35] The fact is that nearly sixty parchment columns separate the one statement (*Flateyjarbók,* col. 223b) from the other (*Flat.,* col. 281b). The various segments of *GS* are not all written consecutively but are interspersed with other matter and inserted into the text at the spots deemed chronologically appropriate by the compiler of the manuscript. This is readily seen by studying the facsimiles in *Corpus Codicum Islandicorum* or Reeves' *The Finding of Wineland the Good.*

This whole business of the dates of the Vinland voyages requires some further study. Haraldur Bessason, citing the "opinion of historians," has decided that "Leifr Eiríksson carried out his explorations in North America about 990."[36] But Earl Eiríkr Hákonarson could scarcely have received Bjarni previous to his assumption of the rule over Norway in 1000. Tornöe, following a suggestion made nearly

[35] "Þat er nú þessi næst, at Bjarni Herjólfsson kom útan af Grœnlandi á fund Eiríks jarls, ok tók jarl við honum vel." Text from *Ísl. fornrit,* IV, 248; cf. note 1 on the same page and note 3 on p. 247, the latter with reference to the disposition of *Flateyjarbók,* at this point.

[36] "Some Notes on Leifr Eiriksson's National Origin and the Sources on Greenland and Vinland," *The Icelandic Canadian,* Winter, 1965, p. 19. Bessason's notes are slightly confused so that the precise documentation intended is unclear.

two hundred years ago by Gerhardt Schöning, wishes to place Bjarni's journey to Norway a dozen years earlier, when "Earl Eirik ruled Vemork in Norway, in conjunction with the Danish king."[37] But Earl Eiríkr's father, the famous heathen Jarl Hákon of Hlaðir, Þrándheimr, whose harshness and concupiscence led to his downfall and death after a quarter century of rule in 995 (Norwegian dates before 995 are not impeccably reliable), was the only person in Norway of sufficient stature to rival a national king and thus fulfill the purpose which I think the saga-writer would deem adequate for dignifying Bjarni. Hákon was in fact succeeded in his territories by Óláfr Tryggvason, whose own defeat and death in 1000 was brought about in part by Earl Eiríkr Hákonarson, who had been out of the country in 995 and who gained revenge and the rule—retaining his title of Earl—at a single blow. But in 988–989—to return to Tornöe's surmise—a very young, tributary, and at that time unimportant ruler could have done rather little to worm his way into a saga about Greenlanders. According to *Heimskringla,* the illegitimate Eiríkr, no favorite of his father Hákon, might have been as much as thirteen-years-old when he made his way to Denmark and soon thereafter was granted the title of Earl and sent by King Haraldr Gormsson blátǫnn nominally to administer, under Danish protection, the Norwegian districts of Vingulmǫrk, inland and north of present-day Oslo. Why—and how—would a Greenland merchant have gone to visit him? Haraldr Gormsson is believed to have died about 985, and by 989 he had been succeeded by Sveinn Haraldsson tjúguskegg. The chronology of the *Flateyjarbók* indicates from the manner of its insertion a voyage no earlier than the year 1000. If Bjarni traveled before 995, the compiler knew nothing of it. In order to be received by the Earl in the latter's capacity as ruler of Norway (after Óláfr's death September 9, 1000 and until 1014), Bjarni would probably have gone to Norway not earlier than 1001 and returned in 1002, and Leifr's voyage could not have taken place before 1003. Bjarni's trip to Norway seems somewhat unmotivated for a so well-established and no longer strictly young man. The voyage cannot be disproved, it is true, but suspicion arises that it may constitute this particular saga-writer's device for assuring Leifr a large, seaworthy, and "pedigreed" ship rather than one of the anonymous vessels of the vintage of 986. At least, a saga-writer of the year 1195 or so might likely be conscious

[37] *Early American History,* p. 47.

of such a theme as the preponderance of trade with Greenland for economic and political reasons came to be carried on in foreign bottoms and as the hard-working Greenlanders, despite their access to prime Markland timber, became progressively more content with small, specialized coasting vessels. As indicated, we accept Bjarni as an historical personage, the first known European to view the American coast, but there is doubt as to his voyage to Norway fifteen years later.

Though the actual provenience of Leifr's ship need not and cannot be determined, one notes in this little incident the saga-writer's artistic concern for logic and for detail. With equal artistry, the criticism which Bjarni allegedly receives, not from mere provincials on Greenland but among the sophisticates of the Norwegian Earl's entourage, is cleverly utilized as an incentive, not for a piqued and certainly competent enough Bjarni Herjólfsson to repair his reputation, but for the oncoming hero Leifr to win *his* spurs. This is at once clever narrative obfuscation and subtle displacement of psychological motivation. Despite a supposition by Halldór Hermannsson, there are no grounds for assuming that Bjarni and his crew members would have had to keep quiet about their American experience during the intervening years.[38]

It will be pertinent at this point to discuss a critical linguistic matter, namely the word *Vínland*. The proper pronunciation of this Icelandic word, with its long vowel, is effectively obscured in translation, but so carefully was, and is, the difference in pronunciation observed between long and short vowels in Icelandic (thus, between *vín,* 'vine, wine,' and any hypothetical *vin,* gen. *vinjar,* 'meadow'—the simplex was archaic long before A.D. 1000) that this sequence of phonemes could surely at no time during the past millenium have grown confused in Icelandic ears. In his well-known study of *vin*-names twenty years ago, Professor Valter Jansson, conceivably cautious in view of Sven Söderberg's earlier surmise as to a form *vinland* (with short *i*), admits the bare possibility of such a form.[39] But *testis unus testis nullus,* and the extensive philological materials analyzed in Jansson's own book argue against, rather than for, any such conclusion. We are not compelled to believe that all "Wineland" voyagers found the grapes so regularly recorded in these sagas once the tradition was started, for some clearly did not. The phrase *Vínland it góða,* "Wineland the Good," is certainly

[38] Hermannsson, "Tyrkir," *Modern Language Notes*, p. 390.
[39] *Nordiska Vin-Namn. En ortnamnstyp och dess historia,* pp. 105ff.

the sentimental increment of a later age. Contrary to Bjarni Þorsteinsson,[40] the phrase is far from any indication of a classical or European derivation of the original *Vínland* from *Insulæ Fortunatæ* or the like. The phrase is rather a later invention, a nostalgic throwback recalling the fatness of the western land but not its dangers. Such phrases in the romantic sagas as *Frakkland hit góða* have exerted influence retroactively.[41] The expression likely derives from *Karlamagnus saga* and is a rendering of *la dulce France, France dulce,* and so on, not least in immediate association with textual references to the fair forests and fields, the fruit trees, ample pasturage, and impressive grapevines of gracious France.[42] It would seem to have entered the Vinland tradition at some point during the two generations that separate *GS* from *ES*. It was therefore not the genesis of the word *Vínland,* as attaching to North America. One lucky strike, made by Leifr Eiríksson's expedition, evidently started the whole tradition of grapes, concerning which none of the later voyages in either saga adds one whit to our essential knowledge. But, in the world of reality, each expedition subsequent to Leifr's would naturally look for grapes; and, just as naturally, in the realm of letters, would saga-writers cling to them as well.

We must remember that all tradition relative to the Vínland journeys must have been transmitted orally for several generations,[43] each successive generation beclouding the factual issue somewhat with its own lack of viticultural expertise, but just as effectively obviating opportunity for misunderstanding of the clearly differentiated syllables, *vín-* and *vin-*. Furthermore, the stories in which *vín, vínber* (in one instance,

[40] Þorsteinsson, "Some Observations," p. 187; cf. p. 191.

[41] "Vinland the Good" appears only in the late *Hauksbók* (Chap. 8); cf. S. B. F. Jansson, *Sagorna om Vinland*, p. 60: "menn skylldv leita vinlanz ens goða" (*Skálholtsbók: leita vinn lanndz*).

[42] See E. Ó. Sveinsson, "Sources and Characteristics," *Viktors saga ok Blávus. Riddarasögur*, II: *Jónas Kristjánsson bjó til prentunar*, p. cix, and the phraseology of the saga text (*Viktors saga*, pp. 39–40): heims(k) war ek þa ek lastada Frackland hit goda. þuiat mier litazt hier alluæner veller ok skemtiliger skogar ok ynniligt alldin. girnilig graus ok virdiligur vijnuidur." See also E. F. Halvorsen, *The Norse Version of the Chanson de Roland*, p. 95.

[43] We do not overlook the probable use of crude contemporary maps and tally sticks among the navigators, but these were not reproduced in mass editions and doubtless enjoyed no long life. Arbman states: "It also seems likely that a rudimentary form of plot of distances and courses run was kept on the perforated 'gaming boards' reminiscent of the medieval transverse board on which a peg was moved the appropriate number of holes to register the distance sailed in various directions in the course of a day" (*The Vikings*, p. 18).

through a reasonable inadvertency in the manuscript, *vínker,* 'wine vessel'), *vínviðr,* and *Vínland* figured strongly reinforced the proper pronunciation of the word, by any reasonable supposition. Þórhallr veiðimaðr's verses may or may not be genuine. Apart from an archaic metrical peculiarity, one argument in their favor is the inappropriate way in which they are inserted into the text, but, as we saw with the misplaced theme of Haki/Hekja, that is an inconclusive mode of argument inasmuch as the Family Sagas contain so many *lausavísur* that are in poor agreement with their prose environment. Objective or even convincing criteria for testing the authenticity of such verses have not been devised. Nevertheless, the first of Þórhallr's two verses expresses his frustration over the nondiscovery of anticipated raw materials for wine-making. If the verses are genuine, they illustrate a highly realistic situation: the uncertainties of Karlsefni and his followers as to distances and directions to the Vínland reported by Leifr.

Again, the men on Iceland who made the earliest written references to Vínland treated it as a known fact of geography and exploration rather than as anything whose existence required explanation or proof. That extraordinary historian Ari the Wise (1068–1148), author of *Íslendingabók,* written before 1132, had among his sources his own uncle, Þórðr Gellir, who had actually spoken with a man who had been to Vínland.[44] Karlsefni and Guðríðr with their son Snorri, born in the New World, resettled on Iceland, carrying with them traditions in which the word *Vínland* must repeatedly have figured. The Danish king Sveinn Úlfsson (or Ástríðarson) had received reports on Vínland by 1068 or so. It was to him that Auðunn vestfirzki gave the polar bear he had himself brought from Greenland, also doubtless bringing reports from there about America which, *nota bene*, could only have been oral, uncontaminated by manuscripts whose supposed insufficiencies might have allowed confusion between a short vowel *i* and an

[44] See Halldór Hermannsson's edition of *Íslendingabók* in *Islandica*, XX (1930), 51f., where speaking of Greenland, the saga states: "Þeir fundu þar manna vistir bæði austr ok vestr á landi, ok keiplabrot ok steinsmiði þat, er af því má skilja, at þar hafði þess konar þjóð farit, er Vínland hefir byggt ok Grœnlendingar kalla Skrælinga." Ari thus implies that the story of Vínland is common knowledge. Cf. the introduction and facsimile reproduction of the work in *Íslenzk handrit* in Vol. I. of *Íslendingabók Ara Fróða. AM. 113a and 113b, fol.* The spot where *Vínland* is mentioned is in Chapter 6 of AM. 113b, which the editor, following Árne Magnússon, calls "A." AM. 113a, the "B" of this edition ("A" and "B" are parallel copies of an earlier vellum, according to Jóhannesson, p. xviii), never previously edited, is slightly defective, and the word *Vínland* has dropped out of the sentence.

intendedly long, but unmarked *i* (that is, written *i* instead of *ij*, a common form of "doubling" to indicate vowel length). This King is the same one who personally, or who through the officials of his court, reported to Adam of Bremen concerning the good wine to be had in the New World, not as a matter of loose opinion but as a matter of firm report. Adam, between 1069 and 1075, recorded the matter thus: "Præterea unam adhuc insulam recitavit a multis in eo repertam oceano, quæ dicitur Winland, eo quod ibi vites sponte nascantur, vinum optimum ferentes. Nam et fruges ibi non seminatas habundare, non fabulosa opinione, sed certa comperimus relatione Danorum."[45]

There is widespread speculation to the effect that Adam's Land of Wine was a learned allusion to ancient myths concerning a place of abundance. This argument omits one dimension of importance, which involves onomastics. We refer to Adam's vocabulary in general when referring to established countries. Adam's treatise is in Latin. Chapters 21 and the following contain such forms as *Dania, Nordmannia, Sueonia, Suedia, Svecia, Westragothia, Ostrogothia,* all fluently Latinized as *terræ* of feminine gender. The Latin of later generations exhibits the forms *Vinlanda* and *Vinlandia* to match. But for Adam, the reference to Vínland was seemingly no received tradition from literary sources, with a neat word to harmonize with that environment. Like *Halsingland, Gronland, Halagland, Island* is the word *Winland,* a handful of awkward thumbs in a Latin text. Not on such evidence will *Winland* be shown as less incontestably existent than the others.

Pertinent to the question of a misunderstanding by later generations of the pronunciation and meaning of a syllable *vín/vin* is the fact that Adam builds his account around a reference to vines and not to pasturage. Adam's remark is clearly the compression of oral conversations, probably in Latin, at the Danish court, which had been informed orally of Greenland and Vínland by Scandinavian visitors whose language

[45] This passage from *Adami Gesta Hammaburgensis Ecclesiæ Pontificium* is quoted from identical texts in Hermannsson, *The Problem of Wineland* (*Islandica*, XXV); V. Lendin, "Vinlandsproblemet," p. 322; G. H. Pertz, *Adami Gesta . . .*, p. 213. The quotation is from Book IV, Chapter 38. The magnificent photolithographic edition of the *Codex Havniensis* of Adam of Breman unfortunately ends shortly before the conclusion of Chapter 21. Finnur Jónsson wonders whether the word *regis* may not at some point in time have dropped out of Adam's narrative between the words *relatione* and *Danorum*. This is possible but should be unimportant in view of Adam's insistence on *certa relatio* (Jónsson, "Erik den Rødes Saga og Vinland," *Norsk historisk Tidsskrift*, pp. 116–147. In Chapter 21 Adam has already assured us: "De quibus narrauit mihi scientissimus danorum Rex" (*Cod. Havn.*, p. 129).

was almost indistinguishable from that of the Danes themselves. Those who still wish to argue the length of the syllable *vín* will perhaps not argue that *vites vinum ferentes* can through a phonetic misunderstanding be extrapolated from a phrase containing *pascum, gramen,* or similar intimation of the *pratensic,* rather than the *labruscine,* features of Leifr's discovery.

The wording of the sagas deserves credence except where scholarship can contradict it. If for a moment we are to suppose that the word intended by the saga is not *Vínland* but *Vinland,* in the sense of 'pasture land,' we must confirm the alternative through performance of a number of simultaneous operations. We must show that Adam, who took extreme pains to be definite regarding so unusual a piece of information, deliberately lied, or that he had been misinformed, for no clear reason, at the Danish court, which had no discernible ax to grind at that moment of history. We must produce credible evidence likewise that the cautious and canny Ari, who also was not being tendentious about grapes, had been hoodwinked by his famous uncle, or the latter by his countrymen and informants. At the same time, since we now consider the *Grœnlendinga saga* to have existed in written form by 1200, with a structure and style revealing clear evidence of early, almost primitive, construction, rather than decomposition and the "late" flavor attributed to it by some researchers,[46] we must show that this saga had managed completely to misinterpret or pervert the oral narratives upon which it is based, *yet had made no attempt to rationalize this with any substitute explanation about "meadows" as the reason for Leifr's name-giving.* We could, of course, assume that a gratuitous and unnecessarily false account of this particular aspect of the Vínland voyages had been propounded by Karlsefni and Guðríðr, who lived with great distinction upon Iceland with their American-born son Snorri, who became the grandfather of one bishop, the great uncle of a second bishop, and the great grandfather of a third. Alternatively, we could assume that the account had been altered by the saga-writer for no real reason, and that he had been clever enough in his manuscript to obliterate all traces of the fraud. Throughout this complex operation, we should likewise

[46] Those who adhere to this view include, among others: G. Storm, "Studier over Vinlandsreiserne, Vinlands Geografi og Ethnologi," *Aarbøger for nordisk Oldkyndighed og Historie . . .*; F. Jónsson, "Opdagelsen af og Rejserne til Vinland," *Aarbøger for nordisk Oldkyndighed;* D. Strombäck, Introduction to *Flateyjarbók. Corpus Codicum Islandicorum Medii Ævi,* XIII; M. Gravier, *La saga d'Éric le Rouge. Le Récit des Grœnlandais*, pp. 24ff.; Hermannsson, *passim.*

be tacitly asserting the absurdity of any discovery of grapes in the first place. And that is the most unreasonable assumption of all.

More than merely to guess and theorize, the skeptic would have to indicate concretely, or at least with great probability, the positive sources of contamination of *GS* by southerly lore—reflecting the Blessed Isles and their liberally available products.[47] Some commentators, confused by translations and conflated editions of the Vínland sagas, have blended the two main variants in their minds until precise details of considerable importance have become blurred. Thus, it is sometimes overlooked that the *combination* of "grapes and self-sown grain" freely associated with these sagas by some literary theorists and historians is not a stable feature of the Vínland tradition at all. The earlier of the two sagas, *GS*, makes no mention whatever of self-sown grain as such. Chapter 5 (Þorvaldr's voyage) does mention at one point some sort of drying bin or storage receptacle for grain, presumed evidence of human habitation. The reference may be literally true, or it may merely reflect European learning and cultivated artistry in literature. The later saga, *ES*, makes several references to self-sown grain, but even here (in the *Hauksbók* ms) the skeptical scribe has at one point converted *sjálfsáit* to *nýsáit*, "newly-sown."[48] Since wild rice, *Zizania aquatica*, has so commonly figured in both older and more modern descriptions of our coastal areas as far north as Newfoundland, it would have been strange if the exploring Greenlanders had not come upon it repeatedly. References to it would thus amount to historical fact.[49] But the circumstance that *GS*, our oldest known version of the Vínland stories, only obliquely acknowledges the existence of anything like grain in the new lands is a reasonable indication at all events that its discovery was not part of the *genesis* of tales about fat lands to the west. The grain has waxed slightly in prominence in that later version, the *ES*, but even there its total absence would not impair the narrative.

We return to *vín/vin*. To disestablish *vín-*, 'vine, wine,' as the base

[47] Hermannsson points out that Nansen's inability to do this, for all his labors in defense of the theory, demonstrates its weakness (*The Problem of Wineland*, [*Islandica*, XXV], p. 55).

[48] S.B.F. Jansson, *Sagorna om Vinland*, par. 296 (p. 64); cf. also p. 140.

[49] If ethnologists assert the contrary, we shall cease to credit the aborigines with devices for the storage and drying of produce collected wild. Winter survival without stores of some sort in the "temperate" zone would seem to limit their winter provender. M. Thórdarson, *The Vinland Voyages*, has a plate (Fig. 21) showing *Zizania aquatica*, "wild rice," tied into sheaves by modern Indians.

element of a nominal complex *Vínland,* we must go even further than to entertain the series of suppositions set forth above. The only suggested or conceivable alternative to *vín-land* is a *vin-land* with the putative connotation of 'meadow-land' or the like. If the word *vin,* 'meadow, grassy place,' remained at all in the vocabulary of Icelanders around the year 1000, it was as a quaint and archaic term. In Norway and Sweden it had very early been employed as a place-name, or an element of such, for certain farms and districts. It occurred sometimes as a simplex (ON *vin,* gen. *vinjar*), occasionally as the first element of a compound, more frequently as the second element in such a compound as *Bjǫrgvin/Bjǫrgyn/Biorgvin,* etc. (modern Bergen). The derivation of many such presumed compounds is uncertain at best, in part because of spelling changes through the centuries.[50] A few names compounded with *vin* are recorded for the Orkney and Shetland islands, those claimed for Denmark seem to be uncertain, and none are known for the Faroes or Iceland where, if they had once existed, they evidently passed away as the word *vin* itself fell out of use.[51] There is a Gothic word *vinja,* this is a translation of Greek νομή, 'pasture' (cf. OHG *winnie,* 'pastus'). In Iceland during the period of the Vínland voyages the word *vin* with short vowel, if known at all, was certainly not "productive," that is, not in active use for purposes of naming or producing compounds. There is strong evidence, furthermore, that the word *vin,* originally doubtless a *naturnamn,* descriptive of a feature of the landscape, early came to designate a settlement named for, and usually consolidated with, this feature.[52] All other considerations aside, it requires considerable imagination to have Leifr Eiríksson at one and the same time looking forward to a thriving settlement in the new country, and investing it with an archaic, backward-looking name. Leifr was surely no antiquarian, nor even a poet. He was clearly a pragmatist with inherited as well as acquired talent at leadership, administration, and propaganda. The PR qualities of so glowing a term as "Wineland" need not be stressed. But the archaic designation of a *mede* now, to quote Chaucer, ". . . a mede/All full of fresh flowers, white and reede," would point ineluctably to a Leifr of hitherto unsuspected predilections.

[50] V. Jansson, *Nordiska Vin-namn, passim.*
[51] *Ibid.*, p. 105.
[52] *Ibid.*, pp. 389ff.

Let us for a moment suppose that the explorers fantastically chose to ignore the grapes which even today are one of New England's most conspicuous natural products; or that they actually never got south of Newfoundland and hence never did discover grapes; that all related traditions have been supplied retroactively by diligent and effective middlemen (of obscure motivation), whose influence corrupted tradition from Greenland to Iceland and from Norway to Denmark, covering "all the angles" and transforming "meadows" into "grapevines" within a time span of sixty years or less following the known Vínland voyages, all this because they assumed that grapes must grow wild in the New World precisely because nobody had found them or thought to report them. Adam of Bremen, writing in Latin and approaching this tradition as pupil rather than as tutor, can have had no material effect upon the Icelanders, even in Snorri Sturluson's day (Snorri himself gives no evidence of a familiarity with Adam's work). As a matter of corollary logic, we will then have to regard Leifr's famous *eyktarstaðr* observation as a gross exaggeration, a later embroidery, or a rhetorical indication merely (*GS,* Chap. 3). However loosely it must nowadays be interpreted as any verifiable exercise in spherical trigonometry, the observation gives evidence of a certain sophistication in the Viking Age in matters of latitude (though not of longitude, in view of the lack of chronometers). The explorers were aware of their being rather far south of the latitudes of Iceland and Greenland: "Here day and night were of more equal length than on Greenland or Iceland; the sun had the mid-morning and mid-afternoon positions on the year's shortest day."[53] Complicated and disputed questions are involved here, concerning (a) the reliability of textual transmission, (b) whether the phrase "equal length" was intended literally or as an intimation merely, (c) how accurately the Greenlandic explorers could and would measure for their purpose, and (d) whether in the usage of the explorers (*ca.* 1000) and/or of the saga-writer (*ca.* 1200) *eyktarstaðr* and *dagmálastaðr* have the meanings assumed, for example, by Almar Næss in *Hvor lå Vinland?*.[54] As far as the saga is concerned, this

[53] "Meira var þar jafndœgri en á Grœnlandi eða Íslandi; sól hafði þar eyktarstað ok dagmálastað um skammdegi" (Hermannsson, *The Vinland Sagas* [*Islandica,* XXX], p. 50; cf. *Ísl. fornrit,* IV, 251 n. 2).

[54] On this see *Tideräkningen,* Vol. XXI of *Nordisk kultur,* ed. Martin P:n Nilsson, particularly the index, p. 142, s.v. *ökt, eykt, eyktamǫrk,* etc., and the article by Nils Beckman, "Isländsk och medeltida skandinavisk tideräkning," pp. 4–57 and notes (tables follow pp. 58–76).

is a case in which the potential exactness of a quantitative science is almost totally at the mercy of rhetorical vagaries and their mediaeval practitioners. Present day philologists can only compare, analyze, suggest, and warn.

But to return to our hypothesis. Having abandoned historical grapes, southerly pushes, and astronomical *obiter dicta,* we must resolutely face a further set of alternative choices. It was Leifr and his company who established the temporary settlement on Newfoundland, perhaps at the very place where Ingstad has uncovered an ancient Scandinavian establishment. (It seems to follow from this that the *Straumfjǫrðr* settlement later made by Karlsefni, which in turn was north of Karlsefni's own second settlement at Hóp, *neither* of these being identical with Leifr's village according to *ES,* was well *north* of the Straits of Belle Isle—a very uncomfortable assumption.[55]) Either Leifr (and his countrymen back on Greenland) propounded no name for this settlement, and a lurid name was supplied by a later generation; or, conversely, the land was very early named after its most striking or useful product, its pasturage, this in accordance with the Söderberg-Tanner-Ingstad (and Þorsteinsson?) hypothesis.[56] The young explorer from Brattahlíð coins in all a series of three words to describe the successive countries visited by him, from north to south: *Hellu-land, Mark-land,* and *X-land.* The first two of these compounds employ as their respective first elements words in regular use among the Icelanders, *hella,* 'flat rock, slab,' and *mark*, 'forest' (slightly variant forms of this last are possible; cf. also the related form *mǫrkr*, 'forest'). For X-*land*, the postulated land of prime pasturage, Leifr (or his onomatologist) does not use a word of comparable prevalence, such as *engi-,* 'meadow,' nor *gras-,* 'grass,' but creates an unusual, outmoded, even puzzling and anachronistic term *vin-,* 'grassy place' (in historical times, according to the best evidence, this would ordinarily be a farm or community embracing such an antecedent topographical feature). But, in both *GS* and *ES,* each and every time the product grass is mentioned in connection with the new lands, the word used is the simplex *gras* n. or its plural form *grǫs*. Of such a form as *vin* there is no trace, nor is

[55] Despite literary conflict for reasons of family interests and superior information in one direction or another, the two sagas seem to be in essential accord as to some southerly push to a land of grapes.

[56] S.B.F. Jansson (*Sagorna om Vinland,* p. 161) points out faulty reasoning by Tanner.

any term employed of which *vin* could serve as a synonym or variant. Once again, therefore, we return to the grapes and grapevines, which alone permit a reasonable interpretation of Leifr's nomenclature. The elimination of Tyrkr from *GS,* as already suggested, strengthens rather than impairs the probability that grapes were discovered. For the grapes were not invented to account for an otherwise quite unnecessary Tyrkr. It was rather Tyrkr who was invented in order to introduce the very palpable grapes, the precise details of which, along with much else in the economical *GS,* had doubtless become lost. The very fact that the find of grapes was not made anonymously is here the strongest evidence of a folkloristic or literary theme. A. H. Krappe, assuming that Tyrkr was alcoholically intoxicated (the term *skapgott,* used by the saga-writer, has been given varying interpretations), regards the likely ultimate source of the motif as Oriental. His assumption, though it cannot be proven on the grounds he adduces, is not unreasonable on the face of it, and he points out amusing—if distant—parallels regarding foreign views on the intoxicating quality of unfermented American fruits down through the eighteenth century. Krappe very sensibly concludes that the presence of such "Oriental themes" at so late a date "has led no one to doubt the reality of the voyages of the eighteenth century travellers."[57] The same logic may be applied to the Vínland sagas.

The corroborative tendency of the Hønen runic inscription from Ringerike, Norway, tentatively dated around 1050, with its emotionally charged reference, assertedly, to dangerous voyages in Vínland waters, is so uncertain and enjoys so shaky a reputation among the philologists of Scandinavia that, particularly since it has long since disappeared, we shall not attempt to place it in evidence.[58] Two rather misunderstood pieces of internal evidence from the *GS* itself that are often employed to discredit *vín-* must, however, be commented on briefly. Many writers have commented sarcastically on the statement, as they consider it, in the saga that Leifr took on a shipload of grapevines for timber and in particular loaded his tow-boat with a cargo of grapes, either in grape season proper, the late summer, following which the grapes would have spoiled before the expedition sailed home in

[57] A. H. Krappe, "Intoxicating Grapes," *Modern Language Notes,* LVIII, No. 4 (April, 1943), 274.

[58] S. Bugge, *Hønen-runerne fra Ringerike.*

spring, or possibly in the spring itself, before the grapes could have formed at all.[59] But in the saga text it is stated that Leifr loaded his ship with "timber," most certainly including a goodly representation of those noble logs of which, as the saga reminds us, houses could be built. As to the filling of the ship's boat with grapes, the time of year for this act of husbandry is not rigidly specified (the ellipses and inversions of saga style pose uncertainties), but, if one follows the natural intimation of the saga itself, the men under Leifr's command immediately after the discovery that summer or fall devote alternate days to acquiring grapes (and grapevines) and to felling trees until they have enough for a shipload ("to make a cargo for my ship"). They obviously had their choice of timber, they were reasonable men, and the meaning is clear enough: they took on a shipload of real timber. The saga goes on to say that they filled their ship's boat with grapes ("Svá er sagt, at eptirbátr þeira var fylldr av vínberjum").[60] This activity is not tied in with any special time, relative or absolute, and we are free to draw the sensible conclusion that they loaded their tow-boat with grapes when the latter were ripe and available. When there was any possibility of gathering and transporting the season's grapes, or any other burden, to the houses by boat, we may be sure that they did so, perhaps repeatedly. Whether they knew anything about the art of making wine, or even of drying grapes into raisins for preservation, is uncertain and even unlikely, the natural suspicion being that most of the luscious orbs rather promptly found their way into the explorers' stomachs *au naturel*. But a maneuvering, or even beached tow-boat full of grapes will leave many crushed exemplars, and after a few days of sunshine who knows but what the rustic Greenlanders (even *sans* Tyrkr) may unwittingly have fermented a heady beverage after all? In any case, the saga does not here allege that they *sailed away* with a load of grapes, much less any leathern flasks of "Chateau Vinlandia." After describing the activities of the summer and fall, the saga reads: "In the spring they prepared ship and sailed away." With due narrative exigency, the vines and grapes have at this point become a *sine qua*

[59] Viz., Hermannsson, *The Problem of Wineland* (*Islandica*, XXV), p. 39.

[60] *GS*, Chap. 4: Hermannsson, *The Vinland Sagas* (*Islandica*, XXX), p. 51; *Ísl. fornrit*, IV, 253; Reeves, *The Finding of Wineland*, p. 148 and facsimile opposite; G. Storm, *Eiríks saga rauða*, p. 59. We are not asserting that the author of the saga had a good understanding of grapes, for in Chapter 7, where Karlsefni's expedition is ready to sail home in the spring, grapes accompany them (*Ísl. fornrit,* IV, 264).

non to the expeditions that follow, and they are mentioned among the trophies brought back to Greenland by the crewmen who survived Þorvaldr Eiríksson, as well as by Karlsefni. Perhaps only token quantities of the exotic wares are indicated, as proof of the explorers' successful strikes. But, performing as they do the literary and stylistic function of tying in these subsequent expeditions and "authenticating" them for readers, the grapes need not be independently tested in terms of historic reality *for each expedition in turn.* Like Leifr's booths or houses, they soon become a stock motif, uncritical rejection or acceptance of which may induce us to throw out the infant with the bath.[61]

IV

Even regarding the physical appurtenances of Leifr's settlement, a word must be said. More than one critic has waxed satirical over the incredible accuracy with which expedition after expedition in *GS* manages to reach Leifsville.[62] Now, when it comes to being recorded, the reasonably successful voyages doubtless have the odds in their favor. In a historical sense, we are dealing with a statistical uncertainty as well as a misunderstanding. The voyage under Þorsteinn, which explicitly failed to reach Leifr's settlement, or indeed to make any new land whatever, may stand for any number of unsuccessful expeditions that for understandable reasons went unrecorded (most would probably be forgotten, purely and simply). But even the recorded voyages call for comment. The frequently made assumption that Leifr's Vínland—that is, the "third" land in succession discovered by Leifr in reversing Bjarni Herjólfsson's sailing direction—is identical with any narrowly restricted spot located or described by Bjarni as his "first" land is quite without foundation. Vínland is doubtless an extensive geographical concept. Bjarni landed nowhere and built nothing, and we consequently eliminate him from this particular calculation. The referent is therefore Leifr's voyage, which, as the measure of all subsequent voyages in *GS,* must likewise be subtracted from any list of coincidences.

According to *GS*, Leifr's expedition was followed within the next

[61] Hermannsson's brilliant and scholarly work with the Vínland voyages suffers repeatedly from categorical assertions (See *The Vinland Sagas* [*Islandica*, XXX], pp. 35–39, 45–47, and *passim*. Though the intervening years facilitate more nuanced views on saga construction, Bj. Þorsteinsson is somewhat categorical in the opposite direction.

[62] Hermannsson, *The Problem of Wineland* (*Islandica*, XXV), p. 46 f.

few years by four others, all described as captained by his relatives or friends, persons who would have had every advantage that advice, planning, and, likely enough, the assistance of crew members from one or more previous expeditions in the series could provide. Though *GS* seems largely to aim at accuracy, it is not a general chronicle or series of historical annals. It is an artistic product, a family saga, with all that the term implies. It would not be surprising, as a pure narrative device, to have expedition after expedition reach Leifr's settlement. Of the four voyages, however, one is stated to have failed miserably. And if it should be that Karlsefni's expedition, contrary to *GS*, did not reach Leifsbúðir (and hence, that the more extensive account of this voyage presented by *ES* is more accurate in so stating), then even that expedition will have to be subtracted from the successful lists for this is a point upon which the conflicting traditional claims of the two families—descendants of Eiríkr rauði and of Karlsefni, respectively—are perhaps evenly matched. That would make two successful "repeats." Lacking decisive corroboration in either direction, we shall be compelled for the present to leave it at that. It seems to me, however, that the much discussed sixth voyage, instigated by Leifr's half sister Freydís, may have to be subtracted from the list as well (on this, see below). This would imply that in a historical sense one, possibly two, expeditions (Karlsefni's being in the doubtful column) of the four that followed Leifr in *GS* managed to find his abandoned colony. Particularly after Karlsefni's brush with the natives, it is reasonable to suppose that any and all Norse structures were pulled down or even burned to the ground by the vengeful Skrælings.

The saga accounts refer indiscriminately to Leifr's "booths" and his "houses." Is this *lapsus calami*? Were they in the same location? In the strictest sense, they can hardly have been interpreted as the same structures by the *sagnamaðr,* for *GS* tells that it was after Leifr and his men had constructed booths,[63] that they decided to winter there and built large houses ("tóku þat ráð síðan at búask þar um þann vetr ok gerðu þar hús mikil"). Most commentators, nevertheless, rather confusingly speak only of "Leif's booths." *GS* calls them *búðir* in the voyage of Þorvaldr and that of Karlsefni.[64] In Chapter 7 Karlsefni reinforces the

[63] If by *búðir* are meant booths similar to those in use at the meetings of the Icelandic Assembly, these would be low walls which could be roofed over for temporary occupancy with hides, cloth, and so on.

[64] *GS*, Chaps. 5 and 7.

borrowed dwellings with a stockade, the saga thus contriving to divide the architectural credit between the two heroes. Since Leifr's *hús mikil* are not recognized as existent by *ES*, its only passage on housebuilding occurs in Chapter 10.[65] *Skálholtsbók* speaks of Karlsefni's structures as *bygðir*, *Hauksbók* calls them *búðir*, and immediately thereafter, in both versions, the term *skálar* is applied to them. In the Freydís story of *GS*, Chapter 8, there is a parallel differentiation in terminology between the *hús* of Leifr, which Freydís refuses to share with her nominal partners, and the *skáli*, which the latter then build at a little distance. Beyond that, there is a remarkable similarity in the phraseology of the two sagas which may strengthen the case for influence on *ES* by *GS*. It has to do with the wording that describes the location of the houses. In *GS*, after moving out their gear, the brothers "gerðu sér skála ok settu þann skála firr sjónum á vatnsstrǫndu, ok bjuggu vel um. En Freydís lét fella viðu til skips síns. Nú tók at vetra . . ." The Karlsefni episode in *ES* reads in *Skálholtsbók*: "þeir havfdv giort bygdir sinar upp fra vatninu ok uoru sumir skalarnir nærr meginlanndinv. enn svmir nærr vatninv. nu voru þeir þar þann vetr."[66] *Hauksbók* emends to: "þeir Karlsefni hofdu gort budir sinar upp fra vatnínu. ok uoru sumir skalarnir nðr vatnínu, en sumir firr. Nu voro þeir þar þann vetr."

This phraseology of *ES* (both mss), and the disposition of the various buildings thus conveyed, deserve to be pondered. Even the altered narrative function of the word *þann* is not without interest; it varies the structure of the (supposedly antecedent) *GS*, while managing, as in so many other places, to conserve one of the latter's building blocks.

In the *þáttr* devoted to Freydís, Leifr's dwellings are called *hús*. The saga implies that the structures, intended to house thirty-five men for one winter, would have sufficed for twice that number or more. That is possible, if not probable. We recall that the author of *GS* housed the sixty-five persons of Karlsefni's expedition there, and might thus farsightedly have had Freydís and the brothers in mind as well. We are of course speaking of narrative techniques. The arithmetical specifications of these sagas are doubtless generalizations whose only control factor is the number of persons who might reasonably have been carried (with their gear and provisions) in ocean-going vessels of the Viking Age, vessels whose maximum and minimum specifications are

[65] S.B.F. Jansson, *Sagorna om Vinland*, par. 341, p. 70.
[66] *Ibid.*

roughly a matter of knowledge.[67] At all events, a tendentious literary purpose may possibly be served by the saga's use of the word *hús* instead of *búð(ir)*. In view of the very remarkable nature of the Freydís story in general, it will be discussed here.

V

The theme of the female hellion and whetter of action and general troublemaker is known to several of the Icelandic sagas.[68] Freydís seems to have excited the imagination of *sagnamenn* at both ends of the Vínland tradition. In *ES* she is the heroine who saves Karlsefni's colony from massacre—a literary *Ehrenrettung* as surmised above. In *GS*, Freydís is blown up into an independent story with horrendous details as the organizer and co-captain of an expedition with the ill-fated brothers Helgi and Finnbogi, whom, with their whole company, she murders. Some critics have been impressed by this story as stark "realism." Some accept it, regretfully, perhaps, but in silence. Still others are so repelled by the Freydís chapter as to attack the credibility of the entire *GS* in consequence.[69] None of these attitudes is warranted. It is not to clear the good names of these rough and ready ancients—as the author of *ES* so patently attempted—that one must pronounce the Freydís *þáttr* in *GS* a total, or almost total, invention.

For a real life account, the tale of Freydís is inadequately provided either with initial motive or with subsequent consequences. The saga-writer's inducement to cook up yet another voyage by an offspring of Eiríkr rauði is evident enough. That this should be a woman is within

[67] See A. W. Brøgger and Haakon Shetelig, *The Viking Ships: Their Ancestry and Evolution*.

[68] On the *hvǫt* 'incitation,' see Theodore M. Andersson, *The Problem of Icelandic Saga Origins: A Historical Survey*, p. 98, cf. p. 97. Such whettings occur in *Brennu-Njáls saga, Vápnfirðinga saga, Hávarðar saga Ísfirðings, Harðar saga, Heiðarvíga saga, Eyrbyggja saga, Laxdœla saga, Þorsteins saga stangarhǫggs*.

[69] Hermannsson is among them. His skepticism (*The Vinland Sagas* [*Islandica*, XXX], pp. xi–xiii) contrasts with the viewpoint of G. M. Gathorne-Hardy, *The Wineland Sagas Translated and Discussed*, pp. 127 ff., cf. p. 130: "Why should this awful libel disfigure the annals of the distinguished house of Eric the Red, if there were nothing in it? Who would dare to invent it, if it were not true?" The answer to his query is—a *sagnamaðr*. Stefán Einarsson considers that in creating a more palatable role for Freydís, the author of *ES* "seized upon a rationalized version of an ancient magic behavior, whose significance he did not know" ("The Freydís Incident in Eiríks Saga Rauða, Ch. 11," *Acta Philologica Scandinavica*, XIII [1939], 256). Einarsson finds parallels in Irish literature, in classical antiquity, and among the Lapps for Freydís' exposure of her body.

the bounds of credibility, if admittedly not too likely. Freydís was no Auðr the Deepminded, brilliantly and courageously acting out of deep necessity in changing abodes and providing for her threatened dependents and the honorable continuance of her line. Freydís is portrayed as an explorer—not a colonist but a seeker after wealth on a wild frontier where the Scandinavians have already suffered loss of life through skirmishes with the savages, if either *GS* or *ES* contains actual reminiscences of the indigenous population, and we do not believe otherwise. The natives are by now on guard, in full war equipment, and prepared to discourage further encroachment on their precincts by the ruthless blond foreigners. Peaceful trading operations for furs are no longer even to be thought of—all that must have gone glimmering. Yet, Helgi and Finnbogi, followed almost immediately by Freydís in her own ship, find Leifr's structures in excellent shape, it would appear, all ready for housekeeping. And indeed, no redmen are sighted that summer, fall, winter, nor the following spring.

We discover that Freydís is a vicious psychotic, not too intelligent despite her trickery in secretly taking along five men more than the agreed-upon thirty men for each of the two shiploads. What did these hidden five, and their fellows, think of this during the sea voyage to Vínland? If this is history rather than fiction, were they a pack of thorough criminals one and all, hardened escapees from some early Devil's Island, rather than the neighbors, friends, cousins, and in-laws of Leifr heppni Eiríksson, chief squire and magistrate on Greenland? The most dreadful feuds between whole clans in saga literature do not match the slaughter reported here. It is obviously Freydís' intention from the beginning to contrive the murder of half the little colony, thirty men desperately needed for labor and strength in gathering riches—the ostensible purpose of the journey—and, likely enough, for holding off the redskins in the bargain. She has already refused them access to Leifr's houses. Another suspicious detail with a fictional flavor is the complete insignificance of Freydís' husband Þorvarðr, aside from his reputed wealth. We ask next, what could have been the purpose in inviting Helgi and Finnbogi in the first place? They were not ancestral enemies but a pair of newcomers to Greenland. The ostensible cause of the trumped-up quarrel was their refusal to sell Freydís their ship, which was larger than hers. It is hard to believe, however, that such a trade could not have been effected through more palatable means than the slaughter of a shipload of people. Though this cannot be shown objectively, the brothers Helgi and Finnbogi strike one as fictional characters to begin with: their names have the suspicious flavor of a fraternal pair in a *fornaldarsaga*. But suppose they are actual characters, from the East Firths of Iceland, as stated in *GS*. The size of the crew they have brought from Iceland (the text says Norway, a seeming repetitious error) is not stated. Undoubtedly they have come to Greenland, some, perhaps, to trade, others to settle down there. It seems not too likely that such an entire crew, women included, would have been minded to sail off so promptly to lands still farther distant in order to gain hazardous riches, and still less to settle down there, against the probable warnings of the Greenlanders. In the event of such a relay expedition, we would consequently expect some shift in personnel. The two ships' crews on a cooperative voyage from Garðar-Brattahlíð and environs would not be entirely comprised of persons unrelated by friendship, marriage, or even birth.

The reckoning exacted at home on Greenland after a mass murder of such dimensions is mild in *GS*, by any manner of reckoning. Leifr, displeased, predicts ignominy for Freydís and her descendants, we are assured—without further evidence that the prophecy came true—and in this bland way the entire matter is dropped. A strangely alien impression is conveyed by Leifr's "torture" of three of Freydís' followers into a full confession. This suspectedly Christian and Continental sophistication is reminiscent of a fictional feature in the much later *Hrafnkels saga Freysgoða*.[70] It is also very similar to what is told us of the stern methods employed on behalf of Christ by Óláfr Tryggvason and Óláfr Helgi, both of them greater heroes than Leifr Eiríksson. Of any general hue and cry for vengeance over the murder of thirty men and some women there is no slightest echo in *GS*, and, in calmly eliminating this shameful voyage by Freydís Eiríksdottir and transforming a woman who may in reality have been a strident and disagreeable virago into a valiant heroine under the aegis of Karlsefni, the author of *ES* may have done less violence to "truth" than could be supposed. The murderous tale of his presumed model, the *GS*, may have

[70] "The torture which Hrafnkell and his men undergo seems to have an un-Icelandic flavor. Here I think we can be confident that we have to deal with foreign subject-matter, although it is open to dispute whether it was obtained from oral tales or from books" (Sigurður Nordal, *Hrafnkels Saga Freysgoða*, trans. R. George Thomas, p. 29). Nordal goes on to cite Saxo Grammaticus, Book VIII. We shall add for our part that the two centuries by which *GS may* precede *Hrafnkatla* argue an importance for the oral tale, if our view is sustained that the Freydís incident is chiefly fiction.

deceived him less than it has the scholars of recent generations. It is, of course, possible that Freydís is an entirely fictional character, created by the writer of *GS*. In that case, we must conclude the writer of *ES* probably accepted her essential historicity and took measures accordingly. And, if he was shrewd enough not to accept Freydís as historical, his modification of her character and role is equally brilliant, if not more so. Whichever possibility be the more likely, each is a magnificent commentary on the artistic methodology of *sagnamenn*. We see meanwhile that *GS*, with its greater claim upon our historical belief than *ES*, yet in general inferior to the latter as a literary composition, is wanting neither in patent unhistoricities nor in skilled literary invention.

As a pure horror story, the sixth expedition of *GS* makes perfect sense. Its seeming relationship to the dreadful experiences on the eastern coast of Greenland found in the story of Snæbjǫrn galti[71] has been noticed by scholarship, but I believe that no one has observed a very strange and anomalous sentence towards the end of *Freydísar þáttr*. After the rival crew has been slain and their ship and property taken over, Freydís should be well situated, under normal conditions. But the sentence in which she threatens her crew with death (for betraying the crime) begins: "If ever we are fated to make Greenland."[72] This curious pessimism speaks for a reminiscence of some persons in desperate straits, doubtless shipwrecked in a desolate spot, destitute of provisions, and so on. A substitution of "Iceland" for "Greenland" would in that case restore the original locale of the story and might also explain why a slightly larger ship than the one Freydís allegedly already had (in *GS*) should become the *casus belli*: in the original story, it was probably the sole remaining vessel.

VI

Recent Icelandic research already referred to has indicated in general outline why the pristine flavor of *GS* entitles it to precedence over *ES* as a more proximate record of American voyages that took place around the year 1000. Though the present study has taken issue at some points with the generalizations of J. Jóhannesson and Bj. Þorsteinsson (for example, regarding the interpretation of the crucial word *Vínland*), it

[71] On Snæbjǫrn Holmsteinsson galti, cf. Hermannsson, *The Vinland Sagas* (*Islandica*, XXX), pp. xi-xiii and 32f.; *Landnámabók*, in *Ísl. sög.*, I, 112–115.

[72] " 'Ef oss verðr auðit at koma til Grœnlands' " (*GS*, Chap. 8).

has attempted to show with a wider and more differentiated spectrum of arguments that their views, as far as they go, come close to the truth. Though we cannot here deal with all the issues that could be discussed, we shall select for examination a few further points, particularly those that shed light on the relationship between the two saga versions.

In *ES*, old Eiríkr's heathendom is emphasized, and, to comport with this, he is made to live for some years after Leifr's discovery, on bad terms with his wife, who has built a Christian chapel meanwhile. Eiríkr's religious attitudes are unspecified in *GS,* according to which he died by the year 1001—one estimates—"before the conversion," as the saga states at the end of the story of Þorvaldr, Chapter 5. The precise chronology of Eiríkr's death cannot be determined. The less picturesque, more conservative account in *GS*, which places his death at the early date, is somewhat strengthened by evidence that Eiríkr's son Leifr rather early entered upon the headship at Brattahlíð, since it was presumably for this reason that he was unable to take active part in further explorations of America. The fact of Þjóðhildr's chapel, long doubted, was confirmed archeologically in 1962.[73] In itself, this asserts nothing as to the date of her husband's death, nor whether this preceded or followed construction of the little chapel.

J. Jóhannesson remarks[74] on the prophecies respecting Guðríðr in *GS* and *ES*. Despite their variation in content, each is inserted in its saga for the purpose of enhancing the Karlsefni-Guðríðr clan and its late descendants. It is strange, says Jóhannesson, that these similar prophecies about the same person—a woman, to boot—should occur independently in two sagas. One agrees fully that this is still another criterion for making *ES* largely dependent upon *GS*. There is another piece of evidence that has a humorous touch to it. *GS* makes Þorvaldr's ship lose a keel in a bad storm. The men spend much labor repairing the ship, which clearly has sustained other damage besides; then, for additional physical exercise, we suppose, they raise the old keel (glued together, or perhaps just a fragment of it—in any case, a waste of the good, hewn oak out of which such keels were fashioned) on the headland to sustain the name Kjalarnes therewith bestowed upon it. Hermannsson very soundly points out the unlikelihood of so trivial an

[73] Cf. Michael Wolfe, "Thjoðhild's Church: The Cradle of Christianity in Norse Greenland," *The American-Scandinavian Review,* LI, No. 1 (Spring, 1963), 55–66. The interior dimensions of the chapel seem to have been about 8 x 16 feet.

[74] "The Date of Composition," p. 68.

origin for a topographical feature.[75] A clever parallel is seen in *ES,* where Karlsefni *finds* such an erected keel on a headland, which he then names Kjalarnes. But, believing *GS* to be younger and inferior to *ES,* Hermannsson does not draw from the double incident the conclusion of direct dependency of *ES* upon *GS*, to which we now feel entitled. The reverse relationship in which a found keel (*ES*) gives rise to a lost keel (*GS*), though not impossible in terms of human imagination, is less likely. Sven B. F. Jansson refers to Haukr's "förtydligande tillägg" in *Hauksbók.* But there is even more to be extrapolated from the unknown author of the manuscript that Haukr himself was clarifying. Something of the mentality of the author of *ES* has become evident through his repeated "compensatory" details, as we might term them, contributed in mute justice to his predecessor. That each saga has indulged in a fiction regarding the keel is in any case clear, and Hermannsson is right in insisting that an actual physical feature of the landscape is typically to be looked for in such instances of naming.

Jóhannesson finds that in spite of dependency upon the earlier saga, the artistic reworking of *ES* is so excellent that a literal repetition of a phrase is found in only one case: "þeir hǫfðu með sér alls konar fénað."[76] The phrase is in both instances associated with the intent of Karlsefni's people to establish a settlement. One notes the similar parallel use of the word *umrœða,* both times when new voyages are being discussed: *mikil umrœða* (*GS*),[77] *miklar umrœður* (*ES*).[78] It has been surmised, now, that the Bjarni Herjólfsson of *GS* was a shadow of the Bjarni Grímólfsson of the other saga, and conversely, that Bjarni Grímólfsson is a substitution for an original Bjarni in *GS.* It has probably not been noticed that the *mikil umrœða/miklar umrœður* in both cases is used in immediate context with a Bjarni, and that in the case of *ES*, unlike *GS* where Bjarni is already an established figure, the phrase (now in the plural form) appears just before Bjarni Grímólfsson is introduced for the first time. This strengthens the impression that Bjarni Grímólfsson was created as a substitute, perhaps even a subconscious apology for the abolition of a (presumably heathen) Bjarni Herjólfsson, for whom the Christianity-oriented *ES* could find no real use. And indeed, the deliberate intrusion of a substitute Squire

[75] *The Vinland Sagas* (*Islandica*, XXX), 35f.
[76] Jóhannesson, "The Date of Composition," p. 61; cf. *ES*, Chap. 8 and *GS*, Chap. 7.
[77] *GS*, Chap. 3.
[78] *ES,* Chap. 7.

Þorkell at Herjólfsnes for Bjarni's Herjólfsson's father, Herjólfr bondi, is not only anachronistic on the face of it (the author of *ES* did not at all events dare to call the well-known place Þorkelsnes!), but tends in the same direction.[79] Equally suspicious, of course, is the knightly courtesy of Bjarni Grímólfsson adrift on the wormy sea. But that pretty story has been discussed at length by others. Even Leifr's mythical voyage to Norway in *ES* was most likely in part invented by its author in order to invest the hero with a palpably recent ship, since he could not be represented as purchasing one from a Bjarni Herjólfsson whom the saga has dispensed with.[80]

In both sagas, Karlsefni's voyage receives the greatest share of the narrative, and in *ES* it has integrated into itself some of the names and activities otherwise attributed in *GS*. For example, the activity of assigning topographical names has been taken from Leifr and from Þorvaldr and attributed to Karlsefni. Freydís is retained, as is Þorvaldr, but now as members of Karlsefni's company. Leifr's booths or houses are never found, since he is not reported to have built anything. The happy discovery of a whale in one saga becomes, in the other, a homily on the testing of man's patience, faith, and even industry by the Christian deity. A picturesque heathen is made to suffer the ultimate penalty for his contumacy; and much more besides. With respect to Þorhallr veiðimaðr, there may, of course, have been a division within Karlsefni's crew, and someone—here, naturally, a deviant in faith and policy—may have broken discipline and run off, or simply become lost. The question arises, what vessel did the defectors depart in? A group of ten men is logical enough for a ship's boat sent out to poke around inlets, islands, rivers, and so on, but it is a slim crew for an ocean voyage in a major ship. We learn from *ES* that there have been been 3 ships and 160 persons on the expedition at the outset, together with livestock and supplies for a colonization attempt. Surely, if the three ships are of comparable size, one of them can scarcely be spared for a return to

[79] *ES*, Chap. 3. Herjólfr and Herjólfsnes are known to *Landnámabók*, Chap. 14 (cf. *Ísl. sög.*, I, 80). Hermannsson thinks the author of *ES* had confused Þorkell with Eiríkr's cousin Þorkell (Hermannsson, *The Vinland Sagas* [*Islandica,* XXX] p. 32 f.). The person whom the author of *ES* "had in mind" (Hermannsson's phrase) was more likely Leifr's son Þorkell, but we consider it an intentional "confusion."

[80] Quite inappropriately, an echo of this appears in *Flateyjarbók* before the beginning of *GS* proper. Magnus Magnusson and Hermann Pálsson ignore it in their translation, *The Vinland Sagas: The Norse Discovery of America. Grænlendinga Saga and Eirik's Saga.*

Greenland (as one of Þórhallr's verses indicates) by so small a party. The ship cannot have been owned by Þórhallr veiðimaðr (though one version calls the ship his), for the chief persons aboard it seem originally to have been Þorvaldr Eiríksson and Freydís with her husband Þorvarðr, while Þórhallr is not depicted as a man of property. It is bootless even to discuss whether this particular ship was seaworthy at all after the battering it had received during the dreadful voyage of Þorsteinn, earlier in the saga. The attribution of so important an item as a ship to some specific person of consequence seems to be a stock feature of these sagas.[81] The saga states that this one had come to Greenland under Þorbjǫrn Vífilsson. Is the ship actually stolen by Þórhallr and his party, despite the author's glossing over of this event by the pretense that Karlsefni—for no practical reason that we can see—accompanied them a way on their northward voyage, being rewarded for this courtesy by a final jibe in verse? In that case, the reminiscence has been confused or the story partially bungled by the author, since enslavement and death in Ireland make more satisfactory poetic justice for mutiny and theft than for bad judgment in geography or even the rough practical joke of the improbably poisonous whale of a species "unknown" to those fishermen and whalers. We do not imply that even experienced explorers cannot be poisoned, however, and Icelandic records do indicate occasional poisonings from whale meat. But *GS* conveys no hint of such a setback, the integral status and function of which are obvious in the *ES* narrative. It occurs to wonder whether this incident could be related in any way to tales of a sorcerer in whale's shape.[82]

There is no formula for ascertaining how large Karlsefni's expedition should have been, but we know that stories wax in the telling, particularly when they come to concentrate on favored characters. The 65 persons associated with Karlsefni's voyage in *GS* are perhaps just as likely as the 160 claimed by *ES*, for the taste for magnificence and ample numbers grew as the saga genre developed. The Skrælings of those sparsely populated areas might have been rather wary of dealing with a host so very large by the standards of their experience. But one must defer to the current opinion of ethnologists as to how large a con-

[81] Hermannsson, *The Problem of Wineland* (*Islandica,* XXV), p. 17, thinks Þorvarðr may have been the captain of the ship; cf. p. 21, where Þórhallr takes off in it.

[82] Sveinsson, "Sources and Characteristics," p. cxxiv, mentions that vicious men often turned into whales in the fictional sagas.

federation the primitives of that time and place might have been able to assemble and manipulate for military purposes. As to the 65 versus 160 colonists, we remark merely that the border between history and a tall tale is usually best preserved through adherence to the less imaginative alternative statistic.

VII

There is one further voyage that the two sagas have in common and that is Þorsteinn's abortive expedition. The number of men involved is roughly similar: twenty-five in *GS*, this figure trimmed to twenty in *ES*. The purpose indicated in *ES* is the exploration of Vínland, and the twenty men are equipped with arms and supplies but little in the way of cattle (*fé*), an indication that no lengthy stay is contemplated. No women are mentioned. In *GS* the purpose of Þorsteinn's sailing is that of bringing back (to consecrated soil, of course)[83] the body of his slain brother Þorvaldr from Krossanes, where the Skrælings had killed him during the separate expedition under his leadership. Additional desiderata, including the fetching of a few prime logs from Markland, might well have played a part. The fancier account in *ES* makes the slayer a uniped, has the hero utter a traditional remark about his fat paunch (though here it is the rich land, rather than a generous prince, which has fed him well),[84] neglects to say anything about his burial, and not only converts the purpose of the unsuccessful voyage into a stereotype search for Vínland but carefully displaces Þorsteinn's voyage to a position antecedent to Karlsefni's sailing, with the effect of obliterating all connection with Þorvaldr's death. This indicates, however, that the author of *ES* believes in Þorsteinn's voyage, or wishes his readers to do so. Other things being equal, the *ES* version of both Þorvaldr and Þorsteinn is clearly a modification and downgrading of that in *GS*. The latter itself, however, is not free of all suspicious detail, for Þorsteinn, carefully selecting twenty-five of the strongest fighting men for what he has reason to believe will be a dangerous under-

[83] There is archaeological evidence that such second burials at Brattahlíð were not uncommon, the corpses having undergone some decomposition between the first and second interment. Cf. Wolfe, "Thjoðhild's Church," pp. 62–63, and traditions of Líka-Loðinn, *Ísl. sög.*, VIII, 441.

[84] Cf. Þórmoðr Kolbrúnarskáld, *Ísl. sög.*, V, 357: " 'Vel hefir konungrinn alit oss, hvítt er þessum karli um hjartarætr'." The skilled adaptation in *ES* has it: " 'Feitt er um ístruna. Gott land hǫfum vér fengit kostum, en þó megum vér varla njóta'." (Hermannsson, *The Vinland Sagas* [*Islandica*, XXX], p. 28).

taking, rather unreasonably brings along his wife Guðríðr. This fulfills the narrative purpose of bringing the couple to the northerly Lýsufjǫrðr on Greenland, where Christianity is still rather feeble. Here Þorsteinn dies and supernatural events occur. One would surmise that in actuality the visit of the newly-weds to Lýsufjǫrðr took place later and, as in *ES*, was not connected with the unsuccessful voyage in search of Krossanes.

The *ES* version of Þorsteinn's voyage has borrowed a notable detail from Leifr's voyage in *GS*, namely, Eiríkr's fall from his horse as he, in response to urging, is about to embark on an expedition (in *GS* as the leader of it) for which he is at his age no longer suited. S. B. F. Jansson and others have commented on this theme and its supposed antecedents in literary history.[85] Contrived or not, the incident does remind one of Gunnarr's fall in *Brennu-Njáls saga,* where, for quite a different reason, Gunnarr decides not to travel.[86] The proverb *Fall er farar heill* seems to be part of an ancient and international tradition related to superstitious modes of thought. One attempts to propitiate fate through inverting a prayer or prediction. "Hals- und Beinbruch!" says the German in order to wish a friend good luck. "A bad rehearsal makes a good performance" is the consolatory phrase among theatrical people. There is some flavor of Christian moralizing in the *ES* version of Eiríkr's buried treasure and his implied attribution of the accident to a moral failing, his own greed. This had never bothered Egill Skallagrímsson nor Ketilbjǫrn gamli, who in an episode similar to that of *Eigla* slew the thrall Haki and the female thrall Bót, as told in *Landnámabók.*[87] *ES* has clearly added superfluous details to an established and perfectly adequate motif—that of a character who desists from some undertaking in the face of an unfavorable omen. In *GS*, Eiríkr rides back home again, and the expedition sails without him. In *ES*, the ambiguous wording of the variant versions makes it unclear as to whether Eiríkr went along. The learned discussion that has resulted

[85] Jansson, *Sagorna om Vinland*, pp. 129–133.

[86] *Brennu-Njálssaga,* Chap. 75: "*Fǫgr er hlíðin*" (cited from the edition by Finnur Jónsson, *Altnordische Saga-Bibliothek,* XIII [Halle: Niemeyer, 1908], 165). One notes that Gunnarr's Hlíðarendi and Eiríkr's Brattahlíð have in common the onomastic element *hlíð*. Concerning the fall and the expression, see Rolf Pipping, "Ett dubbeltydigt omen," *Budkavlen*, Årg. XV, No. 1 (1936), pp. 80–82.

[87] *Egils saga Skallagrímssonar,* Chap. 85: "En hvarki kom aptr síðan þrælarnir né kisturnar." Cited from *Saga-Bibliothek*, III, zweite Auflage (Halle [Saale], 1924), p. 292. Cf. *Landnámabók*, in *Ísl. sög.*, I, 228.

from this, discussion about whether Eiríkr would or would not have set sail after his accident, is chiefly irrelevant. For the theme is studded with fiction at all points, one sample of which, to the best of my belief, has never been noticed before. In real life, is it likely that Eiríkr would have been able to preserve a chest of gold and silver? Preparations for the settlement of Greenland would surely have consumed all the ready cash that he and his well-to-do wife had ever been able to accumulate or retain during years of adversity on Iceland, and the *in natura* transactions typical of Greenlandic existence would scarcely have swelled his coffers. Precise facts being unascertainable in any case, we lean upon the more modest conjecture.

There is another question, likewise ignored in discussions, insofar as we know. Would Eiríkr actually have *ridden* to a ship almost in his front yard? This involves considerations that cannot be precisely quantified, but the question itself heightens suspicion that we are dealing with a fictional theme. A few horses, chiefly pack animals, were kept by the Greenland colonists. The historicity of the incident under discussion is related to two real-life factors. One of these is the location of the stables, the other is the problem of where a ship would be kept while being readied for a voyage. We do not know whether it would have been drawn up in front of the hall, or farther up the fjord at or near the *naust*, 'boathouse.' For transportation of goods to and from the latter, pack animals would have been used by Eiríkr if the importation began in his day. Magnus Degerbøl writes that "of . . . *Equus*, Horse, there are a few bones. This find too seems to show that the horse was only rarely kept in Norse times in Greenland."[88] Nørlund and Stenberger have published a detailed sketch of the arrangements at Brattahlíð, but are undecided as to which buildings are the horse stables.[89] In our day, two hundred metres is the average distance of hall and stables from the shore line. But there has been a land submergence of

[88] "Animal Bones from Inland Farms in the East Settlement," in C. L. Vebæk, *Inland Farms in the Norse East Settlement,* p. 114. Cf. Degerbøl's article on animal remains at Brattahlíð, in Paul Nørlund and Mårten Stenberger, *Brattahlid,* p. 155, listing bones of *Equus caballus*; and p. 151 and Fig. 106 on p. 152, description of a small horse.

[89] In *Brattahlid*, the hall of Brattahlíð appears as part of Farm "A," Plate 1 following p. 161 (cf. detailed sketch in Fig. 24, p. 48); cf. p. 81: ". . . the riding horses should be rather close to the farm house, whereas the pack horses could be stabled farther away."

undetermined extent.[90] The authors assume that the ships would have been readied for sailing at some distance from the farm. Unfortunately, this opinion is based, not on archaeological evidence, but on the literary criteria which we are here attempting to test: the saga statements about Eiríkr's fall.[91]

There are dozens of further details for which textual analysis can show with maximal probability that *ES* used or modified features of *GS*, rather than the reverse situation, for which so many scholars have vouched. But the argument we have already advanced, that the author of *ES* may have had access to authentic details (we speak now of real-life reminiscences rather than faithfulness in the transmission of literary inventions common to both sagas), is confirmed by certain appearances. The deer marrow, or pemmican, mentioned in *ES* (Chap. 11) as being found during the expedition by Karlsefni, is one striking example. The rather great length of the Karlsefni expedition in *ES*, three times the length of the same voyage in *GS*, accounts for the inclusion of many things, but out of what would this unusual feature have been expanded except out of some genuine observation, if not by Karlsefni or the others known to the saga, then by some other early but unidentified Norse expedition? To so fruitless a speculation one may oppose the possibility that the pemmican, too, was derived from some version, now lost, of *GS*. The "cakes of dung" of *ES* are likely enough an original feature which *GS* has lost.[92] Karlsefni's battle with the Skrælings is narrated differently in the two sagas (*GS*, Chap. 7; *ES*, Chap. 11). We must ask: did *ES* invent, or was it *GS* that forgot, the identity of the man (Þorbrandr Snorrason) assertedly killed by an axe, or flintstone, during the battle? Can this "attrition" theory be applied to the *GS* version of the bartering with the natives? Thórdarson thinks that bartering was natural among the Indians.[93] Arbman is "reminded of the Scandinavian merchants in the Near East (though there they had been the sellers of the furs) trading with the Arabs for strips of silk."[94] These two points of view need not be in conflict. We think

[90] *Ibid.*, p. 24: "Some of the land has been lost by submergence . . ."; p. 117: ". . . distance to water [was] much greater than it is now."

[91] *Ibid.*, p. 116 n. 1.

[92] *ES*, Chap. 11: "var nesit at sjá sem ein mykiskán væri."

[93] *The Vinland Voyages*, p. 50.

[94] *The Vikings*, p. 115.

merely that the strips of red cloth were contributed to the narrative as an invention by the sophisticated author of *ES*: ". . . as Painter points out, some saga details from around the year 1000 are sufficiently anachronistic to reflect the accumulated experiences of three or four generations of intermittent or continual contact with the skrælings. Such a possibility competes with the opinion of the reviewer and others, that certain sophistications in the Norsemen's trading activities with the natives, the building of a stockade, etc., may reflect cultural and literary influences from (or via) Europe upon the sagawriters of the thirteenth century."[95]

Very little attention has been paid by its adherents or its detractors to the fact that *GS*, too, must have shed some of its pristine details. Was it clumsiness of conception, or such a shedding of detail, that makes the *Skrælings* in *GS* (Chap. 8) show up with loads of furs for trading purposes, without any previous visit of inspection on their part? The more thoughtful account in *ES* (Chap. 11) makes such provision. The savages that slay Þorvaldr, whose men have slaughtered several isolated members of their tribe asleep on a beach, arrive with phenomenal promptness as a great throng. The lack of transition indicates a loss of some significant details in *GS*. And other abridgements are discernible. We know that the original beginning of *GS* became lost at some point, for its substitute opening chapter is manifestly borrowed from Sturla Þórðarson's *Landnámabók* (Sturla died in 1284), from which, thus, nothing in the original saga can be determined. We realize as well that, although the saga knows Þjóðhildr and Guðríðr, Leifr's wife's name can nowhere be learned. From other sources, we know the name of his son and heir, Þorkell.[96] The substitution of "Þorkell bondi" for "Herjólfr bondi" at Herjólfsnes in *ES* is probably another of the pious little compensatory frauds perpetrated by its author.[97] We may consider it likely that the Þórir austmaðr rescued by Leifr from the reef was neither a historical personage nor the first husband of a thus thrice-married Guðríðr, whose antecedents are so differently explained in the rival saga. This leaves open the question of whether this divergency was a deliberate invention or the mere result of expediency

[95] E. Wahlgren, review of Skelton *et al., The Vinland Map and the Tartar Relation* (*Scandinavian Studies*, XXXVIII, No. 1 [February, 1966], 66–67).

[96] Cf. *Fóstbrœðra saga, Ísl. sög.*, V, 326. Leifr seems to have died between 1019 and 1025.

[97] See note 79.

in the face of ignorance. Þórir becomes in any case removed from the story through death during an epidemic the very first winter, the winter in which Eiríkr dies as well. We may find it regrettable that *GS* knows so little of Eiríkr and Þjóðhildr as a married couple[98] (Eiríkr had illegitimate children). Nor do we hear much of the details of life on Greenland, such omissions likely enough being omissions through choice. The sagas, after all, were written on Iceland. The search for Vínland was remarkable enough to sustain an interest in its recording during the Saga Age. But the family feuds, if any, the slow character development, the life stories of heroes on remote Greenland were marginal, lacking alike in central interest and adequacy of recorded detail. Greenland furnished small literary nourishment except as an escape hatch, a place of adventure, and an exotic locale for occasional later stories.

The wording and circumstances of *GS* often lead to the surmise that, somewhere along the line, transmitted material was redactionally compressed and shorn of detail. Contrary to the case with *ES*, whose two main variants could be juxtaposed and compared line for line by Jansson, material for massive internal comparison is not extant.

The present work has not struggled with the vastly intricate problem of geographical identifications (these have been usefully summed up by I. R. Swanton).[99] The nature and restricted bulk of the philological *corpus* render impossible the ascertainment of "average" sailings during the Vinland voyages. Hermannsson points out that the heavily laden ships of the colonists would not have conformed to the distances and sailing speeds so facilely assumed by many writers. And Hovgaard reminds us of the additional complications posed by mirages.[100]

Chapters and whole books have been devoted to landfalls, and a welter of more or less precise assertions has been made, both by scholars of repute and by popular writers who, dwelling in sainted ignorance

[98] Freydís is portrayed as illegitimate, and it is possible that Þorvaldr, too, was illegitimate. The Icelander Guðmundr Kamban has carried out psychological themes in his novel about the Vinland discovery, *Jeg ser et skjønt Land*, translated as *I See a Wondrous Land*.

[99] *The Wineland Voyages*.

[100] William Hovgaard writes: "Here [on Resolution Island, Meta Incognita, etc.], as well as on the coast of Labrador, refraction is very pronounced, and mirage is common and characteristic of the few fine days of summer. Often land is seen from far greater distances than in the ordinary state of the atmosphere" (*The Voyages of the Norsemen to America*, p. 193).

of philological complexities, cite *ad hoc* the jumbled, contradictory, and translated texts that loom up on their horizons, almost as if these, in sooth, were post-Nicene Holy Writ. One such writer will accept the proposition that practically everybody discovered America. Another, with the aid of Boy Scouts, archaeology enthusiasts, and great proficiency in the misreading of Icelandic texts, can show us not only where the mythical Helgi and Finnbogi built their boatshed in New England, but where they stacked their weapons, and—with diagram—how many inches each man and woman of the expedition—in snug harmony—employed for lateral sleeping space. A third cites astronomical evidence derived from "a man named Loki" in the *Edda.* And several make it clear that those who challenge bogus inscriptions are acting from motives too sinister to be specified in print. On the whole, there has been what James M. Lufkin has termed "a more or less continuous 'dialogue of the deaf' between the scientific community on one hand and a group of interested laymen on the other."[101]

After a century of dispute, physical descriptions have now given us some firm *points d'appui* for geographical constructions. These ascertainments can eliminate old errors, while perhaps giving rise to some new ones. The inseparable twin poles of the Vínland problem are literature and history: fancy and fact. It is hoped that the philologically oriented arguments of the present treatise have suggested, at some points even determined, where the boundary between them best should be drawn. A saga as a work of literature, however, is greater than the sum of its identifiable parts, just as a melody is more than the sum of its notes and a poem greater than the sum of the words it contains. In all three cases, the *relationship* between the constituent elements is itself a prime element,[102] and this is true whether one approaches the problem from a scientific, or from a chiefly appreciative, point of view. "The real significance of the sagas," write Magnusson and Pálsson, "is that they so greatly enlarge our knowledge and understanding of the event itself: they illuminate history with humanity."[103]

[101] Untitled editorial in *The Minnesota Archeologist,* XXVII, No. 3 (1965) 96. Lufkin is speaking in particular of the discussion over alleged runic inscriptions.

[102] We quote Alan Dundes: ". . . certainly a vague unit such as motif cannot be used as an adequate structural unit in any scientific study of folklore" (*The Morphology of North American Indian Tales*, p. 54).

[103] *The Vinland Sagas*, p. 29.

SELECTED BIBLIOGRAPHY

Adam of Bremen. *Adami Gesta Hammaburgensis Ecclesiae Pontificium.* Ed. G. H. Pertz. Hannoverae: Hahn, 1846.

———. *Adamus Bremensis. Gesta Hammaburgensis ecclesiae pontificium. Codex Havniensis.* Introduction by C. A. Christensen. Published in photolithography. Copenhagen: Rosenkilde and Bagger, 1948.

Ágrip af Noregs konunga sögum. Diplomatarisk utgave ved Verner Dahlerup. København: Møller, 1880.

Alfræði Íslenzk. Islandsk encyclopædisk Litteratur, I. *Cod. Mbr. AM. 194, 8vo. Udgivet ved Kr. Kålund.* København: Møller, 1908.

Anderson, Rasmus B. *The Norse Discovery of America.* London: Norrœna Society, 1907.

Andersson, Theodore M. *The Problem of Icelandic Saga Origins: A Historical Survey.* New Haven and London: Yale University Press, 1964.

Andrews, A. LeRoy. "Philological Aspects of the 'Plants of Wineland the Good'." *Rhodora: Journal of the New England Botanical Club.* XV, No. 170 (February, 1913), 28–35.

Annales Danici Medii Ævi. Editionem nouam curavit Ellen Jørgensen. Udgivne af Selskabet for Udgivelse af Kilder til Dansk Historie med Understøttelse af Carlsbergfondet. København: Gad, 1920.

Antiqvitates Americanæ. . . . SEE Rafn, C. C.

Arbman, Holger. *The Vikings.* Trans. and ed. with an Introduction by Alan Binns. New York: Praeger, 1961.

Ari Fróði (Þorgilsson). SEE *Íslendingabók Ara Fróða;* Hermannsson, Halldór.

Babcock, William H. *Early Norse Visits to North America.* "Smithsonian Miscellaneous Collections," LIX, No. 19 (Publication 2138). Washington, 1913.

Barðar saga Snæfellsáss. SEE *Íslendinga sögur,* III.

Beckman, Nils. "Isländsk och medeltida skandinavisk tideräkning," *Tideräkningen: Nordisk kultur,* XXI. Ed. Martin P:n Nilsson. Stockholm: Bonnier, 1934. Pp. 4–57.

Bessason, Haraldur. "Some Notes on Leifr Eiriksson's National Origin and the Sources on Greenland and Vinland," *The Icelandic Canadian* (Winnipeg), Winter, 1965, pp. 13–20.

Biskupa Sögur gefnar út af Hinu Íslenzka Bókmentafélagi, Fyrsta Bindi. Kaupmannahöfn, 1858.

Bogason, Sigurður Örn. *Ensk-Íslenzk orðabók.* Reykjavík: Ísafold, 1952.

Brennu-Njálssaga (Njála). Herausgegeben von Finnur Jónsson. Altnordische Saga-Bibliothek, XIII. Halle (Saale): Niemeyer, 1908.

Brøgger, A. W. *Vinlandsferdene.* Oslo:Gyldendal, 1937.

——— and Shetelig, Haakon. *The Viking Ships: Their Ancestry and Evolution.* Oslo: Dreyer, 1953.

Brown, Madelaine R., and Magoun, Francis P. "Tyrkir, First German in North America," *Modern Language Notes,* LXI, No. 8 (December, 1946), 547–551.

Brøndsted, Johannes. "Problemet om nordboer i Amerika før Columbus," *Aarbøger for nordisk Oldkyndighed,* 1950 (1951), 1–152.

Bugge, Sophus. *Hønen-Runerne fra Ringerike* [a preliminary fascicle of *Norges Indskrifter med de yngre Runer*]. Kristiania: A. W. Brøgger, 1902.

Clarke, A. H. "Littorina littorea as an Indicator of Norse Settlements," *Science,* CXLII (November 22, 1963), 1022. [Rejoinder on same page by N. Spjeldnæs and K. Henningsmoen.]

Corpus Codicum Islandicorum. SEE *Flateyjarbók.*

Crone, G. R. "How Authentic is the 'Vinland Map'?" *Encounter,* February, 1966, pp. 75–78.

Dahlerup, Verner. SEE *Ágríp af Noregs konunga sögum.*

Degerbøl, Magnus. "Animal Bones from Inland Farms in the East Settlement." C. L. Vebaek, *Inland Farms in the Norse East Settlements* (*Meddelelser om Grønland,* Bd. 90, No. 1). København: Reitzel, 1943. Pp. 113–119.

Dundes, Alan. *The Morphology of North American Indian Tales,* "Folklore Fellows Communications," No. 195. Helsinki, 1964.

Eeden, W. van. "Vínland-Studiën. I–III," *Tijdschrift voor Nederlandsche Taal- en Letterkunde,* XLI (1922), 49–64, 287–301; XLVI (1927), 65–80.

Egils saga Skallagrímssonar. SEE Jónsson, Finnur.

Einarsson, Stefán. *A History of Icelandic Literature.* New York: Johns Hopkins Press, 1957.

———. "The Freydís Incident in Eiríks Saga Rauða, Ch. 11," *Acta Philologica Scandinavica,* XIII (1939), 246–256.

Eiríks saga rauða [one of the *Grœnlendinga sögur*]. SEE *Flateyjarbók*; Gravier, Maurice; Hermannsson, Halldór; *Íslendinga sögur,* I; *Íslenzk fornrit,* IV; Reeves, Arthur Middleton; Storm, Gustav.

Eyrbyggja saga. SEE *Íslendinga sögur,* I; *Íslenzk fornrit,* IV.

Fernald, M. L. "Notes on the Plants of Wineland the Good," *Rhodora: Journal of the New England Botanical Club,* XII, No. 134 (February, 1910), 17–38.

Fischer, Joseph. *The Discoveries of the Norsemen in America with special relation to their early geographical Representation.* Trans. Basil H. Soulsby. London: Henry Stevens, Son and Stiles, 1903.

The Flatey Book and Recently Discovered Vatican Manuscripts Concerning America as Early as the Tenth Century. London: Norrœna Society, 1906.

Flateyjarbók. Codex Flateyensis. MS No. 1005 in the Old Royal Library of Copenhagen. Introduction by Finnur Jónsson. Copenhagen: Levin and Munksgaard, 1930.

Flateyjarbók. Corpus Codicum Islandicorum Medii Ævi. XIII: *The Arna-Magnæan Manuscript 557 4to Containing inter alia the History of the First Discovery of America.* Introduction by Dag Strömbäck. Copenhagen: Levin and Munksgaard, 1940.

Fóstbrœðra saga. SEE *Íslendinga sögur,* V.

Friederici, Georg. Review of Vinland treatises by P. Nørlund and H. Hermannsson. *Göttingische Gelehrte Anzeigen,* CCI, No. 2 (February, 1939), 69–88.

Fritzner, Johan. *Ordbog over Det gamle norske Sprog. Nytt uforandret Opptrykk av 2. Utgave (1883–1896). Med et Bind Tillegg og Rettelser redigert av Didrik Arup Seip og Trygve Knudsen.* 3 vols. Oslo: Tryggve Juul Møller Forlag, 1954.

Gathorne-Hardy, G. M. *The Wineland Sagas Translated and Discussed.* Oxford: Clarendon Press, 1921.

Gravier, Maurice. *La saga d'Éric le Rouge. Le Récit des Grœnlandais. Texte islandais avec introduction, traduction, notes et glossaire.* Paris: Aubier, 1955.

Grönländer und Färinger Geschichten. Übertragen von Felix Niedner (Thule, Band 13: *Altnordische Dichtung und Prosa*). Düsseldorf-Köln: Eugen Dietrichs Verlag, 1965.

Grœnlendinga saga (sögur). SEE *Flateyjarbók;* Gravier, Maurice; Hermannsson, Halldór; *Íslendinga sögur,* I; *Íslenzk fornrit,* IV; Reeves, Arthur Middleton; Storm, Gustav.

Halvorsen, E. F. *The Norse Version of the Chanson de Roland.* (*Bibliotheca Arnamagnæana,* XIX). København: Ejnar Munksgaard, 1959.

Hannesson, Jóhann S. *The Sagas of Icelanders (Íslendinga Sögur). A Supplement to Islandica I and XXIV.* (*Islandica,* XXXVIII). Ithaca: Cornell University Press, 1957.

Haugen, Einar. "The Sources of the Vinland Map," *Arctic: Journal of the Arctic Institute of North America,* XIX:14 (December, 1966), 287–295.

———. *Voyages to Vinland. The First American Saga, Newly Translated and Interpreted.* New York: Knopf, 1942.

Heggstad, Leiv. *Gamalnorsk ordbok med nynorsk tyding.* Oslo: Det Norske Samlaget, 1930.

Heimskringla. SEE Snorri Sturluson.

Helgason, Jón. *Arngrímur Jónsson Gronlandia 1688.* Published in Facsimile with an Introduction in English. Copenhagen: Ejnar Munksgaard, 1942.

Hellquist, Elof. *Svensk etymologisk ordbok.* Tredje upplagan. Band II: *O:Ö.* Lund: Gleerup, 1957.

Hermannsson, Halldór. *Bibliography of the Icelandic Sagas and Minor Tales* (*Islandica,* I). Ithaca: Cornell University Press, 1908.

——— (ed. and trans. with an introductory Essay and Notes). *The Book of the Icelanders (Íslendingabók) by Ari Thorgilsson* (*Islandica,* XX). Ithaca: Cornell University Press, 1930.

———. *The Northmen in America* (*Islandica,* II). Ithaca: Cornell University Press, 1909.

———. *The Problem of Wineland* (*Islandica,* XXV). Ithaca: Cornell University Press, 1936.

———. *The Sagas of the Icelanders* (*Islandica,* XXIV). Ithaca: Cornell University Press, 1934.

———."Tyrkir, Leif Erikson's Foster-Father," *Modern Language Notes,* LXIX, No. 6 (June, 1954), 388–393.

———. *The Vinland Sagas* (*Islandica,* XXX). Ithaca: Cornell University Press, 1944.

Historia Norwegiæ. SEE Storm, Gustav.

Hollander, Lee M. SEE Snorri Sturluson.

Hovgaard, William. *The Voyages of the Norsemen to North America.* New York: The American-Scandinavian Foundation, 1914.

Ingstad, Helge. *Landet under leidarstjernen. En ferd til Grønlands norrøne bygder.* Oslo: Gyldendal, 1960.

———. *Land under the Pole Star: A Voyage to the Norse Settlements of Greenland and the Saga of the People that Vanished.* Trans. Naomi Walford. New York: St. Martin's Press, 1966.

———. "Vinland Ruins Prove Vikings Found the New World," *National Geographic,* CXXVI, No. 5 (November, 1964), 708–734.

Islandica. SEE Hannesson, Jóhann S.; Hermannsson, Halldór.

Islandske Ættesagaer. Under redaksjon av Hallvard Lie. III. [Includes *Eirik Raudes saga, En Saga om Grønlendingene, Grønlendingetåtten*]. Trans. Anne Holtsmark. Oslo: Aschehoug, 1953.

Íslendingabók (Are hinn Fróðe Þorgilsson). *Tilegnet Islands Alting 930–1930 af Dansk-Islandsk Forbundsfond. Udgiven ved Finnur Jónsson.* København: Jørgensen, 1930.

Íslendingabók Ara Fróða. AM. 113a and 113b, fol. Introduction by Jón Jóhannesson. Reykjavík: University of Iceland, 1956. SEE ALSO Hermannsson, Halldór.

Íslendinga sögur. I, III, V. *Guðni Jónsson bjó til prentunar.* [I (1953) includes *Íslendingabók, Landnámabók, Kristni saga, Eiríks saga rauða, Grænlendinga saga, Grænlendinga þáttr*; III (1958) includes *Eyrbyggja saga, Barðar saga Snæfellsáss*; V (1953) includes *Fóstbræðra saga.*] Reykjavík: Íslendingasagnaútgáfan.

Íslenzk fornrit. IV: *Eyrbyggja saga, Grænlendingasögur. Einar Ól. Sveinsson og Matthías Þórðarson gáfu út.* Reykjavík: Hið Íslenzka Fornritafélag, 1935.

Jansson, Sven B. F. *Sagorna om Vinland.* I: *Handskrifterna till Erik den Rödes saga.* With an English Summary (*Kungl. Vitterhets Historie och Antikvitets Akademiens Handlingar, Del* 60:1). Stockholm: Wahlström & Widstrand (i kommission), 1945.

Jansson, Valter. *Nordiska Vin-Namn. En ortnamnstyp och dess historia* (*Skrifter utgivna av Kungl. Gustav Adolfs Akademien,* 24). Uppsala-København, 1951.

Jóhannesson, Jón. "The Date of the Composition of the Saga of the Greenlanders," *Saga-Book of the Viking Society for Northern Research,* XVI, Part I. London: The Viking Society for Northern Research, 1962. Pp. 54–66. SEE ALSO *Íslendingabók Ara Fróða.*

Jones, Gwyn. *Eirik the Red and other Icelandic Sagas: Selected and Translated.* London: Oxford University Press, 1961.

———. *The Norse Atlantic Saga: Being the Norse Voyages of Discovery and Settlement to Iceland, Greenland, America.* London: Oxford University Press, 1964.

Jónsson, Finnur (ed.) *Egils saga Skallagrímssonar nebst den grösseren Gedichten Egils.* Zweite neubearbeitete Auflage. *Altnordische Saga-Bibliothek,* III. Halle (Saale): Max Niemeyer, 1924.

———. "Erik den Rødes Saga og Vinland," *Norsk historisk Tidsskrift udgivet av Den Norske Historiske Forening,* Femte Rekke, Første Bind (Kristiania, 1912), 116–157.

———. "Opdagelsen af og Rejserne til Vinland," *Aarbøger for nordisk Oldkyndighed,* 1915, pp. 205–221.

———. *Den norsk-islandske Skjaldedigtning. A. Tekst efter Håndskrifterne.* I. Bind. København og Kristiania: Gyldendal, 1912.

Jónsson, Guðni. SEE *Íslendingasögur; Konunga sögur.*

Kålund, Kr. SEE *Alfræði Íslenzk.*

Kamban, Gunnar. *I See a Wondrous Land.* New York: Putnam, 1938.

Konunga sögur. I. *Guðni Jónsson bjó til prentunar.* Reykjavík: Íslendingasagnaútgáfan, 1957.

Krappe, A. H. "Intoxicating Grapes," *Modern Language Notes,* LVIII, No. 4 (April, 1943), 268–274.

Krause, Wilhelm. Review of A. W. Brøgger, *Vinlandsferdene. Göttingische Gelehrte Anzeigen,* CCI, No. 2 (February, 1939), 53–69.

Kristni saga. SEE *Biskupa Sögur . . .*; *Íslendingasögur,* I.

Landnámabók Íslands. Udgiven efter de gamle Håndskrifter af Det kon-

gelige nordiske Oldskriftselskab til Minde om dets hundrede År 1825–1925. København: Thiele, 1925. SEE ALSO *Íslendinga sögur,* I.

Lendin, Valdemar. "Vindlandsproblemet. En översikt över nyare litteratur rörande källorna," *(Svensk) Historisk Tidskrift,* Andra följden. Fjortonde årgången, Häfte 3 (1951), 322–338.

Lufkin, James M. Editorial on alleged Scandinavian antiquities in America. *The Minnesota Archaeologist,* XXVII, No. 3 (1965), 96.

Magnusson, Magnus, and Pálsson, Hermann. *The Vinland Sagas. The Norse Discovery of America. Grænlendinga Saga and Eirik's Saga.* Translated with an Introduction. Baltimore: Penguin Books, 1965.

Magoun, Francis P. SEE Brown, Madelaine R., and Francis P. Magoun.

Meddelelser om Grønland. SEE Nørlund, Paul, and Mårten Stenberger; Vebæk, C. L.

Næss, Almar. *Hvor lå Vinland?* Oslo: Dreyer [1954].

Nansen, Fridtjof. *In Northern Mists: Arctic Explorations in Early Times.* Trans. Arthur G. Chater. 2 vols. New York: Frederick Stokes, 1911.

Njála; Njál's Saga. SEE *Brennu-Njálssaga.*

Nordal, Sigurður. *Hrafnkels Saga Freysgoða: A Study by Sigurður Nordal,* trans. R. George Thomas. Cardiff: University of Wales Press, 1958.

———. "Sagalitteraturen," *Nordisk kultur.* VIII:B. (Stockholm: Bonnier, 1953), 180–273.

Nørlund, Paul, and Mårten Stenberger. *Brattahlid (Meddelelser om Grønland,* Bd. 88, Nr. 1.) København: Reitzel, 1934.

Óláfs saga Tryggvasonar. SEE *Heimskringla.*

Oleson, Tryggvi J. *Early Voyages and Northern Approaches, 1000–1632.* The Canadian Centenary Series. London and New York: Oxford University Press, 1964.

Pálsson, Hermann. SEE Magnusson, Magnus.

Pertz, G. H. SEE Adam of Bremen.

Pipping, Rolf. "Ett dubbeltydigt omen," *Budkavlen,* XV, No. 1 (1936), 80–82.

Rafn, C. C. *Antiqvitates Americanæ sive Scriptores Septentrionales Rerum ante-Columbianarum in America. Samling af de i Nordens Oldskrifter indeholdte Efterretninger om de gamle Nordboers Opdagelsesreiser til America fra det 10de til det 14de Aarhundrede.* Edidit Societas Regia Antiqvariorum Septentrionalium. Hafniæ: Schultz, 1837.

Reeves, Arthur Middleton. *The Finding of Wineland the Good: The History of the Icelandic Discovery of America, Edited and Translated from the Earliest Records.* London: Henry Frowde, 1890.

Riddarasögur. SEE Sveinsson, E. Ó., "Sources and Characteristics."

Sawyer, P. H. *Age of the Vikings.* London: L. E. Arnold, 1962.

Skelton, R. A., Thomas E. Marston, and George D. Painter. *The Vinland*

Map and the Tartar Relation. For the Yale University Library with a Foreword by Alexander O. Vietor. New Haven and London: Yale University Press, 1965.

Snorri Sturluson. *Heimskringla: History of the Kings of Norway.* Trans. with Introduction and Notes by Lee M. Hollander. Austin: University of Texas Press, 1964.

Söderberg, Sven. "Vinland," *Sydsvenska Dagbladet Snällposten,* No. 295 (Malmö, October 30, 1910).

Spjældnæs, Nils, and Henningsmoen, Kari E. "Littorina littorea: An Indicator of Norse Settlements in North America?" *Science,* CXLI (July 19, 1963), 275–276. SEE ALSO Clarke, A. H.

Steefel, Lawrence D. Remarks on the bibliography of the Kensington inscription. *The Minnesota Archaeologist,* XXVII, No. 3 (1965), 97–115.

Storm, Gustav. *Eiríks saga rauða og Flatøbogens Grœnlendinga þáttr samt Uddrag fra Óláfssaga Tryggvasonar udgivne for Samfund til Udgivelse af Gammel Nordisk Litteratur.* København: Møller, 1891.

———. *Historia Norwegiæ, Monumenta Historica Norwegiæ. Latinske Kildeskrifter til Norges Historie i Middelalderen.* Kristiania: Brøgger, 1880.

———. *Islandske Annaler indtil 1578. Udgivne for det norske historiske Kildeskriftfond ved Dr. Gustav Storm.* Christiania: Grødahl, 1888.

———. "Studier over Vinlandsreiserne, Vinlands Geografi og Ethnologi," *Aarbøger for nordisk Oldkyndighed og Historie, udgivne af Det Kongelige nordiske Oldskriftselskab.* II. Række, 2. Bind, 4. Hefte (1887), pp. 292–373.

Stenberger, Mårten. SEE Nørlund, Paul, and Mårten Stenberger.

Strömbäck, Dag. SEE *Flateyjarbók. Corpus Codicum Islandicorum.*

Sveinsson, E. Ó. "Íslendingasögur," *Kulturhistorisk Leksikon for nordisk middelalder,* Bind VII (København: Rosenkilde og Bagger, 1962), 495–514.

———. "Sources and Characteristics," *Viktors saga ok Blávus. Riddarasögur. II. Jónas Kristjánsson bjó til prentunar* (Reykjavík: Handritastofnun Íslands, 1964), pp. cix-ccxii. SEE ALSO *Íslenzk fornrit,* IV.

Swanton, I. R. *The Wineland Voyages* ("Smithsonian Miscellaneous Collections," CVII, No. 12 [Publication 3906]). Washington, 1947.

Tanner, Väinö. *De gamla nordbornas Helluland, Markland och Vinland. Ett försök att lokalisera Vinlandsresornas huvudetapper i de isländska sagorna* (*Bukavlen,* XX, No. 1). Åbo, 1941.

Thorarinsson, Sigurður. "Några reflexioner med anledning av V. Tanners skrift," *Ymer. Tidskrift utgiven av Svenska sällskapet för antropologi och geografi,* LXII, No. 1–2 (1942), 39–46.

Thórdarson, Matthías, *The Vinland Voyages.* American Geographical So-

ciety Research Series, No. 18. New York: American Geographical Society, 1930.
Þorsteinsson, Björn. "Some Observations on the Discoveries and the Cultural History of the Norsemen," *Saga-Book of the Viking Society for Northern Research,* XVI, Parts 2–3. London: The Viking Society for Northern Research, 1963–1964. Pp. 173–191.
Tiderakningen. SEE Beckman, Nils.
Tornöe, J. Kr. *Early American History: Norsemen Before Columbus.* Oslo: Universitetsforlaget, 1964.
Turville-Petre, G. *Origins of Icelandic Literature.* Oxford: Clarendon Press, 1953.
van Eeden, W. SEE Eeden, W. van.
Vebæk, C. L. *Inland Farms in the Norse East Settlements* (*Meddelelser om Grønland,* Bd. 90, No. 1). København: Reitzel, 1943.
Viktors saga ok Blávus. SEE Sveinsson, E. Ó., "Sources and Characteristics."
Vilmundarson, Thórhallur. "Reflections on the Vinland Map," *American-Scandinavian Review,* CIV, No. 1 (Spring, 1966), 20–25.
Wahlgren, Erik. *The Kensington Stone, a Mystery Solved.* Madison: University of Wisconsin Press, 1958.
———. Review of Ingstad, *Land Under the Pole Star. Scandinavian Studies,* XXXIX, No. 2 (May, 1967), 182–186.
———. Review of Skelton *et al., Vinland Map and the Tartar Relation. Scandinavian Studies,* XXXVIII, No. 1 (February, 1966), 62–67.
———. "Further Remarks on *Vínland,*" *Scandinavian Studies,* XL, No. 1 (February, 1968), 26–35.
Zoëga, Geir T. *A Concise Dictionary of Old Icelandic.* Oxford: Clarendon Press, 1926.
Wolfe, Michael. "Thjoðhild's Church: The Cradle of Christianity in Norse Greenland," *American-Scandinavian Review,* LI (Spring, 1963), 55–66.

Some Observations on the Influence of *Tristrams saga ok Ísöndar* on Old Icelandic Literature

PAUL SCHACH

Scholars have long been aware of the pervasive influence of the Tristan story on the medieval and early modern literature of Scandinavia. Although the full scope of this influence remains to be determined, the stimulating pioneering studies of Henry Goddard Leach and Margaret Schlauch provide a substantial amount of information as well as a sound basis for a more penetrating and extensive investigation of the problem.[1] These two studies reveal that themes, names, situations, and motifs associated with the Tristan legend occur over a wide geographical area and a long period of time. Reminiscences of that tragic legend are found, for example, in ballads from Denmark, Norway, Iceland, and the Faroe Islands.[2] The impact of the Tristan story seems to have been especially strong and persistent in Iceland. Here the story of the two hapless lovers, in whole or in part, was imitated, parodied, and plagiarized from about the middle of the thirteenth century to modern times. To judge from the number of borrowings and

[1] Leach, *Angevin Britain and Scandinavia* (Harvard Studies in Comparative Literature, Vol. VI [Cambridge, Massachusetts: Harvard University Press, 1921]), esp. Chap. 7, "Tristan in the North," pp. 169–198; Schlauch, *Romance in Iceland* (Princeton: Princeton University Press, 1934), pp. 149–169 and *passim*.

[2] On the Tristan ballads see Paul Schach, "Tristan and Isolde in Scandinavian Ballad and Folktale," *Scandinavian Studies*, XXXVI (1964), 281–297.

adaptations, interest in the Tristan story must have been at its height in the fourteenth and fifteenth centuries; but the recent date of the three extant paper transcripts of *Tristrams saga ok Ísöndar* bears witness to a continued interest in that work at least as late as the mid-eighteenth century.[3] And the many and widely varying versions of the folktale *Tristram og Ísól* current in Iceland today preserve not only distinct echoes from the medieval romance but also a number of verbal similarities with *Tristrams saga,* even after several generations of oral transmission.[4]

Despite the fact that *Tristrams saga* is the only version of the Tristan romance known to have existed in Scandinavia during the Middle Ages, scholars have been strangely reluctant to derive the numerous Tristan reminiscences, loans, and adaptations in Old Norse literature from the saga itself. Margaret Schlauch, for instance, speaks of the "many traces of the influence of the Tristan story in the North, apart from the Norse translation of it."[5] In regard to the so-called *Spesar Þáttr* in *Grettis saga,* the best-known Tristan analogue in the *Íslendingasögur* (Sagas of Icelanders), the most ingenious hypotheses have been advanced, several of which will be discussed later on. The Icelandic *Saga af Tristram ok Ýsodd,* which I have recently shown to be a burlesque imitation of *Tristrams saga,*[6] was once believed by Gísli Brynjúlfsson to be based on a Tristan tale heard by an Icelander abroad—probably in the British Isles.[7] More recently, the Irish literary historian James Carney declared that *Kormáks saga,* which can now be enjoyed in an excellent translation by Professor Hollander,[8] is "obviously secondary to some Irish adaptation" of the Tristan story.[9] This thesis was further

[3] For a discussion of the manuscripts see Paul Schach, "Some Observations on *Tristrams Saga,*" *Saga-Book,* XV (1957–1959), 102–129.

[4] Cf. Einar Ól. Sveinsson, *Um íslenzkar þjóðsögur* (Reykjavík: Hið íslenzka bókmentafélag, 1940), p. 254: "Enn er getið um græðsluhús, og má það vera komið úr Tristramssögu." Another version of the folktale has *græðslusmyrsl,* whereas *Tristrams saga* (Chap. 30) uses *græðingarsmyrsl.*

[5] *Romance in Iceland,* p. 150.

[6] Paul Schach, "The *Saga of Tristram ok Ýsodd*: Summary or Satire?" *Modern Language Quarterly,* XXI, No. 4 (1960), 336–352.

[7] For this hypothesis (one of three advanced by Gísli on the origin and genesis of the Icelandic saga), see his edition of *Tristrams saga* (Det Kongelige nordiske Oldskriftselskab, No. 7 [København: Thiele Bogtrykkeri, 1878]), p. 300.

[8] *The Sagas of Kormák and the Sworn Brothers* (Princeton: Princeton University Press, 1949).

[9] *Studies in Irish Literature and History* (Dublin: The Dublin Institute for Advanced Studies, 1955), p. 197.

developed by Bjarni Einarsson, who concluded that the author of *Kormáks saga* used "some story about Tristan" as the "chief source" of his saga and portions of it as "models for several scenes" of his work. This Tristan story, however, must have been more highly developed and more sophisticated than the Irish tales Carney refers to. Bjarni Einarsson further suggests that the author of *Kormáks saga* and the writers of other "sagas of skalds" may have been acquainted with several versions of the Tristan story, some of which are no longer extant.[10]

A notable exception to this reluctance to consider *Tristrams saga* as the most likely source of Tristan influence in Old Norse literature is the Danish scholar Paul V. Rubow, who as early as 1928 suggested that a monument be erected to Friar Róbert, the translator of *Tristrams saga,* as the founder of Old Norse prose fiction.[11] According to Rubow, *Tristrams saga* provided the Icelanders with both the model and the impetus for the literary re-creation of the lives and times of their illustrious forebears. In view of the fact that several Sagas of Icelanders (*Heiðarvíga saga, Fóstbræðra saga, Kormáks saga,* and *Grænlendinga saga*) probably antedate Friar Róbert's translation by a decade or two, Rubow's contention that *Tristrams saga* marks the inception of Icelandic saga-writing is untenable.[12] The rejection of this thesis, however, in no wise detracts from the general merit of Rubow's observations on the nature and manner of composition of the *Íslendingasögur,* nor does it, as Ole Widding recently pointed out, preclude the possibility of the ultimate French origin of Icelandic prose literature by way of Norway.[13] Even though *Tristrams saga* did not provide the original model

[10] *Skáldasögur: Um uppruna og eðli ástaskáldasagnanna fornu* (Reykjavík: Bókaútgáfa Menningarsjóðs, 1961), pp. 45 ff. and *passim.*

[11] "Den islandske Familieroman," first published in *Tilskueren* I (1928), 347–357; reprinted in his *Smaa kritiske Breve* (København: Gyldendal, 1936), pp. 7 ff., and in English translation in his *Two Essays* (Copenhagen: Gyldendal, 1949). For a concise summary of Rubow's interesting views see Theodore M. Andersson, *The Problem of Icelandic Saga Origins* (New Haven and London: Yale University Press, 1964), pp. 70–71.

[12] On the relative chronology of the Sagas of Icelanders see Sigurður Nordal, "Sagalitteraturen" (*Nordisk kultur,* Vol. VIII–B [København, 1953]). The early date of *Grænlendinga saga* was recently established by Jón Jóhannesson in an article entitled "Aldur Grænlendinga sögu," in the Nordal Festschrift, *Nordæla* (Reykjavík, 1956). An English translation by Tryggvi J. Oleson appeared in the *Saga-Book,* XVI (1962), 54–66. See also the excellent Introduction to *The Vinland Sagas,* trans. Magnus Magnusson and Hermann Pálsson (Baltimore: Penguin Books, 1965).

[13] "Islændingesagaer," *Norrøn Fortællekunst: Kapitler af den norsk-islandske*

for Icelandic saga-writing, it did, as we shall see, exert a significant influence on both the style and substance of Old Norse literature during the classical and post-classical period of saga-writing.

It would be futile at the outset of this investigation to attempt a critical review of the many speculations, most of them farfetched and many of them mutually contradictory, regarding hypothetical Tristan influences "apart from the Norse translation." Instead, let us begin our discussion by summarizing briefly a few pertinent facts about *Tristrams saga* itself. Although Thorkil Damsgaard Olsen has recently suggested the possibility that the statement regarding the date of translation and the name of the translator found in the prologue to this saga may be "pure fabrication,"[14] *Tristrams saga* is generally accepted as a translation of the Anglo-Norman Tristan romance of Thomas of Brittany made by a certain Friar Róbert in 1226 at the request of King Hákon Hákonarson—probably, as Leach suggests, on the occasion of the Norwegian monarch's marriage to Margrét, daughter of Snorri Sturluson's friend Duke Skúli.[15] It is further generally accepted that *Tristrams saga* was the first of a series of translations of southern romances of chivalry made at the Norwegian court and that Friar Róbert, who later translated *Elis saga ok Rósamundu,* was thus the originator of the rhetorical "court prose" used with individual modifications in subsequent translated romances and in Icelandic imitations of them.[16] In view of the

---

middelalderlitteraturs historie, af Hans Bekker-Nielsen, Thorkil Damsgaard Olsen, og Ole Widding (København: Akademisk forlag, 1965), pp. 76–77. On the influence of medieval literature, and especially of Latin literature, on the Sagas of Icelanders see Lars Lönnroth, *Tesen om de två kulturerna: Kritiska studier i den isländska sagaskrivningens sociala förutsättningar,* (*Scripta Islandica,* Vol. 15 [Uppsala and Stockholm: Almqvist och Wiksell; København: Ejnar Munksgaard, 1964]). Although Lönnroth does not make a very strong case for his thesis (published in the form of four monographs plus an English summary: see Peter Hallberg's rejoinder in *Sammlaren* [1965, pp. 157–184]), it is hoped his studies will stimulate further investigation of the relationship of the Sagas of Icelanders to earlier and contemporary European literature. It is not possible to isolate this *genre* completely from the Sagas of Kings and the episcopal sagas, from the thirteenth- and fourteenth-century romantic sagas, from the translations of chivalric romances, or from the historical and hagiographic Icelandic writings of the twelfth century. Both the "sameness" of the Sagas of Icelanders as a *genre* and the uniqueness of the *genre* have been grossly exaggerated in the past. Cf. also Sigurður Nordal, "Sagalitteraturen," pp. 207–208.

[14] *Norrøn Fortællekunst,* p. 116.

[15] *Angevin Britain and Scandinavia,* pp. 183–184.

[16] For a concise historical survey of the translated romances see E. F. Halvorsen, *The Norse Version of the Chanson de Roland* (Bibliotheca Arnamagnæana, Vol. XIX [København: Ejnar Munksgaard, 1959]), pp. 1–31.

close cultural ties between the two countries, it seems reasonable to assume that some of these *riddarasögur* found their way to Iceland soon after they were translated in Norway. Indeed, some of the translations were made by Icelanders, and the earliest Icelandic imitations of the translated romances date from the second half of the thirteenth century.[17] That *Tristrams saga* should have found immediate favor in both Norway and Iceland is not surprising, for in a unique manner it combines the elements of tragedy and fate characteristic of the indigenous literature of the North with the splendor and color and the erotic element of the chivalric romances of the South.[18] Two of the most important derivatives of *Tristrams saga,* the poignantly beautiful ballad *Tristrams kvæði* and the somewhat pedestrian and burlesque *Saga af Tristram,* were written about 1400.[19] *Tristrams saga* itself is preserved in five manuscripts: in two vellums from the second half of the fifteenth century, of which only four leaves are extant, and in three complete or nearly complete paper transcripts, two of them from the last quarter of the seventeenth century and the third from the year 1729.[20] There is also extant a transcript of the *Saga af Tristram ok Ýsodd* from the year 1850, while the earliest preserved vellum of this derivative of *Tristrams saga* stems from about 1450. In view of these data, it would seem reasonable, when obvious Tristan analogues or loans occur in medieval and early modern Icelandic literature, to consider the possibility of direct or indirect derivation from this well-known and repeatedly copied literary monument before speculating on less tangible sources which are more distant in time and space, if, indeed, many of them even existed at all.

It is quite possible, of course, that certain Tristan themes and motifs reached the North independently of *Tristrams saga,* and even that some

[17] On the dates of the translated romances and of the Icelandic romantic sagas, see the Introductions to the six-volume edition of the *Riddarasögur* by Bjarni Vilhjálmsson (Reykjavík: Íslendingasagnaútgáfan, 1954).

[18] The similarity between *Tristrams saga* and the native literature of the North has frequently been commented on. Jan de Vries, in *Altnordische Literaturgeschichte* (Grundriss der Germanischen Philologie, Vol. 15 [Berlin and Leipzig: Walter de Gruyter u. Co., 1941]), Part 2, p. 347, makes the interesting observation that Tristan is a kind of "anti-Sigurd."

[19] Schach, "Tristan and Isolde," *Scandinavian Studies,* pp. 286 and 296, and "The *Saga af Tristram ok Ýsodd,*" *Modern Language Quarterly,* p. 337.

[20] For a brief discussion of the dates of the manuscripts and their relationship to each other see the *Saga-Book,* XV (1957–1959), 104–112. [The vellum leaf discovered in 1966 will be published by Schach in Iceland in 1969. Ed.]

vernacular adaptation of the romance other than the preserved saga may once have existed in Iceland, as Bjarni Einarsson seems to assume. In view of this possibility, we must be careful not to fall victim to the opposite extreme of uncritically regarding all Tristan reminiscences in Icelandic literature as derivations from Friar Róbert's translation. It is not unthinkable, for example, that the *Spesar þáttr* in *Grettis saga* might have been modeled on the ambiguous-oath scene in Béroul's Tristan novel, with which it seems to have a few superficial points of resemblance. Nor are we justified in jumping to the conclusion that all stories constructed on the framework of the Tristan romance are necessarily modeled on *Tristrams saga,* even when they include a combination of the three basic themes of proxy-wooing, bridal substitution, and quest for healing.[21]

In attempting to assess the strength and the extent of the impact of *Tristrams saga* on the medieval literature of the North and especially of Iceland, it therefore seems advisable to consider first such themes and situations as are unique to the Thomas branch of the romance. The major derivatives of Thomas beside *Tristrams saga* are the magnificent but incomplete Middle High German adaptation of Gottfried von Strassburg (about 1210) and the late Middle English *Sir Tristrem* (after 1300). Since direct influence from Gottfried's *Tristan* on Norwegian and Icelandic literature of the Middle Ages must be regarded as rather unlikely, it seems plausible to assume that parallels to situations unique to Thomas represent loans or adaptations from *Tristrams saga.*

One such situation is the Hall of Statues episode, which is believed to be an innovation and possibly the invention of Thomas.[22] According to Roger S. Loomis, the closest known analogue to this episode is Geoffrey of Monmouth's story of the subterranean chamber which King Locrinus had constructed and in which he secretly visited his mistress Estrildis for seven years.[23] The episode, which has only the most tenuous connection with the action of the Tristan story, is related at length

[21] That the combination of these three basic themes constitutes evidence of connection with the Tristan story seems a reasonable assumption. On this point, see Leach, *Angevin Britain and Scandinavia*, p. 193.

[22] Cf. A. T. Hatto's comment in his translation of Gottfried's *Tristan* (Baltimore: The Penguin Classics, 1960), p. 360. Gertrude Schoepperle mentions the curious *salle aux images* episode only briefly in her comprehensive book *Tristan and Isolt: A Study of the Sources of the Romance* (2nd ed.; New York, 1960,) I, 130.

[23] See his "Survey of Tristan Scholarship after 1911" in Miss Schoepperle's *Tristan and Isolt*, II, 579–580.

and with minute detail by Friar Róbert (Chaps. 79–81 and 84), but without the moralizing and psychological analysis of Thomas.

After subduing the giant Moldagog, Tristram in great haste and absolute secrecy has carpenters and goldsmiths summoned to renovate a subterranean hall deep in a forest, which had belonged to the giant. He has them fashion statues of Ísönd, her companion Bringvet, the scheming dwarf, the giant Moldagog, the king's evil counselor, a huge lion, and Ísönd's dog Petecru (unnamed in the saga). After sending the artisans home, Tristram and the giant assemble and arrange the figures, which are so lifelike that "no one who happened to see them could help believing that they were alive." Tristram frequently repairs secretly to his subterranean hall to visit the statues.

> And whenever he came there he kissed the image of Ísönd and embraced her and put his arms about her as though she were alive, and he spoke many ardent words to her about their love and their grief . . . But when he was angry or depressed in the recollection of their grief and pain, and of the hardship and affliction which he had endured for the sake of those who had slandered and defamed him and his beloved, he vented his wrath on the statue of the evil counselor.[24]

When Kardin discovers that the marriage of his sister Ísodd to Tristram has remained unconsummated, he accuses his brother-in-law of insulting his family. To placate Kardin and to prove to him that his neglect of Ísodd is due to his love for a more beautiful woman, Tristram takes him to his secret hall. The first figure Kardin sees is that of the giant Moldagog, and he is so terrified by it that he swoons. Upon recovering he watches in wonder as Tristram addresses and caresses the image of Ísönd, and he falls in love at first sight with the likeness of Bringvet. Only when he attempts to take a goblet of wine from her outstretched hand does he realize that the figure is not a human being. When Kardin demands to see the living model of this lovely statue, the two companions set out for England.

In the Hall of Statues episode, the following traits are significant. The statues are created in haste, in secrecy, and from the memory of the hero. They are so lifelike that they are mistaken for identifiable

[24] In this episode we find a significant revision made by Friar Róbert, which consists in letting Tristram vent his wrath on the image of the evil counselor. According to Thomas, the hero vents his hatred on the statue of his sweetheart because of the maddening suspicion that she has forgotten him and has transferred her affection to the knight Cariado.

living beings. The postures and attire of the figures have symbolic or characteristic significance. (Ísönd is dressed in purple, for purple "signifies the grief, fear, distress, and misery which she endured because of her love for Tristram"; the scheming dwarf lies cringing at the feet of Ísönd; the giant and the lion are depicted in threatening postures; and Bringvet, as already indicated, stands with a goblet in outstretched hand.) Tristram frequently visits the Hall of Statues to converse with the figures of Ísönd and Bringvet, to kiss and caress the likeness of his beloved, and to vent his wrath on the image of his adversary, the evil counselor.

An obvious imitation of this episode from *Tristrams saga* occurs in *Rémundar saga keisarasonar,* which is believed to have been written in Iceland shortly before 1350 by a man well versed in the sagas and especially in the translated romances.[25] Rémundr, son of Rikarðr, emperor of Saxland, falls in love with a woman who appears to him in a dream. He wants to set out at once in quest of his dream girl (a popular motif in the *lygisögur*), but his parents, fearing that the dream woman might be an ogress, refuse to permit this despite the lovelorn youth's piteous pleas.

Several days after their conversation Junkeri Rémundr secretly summoned his favorite page and said to him:

"You are to ride throughout Saxland and search for the most skilful painter you can find. Bring him to me here in the castle in secret and without anyone's knowledge. And make your journey as quickly as you possibly can."

The page did as he was ordered. He soon located the place where the man was, told him the command and request of the emperor's son, and the man agreed to it.

In due time they came into the presence of Rémundr, and he gave them a cordial welcome.

Shortly after this something strange happened. Rémundr disappeared daily from his men, and this continued for half a month.

And one morning after this, as the king was going to church very early with his bodyguard, he saw a maiden standing in the vestibule of the church, who was so fair and beautiful, polite and elegant, that all believed they had never seen her equal. He went to her and greeted her courteously. But even though the emperor was very powerful, the maiden would not return his greetings, but remained silent.

[25] The standard critical edition of *Rémundar saga* is that of Sven Grén Broberg in the *Samfund til Udgivelse af Gammel Nordisk Litteratur* (København, 1909ff.). Broberg has made extensive studies of the sources of this saga.

Then Junkeri Rémundr approached and said to his father: "My dear father, this is not, as it seems to you, a woman created by God, but a statue made in the image of the woman who appeared to me as I slept. And this statue is but smoke and ashes compared with what she really looks like. Perhaps you will be more inclined to have compassion with me, now that you have seen this statue, even thought it is worthless compared with her.

The emperor now grew silent and went away without speaking a word. But Junkeri Rémundr took the statue in his arms and kissed it with great joy. And here you can see what ardent love really is. And now a long time passes, during which Rémundr finds his greatest pleasure in taking the statue with him wherever he goes and thus alleviating his distress.

Rémundr soon gets into the habit of riding into the woods every day with twelve companions and his statue. "And every day he sits in a clearing, embracing and gently kissing it and sometimes laying it down beside him and gazing at it and after a while lifting it up again." This goes on for many years, and people throughout the realm—especially women—are deeply grieved at the plight of this courteous and accomplished young knight. One day when Rémundr rides out into the clearing he takes his sword, Nöðrubítr, with him. "And he takes his statue and amuses himself with it, as was his wont, sometimes laying it down and kissing it with gentle embrace." In the midst of this love play, Rémundr is rudely interrupted by a knight in full armor, who challenges him to a duel. The knight is Eskupart, the son of Agamenon, who has come to avenge this disgrace to his sweetheart, for she is the model of the statue. Rémundr slays Eskupart with his trusty sword, Nöðrubítr, but in doing so receives a head wound which necessitates a long quest for healing.

The similarities between this passage and the Hall of Statues episode are so striking as to suggest that the author of *Rémundar saga* wrote this portion of his story with Friar Róbert's translation before him. As in *Tristrams saga,* the statue is created in haste and secrecy by a skillful artisan on the instructions and from the memory of the hero. Rémundr mysteriously absents himself from the court every day while the figure is being fashioned, just as Tristram daily rode to and from the subterranean chamber on forest paths known only to him. Like Kardin, King Rikarðr is completely deceived by the statue. The erotic element in *Rémundar saga* is even stronger, or at least more unadulterated and cloying, than in *Tristrams saga.* Even in style and phraseology the similarity of the borrowing is so striking that there can be no doubt as to its major source. But, although the author of *Rémundar saga* made no attempt to disguise his plagiarization of Friar Róbert's translation, he did make a number of interesting additions and modifications. One of these is the appearance of the beautiful woman to the hero in a dream, a motif which, as already noted, this saga shares with a number of other Icelandic imitations of southern romances of chivalry. More surprising is the substitution of the rather unusual loan word *penturr* "painter," for the word *smiðr,* "artisan," or *trésmiðr,* "carpenter," especially since we are dealing here not with a painting but with a life-sized statue, presumably carved from wood.[26] Several additional changes consist in the modification of other well-known Tristan motifs. Whereas in *Tristrams saga* a fragment of the hero's sword remains imbedded in the skull of the vanquished Irish champion, in *Rémundar saga* the hero has to go in search of healing with a piece of Eskupart's envenomed sword lodged in his own head. This trait, incidentally, which is reminiscent of Þórr's battle with the giant Hrungnir in Snorri's *Skáldskaparmál* (Chap. 17), was in turn borrowed from *Rémundar saga* by the author of the *Saga af Tristram ok Ýsodd.* A second change consists in the telescoping of the quest for healing and the bridal quest into one journey, for the woman physician, to the surprise of no one, turns out to be none other than the girl of Rémundr's dream. And this quest for healing and for the hero's beloved is not made by ship, as in all versions of the Tristan story, but by land. It might be added that during this long, hard journey Rémundr is known as *hinn kranki kerrumaðr,* "the sick man of the cart," a faint reminiscence of Lancelot *(Le chevalier de la charrette),* and that his faithful companion and guide during this quest bears the fitting name Víðförull, evidently a loan from the earlier and shorter version of *Mágus saga jarls.* As a final point of contact between *Tristrams saga* and this portion of *Rémundar saga,* it should be noted that Víðförull is himself a skilled craftsman who in absolute secrecy and in a hall constructed precisely for that purpose builds the cart or chariot in which he and Rémundr go on their quest for healing and for Rémundr's bride. Whereas the extraneous Hall of Statues episode has only the most tenuous connection with the plot of the Thomas Tristan novel and Friar Róbert's translation of it, the author of *Rémundar saga*

[26] The loan word *penturr* occurs also in the description of the castle of the King of Babylon in *Flores saga ok Blankiflur* (Chapter 16). This saga can be read in Modern Icelandic spelling in *Riddarasögur*, ed. Bjarni Vilhálmsson IV, 137–194.

has succeeded rather well in incorporating his plagiarism of that episode into the action of his story.

I have dwelt at such length on this borrowing from *Tristrams saga* for several reasons. In the first place, the structure of this episode in *Rémundar saga,* which blends undisguised, almost word for word plagiarism with variously modified loans from *Tristrams saga* and other sources, reflects the composition of the saga as a whole. Secondly, the treatment of the various Tristan loans in this saga, ranging as they do from almost literal borrowing to the reversal of roles, the substitution of a journey by cart for a voyage by ship, and the telescoping of two or more themes into one, illustrates the diversity with which situations and motifs are borrowed and adapted from one saga to another according to the need, the skill, and the caprice of the individual author. And finally *Rémundar saga* as a whole and in its various parts, especially the one under consideration, provides an especially lucid and transparent example of the craft of constructing unified, more or less well-rounded stories from elements borrowed and adapted from a multitude of widely differing sources. However severely we may condemn these fourteenth- and fifteenth-century romantic tales from the standpoint of artistic merit, they do not seem to differ essentially in their manner of construction and composition from the more realistic and aesthetically more pleasing sagas about Norwegian kings and Icelandic chieftains written during the thirteenth century.

An interesting variation of the motif of falling in love with a person from seeing him in effigy is found in *Jarlmanns saga ok Hermanns,* an Icelandic romantic saga composed about or shortly after 1400.[27] Jarlmann travels to Miklagarðr as the bridal emissary of his friend and foster brother, Prince Hermann of Frakkland. By feigning illness he gains access to the castle of Princess Rikilát, who, like Queen Ísönd, is famed for her skill as a physician. In due time he reveals his true identity and purpose and praises the handsome appearance and the outstanding accomplishments of his foster brother.

Then the princess said, "Do you think you could paint a picture in his image on the wall to amuse me?"

"I can try, princess," he replied.

He took his brush and drew a picture or likeness in Hermann's image on

[27] *Jarlmanns saga ok Hermanns* is included in *Riddarasögur* (VI, 173–235).

the wall, with excellent craftsmanship and great skill, and then asked the princess to look at it. She regarded it thoughtfully and said, "You are certainly a great master, and I cannot imagine that any woman would not choose him if the choice were hers."

"You would be pleased even more," said Jarlmann, "if you were looking at Hermann himself." (Chap. 6)

Here, as in *Rémundar saga,* the concentration of Tristan themes makes ultimate derivation from *Tristrams saga* almost certain. Various details and verbal similarities, however, suggest that the loan probably came not directly but by way of *Rémundar saga.* Jarlmann uses a *pincer,* "paint brush" (which he conveniently has with him), to sketch or paint Hermann's *mannlíkan eða líkneski,* "image or likeness," on the wall, while Rémundr employed a *penturr* rather than a *smiðr* to fashion his statue. Princess Rikilát's request that Jarlmann draw " 'a picture in his image for my amusement' " *("eitt líkneski eftir hans mynd mér til skemmtunar")* echoes the statement that Rémundr frequently takes the statue of his unknown sweetheart "and amuses himself with it" *(ok skemmtir sér við hana).* And the assurance of Jarlmann that Hermann in the flesh would be even more pleasing to Princess Rikilát than his picture is a pale but clear reflection of Rémundr's assertion to his father that the image of his beloved was but "smoke and ashes" compared with the beautiful vision he had experienced.

A somewhat more imaginative adaptation of this motif occurs in *Mágus saga jarls hin meiri,* which dates from the second half of the fourteenth century.[28] Vilhjálmr Laisson, King of Valland, sends his friend Sigurðr Hringsson to sue for the hand of Oktavía, daughter of Jarl Roðulgeirr, coruler of Smálönd with his brother Galifreyr. Galifreyr advises his brother to accede to the request, but Roðulgeirr refuses and makes ready to repulse Vilhjálmr's anticipated attack.

Roðulgeirr summoned craftsmen and had a strong castle built with great skill. Oktavía gave Sigurðr a little box of ash-wood and asked him to take it to Vilhjálmr—"and then he will know my will."

Sigurðr sailed home and gave him the box. He unlocked it and saw a figure. It was fair and beautiful, and yet there was something strange about it: it was so fashioned that it was looking backward.

Vilhjálmr said, "Fair and beautiful is the woman after whom this statue

[28] *Riddarasögur*, II, 137–429. On the date of the saga, see the Introduction, pp. ix–xi.

was made, and I see that she wishes to follow her father's counsel, yet she does not wish to reject our suit. She has now shown us what her will is, and I swear this solemn oath: I shall either win her or lose my life." (Chap. 66)

Like the author of *Rémundar saga,* the writer of *Mágus saga jarls* and the redactor of the expanded version of the story from which this passage is taken were both well versed in saga literature.[29] But, although this adaptation could stem from a number of sources, several features indicate that it was inspired by *Tristrams saga.* As mentioned previously, the figures in the Hall of Statues, through their dress or their postures, all express various emotions or desires. So, too, the figure of Oktavía expresses both her unwillingness to disobey her father and the hope that Vilhjálmr will not abandon his suit for her hand. As in *Rémundar saga* and *Jarlmanns saga,* we find here a complex of Tristan motifs, including the proxy-wooing of Sigurðr for his friend and liege lord Vilhjálmr. Furthermore, the description of the magnificent hall near the beginning of *Mágus saga* (Chap. 15) bears a close resemblance to that of the renovation and decoration of Tristram's vaulted subterranean chamber. And finally, the rare loan word *kompásaðr,* "round, circular" occurs both in the latter passage from *Mágus saga jarls* and in the Hall of Statues episode in *Tristrams saga.*[30]

Several interesting analogues to the Hall of Statues episode occur in *Þiðreks saga,* which was probably compiled at the Norwegian court not long after the translation of Thomas's Tristan romance.[31] The first of these is found in that portion of the compilation known as *Velents þáttr,* a novelistic development of the story told in *Völundar kviða.* According to this novella, the giant Vaði from Sjóland has his son Velent apprenticed to two dwarfs who are exceedingly skillful in work-

[29] The author of the older version has drawn on *Þiðreks saga af Bern* for substantial portions of his story, as well as on *Karlamagnús saga*, *Hálfs saga*, and *Nornagests þáttr*, while the writer of the greatly expanded version has used a wide variety of historical and literary sources, some of which can readily be identified from the content and some of which he mentions by name. The older version, called *Mágus saga jarls*, is included in the volume *Fornsögur Suðrlanda*, ed. Gustaf Cederschiöld (Lund, 1884).

[30] *Riddarasögur*, II, 156.

[31] The standard critical edition of *Þiðriks saga af Bern* is that of Henrik Bertelsen in the *Samfund til Udgivelse af Gammel Nordisk Litteratur* (København, 1911). The saga can be read most conveniently in the two-volume edition with normalized spelling by Guðni Jónsson (Reykjavík: Íslendingasagnaútgáfan, 1954). Unless otherwise indicated, references are to Guðni's edition.

ing gold, silver, and iron. When Velent discovers that the treacherous dwarfs plan to kill him, he overcomes them both and acquires their money and their tools, with which he builds a submarine from a tree trunk. Setting out at random, he finally lands at the court of King Niðungr in Jótland. Here, Velent's money and tools are stolen from him. On the smith's assurance that he can recognize the thief, whose name he does not know, from his appearance, King Niðungr has all the men of his court assembled. Rebuked by the king for failing to identify the thief, Velent hits upon another scheme.

> Some time later Velent created a work of art (*smíð*), and this was an image (*mannlíkan*), fashioned exactly like a human being, with hair on its head. Then one evening Velent returned to the castle, set the figure in a corner which the king had to pass on the way to the privy, and then went into the hall and performed his services with the other attendants.
>
> When the king wished to leave the hall with all his men, Velent walked before the king with a candle.
>
> The king glanced to his right and said to the statue: "Hail and welcome, my good friend Reginn. Why are you out here alone? When did you get back from Sweden, and how did you succeed there in the errand I sent you on?"
>
> Then Velent said, "My lord, this man must seem haughty to you, since he will not answer your questions. I fashioned this statue from memory, and that is the name of the man, Sire, who took my tools and my gold." (Chap. 66)

Despite the absence of the erotic element, the points of similarity between this farcical interlude from *Velents þáttr* on the one hand and the Hall of Statues episode and its imitation in *Rémundar saga* on the other are striking indeed. The skillful smith Velent fashions his likeness of Reginn in secret and from memory. He puts it in a place where King Niðungr cannot help seeing it, and the king mistakes it for his counselor. The burlesque character of this episode and its close resemblance to the Tristan borrowing in *Rémundar saga* suggest that it might be a travesty on the latter, but considerations of chronology alone make this impossible. Furthermore, other internal and external evidence, as we shall see, clearly establishes *Tristrams saga* as the source of this scene in *Þiðreks saga*. It is not at all unlikely, however, that the author of *Rémundar saga* drew on both the Hall of Statues episode and the humorous adaptation of portions of it in *Velents þáttr*—the latter with considerably more skill than the former. As in *Tristrams saga,* the extraneous interlude of the loss and recovery of the smith's tools and money (which Reginn had merely appropriated "for fun") is only loosely woven into the action of the *þáttr* of Velent the Smith.

Another interesting variant of the recognition trait is found in *Herburts þáttr ok Hildar.* Herburt has been sent as bridal emissary to sue for the hand of Hildr Artússdóttir for his uncle, King Þiðrekr. After hearing the proposal of marriage, Hildr asks Herburt what sort of man Þiðrekr is and what he looks like. Herburt praises his uncle's wealth, power, and accomplishments, but refrains from saying anything about his appearance.

> She asks, "Can you trace (*skrifa*) his face here on the stone wall?"
>
> He replies, "My lady, I can do that with my hands in such a way that anyone who has never seen King Þiðrekr before will be able to recognize him."
>
> And now he draws a large and dreadful face on the stone wall and says, "My lady, here you see the face of King Þiðrekr af Bern. And so help me God, the face of King Þiðrekr is far more dreadful than the picture."
>
> Thereupon she replies, "May God not be so angry with me that this dreadful devil should ever possess me."
>
> And then she says, "My lord, why do you woo me for King Þiðrekr af Bern and not for yourself?" (Chap. 283)

At first blush, this portion of *Herburts þáttr* looks like a loan from *Jarlmanns saga* with a type of modification which is very common in the sagas. In both stories the prospective bride requests the proxy-wooer to draw a picture in the likeness of the actual suitor. But whereas Jarlmann, like Sigurðr in *Mágus saga jarls,* remains true to his friend and liege lord, Herburt, like Tristram, betrays his uncle. Again, however, considerations of chronology make this obvious interpretation impossible. The compiler of *Þiðreks saga* borrowed directly from *Tristrams saga,* and if there is a connection between this episode in *Herburts þáttr* and the corresponding passage in *Jarlmanns saga,* it is the latter which must be regarded as the borrower. *Herburts þáttr* is a typical example of the manner in which saga-writers frequently sought to embellish a somewhat pedestrian account by suggesting to their audiences points of contact with similar stories about more illustrious literary figures. The proxy-wooing of Herburt for his uncle, King Þiðrekr, which seems to derive from the same source as the tale of King Herbort of Denmark in the MHG *Biterolf,* closely parallels the more famous story of Tristram.[32] To enhance the importance of his own story of the unfaithful wooer, the author of this portion of *Þiðreks saga* adapted portions of *Tristrams saga* to his own purpose. And just to make sure that even the least sophisticated among his audience did not miss the point, the author bestowed the name Tristram on Herburt's younger brother and the name Ísodd on his mother, the wife of King Þiðrekr.[33]

It might be added here that the compiler of *Þiðreks saga* had a predilection for statues, just as Friar Róbert had a fondness for the words *líkneski* and *líkneskja.* Shortly after being crowned king in Rómaborg, Þiðrekr "had a statue cast of his horse Fálki and himself. This is made of copper. He had another statue made north of the city. There he stands in a tower, pointing his sword Ekkisax toward the stone arch which extends across the river" (Chap. 415). Although there is no motival connection between this passage and the Hall of Statues, it is of interest to note that several pages further on Þiðrekr slays a dragon and marries the widow of the dragon's victim, King Hernið. The name of the woman is Ísodd (the second wife of Þiðrekr so named!)—a circumstance which suggests that the writer again wanted to strengthen the faint similarity with *Tristrams saga.* And, in the Swedish chronicle we read that Viðga "had a statue made in the image of Þiðrekr af Bern and forbade his ferryman to convey anyone over the sound who had such an appearance." This is clearly an echo of the recognition trait as found in the stories of Velent and Herburt.

An analogue of an altogether different kind occurs in *Írons þáttr jarls,* a novella about a man who neglects his wife because of his passion for the chase. One morning early, the neglected and offended wife hears her Nimrod husband preparing to go off on another hunting expedition.

[32] Apparently William J. Paff accepts the farfetched supposition of de Vries (*Altnordische Literaturgeschichte*, II, 432) that Celtic names were reincorporated into *Herburts þáttr* by a Norwegian scribe or singer who noted its similarity to the Celtic story of Tristan (*The Geographical and Ethnic Names in the Þiðriks Saga: A Study in Germanic Heroic Legend* [Cambridge, Massachusetts: Harvard University Press, 1959], p. 109).

[33] Margaret Schlauch overlooked the frequent occurrence of the name Ísodd (Ísollde) in *Þiðreks saga,* the identical spelling of the names Tristram and Ísodd in this work and in *Tristrams saga*, and the concentration of Tristan motifs in *Herburts þáttr*, when she commented (*Romance in Iceland*, p. 152) that it "is possible that the loves of Tristan and Iseult also influenced one minor episode of the *Þiðreks saga* . . . Two minor characters in this section are actually called Tistram and Isolda [*sic*!]."

Shortly after the jarl has gotten out of bed, his wife arises and leaves the castle. Not far from the castle there is a fair linden tree. She goes beneath the tree and takes off all her clothing. Then she spreads out her arms and lets herself fall down lengthwise in the snow. After this she gets up and puts on her clothing again. She sees her likeness (*líkneskja*) in the snow, and all the signs that a woman had been lying there. She returns to the castle and approaches the jarl, who is eating his breakfast.

She says, "Why are you eating so early, my lord? What do you intend to do?"

The jarl replies, "My lady, I plan to ride out into the forest to hunt, as is my custom."

Then she asks, "Why must you always ride out into the wilderness? Why don't you hunt the animals which are close by, so that you can come home at night and sleep in your own bed?"

The jarl replies, "There is no game near the castle which is worth hunting. I don't want to have my dogs chasing such small animals as run around here."

When all other efforts at persuasion fail, the jarl's wife takes him out to the linden tree and asks him if he can identify the creature whose tracks and outline can be seen in the snow.

The jarl looks at the place in the snow and sees that a woman has lain down there.

Then his wife says, "My lord, do you think you have ever seen such a creature as that? If you do not wish to pursue it, some other man will."

The jarl replies, "My lady, no one but myself is to pursue this creature,"— and he returns to the castle and orders his men to unsaddle the horses and tie up the dogs. Now he no longer desires to ride out into the forest. (Chap. 255)

According to A. H. Krappe, this episode is unique in Germanic heroic legend.[34] The closest parallel in medieval literature is found in *Aucassin et Nicolette,* where Nicolette asks some shepherds to tell Aucassin that there is a rare and marvelous animal in a certain forest. She means herself, of course, and is certain that Aucassin will understand the metaphor, just as Īron understands the slightly veiled hint of his wife. Ultimately the motif derives from the Orient, probably by way of Greece. There can be little doubt of the influence of *Tristrams saga* on the version of this motif in the Īron story in *Þiðreks saga.* Not only

[34] "Sur une forme norroise d'un épisode d'*Aucassin et Nicolette,*" *Romania* LV (1929), 260–263.

does the name Íron occur in *Tristrams saga* immediately preceding the Hall of Statues episode, but the wife and daughter of Íron in *Þiðreks saga* both bear the name Ísodd. Even if the writer had not given us this broad hint, the general resemblance of the episode to several scenes in *Tristrams saga* and the erotic significance of the *líkneskja* would justify the assumption of influence from the translation of Friar Róbert.

Without suggesting a possible connection with *Tristrams saga,* Kölbing refers to a curious parallel in *Landnámabók* (IV, 4), where a man named Tjörvi inn háðsemi (the Mocker) gives expression to his affection and vents his wrath in a manner similar to that of Tristram.[35] Tjörvi, a nephew of Hróarr Tungugoði, sues for the hand of Ástríðr mannvittsbrekka Móðólfsdóttir, but her brothers reject his suit and marry her instead to a man named Þórir, a son of Ketil flatnefr.

Then Tjörvi drew their pictures (*líkneski*) on a wall of the privy; and every evening when he and Hróarr went to the privy, he spat in the face of Þórir's image and kissed her image until Hróarr scraped them off the wall. Thereupon Tjörvi carved them on the handle of his knife and spoke this verse:

First we drew the likeness of this
young woman on the wall with the
likeness of Þórir. Now I have carved
her picture on the handle of my knife.
Much have I spoken with this woman.

This led to the death of Hróarr and his nephews.

Hróarr, who was the grandson of Garðar, discoverer of Iceland, was a well-known man, but there is no other mention of Tjörvi anywhere, not even in *Reykdæla saga,* which relates the death of Hróarr and the outlawry of Þórir. Whatever historical truth may be in this tale from *Landnámabók,* it is difficult to believe that the editor responsible for its final form was not acquainted with *Tristrams saga* and *Velents þáttr.* Tjörvi's purpose in creating the two effigies is similar to that of Tristram, and his location of them is like that of Velent. Another possibility is that the loan may have come indirectly, by way of a lost *Hróars saga Tungugoði* from which, Jón Johannesson suggests, Sturla

[35] *Tristrams saga ok Ísondar,* Mit einer literarhistorischen Einleitung, deutscher Übersetzung und Anmerkungen zum ersten Mal herausgegeben von Eugen Kölbing (Heilbronn: Verlag von Gebr. Henninger, 1879), p. 213 (note to p. 94, 36ff.). Kölbing cites only five lines of prose, with almost no comment.

Þórðarson seems to have gotten most or all of his information about Uni Garðarsson and Hróarr Tungugoði.[36]

The use of traits borrowed from the Hall of Statues episode in three different *þættir* of *Þiðreks saga,* one of which is made up of a whole complex of Tristan names and themes, suggests that the Tristan story has left more of a mark on this compilation than the slight trace of which Margaret Schlauch speaks.[37] It is quite apparent that the compiler of *Þiðreks saga* was well acquainted with *Tristrams saga,* and his use of the names Tristram and Ísodd (or Ísollde) clearly indicates that he sought to enhance parts of his own work through embellishments which establish an affinity between it and the most famous and popular love story of the Middle Ages. The adaptations of traits from the Hall of the names Tristram and Ísodd (or Ísollde) clearly indicates that he *Hermanns,* and *Mágus saga jarls hin meiri* provide additional support for my earlier assertion that *Tristrams saga* must have been especially popular in Iceland during the fourteenth and fifteenth centuries. The curious analogue from *Landnámabók* is further evidence of the popularity of both *Þiðreks saga* and *Tristrams saga* in Iceland around the middle of the thirteenth century.[38] Additional adaptations of the Hall of Statues episode, especially from the Icelandic romantic sagas, could be cited, but these will suffice for the present.[39]

In the Introduction to his translation of *Kormáks saga,* Lee M. Hollander emphasizes that this story is "remarkable among the sagas of Iceland for the sentimental theme running through it" and refers to the widely held view that there seems to have been little or no local tradition about Kormákr.[40] Several scholars, noted earlier, have gone

36 *Gerðir Landnámabókar* (Reykjavík: Félagsprentsmiðjan, 1941), pp. 117–120.

37 See note 33.

38 Since Sturla Þórðarson died in 1284, his redaction of *Landnámabók* can be dated at about 1280; *Laxdœla saga,* whose author drew on both *Þiðreks saga* and *Tristrams saga,* was probably written between 1244 and 1248 (on the date of *Laxdœla* see A. Margaret Arent trans. *The Laxdœla Saga* [Seattle: University of Washington Press; New York: The American-Scandinavian Foundation, 1964], p. xxiii).

39 One additional example is a close parallel with *Rémundar saga* in *Þjalar-Jóns saga.* See Einar Ól. Sveinnsson's essay "Sources and Characteristics" in *Viktors saga ok Blávus* (*Riddarasögur,* Vol. II [Reykjavík: Handritastofun Íslands, 1964]), p. cxxvii f.

40 *The Sagas of Kormák,* p. 9. Hollander does not accept this assumption, arguing that the "preservation, in fairly orderly arrangement," of the verses compels us "to reckon with a tradition, however slender." The occasional discrepancies between the

so far as to propose that *Kormáks saga* is a novel modeled on some version of the Tristan legend. The most recent and detailed comparison of *Kormáks saga* with the Tristan story is that of Bjarni Einarsson.[41] Beside the general theme of the lifelong love of the hero for a married woman, his death in a foreign country with the name of his sweetheart on his lips, and various other parallels of varying degrees of significance, Bjarni Einarsson emphasizes three episodes in *Kormáks saga* which he believes were constructed on incidents related in the Tristan romances. The first of these is the attempt of Steingerðr's father and two accomplices to ambush Kormákr in the hall of his house (Chapter 5), which Bjarni regards as an adaptation of the well-known motif of the sharpened blades as found in the *Tristrant* of Eilhart von Oberge (ll. 5285–5487).[42] But these two passages seem to me to have little in common. In the saga we read that "Þorkell had placed an unsheathed sword on one side of the door, and Narfi had placed a long-handled scythe on the other side." The scythe falls down and strikes the sword, knocking a piece out of it. If this is a reminiscence of the sharpened blades motif, it is a very vague and distorted one. It is not even clear just what role the sword and scythe were meant to play in the action of the story, but there seems to be little resemblance between this situation and the scene in Eilhart's *Tristrant,* where King Mark had "mit wulfesîsen ein bloch . . . beslân" (ll. 5304f.), on which Tristan and all the knights of King Arthur cut themselves.[43] The second major episode which Bjarni believes to be modeled on a situation in the Tristan story is the *hólmganga* between Bersi and Kormákr (Chaps. 10 and 11). The three points of similarity he emphasizes are Bersi's offer to heal Kormákr, the healing of the hero's wound by his mother, and

---

verses and the prose narrative, which Hollander concedes, seem to speak against any coherent tradition. Furthermore, many of the verses are probably spurious.

41 *Skáldasögur,* pp. 52–164.

42 *Ibid.*, pp. 71–76.

43 Crucial to Bjarni's argument are three lines in Béroul (3546–3548):

> Menbre li de l'espié lancier,
> Qui fu en l'estache feru;
> Ele savra bien ou ce fu.
>
> ("May she remember the thrown lance which was hurled into the post; she will well know where it was.")

These words, spoken by King Artus to Perinis, are assumed by Bjarni to be an allusion to the sharpened blades episode. But see also Miss Schoepperle, *Tristan and Isolt,* I, 220.

the notch in the bewitched sword Sköfnung caused by Kormákr's unskillful handling of it. Again the parallels are too general to justify derivation from the Tristan story. The same features occur in many tales, including a number of the sagas. Bersi's generous offer of help to his hotheaded rival serves to point up the basic nobility of his character, and has no connection with the action of the story, whereas Morhold's reference to his sister as the only possible source of help for Tristram is a form of epic anticipation which requires fulfillment later on in the story. It is only natural that Kormákr's mother should heal her son after he had foolishly rejected the help of Bersi. And the role of the notched blade in *Kormáks saga* is quite different from that in the Tristan story, where it serves as a token of identification. Thus, in this episode too, the points of difference between *Kormáks saga* and *Tristrams saga* far outweigh the points of resemblance.

The third parallel which Bjarni cites, however, is most striking. Following Kormákr's second duel with Þorvarðr (Chap. 23), the action of the story seems to disintegrate—a circumstance which led a number of scholars, including Guðbrandur Vigfússon, to suspect extensive interpolation.[44] Kormákr and his brother Þorgils skarði set off for Norway, and Þorvaldr tinteinn follows with his wife Steingerðr. During the voyage some vikings try to rob Þorvaldr and abduct Steingerðr, but Kormákr rushes to their rescue. At the court of King Haraldr gráfeldr, Kormákr continues to force his attentions upon Steingerðr and once even tries to carry her off bodily, but the King always intervenes and prevents bloodshed between Kormákr and Steingerðr's second husband. After returning from an expedition with King Haraldr to Bjarmaland, during which Þorvaldr was knocked senseless by Kormákr, who in turn had his ship rammed and capsized by Steingerðr, the married couple set out for Denmark (Chap. 26). Kormákr and his brother follow. At the Brenneyjar (Brenn Islands) they overtake Þorvaldr and learn that Steingerðr has been abducted by vikings.

Now Þorvaldr and Kormákr met, and Kormákr asked whether they had had any trouble. He replied, "Things have not turned out for the best."

Kormákr asked, "What happened? Is Steingerðr gone?"

Þorvaldr replied, "Steingerðr is gone and all of our possessions."

Kormákr asked, "Why don't you go after them?"

Þorvaldr said, "We don't have a strong enough force for that."

[44] *Origines Islandicae* (Oxford: The Clarendon Press, 1905), II, 316–318.

Kormákr asked, "Are you saying that you're too weak to do it?"

Þorvaldr replied, "We aren't strong enough to fight Þorsteinn, but if you have the necessary strength, go get her and keep her for yourself."

Kormákr said, "That's just what I intend to do."

During the night the brothers took a boat and rowed to the viking ship and climbed aboard. Steingerðr was on the raised afterdeck and was married to a man,[45] but most of the crew were on land warming themselves by the fires. Kormákr questioned the cooks, and they told him all the brothers wanted to know. They boarded the ship by the stern gangplank. Þorgils dragged the bridegroom on deck, and Kormákr killed him against the side of the ship. Þorgils leaped overboard with Steingerðr and swam to land. When Kormákr had almost reached shore, eels wound themselves around his arms and legs so that he was drawn under. . .[46]

Kormákr made it to land and returned Steingerðr to Þorvaldr. Þorvaldr told Steingerðr to go with Kormákr, since he had rescued her so valiantly, and Kormákr said that he wanted her to do so. But Steingerðr declared she would not be bartered off like that. And Kormákr too thought that they were not destined for each other. He said that wicked spirits or evil spells had prevented that from the very beginning. . . .[47] Kormákr asked Steingerðr to remain with her husband.

Þorvaldr and Steingerðr return to Iceland, while Kormákr and his brother acquire great fame through harrying in the British Isles. After founding the fortress of Skarðaborg (Scarborough)[48] in England, the brothers proceed to Scotland. Here Kormákr slays an uncanny Scottish giant, but in the fierce encounter his ribs are staved in. After lying wounded for some time, Kormákr dies while composing a skaldic verse which concludes with the words *greipa glóðar Gerðr*. This is a kenning for "woman," but can also be interpreted as a circumlocution meaning

[45] This is the literal translation of the Icelandic *Steingerðr var í lyftingu ok gift manni*. Hollander (*The Sagas of Kormák*, p. 69) translates the last three words "and had fallen to the share of a man." It can be safely assumed, I believe, that she was in the embrace of the viking leader.

[46] Verse 80, which occurs at this point, may be the source of the eels in the prose account. Guðbrandur Vigfússon (*Origines Islandicae*, II, 316–317) regards the eels as an echo of the Irish tale about Cuchulainn (in the *Tain bo Cuailgne*). Hollander (*The Sagas of Kormák*, p. 204 n. 3 to Chap. 26) suggests the eels may represent sea creatures sent out by the witch Þórveig to drown Kormákr.

[47] Here verse 81 is inserted into the story, but it contrasts sharply in tone and spirit with the prose. In the verse, Kormákr chides Steingerðr and insults her husband.

[48] Skarðaborg is derived by the author from Þorgil's nickname *skarði* (harelip). The place-name also occurs in *Jómsvíkinga saga* and in the form Skörðuborg in *Hálfdanar saga Brönufóstra*.

"Steingerðr."[49] Thus Kormákr, like Tristram, dies with the name of his sweetheart on his lips.

Even the most casual reader of this awkwardly constructed portion of the story cannot fail to be surprised at the sheer incredibility of the whole sequence of events or puzzled by the repetition and the real and apparent contradictions of motifs. I shall review briefly only a few of the many incongruities. At the mere whim of his wife Steingerðr, Þorvaldr tinteinn undertakes a voyage from Iceland to the court of King Haraldr gráfeldr of Norway, whose chief role in the story is to serve as arbiter in the domestic quarrels of an Icelandic farmer whose wife doesn't seem to be overly fond of either her feckless husband or her impulsive but irresolute lover. Within two short saga chapters the abduction motif occurs three times: first Kormákr prevents the abduction of Steingerðr by vikings, then he himself is prevented by King Haraldr from abducting her, and finally he rescues her from her viking abductors, only to give up his hard-won booty without an argument. And what is most puzzling of all, the two brothers, after boarding the ship and finding Kormákr's sweetheart in the arms of a viking, first go ashore and question the cooks before coming to the rescue of the damsel in distress, and then, to cap the climax, they choose to swim ashore with her after having come aboard by the gangplank!

This abduction and rescue of Steingerðr is correctly equated by Bjarni Einarsson with the so-called Harp and Rote episode of the Tristan story.[50] He emphasizes the following five parallels: (1) Neither Þorvaldr tinteinn nor King Markis feels he has sufficient forces to engage the abductor in battle; (2) Like Tristram, Kormákr arrives on the scene after the abduction and is informed about it by the husband; (3) in both accounts the scene of the rescue is a ship at anchor; (4) in *Kormáks saga* the heroine is *í lyftingu ok gift manni,* while in *Tristrams saga* she is in the embrace of the Irish baron in a tent by the ship; (5) both Kormákr and Tristram return their rescued sweethearts to their husbands. To this we might add that in both stories the husband is rebuked by the doughty rescuer—in *Kormáks saga* before the rescue and in *Tristrams saga* afterward.

The two accounts also exhibit several interesting points of difference.

[49] See *Skáldasögur*, p. 161 n. 1.
[50] *Ibid.*, pp. 155–157.

In *Tristrams saga,* as in several Arthurian stories and numerous other medieval romances, the king loses his wife to the abductor as the consequence of a rash boon—a trait which would have been out of place in even such a fanciful saga of native heroes as *Kormáks saga.* The original purpose of the episode, which was introduced into the Tristan story by Thomas, was, as Hatto expressed it, "to tone down the double offense of adultery with lese-majesty."[51] In *Kormáks saga* the husband clearly acknowledges the right of the hero to his hard-won booty, whereas in *Tristrams saga* this right is obliquely expressed in the hero's stern rebuke of the King. Kormákr's failure to take what is rightly his climaxes and emphasizes the basic theme of his unhappy fate; by contrast, Tristram returns Ísönd to King Markis only after "dallying" with her for a night "among the flowers" (Hatto). And finally, Tristram resorts to a stratagem to rescue Ísönd from her abductor, while Kormákr and his brother use force. On only one point, and that a minor one, must I disagree with Bjarni Einarsson: a comparison of the preserved fragment of the text of Thomas with the corresponding adaptation in *Tristrams saga* reveals that Friar Róbert, through a restructuring of the episode and the clever use of certain rhetorical devices, has subtly shifted the emphasis in such a way as to diminish considerably the opprobrium of cowardice against King Markis.[52] He was, after all, writing at the "command and behest of worthy King Hákon"!

Precisely at this point in the action *Tristrams saga* sheds welcome light on the confused and confusing account in *Kormáks saga.* According to the text as it now exists, Kormákr and his brother boarded the abductor's ship twice—once from their boat and later by the stern gangplank. Quite as puzzling to the reader is the statement that the two had to swim to shore with the rescued heroine—apparently within a few minutes after having come on board. In *Tristrams saga* the wily hero plays his fiddle for the Irish baron and his newly acquired lady *(frú).* "And in the meantime the tide had come in, so that it was not possible to reach the gangplank because of the high tide, for by then the gangplank was floating out past the ship." The Irish baron at first wants to wait for the tide to recede, but finally accepts Tristram's offer to carry

[51] Gottfried's *Tristan,* trans. Hatto, pp. 360–361. But see also Schoepperle, *Tristan and Isolt,* pp. 429–430.

[52] For an analysis of this episode see Paul Schach, "The Style and Structure of *Tristrams saga,*" *Scandinavian Studies* (Seattle: University of Washington Press; New York: The American-Scandinavian Foundation, 1965), pp. 68–69.

Ĭsönd out to the ship on his horse. Instead, Tristram, deriding the duped abductor, rides away with Ĭsönd.

This model permits us to reconstruct the garbled rescue episode in *Kormáks saga.* Kormákr and his brother in the evening row to the place where the abductor's ship is lying at anchor. Here they take the cooks by surprise and compel them to divulge the whereabouts of Steingerðr. After boarding the ship by way of the stern gangplank, they overcome those of the crew who have not gone ashore. Finally they reach the abductor, pull him onto the deck, and kill him. Meanwhile the tide has come in, so that their only possibility of getting to land is to swim. Presumably Kormákr was slightly wounded or else had to fight a rearguard action so that not he but his brother Þorgils swims to shore with Steingerðr. The completely irrelevant reference to the eels may be due to a scribal error or, as Bjarni Einarsson suggests, to the caprice of the author.[53] Gertrude Schoepperle long ago emphasized the striking resemblance of this episode in *Kormáks saga* to the Tristan episode.[54] In my opinion the points of resemblance are strong and numerous enough to justify regarding this portion of *Kormáks saga* as a loan from *Tristrams saga.* Indeed, as we have just seen, it is almost impossible to make any sense out of the sketchy account and the confused sequence of events in *Kormáks saga* in its present form of preservation without reference to its clearly narrated and well-preserved model in *Tristrams saga.*

We are not surprised to find that the mournful death of the two star-crossed lovers has left its mark on Scandinavian song and story, especially since it bears such a strong resemblance to the fate of Hagbard and Signe, Sigurðr and Brynhildr-Guðrún, and Randvér and Svanhildr in the autochthonous literature of the North. To be sure, the death scene is avoided in the post-classical escape literature of Iceland. Even in *Haralds saga Hringsbana,* which preserves most of the basic motifs of its model, the story concludes with the multiple marriage characteristic of the Icelandic romantic sagas. But the Scandinavian ballads and the more austere prose fiction of the North imitated the death of the lovers with considerable skill and variation.[55] The most faithful and poignant recreation of that memorable scene is found in the Icelandic ballad

[53] *Skáldasögur*, pp. 157–158. See also note 46 above.

[54] Schoepperle, *Tristan and Isolt,* II, 544–545.

[55] For a fuller discussion of the ballads, see Schach, "Tristan and Isolde in Scandinavian Ballad and Folktale," *Scandinavian Studies.*

Tristrams kvæði.[56] After having caused her husband's death by telling him that " 'svört eru segl á skipunum, en ekki blá' " ("black are the sails on the ships, and not blue"), Ísodd svarta, driven by jealousy and hatred, has Tristram and Ísodd bjarta buried on opposite sides of the church with the imprecation: " 'Þið skuluð ekki njótast dauð, ef ég má nú' " ("You shall not enjoy each other's love after death, if I can prevent it"). But the ballad concludes with the stanza

Uxu upp þeirra af leiðunum
lundar tveir;
fyrir ofan miðju kirkju
mættust þeir.

(Up from their graves there grew two trees;
above the middle of the church they entwined.)

In one version of the ballad each verse is followed by the refrain "Þeim var ekki skapað nema að skilja" (For them it was fated only to sever). The other version has the refrain "Og er sá sæll, sem sofna náir hjá henni" (And he is blessed who is favored to fall asleep beside her).[57]

The beautiful Norwegian ballad *Bendik og Årolilja* has preserved so many details of the death scene that Paasche was led to suggest a direct influence from *Tristrams kvæði*.[58] Bendik is slain outside the church; inside, before the altar, his *"vene viv"* falls over dead. Bendik is buried to the north of the church, and Årolilja to the south.

De voks upp av deires grefti
dei fagre tvo liljeblomar;
dei krøktest ihop ivi kyrkjesvoli—
der stend dei kongjen til domar.
—Årolilja, kvi søv'e du so lengje?

(Up from their graves grew two lilies;
they entwined above the church gable—
there they stand in judgment of the king.
—Årolilja, why do you sleep so long?)

[56] The two versions of *Tristrams kvæði* are found in Jón Helgason's edition of *Íslenzk fornkvæði (Islandske Folkeviser)* Vols. I, III, and IV (Editiones Arnamagnæanæ, Series B, Vols. X, XII, and XIII [København: Ejnar Munksgaard, 1962–1963]).

[57] This version of the ballad, which is only two-thirds as long as the other, is prefaced by a four-line verse concluding with the line quoted here.

[58] Frederick Paasche, *Norges og Islands Litteratur inntil Utgangen av Middelalderen* (*Norsk Litteratur Historie*, Vol. I), Ny utgave ved Anne Holtsmark (Oslo: H. Aschehoug og Co., 1957), pp. 517–519.

The substitution of *liljeblomar* for the trees of the saga and of the Icelandic poem was apparently suggested by the name of the heroine. The refrain bears a certain resemblance to that of the second version of *Tristrams kvæði.*

In the Faroese ballad *Tístrams táttur,* however, the details have become obscured through amalgamation with motifs from the Ambales and the Hagbard and Signe stories and through the inevitable erosive effect of oral transmission over a rather long period of time.[59] At the instigation of Tístram's parents, the hero is hanged by the King of Frakkland because of his refusal to marry the King's daughter. Tístram's sweetheart, Frú Ísin, sails to Frakkland and exacts bloody vengeance for his death. Then she cuts him down from the gallows, gives him a fitting burial, and dies of grief over his grave. In the earliest version of the Danish ballad of Tristrum and Jomfru Isoldt, the process of degeneration is even more pronounced. Here the lovers, who are really brother and sister, are poisoned by the Empress of Rome because of an incestuous union she and their parents were unable to prevent. The poem ends with Isoldt "döde y her Tristrums arrum." The incest motif of the Danish ballad (and possibly also of the Faroese poem) may have been suggested by an inadvertence of Friar Róbert, for in Chapter 16 of *Tristrams saga* he mistakenly wrote that Róaldr asked his *sister* (instead of his wife) to pretend she had given birth to the infant Tristram.[60]

In Icelandic prose literature the closest parallel is found in the *Saga af Tristram ok Ýsodd.* Here, as in the Norwegian ballad, the dead lovers are buried on the north and south sides of the church respectively. The two trees which grow from their graves are laden *með hinum fegursta ávexti* (with the fairest fruit). According to this derivative of *Tristrams saga,* the trees are still standing as proof of the nobility of the two lovers who were intended by God himself for each other, a trait similar in thought to the last line of the Norwegian ballad. The pious

[59] This ballad, which unfortunately has been preserved in only one version, is found in V. U. Hammershaimb's *Færøsk Anthologi* (Copenhagen, 1891), I, 216–222.

[60] AM 543 4to and the editions of Kölbing and Gísli Brýnjúlfsson all have *systur.* In ÍB 51 fol., which derives from the same text as AM 543 (which in turns goes back to the vellum AM 567 4to), the scribe first wrote *systur.* He then corrected the text by partially erasing *systur* and superimposing *konu* upon it; the result is a somewhat blurred *kosnnu,* which the copyist of JS 8 fol. correctly interpreted and rendered as *conu.* Since there is no reason to attribute *systur* to the writer of the extant vellum, it may be inferred that the mistake goes back to Friar Róbert himself.

author of this tale expresses the fond hope, in the form of a prayer, that Tristram and Ýsodd fagra might be united after death: "Nú þó at þau mætti ekki njótast lifandi . . . þá biðjum vér þess guð sjálfan, at þau njótist nú með ást ok vingan" (Although they could not enjoy each other's love while alive, we pray to God that they may now have joy of each other in love and friendship). The striking verbal similarity between this passage and the hope of Ísodd svarta in the Icelandic ballad that Tristram and Ísodd bjarta should *not* be united in death suggests that a similar sentence must originally have been found in *Tristrams saga,* possibly as part of the final paragraph of the story, which reads as follows in its present state of preservation:

> Then they were buried. And it is said that Ísodd, Tristram's wife, had Tristram and Ísönd buried on opposite sides of the church so that they should not be close to each other after death. But it so happened that a tree grew up from each of their graves, so high that their crowns intertwined their branches above the church gable. And from this one can see how great was the love they had for each other.

We are almost startled at the abrupt conclusion of the chapter and especially at the laconic observation regarding the great love of Tristram and Ísönd. This love is fittingly symbolized, to be sure, by the meeting and entwining of the crowns of the two trees above the church; but the sombre tone of the entire scene, the fervent prayer of Ísönd for forgiveness, and her final words to her dead sweetheart require a verbal as well as a symbolic assurance of divine approval of their immortal love. I believe that the last sentence of *Tristrams saga* has been truncated, and that the saga originally ended with the declaration that "they should now enjoy in death the love that was denied them while alive."

A striking analogue to the death scene is found in the love story of Hjálmarr and Ingibjörg as related in *Örvar-Odds saga* (Chap. 31). The story itself was probably borrowed from *Hervarar saga ok Heiðreks.* In the most primitive form of the story, Ingibjörg takes her own life when she hears of the death of Hjálmarr in the battle of Sámsey.[61] A more modern version of the death of Ingibjörg is found in a younger redac-

[61] *Saga Heiðreks Konungs ins Vitra,* ed. and trans. Christopher Tolkien (Nelson's Icelandic Texts [London: Thomas Nelson and Sons Ltd., 1960]), p. 10: "Eptir þat deyr Hjálmarr. Oddr segir þessi tíðindi heim í Svíþjóð, en konungsdóttir má eigi lifa eptir hann ok ræðr sér sjálf bana" [After that, Hjálmar died. Back in Sweden, Oddr told these tidings; but the king's daughter could not live on after Hjálmarr, and she took her own life].

tion of the saga. Here Örvar-Oddr brings not only the report of Hjálmarr's death but also his body back to Sweden, "and when Princess Ingibjörg saw Hjálmarr's body, she fell down dead, and they were buried together at Uppsala."[62] Under the influence of *Tristrams saga* the author of *Örvar-Odds saga* expanded this bare account into a dramatic and highly effective scene. Oddr sails to Sweden with Hjálmarr's body.

He drew his ship ashore, took Hjálmarr on his back, and carried him to Uppsala. He laid him down outside the hall door and went inside. He had Hjálmarr's coat of mail and his helmet in his hands, and he laid them down on the floor of the hall before the king, and told him the news of what had happened. Then he went to where Ingibjörg was sitting on a chair, sewing a kirtle for Hjálmarr.

"Here is the ring," he said, "which Hjálmarr sent you before he died, along with his greeting."

She took the ring and gazed at it, but answered not a word. Then she sank back against the chair post and was dead.

Then Oddr uttered a grim laugh and declared, "Things have not been going well for the most part recently. Now they shall have the joy of each other in death which was denied them while they were alive." Then Oddr took her in his arms and carried her out of the hall and laid her in Hjálmarr's embrace. (Chap. 31)

To be sure, the tree symbolism and the burial in separate graves associated with the Thomas branch of the Tristan story are lacking in *Örvar-Odds saga;* but these are traits which would be quite as incongruous in this heroic saga of the North as the rash-boon motive would be in a saga of Icelandic heroes such as *Kormáks saga.* (We must furthermore keep in mind the fact that the death of the hero and heroine of *Tristrams saga* was prefigured by the almost equally dramatic death of Tristram's parents, Kanelangres and Blensinbil, and that saga-writers familiar with this story could draw upon both death scenes in the construction of their own works.) Both the general situation, however, as well as a number of details so strongly resemble the death scene in *Tristrams saga* that it is difficult to escape the conclusion that the author of *Örvar-Odds saga* was acquainted with the translation of Friar Róbert. Like Tristram and Kormákr, Hjálmarr perishes of his wounds in a distant land with the name of his sweetheart on his lips; and like Ísönd,

[62] See *Örvar-Odds saga*, ed. R. C. Boer (*Altnordische Saga-Bibliothek*, Vol. II [Halle a. S.: Max Niemeyer, 1892], p. 60, note to secs. 4–7.

Ingibjörg dies of a broken heart when she learns of her lover's death. In *Tristrams saga* we read that Īsönd "lay down on the floor and kissed him and put her arms around his neck, and thus she died." In *Örvar-Odds saga* Oddr places Ingibjörg in Hjálmarr's arms; and his declaration " 'Nú skulu þau njótaz dauð, er þau máttu eigi lifandi' " is almost identical with the hope expressed by the author of the *Saga af Tristram.* Additional evidence for the influence of *Tristrams saga* on the tale of Örvar-Oddr is an analogue of quite a different kind. The longer recension of *Örvar-Odds saga* briefly refers to a cape which Ögmundr Eyþjólfsbani had made from the beards and mustaches he received yearly as tribute from all the kings in the Baltic. This is evidently an adaptation of the bizarre tale related in *Tristrams saga* about King Artús and an African giant who went about slaying kings and dukes and other chieftains for their beards (Chap. 71).[63]

The *Īslendingasögur*, too, contain a number of passages reminiscent of the death scene in *Tristrams saga.* As noted above, Kormákr, whom Bjarni Einarsson calls the "Icelandic Tristan," died of his wounds in a distant land with the name of his sweetheart on his lips. A closer parallel is found in *Gunnlaugs saga.* Here too the hero dies of his wounds in a distant country, while his sweetheart, Helga hin fagra, dies as she gazes at a cloak given to her by Gunnlaugr. Although we are told that Helga's death was caused by an illness, the elegiac tone of the episode suggests that she really died of grief. And in *Laxdœla saga,* the author strongly suggests that Hrefna died of grief following the slaying of her husband Kjartan:

> Þorsteinn Kuggason took Kjartan's son Ásgeirr for fostering as a consolation to Hrefna, but Hrefna accompanied her brothers to the north and was very depressed. And yet she bore herself with dignity, and spoke pleasantly to everyone. Hrefna did not marry again after Kjartan's death. She lived only a short time after she came north, and people say that she died of a broken heart. (Chap. 50)

Like the text of *Kormáks saga* (and, in varying degrees, of practically all sagas), the translation of Friar Róbert has undergone considerable change during its rather long scribal transmission, thanks to the penchant of Icelandic scribes to regard themselves as editors rather than as mere copyists. I have discussed elsewhere some of the more interesting textual differences between one vellum (V) and the three paper

[63] See Kölbing's edition of *Tristrams saga,* pp. 211–212.

transcripts *(A, B, C)*.[64] For the most part, the changes made by the various scribes consist in a modernization and shortening of the text: obsolete words and constructions are replaced by current ones, and the text is condensed through the omission of words, phrases, and entire sentences and through the reduction of alliterative or other collocations to single words, especially in long descriptive or emotive passages. But the text of *Tristrams saga* has been tampered with in other respects also. Although *B* in general is more faithful than *A* to the vellum in phraseology, it contains more careless errors (including the introduction of a new character through the erroneous expansion of an abbreviation and the attribution of statements to the wrong characters through the inadvertent omission of an entire line) as well as a large number of interlinear and marginal emendations. The writer of *C* severely compressed the text of *B,* while at the same time incorporating almost all the emendations into the text itself. Consequently, the style of *Tristrams saga* taken as a whole is quite uneven, and several passages in it are almost as unintelligible as the episode from *Kormáks saga* discussed above. A case in point is the treatment of the ambiguous-oath motif. Here the relationship between the model and the loan is almost an exact inversion of that between *Tristrams saga* and *Kormáks saga* in that the somewhat jumbled condition of the passage in *Tristrams saga* may shed some light on several points of difference between it and the much-discussed adaptation in the so-called *Spesar þáttr* of *Grettis saga.* The story, which is told in Chapters 84–92 of that saga, is as follows.

After being outlawed for the slaying of Grettir, Þorbjörn öngull sails to Norway. Learning of the presence in that country of Grettir's brother Þorsteinn drómundr, Þorbjörn proceeds to Miklagarðr (Constantinople), where he joins the Varangian guard. Þorsteinn follows his brother's slayer, recognizes him by the notched blade of his sword, and exacts vengeance for Grettir's death. Unable to prove his identity as Grettir's brother, Þorsteinn is thrown into a dungeon to starve to death. Here he reveals himself to be, like Tristram, an excellent singer. Spes, a woman of good family who was married to a man of lower social standing for his money, is charmed by Þorsteinn's beautiful voice and has him ransomed. Her husband Sigurðr soon suspects Spes of being in love with another man. After twice failing to catch them together, he decides to set a trap. Pretending, like King Markis, to go on a journey,

[64] *Saga-Book,* XV (1957–1959), 104–112. A discussion of the recently discovered second vellum will appear shortly.

he lies in wait with a large group of witnesses. Sigurðr and his men see Spes and Þorsteinn together in her room, but when they break in, they find her alone, since Þorsteinn has escaped by means of a trapdoor from her *sjávarlopt,* just as King Haraldr hinn harðráði Sigurðarson did in the story told about his love affair with Maria, the niece of the Byzantine emperor, in the compilation of Sagas of Kings known as *Morkinskinna.*[65] When Sigurðr demands that she prove her innocence of his charges of adultery and of having supplied her lover with money, Spes replies that he is demanding the very thing she was about to propose. She has the bishop set the time and place for her trial, and makes the necessary arrangements with Þorsteinn.

Time now passed until the day arrived on which Spes was to take the oath. She invited all her friends and relatives, and dressed in the finest clothing she owned. Many high-born ladies accompanied her. There had been heavy rains, so that the street was wet, and there was a large pool of rain water to be crossed before they could reach the church. And when Spes and her bevy of followers arrived at the pool, they found a large crowd there, including many poor people begging alms, for that was the main street. All of them felt obliged to greet her as warmly as they could and to wish her well, since she had so often been of help to them. Among these poor people there was a tall beggar with a long beard. The ladies stopped at the edge of the pool, since it seemed difficult to cross without getting muddy. And when the tall beggar caught sight of Lady Spes, who was more richly attired than the other women, he addressed her.

"Good woman," he said, "will you condescend to let me carry you across this pool? We beggars are obliged to serve you as best we can."

"How do you expect to carry me," she said, "when you can scarcely carry yourself?"

"It would be proof of your humility," he said. "I can do no more for you than for myself. Things will go all the better with you for not having scorned the help of a poor man."

"You can be sure of one thing," she said. "If you do not carry me across safely, I'll have you skinned alive and disgraced in other ways too."

"I am happy to take that risk," he said, and stepped out into the pool.

She acted as though she were not very happy about having him carry her, but she got up on his back nevertheless. He hobbled very slowly on his two crutches, and when he reached the middle of the pool, he staggered around in all directions. She told him to pull himself together.

[65] *Grettis saga Ásmundarsonar,* ed. Guðni Jónsson (*Íslenzk fornrit,* Vol. VII [Reykjavík: Hið íslenzka fornritafélag, 1936]), pp. lv ff.

"If you drop me here," she said, "you will experience something the likes of which you have never experienced before."

The poor wretch struggled on and strove with all his might. By exerting all his strength he managed to get near the edge of the pool. But then he stumbled and fell forward in such a way that he heaved her up on the bank, but he himself landed full length in the pool up to his armpits. And as he fell in this position, he grabbed for Spes, but was unable to catch hold of her clothing. His muddy hand grasped her knee and slipped all the way up to her bare thigh. She sprang to her feet, scolding and saying that she never had anything but trouble from such worthless vagabonds.

"You deserve to be beaten half to death," she said, "but that seems a pity to me because of your wretched condition."

He replied, "Fortune is fickle. I intended to do a good deed, and hoped to receive alms from you in return, but instead of something good I get nothing from you but insults and threats." And he behaved as though he were quite distressed.

Many persons pitied him, but Spes declared he was a cunning rascal. But since so many pleaded for him, she took her purse, which was full of coins, and shook it out.

"Take these, old man," she said. "It wouldn't be right for you not to have full compensation for the scolding you got from me. And now we shall part company after all in such a way as you deserve."

He picked up the gold coins and thanked her kindly for them.

Spes proceeded to the church, where there was a large crowd of people waiting. Sigurðr stated his case energetically and challenged her to refute the charges he had brought against her.

Spes replied, "I am not concerned about your accusation. Who is the man you claim to have seen in my room with me? It often happens that worthy men visit me, and I see no reason to be ashamed of that. But I am willing to swear that I never gave money to any man, nor have I suffered bodily defilement from any man except my husband and that wretched beggar who put his filthy hand on my thigh when I was carried across the pool of water today."

Now many agreed that this was a lawful oath, and that it could not be regarded as a blemish on her character, because the fellow had unexpectedly seized her. She said that the truth could be told. Then she swore the oath which was worded as described above. Many said that she would prove the proverb that "little should be left unsworn in an oath." She replied that she thought no sensible people would believe that there was anything suspicious about it. Then her kinsmen declared that it was a great vexation to women of high birth to have such false accusations remain without redress, for it was a deed punishable by death if a woman were convicted of infidelity against her husband. Spes thereupon requested the bishop to grant her a divorce from Sigurðr, for she declared she could no longer endure his false accusations. Her kinsmen supported her request. With their assistance and gifts the divorce was arranged in such a way that Sigurðr received but little of their property and was forced to leave the country. Here it happened again, as it so often does, that "the weaker have to yield." Sigurðr was able to accomplish nothing even though he was in the right.

Spes now took all their money and was regarded as a great and distinguished woman. When people thought about the wording of her oath, it seemed to them as though there had been something suspicious about it, and they concluded that clever men must have contrived its formulation for her. Later they succeeded in digging up the fact that the beggar who had carried her over the pool was Þorsteinn drómundr. Nevertheless Sigurðr received no redress for this injustice, and he is now out of the story. (Chap. 89)

Spes and Þorsteinn marry and go to Norway, where Þorsteinn is cordially received by King Magnús. After nineteen years of happy married life, Spes and Þorsteinn begin to suffer remorse for their duplicity. Like Kári Sölmundarson in *Njáls saga,* Sturla Sighvatsson in *Sturlunga saga,* and many other historical and fictional characters in saga literature, Spes and Þorsteinn make a pilgrimage to Rome to obtain absolution for their sins. Thereupon they proceed to the Holy Land, where they renounce married life and, each in his own hermitage, await the pleasures of the life to come.[66]

As indicated at the beginning of our discussion, this adaptation of the equivocal-oath motif has been the subject of much scholarly controversy. Many regard the Spes episode as an addition to the story of Grettir supplied by one or the other of various assumed redactors. Boer, for example, first attributed the emendation to the "second interpolator" of the saga, but later surmised that it must have been the *third* one who contrived and added the *þáttr.* On the basis of the loan word *speja,* "to spy," he assumed a German source for the equivocal oath, while at the same time recognizing the story about King Haraldr hinn harðráði Sigurðarson mentioned above as the model for the episode as a whole.[67]

66 After the marriage of her son Snorri, Guðríðr Þorbjarnardóttir in *Grænlendinga saga* goes on a pilgrimage to Rome and then becomes an anchoress in Iceland. The motif of both husband and wife entering a hermitage in the Holy Land is common in the Icelandic romantic sagas. In the *Saga af Tristram ok Ýsodd* the king does so after the death of Ýsodd.

67 R. C. Boer, "Zur Grettissaga," *Zeitschrift für deutsche Philologie,* XXX (1898), 1–71, esp. p. 30.

Noting that the treatment of the ambiguous-oath theme in *Grettis saga* differs from those in both the Thomas and Béroul branches of the Tristan story, Golther suggested the possibility of transmission through a lost Norman *Spielmannsepos*.[68] Since Spes does not actually undergo the ordeal of the hot iron, Paul Herrmann argued that the loan must have been made before 1150; later, he specified a lost French lai as the probable source.[69] In opposition to Boer, Heinz Dehmer declared that the *þáttr* is really an independent novella, too skillfully and compactly constructed to be the work of an Icelander. He insisted that this novella must have been borrowed in its entirety and hinted that the "name Spes may perhaps give us a clue" to its origin.[70] The most ingenious hypothesis of all is that advanced by Henry Goddard Leach. Leach points out the fact that a version of the unfaithful wife's ambiguous oath, namely the "popular Byzantine romance of the loves of *Clitophon and Leucippe*," was current in Byzantium during the first half of the eleventh century and conjectures that such a tale may have come to be associated with a Norseman in the Varangian guard. Transmitted orally to Iceland and transferred to Grettir's brother Þorsteinn, this tale formed the nucleus of the *Spesar þáttr* which may, Leach concedes, have been "colored" by Friar Róbert's *Tristram*.[71] Bjarni Einarsson, on the other hand, holds that the equivocal-oath motif in *Grettis saga* derives from some form of the Tristan story, but insists that it cannot have come from any version of the Thomas branch because of certain details in which the *Spesar þáttr* differs from Thomas.[72]

A study of the statements mentioned above finds the scholars in complete agreement in the assumption that the ambiguous-oath motif in *Grettis saga* cannot have been borrowed from *Tristrams saga* but in complete disagreement regarding the ultimate source and the manner of transmission of that motif. It is also clear that they base their shared belief on the hypothesis that *Spesar þáttr* is not an organic part of *Grettis saga* and that in their search for sources other than Friar Róbert's

[68] W. Golther, *Tristan und Isolde in den Dichtungen des Mittelalters und der Neuen Zeit* (Leipzig: Hirzel, 1907), pp. 14–29.

[69] See *Die Geschichte von dem starken Grettir, dem Geächteten* (Sammlung Thule, Vol. V), trans. Paul Herrmann (Jena: Eugen Diederichs, 1913), p. xxiv, and the edition of 1922, p. xxiv.

[70] *Primitives Erzählgut in den Íslendinga-Sögur* (Von Deutscher Poeterey, Vol. II [Leipzig: J. J. Weber, 1927]), p. 116.

[71] Leach, *Angevin Britain and Scandinavia*, p. 189.

[72] *Skáldasögur*, p. 45.

translation they exaggerate the importance of relatively insignificant details. If, therefore, it can be shown that *Spesar þáttr* is not the addition of a second or third or fourth redactor but part of the author's original, overall plan for his work about Iceland's most famous outlaw of olden times, the chief argument against deriving the equivocal oath from its most likely source loses its validity.

If we assume, for the moment, that *Spesar þáttr* is a later addition to the saga, we are faced with the problem of where and how the saga originally ended. The slaying of Þorbjörn öngull by Þorsteinn drómundr was certainly part of the original story, not only because it was a necessary act of vengeance, but because the author promised much earlier in the story that Þorsteinn would avenge his brother's death.[73] It also seems unlikely that the author would describe Grettir's avenger as a *raddmaðr mikill,* "a man with a very fine voice" (Chapter 13), unless he intended Þorsteinn to use his voice for some purpose. Nor does it seem likely that the story originally ended with Þorsteinn's ransom from prison by Spes; the very manner in which she is introduced into the story precludes that possibility. Chapter 86 ends with Þorsteinn singing loudly and merrily in his dungeon cell; Chapter 87 begins with this description of Spes:

> Spes was a prominent woman in the city, quite well to do and of distinguished lineage. Sigurðr was the name of her husband, who was wealthy but of a lesser family than she. She had been married to him for his money. There was no great love between the two, and she regarded her marriage as a terrible mésalliance. She was a high-spirited and very haughty woman.

Obviously this high-spirited, unhappily married woman will have more to do with Þorsteinn than merely effect his release from prison. The author of *Grettis saga* might possibly have ended his story with Spes and Þorsteinn happily married in Norway—except for the demands of justice. Spes had deceived and divorced her husband in such a shabby and high-handed manner that both she and Þorsteinn are finally (after nineteen years of married life!) overcome with remorse. Unable to make amends in any other way for their crimes and sins, they dispose of their worldly goods, arrange for the care of their children, obtain

[73] *Grettis saga*, Chapter 41. In this well-constructed scene, the discrepancy between Grettir's almost superhuman strength and his lack of good luck are effectively contrasted as a parallel to the contrast between his muscular arms and the slender arms of his brother and future avenger.

absolution from the Pope in Rome, and end their days in their hermit cells in the Holy Land.

There is still another reason for regarding the so-called *Spesar þáttr* as an integral part of the overall design of the author: it is the exact and necessary counterpart to Chapter 39 of the saga, in which Grettir appears before King Óláfr the Saint to request permission to undergo the ordeal of the hot iron to prove his innocence of the charge of having with malice aforethought burned the sons of Þorir Skeggjason to death. Although the King grants this request, Grettir is prevented from bearing the hot iron through the mysterious arrival of a youth of strange appearance (some believe him to be "an unclean spirit, sent as an ill omen to Grettir"). When this apparition curses and denounces Grettir, he knocks it down, causing a great commotion in the church. Because of Grettir's impetuous behavior, the king declares that the ordeal cannot be carried out:

> "You are a man of great adversity, Grettir," said the king. "The ordeal, for which all preparations were made, cannot now be carried out. It will be impossible for you to withstand your ill fortune . . . I see that few men are your equal in strength and bravery, yet your misfortune is even greater, and for that reason you cannot remain here . . . If ever a man has been under a curse, it is you above all others."

Grettir's failure to clear himself of the charge of having deliberately caused the death of Þorir's sons marks a major turning point in his life, for upon his return to Iceland he is outlawed and eventually slain for this inadvertent deed.

Before returning to Iceland, however, Grettir pays his brother Þorsteinn a visit after first having freed a nearby farm of a formidable *berserkr*. Þorsteinn greets him with the significant words "You could accomplish great things in life, kinsman, if only they were not followed by disaster." To this Grettir replies, "And yet one must relate things as they happened." In the following chapter Þorsteinn makes his prediction that he or no one will avenge the death of Grettir, despite the striking difference between the two brothers in strength and dexterity. At the very end of the story this prophecy is fulfilled, for Þorsteinn is endowed with good luck to the same degree that Grettir was pursued by misfortune. Although Grettir's intentions were good, his prodigious feats of strength and bravery inevitably brought disaster to himself and others. For Grettir, a heroic and magnanimous deed resulted in nineteen years of hardship ending in a terrible death. By contrast, Þorsteinn's deceitful conniving brought him nineteen years of luxurious and happy married life followed by the absolution of his sins and the prospect of an even happier life to come. Whereas even Saint Óláfr was powerless to exonerate Grettir from the false accusation of murder, tyrannical King Haraldr had no difficulty in effecting the exoneration of Þorsteinn and Spes from the true charge of adultery. Thus, the *Spesar þáttr* is the culmination of the entire story, the necessary counterpart of the confrontation of Grettir and Saint Óláfr, the final fulfillment of events foreshadowed throughout the saga and the realization of the tragic basic theme that "good luck and accomplishments are two different things altogether."[74] The equivocal oath and the many other ambiguities and double entendres throughout the episode reflect and symbolize the enigma of Grettir's existence, the substance of which is summarized in the words of Saint Óláfr and in Þorsteinn's greeting to Grettir and repeated ironically in Þorsteinn's retort to Spes's scolding: "Fortune is fickle. I intended to do a good deed . . ."

Since the *Spesar þáttr* is obviously an organic, necessary, and integral part of *Grettis saga,* it now remains to discuss briefly the various minor objections to deriving the ambiguous-oath motif from *Tristrams saga.* As we have already seen, Boer based his assumption of a German source on the occurrence of the loan word *speja,* "to spy," in Chapter 88. But this verb and the related noun of agent *spejari* are not at all unusual in Old Norse; indeed, they occur even in *Stjórn,* an Old Norwegian Bible translation dating from about 1190. The supposition that Béroul's Tristran, like Þorsteinn drómundr, was disguised as a beggar is used by Bjarni Einarsson to demonstrate the impossibility of derivation from *Tristrams saga,* since Friar Róbert's hero appears in this scene as a pilgrim. But the hero of the various Tristan stories appears so often in so many different disguises that this detail is of little significance. And anyway, Béroul's Tristran disguises himself not as an ordinary beggar but as a leper. Not only is he addressed and described at least twenty times as (*lis*) *ladres*; Béroul's Tristran even explains in great detail to King Marc how he contracted this disease from his mistress.

Several scholars have emphasized the fact that the heroine is sub-

[74] This formulation of the basic theme of the saga is found in Chapter 34. With these words Grettir's friend and kinsman Jökull Bárðarson tries to dissuade him from attempting to lay the ghost Glámr. As a result of this heroic deed, Grettir is cursed with fear of darkness and loneliness.

jected to the ordeal of carrying the hot iron in the Thomas branch of the Tristan story but not in Béroul or *Grettis saga.* This they regard as evidence that the ambiguous-oath motif must have been borrowed from a pre-Thomas stage of the story. Two fallacies are in this conclusion. In the first place, the religious ordeal known as *járnburðr,* which was introduced into the North together with Christianity from Germany and England and was abolished in Norway in 1247, seems to have been restricted to men (Grettir, in the counterpart of this episode, wished to undergo this ordeal);[75] the corresponding ordeal for women was the *ketiltak,* which consisted in taking a stone out of a kettle of boiling water.[76] In the second place, it is preposterous to believe that a haughty noblewoman like Spes would submit to an ordeal. What is involved here is compurgation by oath, and from the outset Spes is clearly confident of winning her case (in good Icelandic fashion) through the overwhelming number and the wealth and social standing of her friends and kinsmen. The only detail of importance is the phrasing of the oath, and it is precisely this detail which is given prominence in both *Tristrams saga* and *Grettis saga.*[77]

And finally, it has been suggested that the general situation in the *Spesar þáttr* is more nearly like that in Béroul than the corresponding passage in *Tristrams saga,* especially since Ísönd is carried from a boat, whereas the boat is lacking in the other two versions. If the missing boat in the Icelandic text must be accounted for, this can easily be done on the basis of the text in *Tristrams saga,* for here the account, as noted previously, is confusing and contradictory. First of all, we are told (Chap. 58) that Tristram is to await Ísönd at "a certain *straumsvað,*" which suggests that she and her retinue intend to wade or ride across the ford. Then we read that Ísönd intends to have Tristram "carry her from the ship when she is brought across the river." At this point the reader may well begin to wonder why and how a ship should be used to cross

[75] Although the *járnburðr* is referred to in the *konungasögur* in paternity tests, it seems to have been almost unknown in Iceland. A noted exception is *Sturlu saga,* where it occurs twice. This is all the more interesting in view of the fact that Sturla Þórðarson, the grandson of the central figure of *Sturlu saga,* is regarded by many scholars as the author of *Grettis saga* in its original form. See note 78.

[76] The *locus classicus* is found in *Guðrúnarkviða* III, where Guðrún's innocence of the false charges of adultery and Herkja's guilt are established in this manner.

[77] The word *eiðstafr,* "oath formulation" occurs in both sagas, and in both passages the heroine and the other participants are much concerned about the exact wording of the oath to be taken.

the shallows or ford of a river. Evidently Friar Róbert was somewhat puzzled too, for a few lines further on Ísönd is in a boat, which she apparently rows across the shallows of the river herself. At least that is what the text literally says: "Því næst lendi hon bátinum" (thereupon she landed the boat). She now calls to Tristram in a loud voice, saying, "Friend, come here and carry me from the boat, for you must be a good sailor." Why Ísönd should use the word *skipari* in addressing a man disguised as a pilgrim standing on a river bank is also obscure. And finally, although horses have not been mentioned previously, Ísönd and her attendants next "leaped on their horses and rode on their way, with much joking and banter about the pilgrim . . ." Surely the sophisticated author of *Grettis saga* would not simply imitate such an awkwardly related account without first simplifying and clarifying the confused and confusing situation. The easiest way to do so was to avoid all reference to ships, boats, sailors, and horses through the simple expedient of having the compurgation take place within easy walking distance of Spes's home in the city of Constantinople.

Thus none of the arguments advanced in support of the derivation of the equivocal oath in the Spes episode from extant or hypothetical sources other than *Tristrams saga* are cogent. It is not absolutely out of the question that the author of *Grettis saga,* writing in the early decades of the fourteenth century, may have had access to a Norman *Spielmanns-epos*, a lost German poem, Béroul's *Tristran*, or a lost pre-Thomas *lai* (all from the twelfth century). It is also possible that he may have heard a tale based on the Byzantine romance of *Clitophon and Leucippe* (from the early decades of the eleventh century). But it seems much more probable that he found his inspiration in the readily available and highly popular *Tristrams saga.* The degree of probability is substantially increased by the following considerations. *Grettis saga* in its present form is regarded by many scholars as an expanded version of an earlier Grettir biography by Sturla Þórðarson,[78] who, as noted earlier,

[78] In his edition of *Grettis saga* (pp. lxviii–lxxv), Guðni Jónsson dates this saga at 1300 or somewhat later and adduces plausible evidence for attributing the work to a priest named Hafliði Steinsson (1253–1319). Nordal, however, argues that so much genuine tradition is embodied in *Grettis saga*, compared with other late works, that the present version of the story must represent a fourteenth-century expansion of an earlier Grettir biography by Sturla Þórðarson, who got his information about the hero from the priest Halldór Oddsson, the last member of one branch of Grettir's family. The one important point of difference is the question of whether the ambiguous-oath motif was originally part of the story. Nordal believes it represents a borrowing

included traits from the Hall of Statues episode in his redaction of *Landnámabók*. The author of *Grettis saga* knew *Þiðreks saga,* which contains previously discussed allusions to and adaptations from *Tristrams saga.*[79] A number of sagas written around the year 1300 are known to have borrowed material from both *Þiðreks saga* and *Tristrams saga.* And finally, although the author of *Grettis saga* adapted the equivocal-oath motif with skill and imagination, he did not efface all traces of his source. A careful reading of the two passages reveals a number of lexical and phrasal similarities between the model and the adaptation. In contrast to the version of this motif found in Béroul, both Þorsteinn drómundr and Friar Róbert's Tristram fall with the heroine after carrying her to dry ground. In *Tristrams saga* Ísönd "hafði . . . upp klæði sín, ok fell hann þegar á hana" (lifted up her skirts, and he at once fell down upon her). A few minutes later she facetiously remarks to her companions: " 'Nú, er þat undr, þó at pílagrímrinn vildi leika sér ok þreifa um hvítu lær mín?' " ("Well, is it surprising that the pilgrim should want to amuse himself by seizing my white thighs?") In *Grettis saga* Þorsteinn is unable to grasp Spes's skirt: "tekr hann þá saurugri hendi upp á kné henni ok allt á lærit bert" (his muddy hand seizes her knee and [slides] all the way up to her bare thigh). After Spes told the literal truth regarding Þorsteinn and her husband, many people are of the opinion that "henni væri þat ekki mannlýti, þó at karl hefði fíflat á henni váveifiliga" (she could not be blamed because the fellow had suddenly tricked her). There can be little doubt about the origin of these passages from *Grettis saga,* especially when we consider the erotic overtones of both *leika sér,* "to play," and *fífla,* which usually means "to seduce." And in both passages, as just noted, there is much concern and comment about the *eiðstafr,* i.e., the precise wording or formulation of the oath.

A brief consideration of the treatment of the proxy-wooing, bridal-substitution, forest-idyll, and quest-for-healing motifs will suffice to

---

from the Tristan romance made by the expander of the saga, whereas Guðni Jónsson argues (correctly, I believe) that the entire *Spesar þáttr* is an organic part of the story. As previously noted, Sturla must have known *Tristrams saga.* My own feeling is that both Nordal and Guðni are partly right: Sturla Þórðarson is the original author of *Grettis saga*, which contained the *Spesar þáttr*, and Hafliði Steinsson is responsible for the present expanded form of the saga according to the A-class of manuscripts. A more detailed study of this problem is in progress.

[79] Chapter 53 of *Grettis saga* seems to have been influenced by Chapter 330 of *Þiðreks saga*. See the edition of *Grettis saga* by Guðni Jónsson, p. 173 n. 2.

round out the picture of the manner and extent of the borrowing of individual scenes or themes from *Tristrams saga.* To be sure, these four motifs, unlike the Hall of Statues episode, are familiar in folklore and history as well as in heroic and courtly epic; and consequently one must consider the possibility of sources other than the Tristan story for such parallels. Not infrequently, however, the loans and adaptations consist not of isolated motifs, but of a complex of motifs or a combination or succession of scenes or events; and occasionally, as in the examples from *Þiðreks saga,* the borrowing author deliberately reveals his source through the use of names. In the complete absence of any compelling evidence in support of the hypothesis of "influence from the Tristan story apart from the Norse translation of it" in the material discussed thus far, it is probably safe to assume that analogues to these four themes also derive directly or ultimately from *Tristrams saga* if their affinity with the Tristan legend can be demonstrated with reasonable certainty.

An interesting example of the bridal-emissary motif occurs in the version of the story of Svanhildr and Randvér as found in *Völsunga saga.*[80] The legend itself, the literary history of which has recently been reviewed and clarified by Hollander,[81] is an old one, going back to Jordanes. A very brief and primitive account of this tragic love story is given in the prose Introduction to the Eddic poem *Guðrúnarhvöt,* where we read that Svanhildr Sigurðardóttir "was married to Jörmunrekkr the Mighty; with him was Bikki. He advised Randvér to take her. This Bikki told the king. The king had Randvér hanged and Svanhildr trampled to death under horses' hoofs." In his *Skáldskaparmál* (Chap. 41), Snorri Sturluson improves on the story by rearranging the sequence of events, strengthening the motivation, and introducing the bridal-emissary motif:

> King Jörmunrekkr the Mighty . . . sent his son Randvér to woo Svanhildr for him. When he came to Jónakr, the maiden was entrusted to him to be brought to Jörmunrekkr. Then Bikki said it would be more fitting for Randvér to have Svanhildr since he and she were both young, whereas King Jörmunrekkr was old. This counsel pleased the two young persons well. But Bikki betrayed this to the king . . .

[80] The standard critical edition is that of Magnus Olsen (*Samfund til Udgivelse af Gammel Nordisk Litteratur* [København: S. L. Møllers Bogtrykkeri, 1908]).

[81] "The Legendary Form of *Hamðismál,*" *Arkiv för Nordisk Filologi*, LXXVII (1962), 56–62.

In *Völsunga saga* the account is substantially expanded. Despite Guðrún's dark premonitions of impending disaster, Svanhildr is betrothed to Jörmunrekkr and accompanies Randvér and Bikki to her new home. Among the added details is a definite reference to a sea voyage. We are told that Svanhildr went aboard ship with high-born attendants and that she sat beside Randvér on the raised deck during the voyage. In commenting on this passage in *Völsunga saga,* Margaret Schlauch feels that "the innovation is probably due to the Tristan story,"[82] and refers in a footnote to the well-known discussion of *Haralds saga Hringsbana* and its relationship to the Tristan and Svanhildr romances by Gertrude Schoepperle and Henry Goddard Leach.[83] Here Miss Schoepperle suggests that the Tristan and Svanhildr traditions may have crossed each other "somewhere in the dim land of literary origins previous to our earliest records." But the wooing-by-proxy motif is not even hinted at in the earliest known versions of the story, nor is it the innovation of the author of *Völsunga saga,* as Miss Schlauch seems to think. Since its first known occurrence is in *Skáldskaparmál,* we are justified in assuming it was introduced by Snorri, together with the comment about the inappropriateness of a union between the young maiden and the aged king, for the purpose of motivation. (It should not be forgotten that the refinement of motivation and the rationalization of incredible or miraculous events were characteristic of Snorri's treatment of both Scandinavian mythology and Norwegian history.) It is not the proxy-wooing motif itself which must be regarded as a loan from the Tristan story but the specific details of the sea voyage, and these details are far more likely to have come from *Tristrams saga,* which is known to have been popular in Iceland at the time when *Völsunga saga* was composed, than from "somewhere in the dim land of literary origins." Like the author of *Örvar-Odds saga,* the writer of *Völsunga saga,* noting the similarity between his own account and *Tristrams saga,* borrowed details for the purpose of expanding and improving his own story.

The motif of the substituted bride appears in various forms in imitation of Friar Róbert's translation. Whereas the bridal substitution was a unique expedient in *Tristrams saga,* in *Haralds saga Hringsbana* the deception is permanent. What looks on the surface like a compromise

[82] *Romance in Iceland,* p. 150f.

[83] "Haraldssaga Hringsbana and the Tristan and Svanhild Romances," *Scandinavian Studies,* II (1914–1915), 264–276.

between these two extremes is found in the *Saga af Tristram,* where the substitution is repeated for three consecutive nights while Tristram and Ýsodd enjoy each other's company in an adjoining room. This I regard as a deliberate rebuttal in the form of a burlesque exaggeration to the traditional gross lascivious nature of King Markis, to whom all women were alike. In these two sagas, as in *Völsunga saga,* the discrepancy between the youth of the bride and of the bridal emissary and the advanced age of the king is emphasized. In *Haralds saga* it is the father of the prospective bride who suggests that a marriage between his daughter Signý and Haraldr would be more appropriate because of the advanced age of Haraldr's father Hringr; in the *Saga af Tristram* the hero's uncle offers to concede his bride-elect to his nephew, but Tristram magnanimously declines to accept what he already posseses (again the irony is obvious). As in *Tristrams saga,* the heroine in the *Saga af Tristram* orders her faithful companion to be slain to prevent the discovery of her deceitful behavior. The Icelandic adaptor, however, has Ýsodd herself save Bringven from death, explaining that she had merely wanted to test Bringven's trustworthiness and loyalty to her. The purpose of this change was probably not so much to rectify a glaring inconsistency in the character of the heroine as to protest against the cruelty of the model by ennobling the character of the imitation.

The forest-idyll theme has also undergone considerable transformation in various derivatives of *Tristrams saga.* The clearest echo of the forest life of Tristram and Ísönd occurs in *Kára saga Kárasonar,* in which the hero and his sweetheart Ingibjörg are banished to an uninhabited island. Here the lovers dwell for a time in great happiness. Like Tristram, Kári is an excellent huntsman and provides food for himself and Ingibjörg by shooting birds with his bow and arrow.[84] In the *Saga af Tristram* the blissful forest idyll has been transformed into a seven-day imprisonment without food in a cave. Unlike the lovers in the Norwegian saga, the hero and heroine refrain from taking advantage of their proximity—probably because Tristram suspects (and rightly so) that they are being observed by the King. A further transformation occurs in the Tristram folk tales, where the heroine is made to fall into a pit with her two servant girls. A faint but unmistakable echo of the motif is found near the end of *Ambales saga,* the late sixteenth-century Icelandic Hamlet story. Ambales is pleasantly surprised to discover that

[84] On *Kára saga,* see Margaret Schlauch, *Romance in Iceland,* p. 152f.

his father's trusty friend Tellus, long believed dead, is alive and well. When asked where he has spent the past several years, he replies that he had been living for some time "in a wilderness with a woman named Ísodd."[85] The form of the name is identical with that of Ísönd's mother and of Tristram's wife in *Tristrams saga.*

Miss Schlauch thinks that the numerous quests for cure from a poisoned wound or from a mysterious illness in the Icelandic romantic sagas probably represent borrowings from "the Tristan story."[86] Among the romances she lists are *Haralds saga Hringsbana,* which was constructed on the plot of *Tristrams saga,* and *Rémundar saga,* which, as we have seen, contains not only motival and thematic, but also lexical and phrasal loans from the translation of Friar Róbert. In the absence of any convincing evidence to the contrary, we will probably not go wrong in assuming direct or indirect influence from *Tristrams saga* on most of the romantic sagas mentioned by Miss Schlauch.

Space does not permit a discussion of entire sagas constructed on the framework of *Tristrams saga.* The two most important imitations of the story as a whole are *Haralds saga Hringsbana* and the *Saga af Tristram ok Ýsodd,* which have already been mentioned. Both of these late works have been treated in detail elsewhere.[87] And both of them, I believe, represent protests against the deceit and duplicity of the lovers and against the blind lasciviousness of the king in the translation of Friar Róbert.[88]

It is much more difficult to demonstrate the influence of *Tristrams saga* on the general spirit of a work or on character delineation than it is to identify specific motifs, especially when these motifs occur in significant combinations or when they are actually associated with the names of the famous hero and heroine. The impact of the translated romances on such stories of native heroes as *Laxdæla saga* and *Gunnlaugs saga* has frequently been pointed out. Much of this influence derives from *Tristrams saga.* As suggested earlier, the popularity of *Tristrams saga* was probably due largely to its similarity to native love stories such as those of Hagbard and Signe, Sigurðr and Brynhildr-Guðrún,

[85] *Hamlet in Iceland,* ed. Israel Gollancz (London, 1898), p. 188.

[86] *Romance in Iceland,* p. 153.

[87] Schoepperle and Leach, "Haraldssaga Hringsbana," *Scandinavian Studies;* Schach, "The *Saga af Tristram ok Ýsodd,*" *Modern Language Quarterly.*

[88] This is especially clear in the final chapter of the Icelandic tale, where the author takes great pains to assure us that the two lovers were destined for each other by God.

and Randvér and Svanhildr, as well as to its unique amalgamation of the element of tragic fate characteristic of the native literature of the North with the exotic, erotic, colorful element of the chivalric romances of the South. We have seen that Kjartan's wife Hrefna in *Laxdæla* died of a broken heart following the slaying of her husband, just as Ísönd did upon finding Tristram dead. Some of the male characters in this saga, too, bear a stronger resemblance to the resplendent, dashing heroes of southern romances than to the rugged but sometimes somewhat uncouth vikings, warriors, farmers, and skalds of earlier stories such as *Egils saga* and *Eyrbyggja.* One of the best examples of the love of the author of *Laxdæla* for color and splendor is the following description of Guðrún's son Bolli:

> Bolli was such a man for show when he returned to Iceland from his journey abroad that he wanted to wear only clothing of scarlet and silk, and all his weapons were inlaid with gold. He was known as Bolli the Magnificent . . .
>
> Bolli rode away from the ship with eleven men. They were all attired in scarlet clothes, and rode in gilded saddles. All were men of gallant bearing, but Bolli surpassed them all. He was dressed in silk clothes which the king of Miklagarðr had given him. He wore a scarlet red cloak, and was girded with Fótbítr; its hilt was inlaid with gold and its haft wound with gold. He wore a gilded helmet and had a red shield at his side, on which a knight was traced in gold. He carried a lance (*glaðel*) in his hand, as was the custom in foreign countries. Wherever they took lodging, the women could not help gazing at Bolli and his companions with all their finery. Such was the courtly style in which Bolli rode on through the west districts . . . (Chap. 77.)

The shield with the knight traced on it in gold may well be a loan from *Knytlinga saga,*[89] but the description as a whole reminds us of Tristram and of his father Kanelangres, who was in some respects even more gallant and dashing than Tristram himself. The next to the last sentence in the above quotation recalls the tournament at which Kanelangres demonstrated his dexterity in all knightly accomplishments before King Markis and his court.

> But Kanelangres was the most valiant of all in the passage of arms and the mightiest in the jousts, for he knew best how to bear his armor and was

89 Rolf Heller, *Laxdæla saga und Königssagas* (*Saga,* Heft 5 [Halle (Saale): Max Niemeyer Verlag, 1961]), p. 13 f. The apparent chronological problem is satisfactorily explained by Heller.

most valorous in all feats of knighthood. Here, too, as always, he gained the greatest fame, for all the maidens and ladies in that large crowd gazed upon him with eyes of affection. All of them desired his love, even though they had never seen him before and did not even know from what country or family he came or what his name was. Yet they inclined their hearts and minds toward him, for that is the way of women.

The characters Kjartan and Óláfr Peacock in *Laxdæla saga* likewise reveal something of the gallant bearing and resplendent color of the heroes of southern romances, as do Gunnar of Hlíðarendi and Kári Sölmundarson in *Njáls saga.* The author of *Njála* must have known a number of translated romances, but it seems unlikely that any of these except *Tristrams saga* would have appealed to the profound creator of the greatest of all Sagas of Icelanders, a work which reflects and symbolizes the deep tragedy of the moral and cultural dissolution of his time.

The stylistic influence of *Tristrams saga* is another problem which cannot adequately be treated until syntactic and stylistic analyses of many more sagas have been made. Friar Róbert, who was not the pedestrian, haphazard translator many people think he was, made deliberate and frequently skillful use of the *figurae* of classical and medieval Latin, such as collocation, alliteration, amplification, parallelism, antithesis, variation, the figura etymologica, and so on, to achieve certain stylistic effects.[90] Although we may not agree with the aesthetic principles by which he was guided, the good friar's virtuosity must be respected. Nor can there be any doubt that this virtuosity was not only respected but highly admired and copied by Friar Róbert's contemporaries. As Jan de Vries expressed it, he created the model for Norwegian translators and their later Icelandic imitators,[91] and even the most casual reading of the translated romances and the Icelandic romantic sagas reveals the stylistic indebtedness of their translators and authors to *Tristrams saga.*[92] Directly or indirectly, the increasingly more frequent use of

[90] Schach, "The Style and Structure of *Tristrams Saga,*" in *Scandinavian Studies.*

[91] *Altnordische Literaturgeschichte*, II, 349: "Bruder Robert hat mit dieser Übersetzung ein Vorbild geschaffen, das für die weitere Entwicklung dieser Kunstrichtung bestimmend war."

[92] Lexical, syntactic, and stylistic analyses of selected *riddarasögur* are now being made by several students under my direction. Preliminary comparisons indicate that de Vries' impressionistic judgment is substantially correct and that *Tristrams saga* was indeed the *Vorbild* for later Norwegian translators and Icelandic imitators of southern romances of chivalry.

loan words such as *riddari* (knight), *glaðel* (lance), and *kurteiss* (courteous, courtly), as well as the employment of alliteration and of synonymous or antithetical collocations in the late sagas of Icelanders, must also be attributed in large part to the initial impact of *Tristrams saga* in Norway and Iceland and to its continued popularity in Ultima Thule.

The purpose in this discussion has been to examine a number of Tristan reminiscences in medieval and early modern Scandinavian literature with a view to determining whether they represent borrowings from *Tristrams saga.* The textual histories of this work and of the obvious derivatives, *Tristrams kvæði* and the *Saga af Tristram ok Ýsodd,* indicate that Friar Róbert's translation was known, copied, and imitated in Iceland during a period of at least six centuries (from about 1250 to 1850). Since our first group of loans were restricted to themes and motifs unique to the Thomas branch of the Tristan story, they can only have come from the work of Thomas itself or from the Middle High German or Old Norse adaptations of it. Although knowledge in the North of Thomas or Gottfried von Strassburg cannot be regarded as impossible, it seems reasonable to assume that Friar Róbert was the source of most of these traces of the Tristan story. We next examined the so-called *Spesar þáttr* of *Grettis saga* and some of the many arguments advanced to demonstrate the impossibility of deriving the ambiguous-oath motif from *Tristrams saga.* Not only are none of these arguments compelling; the suggested sources of this motif were either purely hypothetical or else too far removed in time and space to be regarded as more likely sources than Friar Róbert's translation. On the positive side, we noted that, despite the careful workmanship of the author of *Grettis saga,* the *Spesar þáttr* reveals lexical and phrasal similarities with *Tristrams saga.* Since the remaining analogues discussed here are common not only to all known versions of the Tristan story but to the folklore and literature of many climes and countries, it might seem that the degree of probability of derivation from *Tristrams saga* would be considerably reduced. Here too, however, most of these analogues were found, not in single occurrences, but in a whole nexus of Tristan motifs or even in imitation of *Tristrams saga* as a whole (for example, *Haralds saga Hringsbana* or the *Saga af Tristram*). The problems of the influence of *Tristrams saga* on the style, the general spirit, and the character delineation of Icelandic sagas written after about

1250, merely touched on here, will have to be reserved for more thorough examination elsewhere. Suffice it to say that it is plausible to attribute, directly or indirectly, to *Tristrams saga* much of the romantic influence in the late Sagas of Icelanders and many of the stylistic features of the Norwegian translations of southern romances and of the Icelandic imitations of them.

In view of this evidence, which is far from exhaustive, it seems difficult to avoid the conclusion that most of the Tristan reminiscences in medieval and early modern Scandinavian song and story derive from *Tristrams saga* and that Friar Róbert's translation of the Tristan romance of Thomas of Brittany was among the best known and most influential works of Old Norse prose literature.

The Heroic Pattern: Old Germanic Helmets, *Beowulf*, and *Grettis saga*

A. MARGARET ARENT

The work of C. G. Jung, K. Kerényi, and M. Eliade has drawn attention to the archetypal nature of motif patterns in myth, fairy tale, and heroic legend. As a consequence, assumptions long held to be determinative for the literary development of the heroic epic have had to undergo revision. The historical core of the hero tale *(Heldensage)*, with which, allegedly, fairy-tale (Märchen) motifs subsequently had become amalgamated, has had to yield its primary position to the nonhistorical ingredient.[1] The new approach focuses squarely on the mythical-religious origins from which the *Heldensage* received its impetus. After lifelong scholarship on the *Heldensage,* Hermann Schneider recognized the far-reaching implications of recent research

[1] Hermann Schneider, *Germanische Heldensage* (*Grundriss der germanischen Philologie*, begründet von Hermann Paul, 10/I; zweite, durch einen Anhang erweiterte sonst unveränderte Auflage [Berlin: Walter de Gruyter & Co., 1962]), I, 22 ff; Otto Höfler, *Kultische Geheimbünde der Germanen,* (Frankfurt am Main: Verlag Moritz Diesterweg, 1934), I, 204 and n. 124; Franz Rolf Schröder, "Mythos und Heldensage," in *Zur germanisch-deutschen Heldensage*, hrsg. von Karl Hauck (*Wege der Forschung*, Vol. XIV [Darmstadt: Wissenschaftliche Buchgesellschaft, 1961]), p. 285. See also Werner Betz, "Die deutsche Heldensage," in *Deutsche Philologie im Aufriss* (zweite überarbeitete Auflage, hrsg. von Wolfgang Stammler [Berlin: E. Schmidt, 1962]), III, cols. 1882 ff.

in adjacent disciplines and, in an entirely new introduction for the study of the *Heldensage,* acknowledged with remarkable forthrightness the reversal of his fundamental premises.[2] In contrast to former romantic explanations which superficially equated the fantasy motifs with mythical conceptions and the heroes with nature deities to account for the symbolic content of the *Heldensage,*[3] the newer "mythological" interpretations reach back to beliefs lived and enacted in cult practices, to universal thought patterns in the human psyche that derive from a sacred rather than a profane experiencing of the world. These are the primordial experiences to which the myth originally gave expression.[4] Reflexes of these thought complexes can be discerned in the plastic and literary arts of the early Germanic period. Some of the pictorial representations in particular bear witness to a former unity of spirit where art was not yet separated from practical function.

Evidence concerning early religious practices and warrior cults in the Germanic world is partially provided (1) by outside observers, notably Tacitus and Ammianus Marcellinus, (2) by analogy with contemporary folk practices and superstitions whose ancient religious associations have been all but lost,[5] (3) by literary references in the later Germanic sources, and (4) by pictorial representations found on weaponry from the period of the Great Migrations. Explicit descriptions of religious customs are noticeably wanting in the Eddas, in skaldic poetry, and in the Icelandic sagas. Yet much can be inferred from incidental remarks, idiomatic expressions, and otherwise obscure comparisons in these texts. Heinrich Beck in a recent monograph[6] has cited many such examples to support the religious interpretation of depictions dating from the Great Migrations. All four of these sources

[2] Schneider, "Einleitung zu einer Darstellung der Heldensage," (Anhang in *Germanische Heldensage*), I, 445–457.

[3] For example: Dietrich von Bern = Donar; Siegfried = der junge Tag; Brünhilde = die Sonnenbraut. Schneider, *Germanische Heldensage,* p. 23.

[4] See Höfler, *Kultische Geheimbünde,* p. 211; Jan de Vries, "Betrachtungen zum Märchen, besonders in seinem Verhältnis zu Heldensage und Mythos," *Folklore Fellows Communications* (Helsinki, 1954), LXIII, No. 150, p. 127: "Was wäre aber ein Mythos, der nicht von Anfang an im Kult verwurzelt ist?"

[5] See particularly the works of Lily Weiser and Otto Höfler. For appraisal of these works, see Jan de Vries, *Altgermanische Religionsgeschichte* (*Grundriss der germanischen Philologie,* hrsg. von Hermann Paul, 12/I and 12/II [Berlin: Walter de Gruyter & Co. [1956–1957]), I, 79–80, 495.

[6] *Einige vendelzeitliche Bilddenkmäler und die literarische Überlieferung* in *Bayerische Akademie der Wissenschaften, Sitzungsberichte, philosophisch-historische Klasse* (München, 1964), Jahrgang 1964, Heft 6, pp. 1–50 and 3 plates.

mutually elucidate one another and afford a glimpse into the recesses of Germanic antiquity.

The deciphering of the bronze helmet plates and bracteates found at Vendel, Torslunda, Valsgärde, Pliezhausen, Gutenstein, Obrigheim, and Sutton Hoo (all dating from approximately the seventh century A.D.) has long intrigued scholars. In the main, the results of their investigations have relied on conjecture and on some untenable hypotheses. Generally the interpretations have tended to rest on the prevailing premise regarding the *Heldensage* itself: if the representations are not of gods, then they are of heroes who can be identified in history and/or epic.[7] This assumption has led to explanations which violate both the artistic unity of the depictions and their apotropaic function. One such argument holds that since the late medieval literary sources attribute deeds of a cult nature to specific heroes, the much earlier pictorial plates must represent these heroes.[8] Obviously circular and faulty, this argument invites correction and makes imperative a re-evaluation of the relationship between the older pictorial motifs and their literary "counterparts," for the similarities between the plastic and the literary representations may rest more plausibly in the common mythical-religious ground from which both have sprung. Interpretations based on these deeply rooted folk beliefs gain in cohesiveness over against those which rely on specific attributes of gods or heroes for identification.

Part I of this essay will deal with the pictorial ornamentations from the Germanic helmets and bracteates found in Sweden (Torslunda, Vendel, and Valsgärde), in south Germany (Gutenstein, Obrigheim, and Pliezhausen), and in England (Sutton Hoo). Investigation of the figural themes should elucidate their archetypal character and confirm their function as *signa sacra.* The discussion will proceed on the assumption that the helmet and bracteate motifs can provide guidelines according to which the Germanic *Heldensage,* and for the present essay *Beowulf* and *Grettis saga* in particular, should be examined. The cul-

[7] Karl Hauck, "Alemannische Denkmäler der vorchristlichen Adelskultur" in *Zeitschrift für württembergische Landesgeschichte* (Stuttgart: W. Kohlhammer Verlag, 1957), Vol. XVI, Jahrgang 1957, Heft 1, p. 7: "Wir übergehen an dieser Stelle *das Faktum* [italics mine], dass diese Riten in dieser Bildüberlieferung stets von ganz bestimmten Helden erzählt werden . . ." See also the remark: "Nachdem sich dartun lässt, dass wir es im Bereich der Bildbleche in der Regel mit Szenen aus der heroischen Überlieferung zu tun haben und nicht mit Götterbildern . . ." (pp. 16–17).

[8] *Ibid.*, pp. 4–5. Hauck suggests that the plates can serve as guide for the reconstruction of earlier forms of the medieval epics.

Plate 1. Torslunda. 2/1. Bronze matrix for making helmet designs. The matrix as pictured is two times the size of the original.

Plate 2. Torslunda. 2/1. Bronze matrix for making helmet designs.

Plate 3. Sutton Hoo. 2/1. Detail from the purse lid.

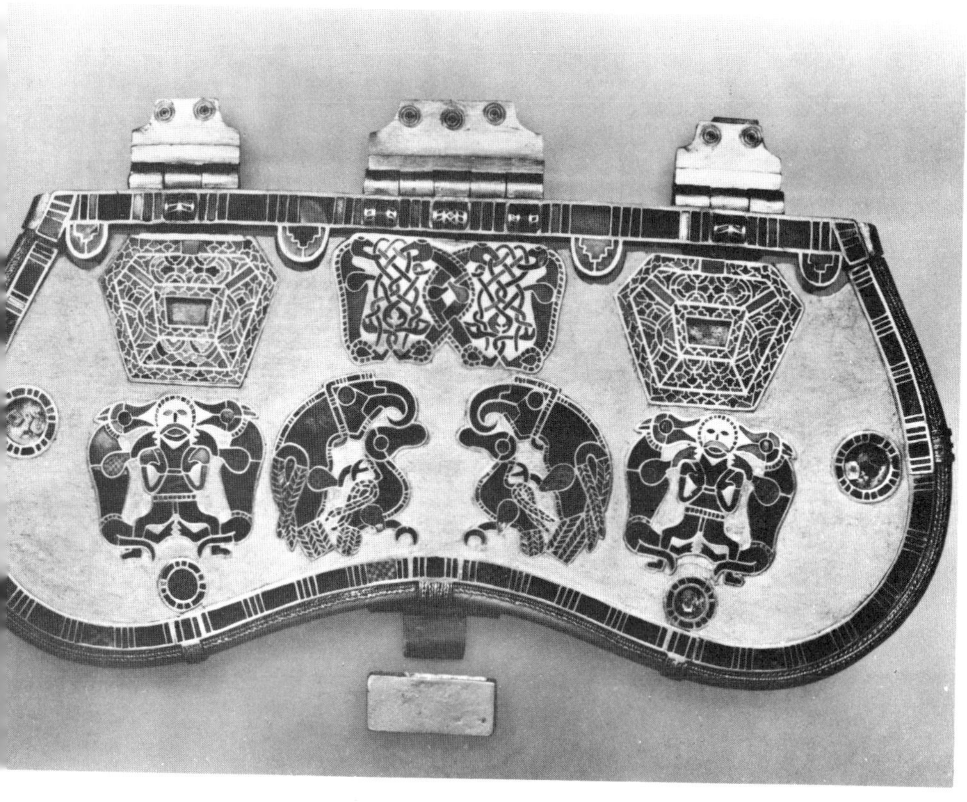

Plate 4. Sutton Hoo. App. 1/2. The purse lid with designs in cloisonné.

Plate 5. Vendel I. 2/1. Motif detail from the helmet.

Plate 6. Vendel I. 1/1. Fragment from the helmet showing detail above left eyebrow.

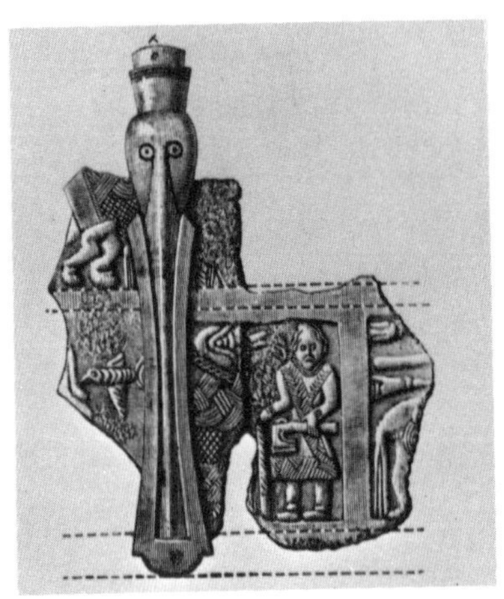

Plate 7. Vendel I. 1/2. Fragment of the helmet,center back.

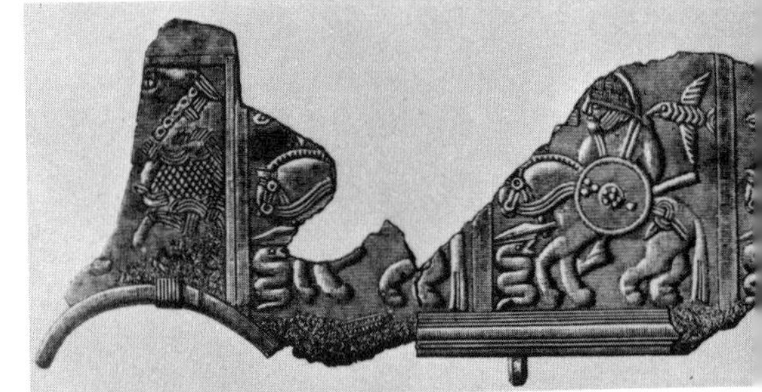

Plate 8. Vendel I. 1/2. Fragment from left side of the helmet.

Plate 9. Valsgärde 8. 1/1. Design from the helmet.

Plate 10. Valsgärde 6. 1/1. Design from the helmet.

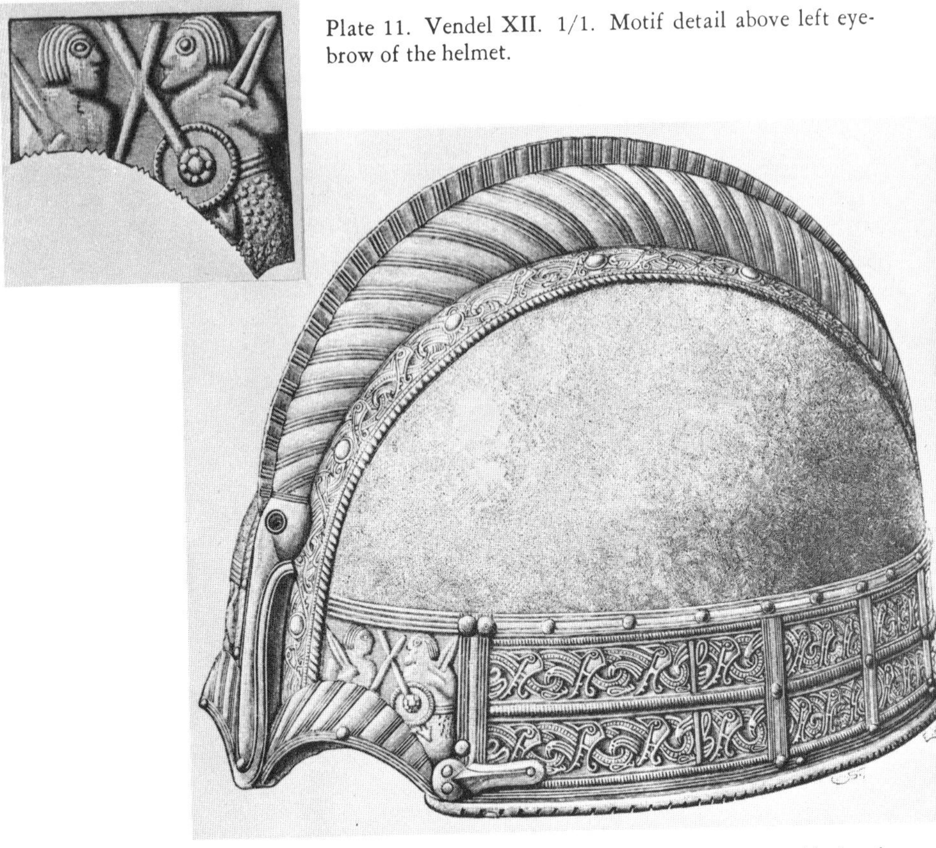

Plate 11. Vendel XII. 1/1. Motif detail above left eyebrow of the helmet.

Plate 12. Vendel XII. 1/2. The complete helmet; the right side has been reconstructed.

Plate 13. Vendel XIV. 1/1. Motif detail above eyebrows of the helmet.

Plate 14. Vendel XIV. 1/3. The complete helm

Plate 15. Torslunda. 2/1. Bronze matrix for making helmet designs.

Plate 16. Gutenstein. 1/1. Fragmentary detail of silver foil design found as sheathing on a sword scabbard.

Plate 17. Gutenstein. 2/3. Reconstruction of the bracteate fragments; drawing by I. Müller.

Plate 18. Obrigheim. 1/1. Reconstruction of the bracteate; drawing by I. Müller.

Plate 19. Sutton Hoo. 1/1. Motif detail from the helmet.

Plate 20. Sutton Hoo. Reconstruction of a motif from the helmet.

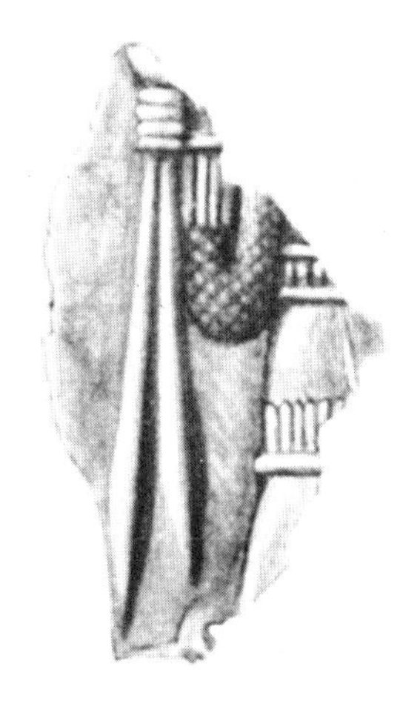

Plate 21. Odin's Hill, Uppsala. 2/1. Fragmentary design.

Plate 22. Vendel I. 1/1. Fragment from the left side of the helmet.

Plate 23. Vendel I. 3/4. Fragment from the right side of the helmet.

Plate 24. Vendel I. 1/2. The complete helmet.

Plate 25. Valsgärde 8. 1/1. Motif detail from the helmet.

Plate 26. Sutton Hoo. 1/1. Motif detail from the helmet.

Plate 27. Pliezhausen. 1/1. Drawing of the bracteate by W. Hilpert.

tural and religious background revealed in the decorative motifs could well shed light on various aspects in the literary works. Yet, without an analysis of the self-contained internal structure of these works, the motifs would merely represent interesting sidelights, but their integral function—the only valid reason for their appearance in the poem or saga—would remain undemonstrated. Through the combined application of these two methods, the cultural and the aesthetic, the genius and uniqueness of the Beowulf poem and the *Grettis saga,* their likenesses and differences, may hopefully be brought out. Part II will deal with *Beowulf,* Part III with the *Grettis saga* in their relationship to the motif-cycle discovered in the pictorial plates. The progression from one part to the next will make apparent the progressive secularization of the once mythical-religious *topoi.*

Old Germanic Helmets and Bracteates

Two thematic cycles on the helmet plates can be differentiated for convenience of discussion: (1) initiation rites for the warrior, and (2) his responsibility and fate.

Initiation Rites for the Warrior

Tribal organization generally includes puberty rites, initiation to full manhood, and the like. These involve tests of strength and valor, introduction to the secrets, history, and responsibilities of the tribe, death of the old life and reawakening to the new. By analogy with this almost universal phenomenon among primitive peoples, and on the basis of what can be gleaned about the religious history of the Germanic tribes from outside sources, such initiation practices and cults can be assumed for the early Germanic period. Tacitus, Ammianus Marcellinus, and Procopius throw some light on customs among various Germanic tribes: among the Taifali, proof of manhood consisted in conquering a wild boar or bear; among the Chatti, in killing an enemy; among the Heruli, in fighting without a protective weapon.[9]

The plates from Torslunda, Sutton Hoo, and Vendel I present almost identical illustrations of the conquering or fettering of a bearlike monster (see Plates 1–3,5). Schück and Stjerna took the Torslunda and Vendel depictions (Plates 22 and 23) to be of the heroes Ragnar Lod-

[9] Ammianus Marcellinus, *Rerum gestarum libri qui supersunt,* III, xxxi, 9, 5 (on the Taifali); Tacitus, *Germania,* Chap. 31 (on the Chatti); Procopius, *History of the Wars,* I, sec. 2, xxv, 27, 28 (on the Heruli).

brok and Beowulf respectively.[10] Recent scholars, however, are quite unanimous in associating the pictures with the cult practices mentioned above, with deeds of bravery to test the initiate.[11] That two monstrous beasts have to be contended with, as shown on one Torslunda depiction (Plate 2) and on the Sutton Hoo purse, where the motif occurs twice as a symmetrical pair on either side of the purse lid (Plate 4), would seem only to increase the champion's prowess. The Torslunda plates are molds from a smithy, used, no doubt, to make plates for helmets similar to the one of Vendel I. On this helmet, the monster-quelling motif occurs as a pair on the frontal side above the eyebrows (see Plates 5, 6, 8, and 23). The fragmentary piece on the left frontal side (Plate 6) apparently presents a slight variation in the posture of the monster and also a reversal of warrior and monster from left to right, which gives symmetrical balance to the frontal presentation. A duplication of the right frontal motif occurs on the back side of the helmet (Plate 7), and fills in the space between the two series of mounted warriors that run along the sides of the helmet as a frieze (Plate 24).

Interesting to note is the stylization of this monster-quelling motif on the Sutton Hoo purse lid, especially in the top center design (see Plate 4). The paired motif of Plate 3 is here repeated in an interlocked design, but, whereas the monsters markedly correspond to those of the more realistic depiction on the lid, the warrior has been resolved into a complex of intertwining lines.

Further development toward abstraction can be seen on the Valsgärde 8 and the Valsgärde 6 helmets. The surface of the helmet from the grave-find of Valsgärde 8 is covered with three horizontally parallel zones of pressed bronze plates and two semicircular fields on either side of the comb. The zoomorphic design shown in Plate 9 appears repeated throughout on the lower band of plates and consequently occurs frontally above the eyebrows. The horse-and-rider motif of Plate 25 forms a frieze in the second or middle zone on the left side, with reversal of direction on the right side. In the third zone, all the larger

[10] Henrik Schück, "Til Lodbroks-sagan," in *Svenska fornminnesföreningens tidskrift*, II (1902), pp. 138–139. Knut Stjerna, *Essays on Questions connected with the Old English Poem of Beowulf*, trans. John R. Clark Hall (Coventry: Viking Club, Society for Northern Research; Extra Series, 1912), III, 44–45 and 47.

[11] See de Vries, *Altgermanische Religionsgeschichte*, I, 363, 492–493, 498, 503. See also Otto Höfler, *Siegfried, Arminius und die Symbolik* (Heidelberg: Carl Winter Verlag, 1961), pp. 87–88, n. 240dd; and Beck, *Einige vendelzeitliche Bilddenkmäler*, pp. 45–48.

fields appear to have depicted the same rider scene as in the second zone. The zoomorphic design of the first zone, however, appears in this third zone in a three-cornered field all the way to the back of the right side. It would thus seem that this animal motif also filled in the frieze design of the rider in the relatively same position as on the Vendel I helmet, but higher up. The middle of the left semicircle in zone four contains the rider motif of Plate 25, and in the semicircle to the right of the comb the zoomorphic design again appears. Since the helmet is badly damaged and corroded, it cannot be determined whether other of the irregular fields in the half circles once contained this pattern.

From the Valsgärde 8 animal design a highly stylized monster motif emerges. Two compositional interpretations suggest themselves. Along the midline, standing in locked combat are either two monsters (the champion having been omitted from the design, otherwise comparable to the Torslunda [Plate 2] and Sutton Hoo [Plate 3] pattern) or monster and champion, the arrangement being the familiar one from Torslunda Plate 1 and Vendel Plate 5. The similarity of the two figures would be noteworthy even with the two unalike adversaries represented. But close observation reveals some differences. The long tail on the right figure for instance, is lacking on the left. The right figure would thus be the monster, the left the champion. This second interpretation would nicely account for "irregularities in the pattern" referred to by Arwidsson, who, expecting the figures to be identical, instead attributes the irregularities to the artisan's lack of skill.[12]

The stylization of the motif on the Sutton Hoo purse would, however, seem to indicate a tendency to eliminate the warrior from the pattern. This process is all but complete in the helmet design from Valsgärde 6 (the contents of this grave-find are younger than those of Vendel I and Valsgärde 8 [the latter two, *ca.* A.D. 650]). The zoomorphic design under discussion appears on Valsgärde 6 in a finer and more elaborate composition of four monsters grouped two against two (see Plate 10). From the degree of stylization and the position on the

[12] Greta Arwidsson, *Die Gräberfunde von Valsgärde,* II: *Valsgärde 8,* (*Acta Musei Antiquitatum Septentrionalium, Regiae Universitatis Upsaliensis IV*, ed. Sune Lindqvist [Uppsala and Stockholm: Almqvist och Wiksells Boktryckeri A. B.; København: Ejnar Munksgaard, 1954], p. 127: ". . . weder eine selbständige Schöpfung noch eine stilistisch gute Arbeit. Durch Unregelmässigkeiten, falsche Ausdeutungen und unachtsames Einfügen füllender Details hat der eine Künstler fast vollständig den eleganten Rhythmus und das feine Gefühl verloren [in contrast to the work on other pieces in the grave-find and to Valsgärde 6].

helmet—a band around the bottom edge and one cutting vertically through the two halves of the helmet on either side—and from the fact that the monsters may appear both sideways and upside down, pure ornamentation would seem to have replaced the more primitive realism of Vendel I or of the Torslunda molds. This perhaps indicates a gradual weakening of the original religious and magic function associated with these *signa sacra.*

The beaded edges on the stylized representations of this motif (Plates 4, 9, and 10) are reminiscent of a scaley hide, and the winglike appendages and tail would suggest a dragon-type creature. Thus it is apparent that this motif may be represented by a range of formidable beasts, real or imaginary: the wild boar (as Tacitus suggests), the bear, the dragon or mythical monster.

The shaggy trousers of the Torslunda warrior in Plate 1, the plaited pattern on the other Torslunda warrior, Plate 2, and the tunic of the Vendel I warrior, with a border of plaiting (Plate 5), suggest the rough coat and plaiting seen also on the monster (Plates 1, 2, and 5). Fragmentary bits of this plaiting as part of the beast also appear on the Vendel I helmet, on the eye-guard (Plate 23) and above the rider frieze center back (Plate 7). These similar patterns bring to mind a certain likeness between the champion and his adversary, as has already tentatively been proposed for the Valsgärde 8 motif. Animal names for individuals and tribes, depictions and later descriptions of the wearing of animal masks, of theriomorphic transformations, of the appearance of ancestors or the dead in animal form, and so on attest to shamanistic beliefs among the Germanic tribes. Such animal affinities found obvious expression in warrior groups like the *berserkir* (bear-skins) or the *úlfheðnar* (wolf-skins).

Two warriors engaged in combat with one another make up another motif. It appears on the helmets of Vendel XII and XIV and on the helmet of Sutton Hoo. On the Vendel XII helmet the representation probably formed a pair on either frontal side above the eyebrows (Plates 11 and 12), as it also does on Vendel XIV (Plates 13 and 14). On the Sutton Hoo helmet, the same theme occurs once on the back side, filling in the series of mounted warrior panels.[13] The two warriors en-

[13] For a description of this helmet, see Karl Hauck, "Germanische Bilddenkmäler des frühen Mittelalters," in *Deutsche Vierteljahresschrift für Literaturwissenschaft und Geistesgeschichte,* Vol. XXXI, Heft 3 (1957), p. 362 n. 37. See Plate 7 for comparable position on the Vendel I helmet.

gaged in hand-to-hand combat might conceivably represent a type of *Zweikampf* or duel, in which the initiate must pit his strength against an enemy, as Tacitus reports concerning the Chatti. Germanic tribes also employed the *Zweikampf* as an augury for the coming battle, that is, as a symbol in miniature for the battle itself. Two warriors, chosen from the opposing sides, fight to the death to win the victory for their tribe.[14] Such a contest has religious connotations, being indicative of what Fate or the gods preordained. It should be noted, however, that the placement of this motif on the three helmets corresponds precisely to that of the monster motif on Vendel I. The warriors on the Vendel XII panel (Plate 11) are dressed like the monster-queller on the Torslunda picture (Plate 1), and one of the warriors on Vendel XIV (Plate 13) has the same attire as the fighter of Vendel I (Plate 5). None of these warriors is helmeted. These correspondences would seem to affirm the explanation that here too initiation rites are depicted.

On one of the molds from Torslunda and on bracteates from Gutenstein and Obrigheim an *úlfheðinn*-type warrior appears in skins, tail, and mask (Plates 15, 16, 17, and 18). The wolf figure to the left on the Gutenstein and Obrigheim fragments (Plates 17 and 18) presents a submissive aspect of the warrior, as seen by his gestures of handing over the sword and sheath with bowed head and of releasing his grasp on the lance. Enough of a pattern remains on these bracteates to reconstruct a wolf-warrior on the right (Plates 17 and 18) in the same attitude as the one on Torslunda Plate 15, who with uplifted head is ready to draw his sword. In addition, a helmeted figure, like the one on the Torslunda plate, can also be surmised between the two wolf figures on the Gutenstein and Obrigheim plates. The donning of bear-skins or wolf-skins, tails, and masks made up part of the initiation ritual; it was carried over into the cults of *berserkir* and *úlfheðnar*, and was commonly associated with the appearance of the *Totenheer* (Host of the Dead) or *wilde Jagd* (Wild Hunt). It was not just an act of costuming; the warrior so attired underwent in fact the transformation, felt and acted like a wolf or bear.[15] The *berserkir* were particularly known for their invulnerability to weapons and fire.[16]

[14] See Höfler, *Kultische Geheimbünde,* p. 155; de Vries, *Altgermanische Religionsgeschichte,* I, 429–431, and II, 13–14.

[15] De Vries, *Altgermanische Religionsgeschichte,* I, 223, 454–455; Höfler, *Kultische Geheimbünde,* pp. 16–22, 56–57, 250–253, 323.

[16] De Vries, *Altgermanische Religionsgeschichte,* I, 493.

The explanation that the wolf figure on the right is about to attack the helmeted figure, as Hauck suggests,[17] does violence to the organic structure of the depiction as a whole and fails to account for the stance of the helmeted figure. It is at once apparent, even from the Torslunda plate alone, that the helmeted figure is not in fighting posture, but rather is leading and drawing the wolf-warrior on. Not only the airy unconcern for an impending attack on his person, but also the lightness of step, with the peculiar curved foot position and the several lances, mark the depiction as a "weapon dance." R. L. S. Bruce-Mitford has correctly interpreted this stance on the Sutton Hoo "twins," where it also appears, as a stylized dance movement (see Plate 20).[18] Comparable to the stance shown on the Sutton Hoo motif is the fragmented depiction from Odin's Hill, Uppsala, showing two spears similarly grasped in one hand (Plate 21). Unfortunately the remainder of the figural motif is obliterated, but the geographic distribution of the motif throughout Germanic territories, north, south, and west, attests to its universal meaning. The Sutton Hoo find illuminates particularly the close connection that still existed between Anglo-Saxon England and Sweden during the sixth and seventh centuries.

Tacitus describes the sword dance as a form of amusement among the Germanic tribes, but it is more likely that such weapon dances belonged to ritualistic mock deaths and initiation rites.[19] Höfler associates the Torslunda wolf (Plate 15), along with the other monster motifs of the Torslunda series, with cult ritual.[20] A sword dancer in wolf's attire appears on a depiction of the Zürich Carneval as late as

[17] Hauck, "Alemannische Dankmäler," pp. 12, 16. Stjerna (*Essays*, p. 49) interprets the Torslunda wolf figure as a "she-wolf" from an episode in *Beowulf* [Grendel's dam?].

[18] R. L. S. Bruce-Mitford, "The Sutton Hoo Ship Burial," in *Proceedings of the Suffolk Institute of Archaeology,* Vol. XXV, No. 1 (1949), p. 50. The identical foot position for the warrior on the Torslunda picture (Plate 2) requires an expansion of the interpretation: the foot position indicates, apparently, not merely a stylized dance movement, but also more generally, perhaps, the ritualistic nature of the acts involved or the ecstatic condition accompanying all these acts. The horn-helmeted figure of the aiding god, as eidolon of a supernatural power, appearing on Valsgärde 8 (Plate 25) also seems to have this foot position.

[19] Tacitus, *Germania,* Chap. 24. See also Robert Stumpfl, *Kultspiele der Germanen als Ursprung des mittelalterlichen Dramas* (Berlin: Junker und Dünnhaupt Verlag, 1936), pp. 254–259; Höfler, *Kultische Geheimbünde,* pp. 32, 154 ff.; de Vries, *Altgermanische Religionsgeschichte,* I, 444.

[20] Höfler, *Siegfried, Arminius,* p. 88 n. 240 dd. Höfler's earlier interpretation (*Kultische Geheimbünde*, p. 57) agreed with Hauck's.

1578.[21] On the Sutton Hoo helmet the sword dancers (Plates 19 and 20) are placed, as one might expect if the theme portrays elements of the initiation rite, on the frontal side above the eyebrows. With primitive peoples the very essence of the dance consists in a mediating between the human and suprahuman sphere, between the realm of the dead and the realm of the living, a function attributable to its ecstasy-inducing power. Such an ecstatic state can also be witnessed in the battle fury of the *berserkir* and *úlfheðnar* and in the wild raging of the *Totenheer* and *wilde Jagd*. As in other primitive tribes, the young Germanic warrior no doubt underwent a ritualistic initiation consisting of a kind of mock death and reawakening which constituted his readiness for the duties of manhood and his being accepted as a full-fledged member of the tribe.[22] It is within this context that the Gutenstein and Obrigheim bracteates (Plates 17 and 18) will find their most coherent explanation: an *úlfheðinn* in two attitudes, subdued as in a mock death and aroused to battle frenzy. The transition from the one to the other is indicated by the mediating sword-dance figure.

The analogous placement of the bear or monster motif, the *Zweikampf*, and the sword dance on all these helmets (frontally above the eyebrows and center back) cannot be merely accidental. Weapons and accoutrements of battle had very special meaning, were handed down from father to son; swords were given names, and helmet, sword, lance, and byrnie were most revered objects.[23] Altogether one can assume that tradition was followed in their making, in what was depicted on them and where it was placed. The practical function of these emblems must not be overlooked. The emblems speak for the hero's success and prowess in battle and thus serve as amulets and bode luck for the fight. Furthermore, any magic function which they served would also demand precise placement of the symbols.

The Warrior's Responsibility and Fate

On the left side of the Vendel I helmet there appears in multiple series a warrior in full gear on horseback, with his lance pointed at a coiled snake (see Plate 22). Chthonic monsters of the serpent-dragon type constitute an almost universal phenomenon in cult rituals and

[21] Höfler, *Kultische Geheimbünde*, pp. 56, 60.

[22] De Vries, *Altgermanische Religionsgeschichte*, I, 459 n. 1, 493, 499, and 501; Höfler, *Kultische Geheimbünde*, pp. 236–237.

[23] See de Vries, *Altgermanische Religionsgeschichte*, I, 372.

mythology all over the world. In times long past the god or gods established cosmic order out of the amorphous chaos by overcoming the monsters. In the Germanic world Thor's fight against the giants and the *miðgarðsormr* is representative of this struggle against destructive forces of evil. Attempts to identify the Vendel rider with Thor have failed, since no literary confirmation exists which could explain the birds in this context.[24] Identification with Odin, on the other hand, has been proposed on the basis of the presence of the two birds, supposedly Huginn and Muninn;[25] but battle with the serpent cannot be attested for Odin, and the two birds are not two ravens but are the birds of prey, the eagle and the raven (note the differences in beaks and body markings). Thus, identity with specific mythical figures cannot be estalished with conclusiveness.

Stjerna's proposal that the depictions on the helmet represent Beowulf and his dragon fight (Plate 22) and his attendant Wiglaf (Plate 23) and that the birds might be connected with the name of Beowulf's death place, *Earnanæs*,[26] can be countered with other, more convincing explanations. First, Beowulf was not mounted on horseback when he proceeded to the dragon's lair. Second, and more important, the eagle and the raven made up a natural component of any battle scene; their accompaniment with the warrior indicated assurance that the enemy would fall to their prey.[27] There is no justification for interpreting these depictions as faithful illustrations of either gods or heroes and their deeds. Such solutions either fail to explain all the attributes in the depiction or destroy the unity and simultaneity of the picture by joining

24 See Beck, *Einige vendelzeitliche Bilddenkmäler*, p. 10.

25 De Vries (*Altergermanische Religionsgeschichte*, Vol. II [1st ed., 1937], sec. 34) states that the serpent remains unexplained in the configuration Odin, Huginn, Muninn. In the second edition, however, he is more decisive in his identification of the pictorial plate with Odin. See I, 318; II, 43, 61–63.

26 Stjerna, *Essays*, pp. 44, 46.

27 See Stjerna, *Essays*, p. 46; Hauck, "Alemannische Denkmäler," p. 17 n. 33; Beck, *Einige vendelzeitliche Bilddenkmäler*, pp. 11, 25–31; de Vries, *Altgermanische Religionsgeschichte*, II, 61–62. The combination raven-eagle-wolf as predators on the battlefield strikingly appears in the Old English poetry (*Beowulf*, ll. 3024–3027; *Brunaburg*, ll. 60–65; *Elene*, ll. 110–114; *Judith*, ll. 204–212), and the Finnsburg fragment mentions birds and the wolf as omens of impending battle (ll. 5, 6, and 34). References to the raven, eagle, and wolf and their role in the battle slaughter are also found in the *Poetic Edda*, the skaldic poetry, and the sagas. For example, the raven appears as a good omen in the *Reginsmál*, verse 20, and in *Njáls saga*, Chap. 79. Thorgils' ditty, verse 3 in the *Laxdœla saga*, Chap. 65, speaks of "feeding the raven" after Helgi Hardbeinsson had been killed.

together a sequence of events. It is, however, still possible to look for an interpretation that unites mythical-religious conceptions with historical-secular happenings.

The overcoming of a chthonic being, monster, dragon, or giant took place not just *in illo tempore,* but was repeated and reactualized periodically to insure the re-creation of order and security. It may, for instance, have been reenacted yearly in rituals symbolizing the change from the old cycle to the New Year, or as an enthronization rite in which the king legitimized his reign by performing anew what the gods did long ago.[28] Here the transference to the political-historical realm is already accomplished. The borderline between myth and history is a fluid one; one only need recall that the Scandinavian kings traced their genealogies back to the gods.

The crushing of the political enemy was another instance of creating and wresting the known order from the destructive and hostile forces around it. Otto Höfler has cited convincing examples from Egypt, Persia, and India of the political enemy being actually visualized as the dragon or monster itself. Victory over the enemy was generally accompanied by ritualistic ceremonies: the Persian hero Ardašir poured molten metal down the throat of the defeated monster; King Mithradates of the Parthians (*ca.* 90 B.C.) performed the same rite on the defeated Roman enemy when General Manius Aquilius had to capitulate; the same fate is reported for Licinius Crassus (53 B.C.), the partner in the Triumvirate of Caesar and Pompeii, although the story may be modeled on that of Manius Aquilius.[29] Thus, warding off the tribal enemy was seen as a reenactment of the mythical struggle against the chthonic monster *in illo tempore.* The fact that historical events were experienced as a series of acts that followed mythical precedents made the shift from the mythical-religious realm to the political-historical scene a natural one, and vice versa. The *imperator imperii* of Roman coins easily made the transfer to *imperator christianissimus,* the emperor being victor for Christ and fighting the enemies of Christendom.

Pictorial representations of the serpent-dragon motif in the Germanic

[28] See Mircea Eliade, *The Myth of the Eternal Return,* trans. Willard R. Trask (London: Routledge and Kegan Paul, 1955), pp. 27–28, 34–35, 37, and *The Sacred and the Profane* (New York: Harper and Bros., 1961), pp. 77–79, 105; also de Vries "Betrachtungen," pp. 159–162; Höfler, *Kultische Geheimbünde,* pp. 249, 322.

[29] Höfler, *Siegfried, Arminius,* pp. 16–20, esp. p. 19. For other examples, see Eliade, *The Sacred and the Profane,* pp. 47–49.

north may have received added stimulus from Roman coins and from the flags of Roman legions which portrayed the "draco."[30] But such a universal symbol no doubt overlapped with indigenous conceptions, for in Germanic literature the Romance *draco* gradually replaced the Germanic *ormr, wurm, lindwurm* (Icel. *dreki,* OHG *dracho*) in the whole gamut of its connotations.[31]

The insignium on the helmet thus depicts a warrior, any warrior (hero or king) who overcomes the enemy, envisioned as the primordial archenemy, and whose act is accompanied by good omens, the birds of prey. As an archetypal representation, the depiction becomes a meaningful whole, whereas former interpretations account only for some individual attributes.

On the right side of the Vendel I helmet, a similar horse and rider proceed to battle with an eidolon-type figure guiding the reins of the horse (Plates 23 and 24). The two birds of prey again appear in the rider's wake. The guiding figure is smaller in proportion to the rider, perhaps in accordance with the artistic principle, common in medieval art, which subordinates related themes to the main subject. The reduced size does not mean that the figure is of lower rank or ultimately of less importance, only of lesser artistic importance within the pictorial context; it possibly renders a psychological reality.[32] Likewise, on the Valsgärde 8, Sutton Hoo, and Pliezhausen plates there appear smaller figures who guide the spear and/or lead the horse (see Plates 25, 26, and 27). These eidolon figures apparently represent numinous powers that aid in the fight. Beck cites numerous literary examples that point to a general religious conception of "guiding powers" unconnected with an invocation of any specific god.[33]

The depictions from Valsgärde 8, Sutton Hoo, and Pliezhausen,

[30] Concerning the influence of Roman coins, see Stjerna, *Essays,* pp. 44 and 167; de Vries, *Altgermanische Religionsgeschichte,* I, 318, and II, 42; Beck, *Einige vendelzeitliche Bilddenkmäler,* pp. 14, 23–24. For references to Roman banners with a dragon, see Ammianus Marcellinus, *Rerum gestarum,* I, xvi, 12, 39; Höfler, *Siegfried, Arminius,* pp. 99 ff.

[31] Höfler, *ibid.*

[32] Hauck ("Alemannische Denkmäler," p. 6) relates the eidolon-like figure to the well-established practice of depicting "ausser- und übermenschliche Wesen" in this manner and notes that these eidolon figures assume the relative position of the *numen victoriae* on Roman coins. Interesting to compare in this context is the dwarflike figure pictured on the Bayeux tapestry who has hold of the horse's reins. Could he represent an eidolon figure rather than a dwarf as hostler?

[33] See Beck, *Einige vendelzeitliche Bilddenkmäler,* pp. 31–32.

however, add another element to this same theme.[34] Along with the helpful gods, there appears another figure that imperils horse and rider. Ammianus Marcellinus, the Roman military writer of the fourth century, reports how foot soldiers at the Battle of Strassbourg, A.D. 357, crept under the mounted warriors of the enemy to deal the horse, and therewith the rider, the death blow.[35] The same practice is referred to in the *Konungs skuggsjá* and the *Gull-Þóris saga*.[36] Plates 25, 26, and 27 give realistic illustration to this situation: the enemy, under the horse, plunging his sword into the horse's belly. Thus, despite the aid of the gods and one's own strength, the outcome of the battle may well hang in the balance, even mean the warrior's doom. The equalized rampant lions on the Pliezhausen bracteate (Plate 27) would seem to indicate this precarious point between victory and defeat.[37] Such a specific war practice must have carried a meaning universally understood, as the wide geographic distribution of these finds—from Scandinavia in the north, to Anglian Britain in the west, to Alemannic territory in the south—would also indicate.[38] Interpretations that see in the rider the historical hero Ermanaric, whom the god Odin himself calls home to Valhalla, fail to take into consideration the evidence from Ammianus, the simultaneity of the depiction,[39] and its traditional character. True, Odin is an unreliable and unpredictable god who can lead his warrior to destruction, but is it then likely that he would function as an apotropaic symbol, as much as the warrior might be desirous of being called home by Odin, of being dedicated and sacrificed to the god?[40] The all-pervasive factor that ruled over both gods and men was

[34] The same depiction occurs on the helmet of Valsgärde 7, which Arwidsson considers much finer in artistic quality (*Die Gräberfunde von Valsgärde*, p. 132).

[35] Ammianus Marcellinus, *Rerum gestarum*, I, xvi, 12, 22.

[36] See *Konungs skuggsjá*, Chap. 38, and *Gull-Þóris saga*, ed. Kr. Kålund (København: Samfund til Udg. af gammel nordisk Litteratur, 1898), p. 37.

[37] Beck, *Einige vendelzeitliche Bilddenkmäler*, p. 40.

[38] Swedish origin or influence in respect to the Sutton Hoo helmet is discussed by R. L. S. Bruce-Mitford, "Sutton Hoo and Sweden," in *Archaeological News Letter*, No. 1–2 (1948–1950), pp. 4–5. The Sutton Hoo grave cannot be dated earlier than A.D. 650; the helmet, however, was already an heirloom when placed in the grave and dates probably from the sixth century.

[39] Hauck ("Alemannische Denkmäler," p. 6) interprets the depiction as the opening of the battle with the traditional hurling of the spear and the battle's close with Odin calling his hero home. On identification with Ermanaric, cf. Hauck, "Germanische Bilddenkmäler," p. 362.

[40] No doubt the aristocratic warrior did desire to be called home by Odin (see Höfler, *Kultische Geheimbünde*, pp. 238, 335–340), but in view of the fact that the

Fate. With it the warrior had to reckon in any case. But how does Fate manifest itself? It can only be experienced in specific moments, especially in unpredictable situations of sudden disaster and almost contrived cunning. The treacherous battle technique attested in the literary sources has all these qualities and aptly carries this meaning on the Valsgärde, Sutton Hoo, and Pliezhausen plates.

The fact that these insignia are found on war gear in such widespread areas, that they allow expansion of the motifs—two guiding figures (Valsgärde variant), two monsters (Torslunda), two sword dancers (Sutton Hoo), and multiplication into a series (the panels of raiders on Vendel I, Valsgärde 8, and Sutton Hoo)—speaks for their repetitive character, suggestive of magic formulae, and hence for their universal significance as archetypes used as apotropaic *signa sacra,* rather than as individualized illustrations of specific gods or heroes. The warrior who went into battle with these emblems on his helmet no doubt sensed the conformity to tradition. He had proved his strength in the cult ordeals, was prepared to defend the tribal order and overcome the enemy in accordance with a precedent established by the gods long ago. Proof of his own prowess, the aid of the gods, the presence of the birds of prey boded good for the outcome of battle. Yet all the while the warrior must be wary of Fate and must accept the possibility of the disastrous alternative.

The life of a warrior may thus be said to follow a pattern: initiation, with mockdeath and reawakening, the undergoing of trials and the performance of deeds of bravery to prove his ability to contend with the enemies of the tribe; periodic transformation into a "werwolf," with ecstatic manifestations of battle fury and great strength, the quelling of monsters and the hated enemy, the dragon; and eventually, after fame, a fateful end in death. The helmet plates and bracteates confront us with this typical lot of the warrior hero, whose life and deeds are to

---

emblems on the helmets serve an apotropaic function, it is scarcely possible to see in the god Odin a protector and guardian. He is not the god who can be invoked, whose blessing and protective powers can be called into action automatically. De Vries seems to misinterpret Höfler's intent when he designates Odin as "Schirmgott" (*Altgermanische Religionsgeschichte,* I, 79). The discrepancy in Odin's character began to be felt as an ethical dichotomy sometime in the seventh and eighth centuries. Starcatherus (Starkaðr), the prototype of an Odin warrior, stands as a pawn between the gods Odin and Thor. Starkad shows regrets in carrying out the sacrifices demanded by Odin when he is liegeman to the kings Ali (Onela), Ingeld, and Vikar. Odin's blessing turns out to be a curse in disguise. See de Vries, "Die Starkadsage," in *Germanisch-romanische Monatsschrift,* N. F., Vol. V, No. 4 (1955), p. 296.

be understood as religious participation in the tribal order and cults. Höfler in his *Kultische Geheimbünde der Germanen* continually warns of too specific an interpretation of the evidence, of equating too readily the *Weihekriegertum* with the cult of Odin.[41] The cult rituals illustrated above precede systematized mythology, they are of a more primordial nature, the stuff out of which literary myths grew. The many-sided and ambiguous figure of Odin and his cult are the summation and final expression of these tribal practices and beliefs with their multiple aspects.

Beowulf

The Germanic *Heldensage* can be said to have received its main impetus from this mythical-religious background of cults and tribal organization. This new premise requires a reevaluation of the relationship of the *Heldensage* to history, myth, and the Märchen.

In contrast to the myth and Märchen, the heroic legend is rooted in a real setting with real actors and takes place in a specific historical period. For example: time = the Great Migration; place = Hreosnabeorh, Hrefnesholt, Heorot (the great hall of the Danes at Leire), [Siegfried of] Xanten, [Hagen of] Troja. Historical personages, often thrown together from different periods and assigned roles contrary to known facts, are nonetheless identifiable in the medieval epics: Arminius, † A.D. 21; Ermanaric, † A.D. 374; Attila, † A.D. 453; Theodoric, † A.D. 526; Hygelac,† *ca.* A.D. 520; Ongentheow, † early sixth century; Ohthere, † A.D. 525; Onela, † early sixth century. The names of the great heroes of history and the place of their remarkable deeds remain peculiarly fixed in memory and transmission, whereas the personal and individual qualities and the outer events surrounding these deeds all melt away.

Primitive peoples experience history as separate instances in time when the numinous is actualized in the profane world rather than as a chain of events in the sequence of cause and effect. Whenever victory over the political enemy was achieved, for instance, the precedential act of the gods in subduing the monster of chaos projected itself into real, secular time. Likewise, only those historical personages in and through whom the archetype could be visualized attained the status of hero.[42]

[41] See Höfler, *Kultische Geheimbünde,* pp. 37–38, 43, 50, 77–80, 172, esp. 199, 211, 239, 271.

[42] "Aus einem geschichtlichen Ereignis entsteht erst dann eine Heldensage, wenn in

The individual and specific attributes would then all but disappear in favor of typical and general qualities.[43] Theodoric became a mythical hero in his lifetime, but usually it takes longer for the real image to fade into the typical *heros*. As resubstantiations of their archetypal referents, historical events assumed, therefore, a similarity and repetitiousness which characterizes the Weltanschauung of early cultures.

Because of the original close interaction between history and myth, historical and political realities constituted reflections of religious conceptions. The divine right of kings, in both its pagan and Christian forms, translated the supranatural world structure into the natural order, and the mythical *Weihekriegertum* had its historical counterpart in the *Gefolgschaft*.[44] Even the obscure references in the literary sources which point to Arminius as the historical Siegfried disclose an inseparable fusion with religious beliefs and the cult.[45] "Die Heldensage widerspiegelt also die Geschichte eines bestimmten Zeitalters, . . . dennoch ist ihr Stoff eigentlich nicht geschichtlich."[46]

When it came to literary writing, history did not always provide a handy example that could merge with the archetype. When the poet needed a hero, he not infrequently created his own after the prototype: Beowulf, for example, is not attested among the lineages of the Geats, just as there probably never was a St. George, or Hamlet, Prince of Denmark. Hetel and Hagen lack historical substantiation, as does Star-

---

seinem Träger ein Archetypus wiedererkannt worden ist" (de Vries, "Betrachtungen," p. 162; see also pp. 78, 126, 161, 163). See also Höfler, *Siegfried, Arminius,* pp. 91, 103–104; Schröder, "Mythos und Heldensage," p. 313; Eliade, *The Myth of the Eternal Return,* pp. 39–44.

[43] It is sometimes difficult to determine whether the process has been one of historization of mythical figures (euhemerism) or of mythologizing of historical persons. For the former, Greek epic offers the best examples; the latter characterizes the Germanic *Heldensage*. De Vries, "Betrachtungen," pp. 131, 165. See also Höfler, *Siegfried, Arminius,* pp. 12, 20.

[44] See Schröder, "Mythos und Heldensage," p. 292; and Höfler, "Die Starkadsage," pp. 296–297.

[45] See Höfler, *Siegfried, Arminius,* pp. 27–29 (on the Cherusker and the symbol of the stag in reference to Siegfried); pp. 69–94 (on Trojaberg [*cf.* Hagen of Troja], its proximity to Xanten and its connection with cult ritual); pp. 107–121 and Anhang, pp. 122–161 (on Gnitaheiði = Knetterheide and its connection with Fáfnir and the Varus battle). See also Höfler, *Kultische Geheimbünde,* p. 187, on theriomorphic names for tribes.

[46] Jan de Vries, *Altnordische Literaturgeschichte* (*Grundriss der germanischen Philologie,* begründet von Hermann Paul, 15/I; zweite, völlig neubearbeitete Auflage [Berlin: Walter de Gruyter & Co., 1964]), I, 66.

catherus, a type that could conceivably exist at any court.[47] It would be vain to seek for their historical counterparts.

The accuracy of personal names and place-names has given to the literary *Heldensage* the appearance of reliability and has led researchers to overemphasize its historical basis. Evidence from outside sources[48] pointed to the existence of substrata (namely, early forms of the *Preislied* and the *Heldenlied*) which could have provided the skeletal facts about national heroes and their deeds. Lachmann, Schneider, and Heusler, among others, set forth their individual theories, continually shading the argument on this point and that, as to how the *Heldensage* developed from these subforms and to what extent it preserved reliable material. Heusler cautiously avoided equating the *Heldenlied* with the more historical *Preislied*. The difference was one of essence, "im Kern," he states, and does not depend on "Umbildung durch Künstlerphantasie."[49] Yet he barely touched upon the real distinction between them, assuming merely the *Heldenlied*'s heroic, that is, non-historical, matter to be the product of naiveté, a childlike way of looking at the world —which, in the light of more recent research and the newer ideas, could be read to mean "archetypal thinking." But this Heusler promptly contradicts. For in the *Heldenlied* and *Heldensage* it is again the creative, the artistic, and the inventive, the conscious and unconscious re-formation, and the use of *Urmärchen* and *Mythenmärchen* in popular circulation that explain the non-historical aspect of the *Heldenlied* and the *Heldensage*. Thus Heusler falls in line with other scholars who were hard put to find an explanation for a real hero fighting a dragon. The fight with a chthonic being is, however, one of the most striking primary features of the hero pattern. It is therefore out of the question that this motif should have been secondarily adopted.

Traditionally, the Märchen has been regarded as a product of the unconscious free play of the folk imagination. It has been defined in terms of its variant motifs and motif complexes. However, when perceived rather as a consciously structured form in which the motifs occur

[47] See Schröder, "Mythos und Heldensage," p. 291; Höfler, "Die Starkadsage," p. 297, and *Siegfried, Arminius*, p. 89.

[48] Tacitus, *The Annals*, II, lxxxviii. Jordanes, *De origine actibusque getarum*, Chaps. 5, 11, and 24; Alcuin, *Epistolae*, No. 81; Einhard, *Vita Caroli Magni*, Chap. 29.

[49] Andreas Heusler, *Die altgermanische Dichtung* (Darmstadt: Wissenschaftliche Buchgesellschaft, 1957), pp. 162–163.

as variables, the Märchen becomes a special literary genre which has at its disposal the same stock of motifs as the myth and *Heldensage*, motifs drawn from a common layer of experience.[50]

It is one thing to say that historical occurrences and characters have been contaminated by extraneous material, distorted or garbled through long transmission, or purposely reorganized for aesthetic reasons, and another to say, as Schneider did later, that a transformation has taken place which sees in the national hero and political events a mythical reenactment.

Cult organization and the warrior's adherence to traditional cult practices and beliefs from youth to death provided a framework for the typical life of a hero (*Heldenleben*). The *Heldenleben*, no matter where it is encountered, in the *Heldensage*, myth, or Märchen, comprises a certain concatenation of elements. The motifs in the schematic pattern reflect former religious rites and the warrior's lot that now have become tags marking the hero:[51]

A. Unusual beginning in life; remarkable youth.
   1. Venerable ancestors; illustrious heritage, usually harking back to some mysterious origin.
   2. Precocious childhood; some connection with a bear; display of phenomenal strength; subduing of wild beasts; similarity of warrior and foe; ecstatic states of battle fury; weapon dances (skill or strength in use of weapons); invulnerability to weapons (on the part of the hero or the foe); fighting without weapons; duels, hand-to-hand struggles.

B. Adventures of Manhood.
   1. Unusually difficult task, involving courage and strength: defending the tribe, aiding a king against a formidable foe.
      a. The enemy may be some demonic being, in which case the adventure usually involves a subterranean journey.
      b. The appearance of good omens for the struggle; aiding or guiding powers; use of ancestral weapons, swords fashioned by the giants, and so on.
   2. Band of faithful followers; usually with a deserter or traitor.
   3. Acquiring of gold and fame, the spoils of victory, the rewards of courage.

[50] See note 116. See also André Jolles, *Einfache Formen* (zweite unveränderte Auflage; Darmstadt: Wissenschaftliche Buchgesellschaft, 1958), p. 233.
[51] See de Vries, "Betrachtungen," pp. 126, 128.

C. Fateful end, brought about by some cunning, some treachery, a curse or the like, as manifestation of Fate.

The pattern may be filled in with a number of variant motifs, and not every hero's life will manifest all the components. The model allows of expansion at any point, particularly variation of the theme into its opposite: the remarkable beginning may mean the child's being subjected to exposure, or sent off helpless in a boat; the child, instead of showing promise, may begin as unruly or a ne'er-do-well who later turns good. Rearrangement and recombining of the elements of the pattern depend on the ingenuity of the individual poet.

Of all the Germanic heroic epics the Beowulf poem stands both chronologically and spiritually closest to the mythical origin. The Christianization of the Germanic tribes no doubt suppressed the complete mythologizing of the Continental Germanic *Heldensage*, making it appear, on the surface at least, predominantly secular and historical. But it is by no means void of genuine mythical motifs. During the period of conversion, pagan and Christian notions were so interfused that the new beliefs often merely substituted for indigenous ones, thus earlier religious conceptions still were allowed to shine through. *Beowulf* in particular is saturated with these themes. Their presence cannot be attributed to the infiltration of Märchen motifs, for the monsters are central in the poem, the historical events peripheral. Indeed, the same motifs are at home in all three of the genres, myth, Märchen, and *Heldensage*, so there is no reason to suppose dependencies. The two religious streams, pagan and Christian, converged in *Beowulf*. The poet was able to salvage and convert much of his traditional material, making it agreeable to the spirit of his times. His hero, Beowulf, rises from the midst of historical kings and chieftains in a specific setting and at a datable time to become both an image and a model of the ideal warrior, the archetypal hero. If the poem is examined from this point of view, it will become apparent that the hero pattern constitutes the main structural basis for the poem, although the poet conceives his theme on many levels and handles his inherited patterns with freedom and imagination.

Beowulf as Archetypal Hero

BIRTH AND YOUTH

Evidence to support Beowulf's historicity cannot be found in external sources. The fact that his name does not alliterate within the known family genealogies further argues against it, and, indeed, the name itself suggests a non-historical origin, for it implies a connection with "bear heroes." The etymology of the name, first proposed by Jacob Grimm and still the most logical one, means "bee-wolf," "foe of the bee."[52] Many a hero in Germanic literature boasts a bear name, for instance Bjǫrn, Bjarni, Bjarki. Such heroes were either conceived or reared by a bear, had thus also the strength of a bear, and often, too, sometime in their life had killed a bear. Well-known bear heroes from other *Heldensagen* include Scyld, Siegfried, Bödvar bjarki, Orm Stórolfsson, Grettir inn sterki.

The bear is associated with early religious beliefs and the cults: initiation rites, vegetation cults, and marriage ceremonies.[53] Fear and reverence account for the tabu-names the bear acquired: German *Bär*, "der Braune"; Old Slavic *medvědĭ*, "honey-knower"; Finnish *mesikämen*, "honey-hand"; Swedish *sötfot*, "sweet-foot."[54] In folk belief the bear sired children by stealing women or wresting the unborn child from pregnant mothers. Bear heroes typically performed feats of great strength: Beowulf, for instance, shows his unusual might in binding five giants and laying low a brood of them and in killing sea monsters (ll. 420–422);[55] in swimming five nights in the sea, killing nine sea monsters (ll. 574–575); in swimming across the sea with thirty suits of armor (ll. 2360–2362). These deeds and his glorious and worthy youth, mentioned in lines 419 ff. and lines 2425 ff., apparently stand to contradict the "sluggish youth" reference deeming Beowulf a slothful and feeble princeling, without honor at the mead-bench when he was young at Hrethel's court (ll. 2183 ff.).[56]

Theriomorphic sympathies and the practice of shamanism constitute well-known aspects of primitive religion. "Bear warrior" and "wolf warrior" (cf. the *berserkir* and *úlfheðnar*) have survived in the Old

[52] Grimm (*Deutsche Mythologie* [2 vols., dritte Ausgabe; Göttingen: Dieterichsche Buchhandlung, 1854], II, 342) gives the etymology of *Beowulf* as *bienenwolf* but interprets it as the *specht* instead of the bear.

[53] See de Vries, *Altgermanische Religionsgeschichte*, I, 362–363.

[54] Friedrich Kluge, Alfred Götze, and Walther Mitzka, *Etymologisches Wörterbuch der deutschen Sprache* (17. Auflage; Berlin: Walter de Gruyter & Co., 1957), pp. 50–51 (s.v. *Bär*); Friedrich Panzer, *Beowulf*, Vol. I of *Studien zur germanischen Sagengeschichte* (München: C. H. Beck'sche Verlagsbuchhandlung, 1910), p. 392.

[55] Line citations and quotations from *Beowulf* are taken from *Beowulf and the Fight at Finnsburg*, ed. Friedrich Klaeber (3rd ed.; Boston: D. C. Heath and Co., 1950).

[56] See pp. 178–179.

English poetic vocabulary as the normal words for hero and warrior: OE *beorn* < **bernu* (ON *bjǫrn,* "the brown animal, the bear") and OE *freca* < **freka* (ON *frekr,* "greedy"; ON *freki,* "the greedy one, the wolf"; ON *freka,* "battle fury").[57] Champions of the *berserkr* and *úlfheðinn* type, as noted earlier, exhibit the same characteristics as their adversary, both physically and psychically. Their terrifying appearance goes hand in hand with their apotropaic function of warding off forces inimical to the tribe, foes of war or nonhuman powers.[58] The Harii, according to Tacitus, painted their bodies and shields black to strike fear into the enemy;[59] and the Roman legions let their dragon banners fly. Thus, in effect, the struggle becomes one of demons versus demons. It has often been noted that Beowulf bears a strong resemblance to his adversary Grendel.[60] Beowulf has a formidable grasp equal to that of thirty men (ll. 379–381); with his bearlike hug and tight grip he wrestles with his foes and crushes them to death (ll. 751 ff., ll. 963 ff., ll. 1533–1534, ll. 2505–2507). Grendel, too, has a mighty grip and a hand with steel-like claws (ll. 835–836, ll. 984–987). Beowulf prefers to fight without a weapon (cf. the Heruli), single-handed, foe against foe (ll. 435 ff., ll. 677 ff.). Weapons would do him no good in any case, for Grendel is impervious to them (cf. the *berserkir*) and thus uses none himself (ll. 433–434, ll. 801–805). Against the dragon, Beowulf would fain not use a weapon, but knows not how to come to grips with fire and venom (ll. 2518–2524). This latter represents a variation on the traditional theme of immunity, such as the *berserkir*, for instance, had against fire. The *Beowulf* poet freely innovates within his tradition-bound material, as he also does with the eagle-raven-wolf motif, to be discussed presently.

The hero and his adversary are extremes, both of which have an affinity with the monstrous. The *Beowulf* manuscript was apparently felt to belong among those of marvels and monsters since it is included in a codex together with the *Wonders of the East* and the *Letter of*

[57] De Vries, *Altnordisches etymologisches Wörterbuch* (Leiden: E. J. Brill, 1961), p. 41 (s.v. *bjǫrn*); p. 141 (s.v. *freki, frekr*).

[58] Höfler, *Kultische Geheimbünde,* esp. p. 249, also pp. 202, 281, 282–283, 291.

[59] Tacitus, *Germania,* Chap. 43.

[60] See R. W. Chambers, *Beowulf: An Introduction to the Study of the Poem* (3rd ed., with a supplement by C. L. Wrenn; Cambridge: University Press, 1957), pp. 56–57; Nora K. Chadwick, "The Monsters and Beowulf," in *The Anglo-Saxons: Studies in some aspects of their History and Culture*, ed. Peter Clemoes (London: Bowes and Bowes, 1959), p. 180.

Alexander on the Wonders of India. Beowulf is no less extraordinary than the Grendel monsters and the dragon. The historical Hygelac must have been remembered as a monster-like creature—presumably because of his gigantic bones, which, posterity notes, were preserved in a grave on an island near the mouth of the Rhine—for he is listed in the compilation *Liber monstrorum* (ms. in Leiden). Although no bear as such appears in the poem, Beowulf's name, his ursine characteristics, his battles with fearful beasts, giants and sea monsters, and his extraordinary strength speak for the connection with initiation and cult practices. These elements, woven into the fabric of the poem, remain as testimony to the pagan origin, uncamouflaged by Christian trappings.

ADVENTURES

That component of a *Heldenleben* which most readily permitted Christianization, the struggle against monsters and the dragon, captured the poet's imagination. He in fact reveals to us one way in which the transition from pagan to Christian concepts was effected: From Cain had descended all the evil broods of earth, ogres and elves, the giants also, who waged war with God for a long time and whom He punished (ll. 111–114). What this punishment was is told later when Hrothgar scrutinizes the hilt of the sword which Beowulf brings up from the mere-wife's lair. It was the ancient work of giants and on it was inscribed the story of the flood and how it had destroyed the brood of giants (*Beowulf*, ll. 1687–1693; cf. Genesis 6: 4–7). The warrior hero, in a manner analogous to that of his ancestors who fought the enemy, the hideous monster of chaos and darkness, could now fight the foes of Christendom, the giants as related in Genesis, Cain and all his brood, and the serpent Leviathan himself. The central significance of the Grendel monsters and the dragon for the Beowulf poem was first convincingly defended by J. R. R. Tolkien in his famous lecture.[61] Part of the greatness of the poem lies in the fact that the adventure of killing a monster or dragon, common in the schematism of a *Heldenleben,* is not just one episode, but is recapitulated and intensified so that the poem reaches a culmination on a yet higher plane. The Grendel monsters are misshapen troll-like creatures, half beast, half human, related to the kin of Cain and the giants. The dragon is the epitome of all dreadful foes. Although he lives in a barrow and guards

[61] "The Monsters and the Critics," in *Proceedings of the British Academy,* Vol. XXII (1936), pp. 245–295.

a hoard, he is more than a "treasure-guarding beast," as Stjerna defines him, more than a "natural creature of God," as Brodeur would have him.[62]

The dragon, even if he is not directly referred to as one of Cain's descendants or as God's adversary, is a chthonic being and belongs to the same generic category as Grendel and his dam. Regin and Fáfnir, after all, are of the race of giants, and Fáfnir turns into a dragon. Substitution from one group of chthonic beings to another merely indicates the potential range of imagery. On the strength of the universality throughout primitive cultures of the dragon symbol, the enemy of man and the gods, that serpent of old in the Bible, assimilation and transfer to Christian ideology was natural. The *Beowulf* poet created a hierarchy of fiends, just as in Biblical representations one finds a plurality of devils but also the archfiend himself. Grendel and his dam are evil monsters; the dragon is the archenemy. Thus, there is a cumulative effect in Beowulf's final struggle. He merges with the mythical archetype, himself almost a god or half-god, fighting the destructive powers of chaos and evil to re-create the cosmos—hence in the secondary sources the frequent comparison of him to a Christ or saint figure. Within the historical sphere, he is lifted above the ordinary warrior fighting a tribal enemy, however implicitly as a reenactment of the paradigmatic act. Beowulf's three main heroic deeds carry the metaphysical dimension explicitly.

Now that the nature of Beowulf's difficult tasks has been defined, the three episodes may be examined for their typical motifs.

Grendel. The purpose of his journey to the Danes is to aid the king in cleansing his hall of a fearful ogre that has been plaguing the region, coming out only at nightfall and apparently the more incensed by revelry and recitation of Christian lays (ll. 86–98). In the gold-adorned hall Heorot, Beowulf lies in wait for the appearance of the monster. A fiery light gleams from Grendel's eyes as he walks toward his prey. Beowulf and Grendel wrestle, breaking up benches and shattering the building. Beowulf succeeds in mutilating the bestial troll by tearing an arm out of the shoulder socket. This means his bane,

[62] Stjerna, *Essays,* p. 166, Arthur Brodeur, *The Art of Beowulf* (Los Angeles and Berkeley: University of California Press, 1959), pp. 217–218: "The dragon, unlike the kin of Grendel, is not of Cain's brood. Monstrous in shape and strength and fury, he is nonetheless one of God's creatures, neither by definition nor by descent an enemy of God."

although Grendel escapes to his lair. Grendel's arm with a pawlike hand, which no hard blade could bite into and which no sword could sever, was put on display (ll. 984–990).

Grendel's Dam. The fight with Grendel's dam occurs in her subterranean den after she has ravaged the hall in revenge for her son. Beowulf must plunge into the gloomy mere infested with sea monsters, against which he struggles. The troll woman clutches at him with her horrid claws. It takes the greater part of a day for him to reach solid bottom. He is dragged into the underwater cave, where a fiery light gleams. He wrestles with Grendel's mother; the sword Hrunting avails him nought. Supernatural powers come to his aid. He espies on the cave wall a magic sword made by the giants, heavier than any normal man could bear in battle (ll. 1557–1562). With it he clefts the merewife through. The poet explains that it was his coat of mail, made by the smith Weland, and the protection of the holy God that brought about victory in battle (ll. 1550–1554). The Danes, waiting above by the fen, see the blood-stained waters and depart, thinking the hero dead. The party of Geats faithfully wait for their lord. Beowulf sees many treasures in the cave, but only brings as booty the hilt of the magic sword and Grendel's head (ll. 1612–1615).

After the two Grendel episodes, the scop draws a comparison between Beowulf and Sigemund. Both are renowned quellers of monsters. Sigemund, it is said, also became famous after his death as the slayer of a dragon, keeper of a hoard. This reference anticipates what is in store for Beowulf: he, like Sigemund, has slain the monsters and has yet to encounter the dragon with the hoard.[63] Victory over this similar but more formidable monster is gained through the hero's own ruin.

The Dragon. Incensed by the theft of some of his hoard, a flying dragon lays waste to the land, even setting aflame Beowulf's royal dwelling. It keeps to its lair by day, stalks its prey by night. The encounter takes place in an inaccessible cavernous lair by the sea. Fiery flame spews out from the den as Beowulf approaches. No supernatural powers come to his rescue: his sword Nægling snaps with the blow from his powerful stroke.[64]

[63] The mythical and historical implications of the hoard with its curse and the fateful end of the hero who gains possession of it will be discussed later. See note 91 on Sigemund as dragon-slayer.

[64] Compare the giant's *heptisax* in *Grettis saga* (Chap. 66) and Kjartan's sword in the *Laxdœla saga* (Chap. 49).

Reference to the failure of the sword Nægling (ll. 2575–2580; ll. 2584–2586; l. 2680) and to the powerful stroke that breaks all blades (ll. 2680–2687) combines two traditional motifs. Hrunting also fails Beowulf in his fight with Grendel's dam, but another sword of wondrous origin and power saves the day. What has already been fated for the hero determines the potency or impotency of the sword employed, and depends on the poet's handling. Alternation between hope and despair, between effectiveness or usefulness of the sword is an elaboration on the theme.

The *Beowulf* poet supports the plausibility of Nægling's failure with yet another reason: the hero's great hand strength. The explanation seems natural enough, since the audience has been conditioned to the idea of Beowulf's powerful grasp. But the powerful handstroke motif probably can be traced to weapon exercises and initiation rites. Beowulf wields the magic sword in the cave of Grendel's dam, a sword heavier than any other man could have managed (ll. 1560–1562), and Nægling snaps under his mighty stroke (l. 2685)—an occurrence well-known to the poet (*mīne gefrǣge*). Sigurd, it may be recalled, breaks all the swords which Regin fashions for him, except the one made of the pieces from his father's ancestral sword (*Vǫlsunga saga*, Chap. 15); and Offa I, according to Saxo, was dull and speechless, but in time of his nation's need proved his strength: no coat of mail was large enough, no sword strong enough for him, except his father's ancient sword which had lain buried the while, the son having been deemed unworthy of it.[65]

Beowulf's band of followers shrink back into the woods, filled with cowardice and fear. One faithful comrade, Wiglaf, comes to his aid and deals the dragon a fatal wound. The treasure gleams in the vaulted cave, mysteriously illumined by a gold banner. Beowulf meets his fated hour, and the poet remarks that it is ever a mystery in what place a hero should find his end (ll. 3062–3068). For Beowulf was ignorant of the curse on the dragon's hoard and of the cunning with which Fate had ordained his end. The victory over the dragon, instead of calling forth a joyous proclamation, prompts an ominous prophecy: raven and eagle, normally good omens for the defeat of the enemy, will contend with the wolf in their eagerness after prey, the doomed Geats themselves (ll. 3024–3027).

[65] See Chambers, *Beowulf: An Introduction*, pp. 32–33, and Panzer, *Beowulf*, p. 281.

The desire for fame and gold, a natural aim of pagan warriors, is tinged in the poem with the nobler virtue of ridding the land of the Danes of devastating monsters and saving the Geats from the dire distress of the dragon. Beowulf's deeds at Hrothgar's court are mainly humanitarian acts, yet he is eager to show his courage and gain renown:

"Ic gefremman sceal
eorlīc ellen, oþðe endedæg
on þisse meoduhealle mīnne gebīdan!" (ll. 636–638)

("I will show courage of a hero, or in this
mead-hall pass my latest day!")[66]

"ic mē mid Hruntinge
dōm gewyrce, oþðe mec dēað nimeð!" (ll. 1490–1491)

("I will with Hrunting gain renown, or
death shall take me off!")

Although Beowulf takes none of the treasures from Grendel's cave, the motif is present. He receives bounteous reward from Hrothgar; these gifts he later presents to Hygelac, "as a good liegeman should." But, the honor and gold he has won mark the traditional hero:

"Þū þē self hafast
dǣdum gefremed, þæt þīn [dōm] lyfað
āwa tō aldre." (ll. 953–955)

("Thou hast brought to pass for thyself by
thy exploits, that thy fame shall live for
ever and ever.")

Him Bēowulf þanan,
gūðrinc goldwlanc græsmoldan træd
since hrēmig; (ll. 1880–1883)

(Then Beowulf, champion brave with gold,
exulting in his treasure, trod the greensward.)

The slaying of the dragon is mainly conceived as a sacrificial act for his land and people. Nonetheless, renown and the hoard play no little role in the motivation:

"Nū sceall billes ecg,
hond ond heard sweord ymb hord wīgan."

[66] The translations are from John R. Clark Hall, *Beowulf and the Finnesburg Fragment* (London: George Allen and Unwin, Ltd., 1963).

Bēowulf maðelode, bēotwordum spræc
nīehstan sīðe: "Ic genēðde fela
gūða on geogoðe; gȳt ic wylle,
frōd folces weard fæhðe sēcan,
mærðu fremman," (ll. 2508–2514)

("Now shall weapon's edge, hand and hard sword, do battle for the hoard."
Beowulf discoursed—spoke a last time with words of boasting:—"I ventured on many battles in my younger days; once more will I, the aged guardian of the people, seek combat and get renown.")

"Ic mid elne sceall
gold gegangan, oððe gūð nimeð
feorhbealu frēcne frēan ēowerne!" (ll. 2535–2537)

("By my valour I will win gold, or war, the dread destroyer of life, shall carry off your lord!")

"Bīo nū on ofoste, þæt ic ǣrwelan,
goldǣht ongite, gearo scēawige
swegle searogimmas, þǣt ic ðȳ sēft mæge
æfter māððumwelan mīn ālǣtan
līf ond lēodscipe, þone ic longe hēold." (ll. 2747–2751)

("Haste now, that I may see the ancient wealth, the golden store, may well survey the bright and curious gems; so that by reason of the wealth of treasure I may leave life more calmly and the people which I ruled over so long.")

"Ic ðāra frætwa Frēan ealles ðanc,
Wuldurcyninge wordum secge,
ēcum Dryhtne, þē ic hēr on starie,
þæs ðe ic mōste mīnum lēodum
ǣr swyltdæge swylc gestrȳnan.
Nū ic on māðma hord mīne bebohte
frōde feorhlege, fremmað gēna
lēoda þearfe;" (ll. 2794–2800)

("I utter in words my thanks to the Ruler of all, the King of Glory, the everlasting Lord, for the treasures which I here gaze upon, in that I have been allowed to win such things for my people before

my day of death. Now that I have given my old life
in barter for the hoard of treasure, do ye hence-
forth supply the people's needs.")

Thus far, Beowulf's heroic exploits have exemplified the complex of motifs typical of a *Heldenleben*: connection with a bear through his name; manifestation of theriomorphic traits and similarity with his adversary; superhuman strength; subduing of fearful beasts, some of whom possess invulnerability; foregoing the use of weapons; use of fabulous weapons of wondrous power; strength in wielding swords; hand-to-hand grapplings; subterranean encounters with supernatural beings (Grendel's dam and the dragon in their cavernous lairs); faithful companions (the Geats at Grendel's mere), and faithless comrades (the Danes at the fen and his cowardly followers at the dragon's cave); winning of fame and gold through his exploits; and an unexpected fateful end through the curse on the hoard.

Additional elements, related to the pagan beliefs and motifs familiar from the helmets, such as the gods who lead the horse and guide the spear and the omnipresence of Fate, underwent, along with the other elements in the poem, partial Christian reshaping. Beowulf may find a magic sword, the work of giants, in Grendel's cave, but it is a light from heaven that penetrates the darkness and the Lord who gives succor in the fight (ll. 1553–1554 and ll. 1570–1572). Pagan elements stand side by side with the Christian notions, just as *Metod* (ordainer of Fate, Providence) and *wyrd* (Fate) alternate with *Fæder alwalda* (the Father Almighty), *Anwalda* (ruler, the Lord), *Frēa ealles* (Lord of All), *Wuldurcyning* (King of Glory), *ēce Dryhten* (the eternal Lord). The coupling of pagan terms, often negative and fateful in their overtones, with more positive and joyous concepts brought about the gradual Christianization of the heathen words: *Metodes hyldo* (God's grace), *dōm sōðfæstra* (the judgment, or glory, of the righteous). In England, Christianization of the vocabulary had already begun earlier, as evidenced by Cædmon's *Hymn*; on the Continent, the same process can be observed somewhat later in the *Hildebrandslied* and the *Heliand*.[67]

[67] Cf. the *Hildebrandslied*: "Welaga nu, waltant got quad Hiltibrant, wewurt skihit" ("Well now, reigning God, said Hildebrand, baleful fate befalls"). On the *Heliand*, see Helmut de Boor, *Die deutsche Literatur von Karl dem Grossen bis zum Beginn der höfischen Dichtung 770–1170,* Vol. I of de Boor and Richard Newald, *Geschichte der deutschen Literatur* (zweite ergänzte und verbesserte Auflage; München: C. H. Beck'sche Verlagsbuchhandlung, 1955), pp. 61–63.

In a transition period during which heathen temples were converted into churches on the same site and Christian holidays were set on pagan feast days, old meanings still clung to the old words. Eradication of former connotations was not accomplished in one fell swoop; the admixture was natural, as was the falling back on idols in times of distress.[68]

Throughout the poem there is an obvious switching back and forth between pagan and Christian phraseology in references to supernatural powers, and this is often coupled with the additional factor of the hero's own strength. Notwithstanding the derived origin of a hero's power (cf. the battle fury and extrahuman strength of the *berserkir* and *úlfheðnar* and Beowulf's superhuman might, referred to as a "God given gift" [l. 1271]), his reliance on himself and his weapons instead of on the gods might be described as a necessary and natural reaction at a time when belief in the old gods was on the wane and acceptance of the new one not yet whole-hearted.[69]

"ðǣr gelȳfan sceal
Dryhtnes dōme sē þe hine dēað nimeð." (ll. 440–441)

("He whom death carries off shall resign himself to God's judgment.")

"Gæð ā wyrd swā hīo scel!" (l. 455)

("Fate goes ever as it must!")

"Wyrd oft nereð
unfǣgne eorl, þonne his ellen dēah!" (ll. 572–573)

("Often fate saves an undoomed man, if his courage is good.")

[68] In lines 175 ff., the *Beowulf* poet either gives a true historical picture of heathen times in the sixth century in Denmark or anachronously attributes to the Danes of that period customs which still prevailed in the Christian England of his own day. Reversion to idol worship was continually combated by the church during the long period of conversion. See Peter Hunter Blair, *An Introduction to Anglo-Saxon England* (Cambridge: University Press, 1959), pp. 120–125; and Klaeber (ed.), *Beowulf,* note to ll. 175–188, p. 135.

[69] Compare *Laxdœla saga*: " 'But to this extent only do I intend to accept the faith in Norway: I'll put but little trust in Thór next winter when I get back to Iceland.' The king smiled and said: 'One can see from the looks of Kjartan that he thinks he had better reason to put trust in his own strength and weapons than in Thór and Ódin' " (Chap. 40).

Hūru Gēata lēod georne truwode
mōdgan mægnes, Metodes huldo. (ll. 669–670)

(Indeed the chief of the Geats trusted firmly in his proud might, and in the favor of the Creator.)

Ac him Dryhten forgeaf
wīgspēda gewiofu, Wedera lēodum,
frōfor ond fultum, þǣt hīe fēond heora
ðurh ānes cræft ealle ofercōmon
selfes mihtum. (ll. 696–700)

(To the people of the Geats, the Lord gave the weaved destiny of success in war, help and support, so that they should all overcome their enemy through the power of one man, through his own strength.)

þǣr him āglǣca ætgrǣpe wearð,
hwæþre hē gemunde mægenes strenge,
gimfæste gife, ðē him God sealde,
ond him tō Anwaldan āre gelȳfde,
frōfre ond fultum; (ll. 1269–1273)

(The monster there had laid hold of him; yet he bore in mind the power of his might, the lavish gift which God had granted him and trusted himself to the Lord for grace, help and support.)

strenge getruwode,
mundgripe mægenes. (ll. 1533–1534)

(He trusted to his strength, the hand-grip of his might.)

Hæfde ðā forsīðod sunu Ecgþēowes
under gynne grund, Gēata cempa,
nemne him heaðobyrne helpe gefremede,
herenet hearde,— ond hālig God
gewēold wīgsigor; (ll. 1550–1554)

(Then the son of Ecgtheow, the hero of the Geats, would have perished under the wide earth, had not his war-corslet, his strong coat-of-mail, furnished him succor, and the

Holy God, the all-wise Lord, brought about
victory in battle.)

Swā mæg unfæge— ēaðe gedīgan
wēan ond wræcsīð sē ðe Waldendes
hyldo gehealdeþ! (11. 2291–2293)

(Thus may an undoomed man,—one who retains
the favour of the Almighty, lightly pass through
both woe and banishment.)

strengo getruwode
ānes mannes; ne bið swylc earges sīð! (ll. 2540–2541)

(And trusted to his own strength—not such is the
coward's way.)

But divine favor and one's own strength were not the only factors in the play of swords. Death and defeat were companions in the fray. Fate had another, disastrous, aspect. The warrior must one day meet his end. With this ultimate alternative Beowulf, too, must reckon. Despite his confident boasts, he envisions a possible gruesome death at the hands of Grendel:

"Nā þū mīnne þearft
hafalan hȳdan, ac hē mē habban wile
d[r]ēore fāhne, gif mec dēað nimeð;
byreð blōdig wæl, byrgean þenceð,
eteð āngenga unmurnlīce,
mearcað mōrhopu;" (ll. 445–450)

("Thou wilt have no need to cover my head in
burial; for he will have me covered with blood,
if death seizes me. He will bear off the bloody
corpse, will set his mind upon devouring it.")

Both possibilities are again weighed before Beowulf begins the battle with Grendel's mother:

"ic mē mid Hruntinge
dōm gewyrce, oþðe mec dēað nimeð!" (ll. 1490–1491)

("I shall with Hrunting gain renown or
death shall take me off.")

And again before the combat with the dragon, Beowulf, heavy with foreboding, knows what may be in store:

"ac unc [furður] sceal
weorðan æt wealle, swā unc wyrd getēoð,
Metod manna gehwæs." (ll. 2525–2527)

("But at the rampart it shall be to us two
as Fate, the lord of every man, decides.")

"Ic mid elne sceall
gold gegangen, oððe gūð nimeð,
feorhbealu frēcne frēan ēowerne!" (ll. 2535–2537)

("By my valor I will win gold; or war, the
dread destroyer of life, shall carry off
your lord!")

It is foreordained that victory is not to be his:

Sceolde *lǣn*daga
æþeling ǣrgōd ende gebīdan,
worulde līfes, ond se wyrm somod,
þēah ðe hordwelan hēolde lange. (ll. 2341–2343)

(The most excellent prince was doomed to
meet with the end of his transitory days—
of this world's life—and the serpent as well,
though he had held the hoarded treasure long.)

Him wæs geōmor sefa,
wǣfre ond wælfūs, wyrd ungemete nēah,
sē ðone gomelan grētan sceolde,
sēcean sāwle hord, sundur gedǣlan
līf wið līce; nō þon lange wæs
feorh æþelinges flǣsce bewunden. (ll. 2419–2424)

(His spirit was sad, restless and ready to
depart. The fate was immeasurably near which
was to wait upon the aged man, to seek the
treasure of his soul, to part asunder life from
body; not long after that was the spirit of the
prince enwrapped in flesh.)

Scyld wēl gebearg
līfe ond līce lǣssan hwīle
mǣrum þēodne, þonne his myne sōhte,
ðǣr hē þȳ fyrste forman dōgọre

wealdan mōste, swā him wyrd ne gescrāf
hrēð æt hilde. (ll. 2570–2575)

(The shield gave its good shelter to the famous chief in life and limb a shorter time than had his longing looked for, if he at that time, that first day, was to command victory in the contest: but Fate did not thus ordain for him.)

Beowulf's end comes to him unbeknown, in ignorance of why the encounter with the dragon should be his downfall. Although Beowulf has premonitions of his heavy fate, the poet includes the traditional theme: a warrior never knows time or place (ll. 3062–3068). Such is the treacherous and sudden aspect of Fate already familiar from the theme of the helmets of Valsgärde 8 (Plate 25), Sutton Hoo (Plate 26), and Pliezhausen (Plate 27). First glory, then death, that is the warrior's lot in life, and so it is summed up in essence by Beowulf and Hrothgar:

"Ūre ǣghwylc sceal ende gebīdan
worolde līfes, wyrce sē þe mōte
dōmes ǣr dēaþe; þæt bið drihtguman
unlifgendum æfter sēlest." (ll. 1386–1389)

("Each of us must expect an end of living in this world; let him who may win glory before death: for that is best at last for the departed warrior.")

"Nū is þīnes mægnes blǣd
āne hwīle; eft sōna bið,
þæt þec ādl oððe ecg eafoþes getwǣfeð,
oððe fȳres feng, oððe flōdes wylm,
oððe gripe mēces, oððe gāres fliht,
oððe atol yldo; oððe ēagena bearhtm
forsiteð ond forsworceð; semninga bið,
þæt ðec dryhtguma, dēað oferswȳðeð." (ll. 1761–1768)

("Now shall the fullness of thy strength last for a while. But soon after it shall be, that malady or sword shall cut thee off from power, or the embrace of fire or welling of a flood, or hideous old age. Or brightness of eyes shall

diminish and grown dim, and at length it shall be
that death shall overpower thee, noble chieftain.")

In *Beowulf*, the Germanic *Heldensage* reached a fuller mythologization than in the Continental epics and lays—this *because of* the Christianization, which here worked together with, not against, the pagan conceptions. The fusion of pagan and Christian attitudes is clearly and neatly displayed in the closing lines of the poem, with their emphasis on the softer virtues coupled with the traditional superlative formulas and inclusion of *lofgeornost*:

cwædon þæt hē wǣre wyruldcyning[a]
manna mildust ond mon(ðw)ǣrust,
lēodum līðost ond lofgeornost. (ll. 3180–3182)

(They said he had been of earthly kings the
mildest, and gentlest of men, the kindest to
his people and most eager for fame.)

The traditional heroic life, with its feats of bravery, proof of prowess, gaining of fame and fortune, and fateful end, has throughout been transmuted into an image acceptable for a Christian warrior to emulate. Just as the shift from monsters to devils, or from Fate to Providence, was accomplished without a complete break with the traditional material, so the Beowulf of the poem could form a link between the not so remote pagan past and eighth-century Christian England. He satisfies the standard for the dauntless pagan warrior, eager for fame and battle, and at the same time embodies the new Christian spirit that strove to imbue this militancy with gentler sentiments of noble sacrifice. Beowulf's almost romantic loyalty to Hygelac, his refusal of the crown in favor of Heardred, the sensitivity of his conscience to any possible wrongdoing on his part that might have brought the disaster of the dragon upon his people, and his supreme selflessness in performing the last duty for the Geats all endow him with ethical nobility to match his physical prowess. But, Beowulf is only on the way to becoming the Christian knight who fights for the right, the soldier of God. He is but a precursor of a later conscious attempt to divert the warlike spirit of the pagan past into open militancy for Christendom—the Crusades, chivalry, knighthood, Sir Galahad, Percival, and St. George.

The central theme of the poem focuses on three adventures of the hero, the first two in prime of youth, the third in old age. Yet, despite an outward advancement in years and position, there is no character development. Beowulf is in the end what he was in the beginning: a model hero, matchless in strength, loyal in duty. The biographical progression is not that of historical biography. The main stream of the action may carry the hero from vassalage to kingship, from youth to old age, but bits of information about his early life and other off-the-scene exploits continually interrupt the sequence as flashback reminiscences and associations throughout the poem. This anachronous structure serves specifically to highlight the moments of Beowulf's life that illustrate his prowess and virtue. Thereby the typical and ideal aspect is brought out most advantageously. Beowulf's life shines forth as a repetition and revitalization of the archetypal *Heldenleben.*

The *imitatio* aspect, however, is twofold: not only realization of the archetype, but also perpetuation of the example. The gentle exhortations "so should a warrior be," "so should a nephew be to his uncle" set Beowulf's life up as an example itself to be followed. By the substance of his deeds and through the didactic element, Beowulf often brings to mind the martyred saint. Furthermore, there obtains a close structural correspondence between a *Heldenleben* and a saint's life. In the latter, also, only certain moments and incidents are selected in order to point up the saint's typical virtues. Hagiographic literature makes use of a pattern very similar to that of the *Heldenleben*: "marvellous infancy and vocation, the struggles and trials by which [the saint] proved himself a true athlete of Christ, an account of his gifts, miracles, and prophecies, the warning of approaching death, a farewell address to the disciples, and the death and miracles at the tomb."[70] Beowulf's presentiments of death, his farewell speeches, and the ritual performance at the burial pyre—elements over and beyond the typical *Heldenleben*—offer a striking parallel to the pattern of a saint's life. The poet blends here as elsewhere pagan traditions with Christian forms. The Sutton Hoo grave find itself shows this merging and may well fall within the poet's ken, being dated some fifty years before the poem.[71] The heroic pattern stood ready to hand when the time came for the

[70] *Lives of the Saints* (The Voyage of St. Brendan; Bede: Life of Cuthbert; Eddius Stephanus: Life of Wilfrid), trans. J. F. Webb (Baltimore: Penguin Books, 1965), Introduction, p. 17. See André Jolles, *Einfache Formen,* pp. 23–41, on the form and structure of a saint's legend.

[71] See R. L. S. Bruce-Mitford, *The Sutton Hoo Ship Burial: A Handbook* (London: The Trustees of the British Museum, 1968), pp. 44–46.

writing of lives of martyred heroes of Christendom. Heroic legends could readily be transformed into saints' lives: one need only mention the amalgamation of the Perseus legend with the life of St. George. For the *Beowulf* poet to accommodate a traditional *Heldenleben* to its Christianized form could not have been more natural at a time when the writing of saints' lives was beginning in England (*Life of St. Cuthbert, ca.* A.D. 699).

History Viewed as Archetypal

Despite moments of glory, death conquers the warrior in the end, *lif is læne eal scæceð, leoht ond lif somod* (life is transitory, all passes away, light and life together). This elegiac theme, one no Christian need despise, as Tolkien put it, permeates the whole poem.[72] Behind the historical events, which serve as background for the personal disaster of the hero, there stands the same inscrutable destiny—war, treachery, feuds bring nations low; their glory, too, passes away:

Līg ealle forswealg,
gǣsta gīfrost, þāra ðe þǣr guð fornam,
bēga folces; wæs hira blǣd scacen. (ll. 1122–1124)

(The fire, greediest of spirits, had consumed
all of those whom war had carried off, of either
people—their glory had passed away.)

Beowulf participates in actual historic events and is meant to be taken as a real person within the framework of the poem, even if he cannot be attested elsewhere. Several arguments speak against his historicalness. As stated earlier, his name does not alliterate within the family genealogies of the Geats. Furthermore, the time scale in the list of reigning kings in Sweden leaves no room for a span of fifty years in which Beowulf supposedly ruled. Hrothgar had ruled the Danes for fifty years when the scourge of Grendel descended on his realm. Beowulf's fifty-year reign over the Geatish kingdom before the dread dragon makes its appearance would seem deliberately created as a poetic parallel. The power of the Geats probably ended with Hygelac's fall, not with Beowulf's. Besides, the fact that after fifty years of such prosperous and successful reign Beowulf's kingdom is ripe for collapse

[72] Tolkien, "The Monsters and the Critics," p. 265.

would seem suspect. The disastrous historical battle (*ca.* A.D. 520) against the Merovingians and Hetware (Chattuarii) in Friesland near the mouth of the Rhine, where Hygelac fell, would more logically be the initiating factor in the dissolution of the Geatish kingdom, the turning point which left the Geats without a powerful leader and enabled their traditional enemy, the Swedes, to establish their supremacy.

The hero Beowulf rises from a background of historical events from roughly the fifth and sixth centuries in the Scandinavian north.[73] Such a historical setting is, as already noted, a distinctive feature of the *Heldensage* in general. The *Beowulf* poet has not only integrated the traditional hero pattern with this history, he has also made history itself archetypal. His mind's eye sees the general in the specific feuds,[74] sees history in its whole sweep, its whole tragedy. He aimed for something quite different from a straightforward account of his hero's destiny or of the feudings among the Geats, Danes, and Swedes. The structure of the poem accords with associative rather than sequential logic. The main action is interspersed with subtle hints, oblique references, and historical allusions.

In the first part of the poem, comprising the two Grendel episodes, subordinate elements evoke comparison and contrast with the main themes and develop their own subplot. The poet's master mind motivates the associations, slipping them in at those points which best serve his purpose.

The linkage in one set of references running through Part I looks something like this: the splendor and sturdiness of Heorot twice calls forth a reversed image—the ultimate destruction of the glorious hall by fire (ll. 81–83; ll. 778–782) and the cause of that conflagration, treachery between son-in-law (Ingeld) and father-in-law (Hrothgar) because of some deadly deed of violence (ll. 83–85).

Unferth is introduced in the narrative as the jealous courtier who would like to belittle Beowulf's accomplishments. The fact, to which Beowulf calls attention, that Unferth had slain his own brothers (ll. 586–588) places him in a long line of other such warriors: Sigemund, Gunnar, Hogni, Atli, Hrothulf, Heorweard, Hnæf, Eadgils, Hæth-

[73] For a full discussion of the historical elements and identification of the personages, see Klaeber (ed.), *Beowulf*, pp. xxix–xlv; Chambers, *Beowulf: An Introduction.*

[74] In contrast, see Schneider, *Germanische Heldensage*, p. 17, and de Vries, *Altnordische Literaturgeschichte*, p. 66, on personalized blood feuds.

cyn, Ermanaric, Hildebrand. And this is not the only trait he shares with traditional characters, for his role as evil counselor (cf. the archetypal Starcatherus) is hinted at when the poet brings together Hrothgar, Hrothulf, and Unferth (who is sitting at the Scyldings' feet) in a reference to the effect that all faith lay in Unferth, though he had not played upright with his kinsmen (ll. 1165–1168). Indeed, at every possible occasion the poet likes to juxtapose Hrothgar and Hrothulf, uncle and nephew,[75] whose apparent present friendship harbors and harbingers a reversal, which is intimated in the remark "for not yet had the Scyldings used treachery" (ll. 1014–1019); or again in the line "Hrothgar and Hrothulf, uncle and nephew, still each to the other was true" (ll. 1163–1165); or in the ironic ring of Wealhtheow's remarks, the first, directed to Hrothulf, indicating her trust in him to requite her sons (ll. 1180–1187) and the second, addressed to Beowulf, saying she knows he will be kind in counsel to her sons and that here at court in Heorot each noble was to the other true (l. 1228). At the end of Part I Beowulf presents his reward gifts to Hygelac, and the poet remarks that so should a nephew be to his uncle and "never weave a cunning snare or contrive death for his bosom friend by secret craft" (ll. 2167 ff.), an obvious reminder of an opposite relationship between uncle and nephew and of what was to happen between Hrothgar and Hrothulf.

These asides about future treachery among the Danish Scyldings serve to develop an undercurrent in Part I that offsets the victorious jubilation over the annihilation of the Grendel monsters and portends the inevitable downfall of the Danes. The reversals and contrasts which the poet sets up, besides the obvious good-evil, light-darkness, joy-sorrow opposites,[76] ultimately illuminate typical circumstances which the poet wishes to emphasize.

Internecine feuds and faithless kinsmen, betrayal and treachery characterize the stuff out of which history was composed, and of these the poet gives us ample examples. Even in the lay of Sigemund, sung by

[75] Tacitus (*Germania,* Chap. 20) points out that the uncle-nephew blood relationship was particularly sacred to the Germanic tribes. The *Beowulf* poet also makes Fitela (Sinfjǫtli) the nephew of Sigemund, whereas in the Volsung tradition he is the incestuous son of Sigemund, but nonetheless his sister's son. Thus it cannot be ascertained whether the *Beowulf* poet was acquainted with the Volsung version.

[76] See Herbert Wright, "Good and Evil, Light and Darkness, Joy and Sorrow in Beowulf," in *Review of English Studies,* N.S., Vol. VIII, No. 29 (1957), pp. 1–11.

the bard to extol Beowulf's deeds, feuds and treacheries (*fǣhðe ond fyrena* [l. 879]) are part of the hero Sigemund's life-tale and also of Heremod's fatal end (ll. 902–904). Hama, it is said, fled the crafty enmity of Ermanaric (ll. 1200–1201).

As part of the revelry to celebrate Beowulf's overcoming of Grendel, Hrothgar's bard tells yet another tale, that of Finn, Hildeburh, Hnæf, and Hengest, of the treacheries between the brothers-in-law Finn and Hnæf and the feud between the Jutes (Frisians) and Danes (ll. 1071–1159). This tale within the tale functions as a further parallel to events already foreshadowed in the oblique references to treachery in the Danish house between uncle and nephew, Hrothgar and Hrothulf, and to betrayal between son-in-law and father-in-law, Ingeld and Hrothgar. That the poet wished the audience to associate the faithless deeds in the Finn episode with those that were to take place between Hrothgar, Hrothulf, and Unferth is seen from the fact that mention of the latter three and their "faithfulness" (ll. 1165–1168) immediately follows the lay of Finn. Unferth, no doubt, was to be associated with the incitor or evil counselor, Hunlafing, of the Finn episode.

That special attention is focused on Wealhtheow, her radiant gown, golden diadem, gracious demeanor, and ale-dispensing among the guests (ll. 612 ff.), and again most particularly after the Finn lay (ll. 1162 ff.), is no coincidence, for through her the theme of the wife as her nation's pledge of peace is woven back and forth between the digressions and the main narrative.

The Finn episode tells of the Danish wife Hildeburh, a weaver of peace between nations, who meets with sorrow and the slaughter of her kinsmen. Such will also be the fate of Freawaru, Hrothgar's daughter, in her match with Ingeld, son of Froda, the Heathobard king, for tribal quarrels will not be patched up through marriage bonds. This is what Beowulf prognosticates in his report to Hygelac concerning affairs at the Danish court (ll. 2024–2031). Significant from the point of view of associative logic is the fact that Wealhtheow appears immediately after the lay of Finn and that the digression on Freawaru and Ingeld is prompted by mention of Wealhtheow, her nation's pledge of peace (*fri usibb folca* [l. 2017]). And curiously at first reading, but not on second thought, Freawaru is depicted here as bearing the ale cup round to the guests, mother like daughter, a detail not previously mentioned when Beowulf was at Heorot, but which he includes here in his report to Hygelac. Finally, in addition to Wealhtheow, Hildeburh, and Freawaru, the poet gives us another example of the peace-weaver wife in Modthryth (*freoðuwebbe*, l. 1942).

In the digression on Freawaru and Ingeld, again an evil counselor enters (Saxo's Starcatherus), inciting Ingeld to revenge. Apart from the fact that a cycle of tales surrounding Ingeld was in the literary repertory of the eighth century and no doubt known to both poet and audience,[77] Beowulf's prognosis is a surmise of the most probable kind, for it was the same old story, a lesson which history had taught time and time again.

The motifs of faithless kinsmen, evil counselors, tribal feudings, and the "peace weaver" bride connect the associations in the digressions and render them meaningful to the whole. As repetitive examples they become interesting for their typicalness rather than for their individuality, at least within this poem.

The poet's predilection for opposites, reversals, parallels, and contrasts, already noted incidentally in the various digressions just discussed, assumes special significance within the pattern he has created. Wealhtheow bestows a wondrously wrought torque on Beowulf, a treasure comparable to the necklace Hama absconded with from Ermanaric's hoard (ll. 1197–1201). A good example of the poet's technique of selecting similar objects from history and legend (for the story he is telling has something in common with other times, other events), it is not unique, but typical. And the poet takes the opportunity to elaborate more by foretelling the fate of the torque at the time of Hygelac's fall, thus forming a link with the second part of the narrative.[78] Hrothgar's words upon Beowulf's departure, theorizing on the possibility that should the Geats be left kingless they would have no better choice for king than Beowulf himself (ll. 1845–1853), also anticipate Part II.

[77] Alcuin's famous remark "Verba dei legantur in sacerdotali convivio; ibi decet lectorem audiri, non citharistam, sermones patrum, non carmina gentilium. Quid Hinieldus cum Christo?" ("In the Refectory the Bible should be read; the lector heard, not the harper; patristic sermons rather than pagan songs. For what has Ingeld to do with Christ?") gives evidence for a popular heroic literature around the figure of Ingeld. See Chambers, *Beowulf: An Introduction*, p. 22.

[78] Beowulf receives the splendid torque from Wealhtheow but presents it to Hygd (ll. 2173), who, we must suppose, gave it to her husband, for Hygelac wore it in battle against the Frisians and Franks, into whose hands it then passed. (ll. 1202–1214).

After drawing the comparison between Sigemund and Beowulf, the scop ends his recital with a reference to Heremod, the reversed image of what a noble chieftain should be (ll. 898 ff.) and hence an admonishment to Beowulf against overweening pride. Hrothgar's high praise of Beowulf (ll. 1709–1724) again calls forth the bad example of Heremod as a warning. The uncle-nephew pair Hygelac/ Beowulf has its negative counterpart in Hrothgar/Hrothulf.

Mention of the good and liberal queen Hygd, wife of Hygelac, prompts the story of the vindictive queen Modthryth, who put to death liegemen because of fancied insult but later turned into a good queen after her marriage to Offa, a victorious and generous king, the opposite of Heremod (ll. 1935–1962).

From the digressions and asides and from their placement by the poet, the purpose of the comparisons becomes clear: they are examples, just as Beowulf's life is exemplary, in a twofold sense.

To join Part I with Part II, the poet deliberately creates parallels, such as Hrothgar's fifty-year reign, after which his land is visited by the Grendel monsters, and Beowulf's fifty-year reign, after which the dragon appears to molest his kingdom; or the prognosis of the destruction of Heorot by consuming flame and the actual burning of Beowulf's royal hall by the fire-spewing dragon; or the gloomy prospect in Part I foretelling the downfall of the Danes and the similar surmise concerning the end of the Geats through future attacks by the Swedes and Franks—"that is the feud and enmity, the deadly hatred of men" (*Þæt ys sīo fǣhðo ond se fēondscipe, wælnīð wera* [ll. 2999–3000]).

Continuing the formal structure of Part I and its themes of blood feud, the poet in Part II includes digressions on the past feuds between the Geats and the Swedes and on the battle with the Franks. In this way, through brief allusions and quick sketches, he fills in for the audience the happenings between the time of the exploits at Heorot and the dread appearance of the dragon and prophesies more feuds in the future. He tells of the tragedy at King Hrethel's court and how Hæthcyn accidentally killed his brother Herebeald (ll. 2435–2443). He recalls the craft and cunning with which the Swedes prepared the treacherous battle trap for the Geats at Hreosnabeorh (ll. 2472–2478) and the Geats' revenge at the battle of Ravenswood (Hrefnesholt), where Hæthcyn was killed by Ongentheow and Ongentheow by Eofor (ll. 2479–2489 and ll. 2922–2998). He mentions the banishment of Eadgils and Eanmund, Ohthere's sons, who flee to Heardred's court, tells how Onela pursues them and kills Heardred (ll. 2379–2390), how Eanmund is slain by Weohstan, father of Wiglaf (ll. 2611–2619), how Eadgils, with Beowulf's support, kills Onela (ll. 2391–2396).

With patient sleuthing scholars have delved into outside sources and archaeological evidence to support the account in *Beowulf* and to date the events. When pieced together, these digressions formed a unified and chronological history. But in the narrative, the happenings are all presented anachronously, and purposely so. Even a single cohesive episode will appear piecemeal in several places. The death of Ongentheow at the hand of Eofor[79] is accompanied by the remark that by that deed one brother avenged the other (ll. 2484–2486), but not until much later (ll. 2961–2981) are the details given as to who the two brothers were and how it came about that Eofor recompensed his brother Wulf. The history of the hoard and how it came to rest in the barrow, another example of piecemeal presentation, will be discussed later.

Episodes connected with Hygelac's battle against the Frisians and Franks (already anticipated in Part I) occur again in two places. In each, Beowulf's strength as a typical hero is highlighted. The first recounts his swimming feat, across the sea's expanse with thirty suits of armour, after the battle in which Hygelac was laid low (ll. 2359–2362). Then further details concerning the battle in Friesland come out when Beowulf in his discoursing mentions the sword he will use to do battle against the dragon, for his deed in that former battle explains how the sword came into his possession—he killed Dæghrefn, Hygelac's slayer, not by force of weapon, but by crushing him with his bare hands (ll. 2499–2504); he then took his battle habiliments. The name of the sword, Nægling, is withheld, however, until line 2680.

Associative logic governs the appearance of the hero motif in lines 2518–2521, where Beowulf, upon mention of his sword, explains why he cannot fight the dragon barehanded as he had Grendel. Mention of Wiglaf's ancestral sword evokes the story of how his father, Weohstan, claimed it as booty after the slaying of Eanmund (ll. 2611–2619), a

[79] The designation of Hygelac as the slayer of Ongentheow (*bonan Ongenþēoẹs*) in line 1968 anticipates the battle of Ravenswood. Although the details differ slightly, Hygelac can be considered Ongentheow's bane, for it was the arrival of his forces that turned the tide of battle.

detail which fills in the previous account of Eadgils' and Eanmund's exile in the land of the Geats.

Thus the technique of associating ideas, of breaking up the discursive sequence, of anticipating and adding to the information bit by bit also characterizes the structural pattern of Part II. Already in Part I, with each retelling of the fight with Grendel and his mother, new details appear, adding each time more of the hero-monster motifs; and in Beowulf's recounting of the banqueting at Heorot, he drops the extra remark that from time to time Freawaru too proffered the ale cup. Among the reward gifts presented to Beowulf by Hrothgar is a corslet or breast armor (ll. 1020 ff.). Its origin as war gear of the Scylding king Hiorogar, however, is first made known in the recapitulation at Hygelac's court (ll. 2153 ff.).

Just as the name of the sword Nægling is not told at first mention, so too the name of Beowulf, the hero, is anticipated first in line 195, then given in line 343; the work of Weland is indicated in line 405, but the smith is not named until line 455; the name of the first Geatish warrior devoured by Grendel (l. 740) is not filled in until line 2076; Æschere's death is described in line 1240, but he is not named until line 1328; Grendel is reported to have slaughtered thirty Danish warriors in line 122—the details are given in lines 1582–1583: "he devoured fifteen on the spot and carried the other fifteen to his den."

On one level it may be said that the digressions produce the effect of epic delay, forestalling and hence enhancing the climax. For the flashbacks, particularly in Part II, interrupt the main action as it pushes forward with its preparations for the fateful encounter with the dragon. But retardation, anticipation, contrastive themes, piecemeal presentation are but concomitant factors, techniques, the means to an end, in the poetic structure.[80]

Digressive material in the form of two "elegies" draws attention to the ultimate aims of the poet in so composing his work. The elegy of the Last Survivor, who conceals the treasure of his race, sets the mood for the comparable situation with Beowulf, who also has no heir, whose kingdom has come to an end, and whose hard-won treasure will also

[80] Adrien Bonjour emphasizes the dramatic and psychological motivation for the digressions, rather than pointing up their literary and structural function (*The Digressions in Beowulf*, Vol. 5 of *Medium Ævum Monographs* (Oxford: Blackwell, 1950).

rust in the earth and do no man good (ll. 2247–2248; l. 2275; ll. 2813–2816; ll. 3166–3169). Such a digression, much like the lay of Sigemund or the lay of Finn, obviously serves to anticipate and associate themes in the narrative. The elegiac "Father's Lament" over his unavenged son hanged on the gallows (ll. 2444–2462) provides commentary on Hrethel's grief over Herebeald, whom he cannot avenge.[81] But what these elegiac lines do in fact is to lift the situation of the grief-stricken father from the specific to the general. This gives us a clue that the elegy of the Last Survivor is also a general, or typical theme.

These hypothetical examples in the elegiac mode also contribute, to be sure, to the overall mournful tone of the poem, with its contrastive elements. In Part I, victory over the Grendel monsters merely delays the inevitable doom of the Danes. In Part II, victory over the dragon heralds the end of the Geats. The tragedy in the political events agrees with the descending gradient in the hero's life. Broadly seen, Part II (tragedy) is played off against Part I (jubilation), just as in miniature in Part I the subplot counters the main theme and the imminent danger of Grendel stalking in the dark offsets the joyous banqueting in the golden bright hall. The dominant theme of *gyrn æfter gomene* (l. 1775)—upon jubilation follows tragic end, all glory passes away—constitutes a proper commentary on life for pagan and Christian alike. And it is the continuity of old and new, the eternal sameness which fired the poet's imagination. For by whatever name the world has been ruled—*wyrd, metod, godes dom*—"so it was then and still is now."

Metod eallum wēold
gumena cynnes, swā hē nū gīt dêð. (ll. 1057–1058)

(The Creator guided all the race of men,
as he still does now.)

holm storme wēol,
won wið winde, winter ȳþe belēac

[81] The parallel between old king Hrethel and the father of the hanged man hinges, according to Dorothy Whitelock, on Anglo-Saxon law, which permitted no vengeance for an executed criminal (*The Audience of Beowulf* [Oxford: University Press, 1951] pp. 17–18). Might it not also have something to do with the hanged men who appear in the *Totenheer,* with sacrificial deaths such as King Vikar's or Odin's, for which also no vengeance would be possible? Herebeald's death can certainly be considered more as a sacrifice than the result of a criminal act, and indeed it has often been compared to the death of Balder.

īsgebinde, oþ ðæt ōþer cōm
gēar in geardas,—swā nū gȳt dêð,
þā ðe syngāles sēle bewitiað,
wuldọrtorhtan weder. (ll. 1131–1136)

(The ocean heaved with storm, contended
with the wind; winter had locked the waves
in its icy bond, until a new spring came
round to the homes of men, and the seasons
gloriously bright, regularly observing their
order, as they still do now.)

wolde dōm Godes dǣdum rǣdan
gumena gehwylcum, swā hē nū gēn dêð. (ll. 2858–2859)

(For men of all degrees God's judgment ruled
their deeds, just as it still does now.)

This refrain sums up the poet's observation on the course of life in this world: whether the gods come or go, whether Christian times or pagan, there is continuity and sameness between past and present deeds, past and present times—this is the essence of his illustrations.

By selecting his examples, setting up parallels, comparisons, and opposites, and by presenting his historical material anachronously the poet achieved a most singular effect. The associative illustrations break the primacy of normal sequence, highlight each event separately as it were, and thus permit the timelessness of hero and of history to emerge. The life of a warrior, the events of this life, follow a precedent set long ago; the history of nations likewise exhibits a recurrent pattern, one felt to be fateful and disastrous. Beowulf is like Sigemund, like the Last Survivor; Wealhtheow, like Freawaru, like Hildeburh, like Modthryth; Unferth, like Hunlafing, like Starcatherus; Hrethel's grief, like the grief of any father in similar circumstances; the fate of Freawaru with Ingeld, like that of Hildeburh with Finn; the betrayals between Finn, Hnæf, and Hengest, like those between Hrothgar, Hrothulf, and Unferth; the feuds among the Geats and the Swedes, like those among the Geats and the Franks—all illustrate a repetitive sameness that reaches back to times immemorial and stretches into the future with its doom-filled prognosis. It is of no matter whence the examples are drawn—from legend, history, or hypothetical surmises created by the poet. His Beowulf is the typical warrior in a world that follows a repetitive and determinative order—both hero and history are paradigmatic.

The fragmenting and dissociating of connected parts, which allows the typical aspects to shine through so effectively, is related to other formal factors in the poem. From the disjoined accounts in the narrative and the adding of bits of information, one has the impression of repetition with elaboration. Formally similar and characteristic for the diction is the use of variation. A series of designations circumscribe the same object. A sampling will suffice to illustrate the technique:

Gyrede hine Bēowulf
eorlgewǣdum, nalles for ealdre mearn;
scolde herebyrne hondum gebrōden,
sīd ond searofāh sund cunnian,
sēo ðe bāncofan beorgan cūþe,
þæt him hildegrāp hreþre ne mihte,
eorres inwitfeng aldre gesceþðan;
ac se hwīta helm hafelan werede,
sē þe meregrundas mengan scolde,
sēcan sundgebland since geweorðad,
befongen frēawrāsnum, swā hine fyrndagum
worhte wǣpna smið, wundrum tēode,
besette swīnlīcum, þæt hine syðþan nō
brond nē beadomēcas bītan ne meahton. (ll. 1441–1454)

(Beowulf arrayed himself with princely armor;
no whit did he feel anxious for his life.
His war-corslet, woven by hand, ample and
deftly worked, was to make trial of the mere.
It had power to shield his body, so that for
him the battle-grasp, the fury's vengeful grip,
might do no damage to his breast, his life!
The shining helmet screened his head, which
was to stir up the watery depths, to tempt
the churning waves. It was adorned with gold,
encircled with lordly bands, as in past days
the weapon-smith had wrought it,—formed it
wondrously, and set it round with boar-images,
so that after that no sword or battle-knife could
ever cut through it.)

Much as Beowulf's typical hero qualities are added to and supported through the sequence of accounts, and much as history gives repeated and similar illustration of betrayals and feudings, so the appositions represent miniature variations on a theme. Brodeur rightly touches on their significance: "This fondness for the accumulation of various designations for a single referent seems to reflect a deep interest on the part of the poet and audience alike, in the contemplation of all the functions, qualities, and values of a person or thing: a desire to savor all its typical aspects."[82] The structural fragmentation, observed on a larger scale, has been carried out down to the smallest linguistic units. Indeed, variation, like the associative and illustrative material, constitutes a displaying of all the typical aspects. The formal arrangement, anachronous and additive, helps convey the archetypal nature of the conceptions basic to the poem. The poetic unity has determined the pertinent use of the traditional thematic and linguistic patterns.

At first glance, some few examples and motifs selected by the poet seem less appropriate or even contradictory to the poet's meaning. Recognition of the structure of the poem and of the inherited patterns will perhaps aid also in elucidating the function of these within the framework of the poem.

The Modthryth digression has always puzzled commentators. Modthryth first of all establishes a contrast with Queen Hygd, but then she herself presents a reversal of temperament. This is a favorite theme of the author: Scyld's fortunes change from bad to good, Heremod turns from good to bad, Modthryth from bad to good. Along with contrasts and reversals, the poet has his mind on types and the typical. Like Wealhtheow, Hildeburh, and Freawaru, Modthryth is the peace-weaver type. She also represents a feminine category familiar from myth and legend: Artemis, Atalanta, and Brünhilde in their inflexible chastity demanded accomplishments of superhuman tasks on the part of prospective wooers or demanded their sacrifice. The figure of Artemis even exhibits the same kind of transformation and change of heart as Modthryth.[83] The fact that this feminine type is universally found outside the poem does not justify the appearance of the motif within the poem, for the poet gives no other example of a woman with this

[82] *The Art of Beowulf,* pp. 19–20. Brodeur mainly explains the artistic device of variation, however, as the vehicle to express emotion or emphasis (see esp. pp. 51, 52, 60, 63), and nowhere does he draw the right conclusion from the splendid observation quoted. For some good insights, see Joan Blomfield's short article, "The Style and Structure of Beowulf," in *Review of English Studies,* Vol. XIV, No. 56 (October, 1938), pp. 396–403.

[83] See de Vries, "Betrachtungen," pp. 31, 168.

cruel bent to indicate that he intended such comparisons. Yet on the basis of the total structure of the poem, with its emphasis on recurrent types, it can be surmised that reference to this trait in Modthryth would not be there unless the characteristic were recognized by the poet as a typical one, like the peace-weaver element. Perhaps he even had Brünhilde in the back of his mind, since he was acquainted with the Nordic tradition of Sigemund.

The poet's predilection for reversals and traditional motifs is again evidenced by his inclusion of the slothful-youth motif, which seemingly discounts Beowulf's early feats of valor and promising boyhood with Hrethel:

hēold mec ond hæfde Hrēðel cyning,
geaf mē sinc ond symbẹl, sibbe gemunde;
næs ic him tō līfe lāðra ōwihte,
beorn in burgum, þonne his bearna hwylc,
Herebeald ond Hæðcyn oððe Hygelāc mīn. (ll. 2430–2434)

(King Hrethel had and kept me, gave me wealth
and food, bore in mind our kinship. Never
through life was I a whit less liked by him
as a warrior within the stronghold than
were any of his sons—Herebeald, Hæthcyn
or my own Hygelac.)

Hēan wæs lange,
swā hyne Gēata bearn gōdne ne tealdon,
nē hyne on medobence micles wyrðne
drihten W*ed*era gedōn wolde;
swӯðe (wēn)don, þæt hē slēac wǣre,
æðeling unfrom. Edwenden cwōm
tīrēadịgum menn torna gehwylces. (ll. 2183–2189)

(For a long time he was contemned, as the
children of the Geats knew him not to be brave,
nor would the lord of the Geats do him much
honor at the meadbench. They very much
suspected he was slothful, a feeble princeling;
but to the glorious man there came a reversal
of all afflictions.)

In the schema of a *Heldenleben,* a bad start in life forms an alternative to the promising-youth motif: the child is abandoned or indolent and sluggish in his early years. Offa I, Egil Skallagrímsson, Orm

Stórolfsson, and Grettir inn sterki, among others, are heroes whose lives begin with the slothful-youth motif. Both of these negative alternatives appear in the Beowulf poem: Scyld's mysterious arrival in a boat as an abandoned babe without worldly goods is reversed at the end of his life when he is laid to rest in a ship and set adrift with much pomp, honor, and wealth (ll. 6–7 and ll. 43–46). Beowulf's supposedly unpromising beginning also takes the opposite turn, as the poet points out. It is as if the poet, realizing the contradiction with his earlier reports, saw a chance to bring in yet another neat reversal in his pattern.[84] Moreover, he no doubt felt constrained to include this motif in order not to miss any of the typical aspects of his hero, in order to define and describe his object from all sides with all the variations. The *Beowulf* poet incorporated the two conflicting elements into the structure of his work and ingeniously accommodated them to his specific purpose.

Concerning the working method of the early poets, Hermann Schneider observes: "Einzelmotive wiederholten sich oft und gerne, und gemäss der Typik des mittelalterlichen Denkens stellten sich kurze Motivkomplexe zwangsläufig ein, sobald die Assoziation einmal ausgelöst war."[85] A similar explanation might also apply to the seemingly dual origin of the dragon's hoard, which first is described as the legacy of the last survivor of a noble race (ll. 2232–2241), and later as a treasure hoarded by illustrious chiefs who put a curse on it (ll. 3069–3073). Out of these two strains Klaeber attempts to piece together a connected history for the hoard.[86] Even if the poet may have felt obliged to include the curse motif simply because it traditionally belonged to the hoard motif, one element in particular speaks for Klaeber's interpretation: the disjointed sequence in which the origin of the hoard is presented would accord with the poet's anachronous technique of breaking up a connected tale or history. If, Klaeber's explanation being assumed, it is true that illustrious chiefs in ages past (l. 3050) buried the hoard in the earth and put a curse on it (ll. 3069–3073), and that at some later time ancestors of the Last Survivor wrested it from the earth (ll. 2248 ff.) and owned it for a time, until war and carnage carried them all off, the lone survivor being left to

[84] See Bonjour, *The Digressions*, p. 5.
[85] Schneider, *Germanische Heldensage*, I, 169.
[86] Klaeber (ed.), *Beowulf*, note to ll. 2231 ff., p. 209.

conceal the treasures once again in the earth—then one might reason further that the noble race of the Last Survivor met with tragedy because of the curse. The Last Survivor's plight and the fate of the hoard —to lie in the ground and rust—create in fact the mood for the analogous situation with Beowulf. He, like the Last Survivor, has no direct heir; and even though he fully expects his people to make use of the wealth (ll. 2800–2801), the curse is fulfilled. He who has attempted to win the gold has thereby lost his life, and the treasure will do no man good. It will only bring disaster upon the Geatish people and the end of their kingdom.

Some have suggested that the Last Survivor transformed himself into the dragon to guard the hoard forever,[87] but this does not accord with the poet's version that the dragon found it lying open, unattended (ll. 2270–2271). The supernatural element surrounding the hoard is referred to in several places in the poem apart from the direct mention of the curse: the barrow is difficult of access because of some craft or cunning (*nearocræftum fæst* [l. 2243]); the barrow or treasure is the work of giants (*enta geweorc* [l. 2274]);[88] the gold is bounded by a spell (*galdre bewunden* [l. 3052]). The curse explains Beowulf's fated end. A warrior's final hour always comes unexpectedly, and through some craft or cunning (compare the Pliezhausen theme). In two passages the poet tells how the curse may be avoided:

Swā mæg unfǣge ēaðe gedīgan
wēan ond wrǣscīð sē ðe Waldendes
hyldo gehealdeþ! (ll. 2291–2294)

(Thus may an undoomed man,—one who retains
the favour of the Almighty, lightly pass
through both woe and banishment.)

þonne wæs þæt yrfe ēacencræftig,
iūmonna gold galdre bewunden,
þæt ðām hringsele hrīnan ne mōste
gumena ǣnig, nefne God sylfa,
sigora Sōðcyning sealde þām ðe hē wolde
—hē is manna gehyld— hord openian,
efne swā hwylcum manna, swā him gemet ðūhte. (ll. 3051–3057)

[87] Panzer, *Beowulf*, pp. 308–309.

[88] By *enta geweorc* either the hoard itself or its stone chamber could be implied (Klaeber [ed.], *Beowulf*, note to l. 2773 f., p. 221).

(At that time the mighty heritage, the gold
store of men of old, was hedged round with a spell,
that no man might touch the treasure chamber, had
not God himself, true king of victories [he is
the shield of men], granted to whom he would to
open the hoard, even to such a man as seemed meet
to him.)

But the pagan ethos remains paramount; God did not favor his loyal servant and break the curse, although the poet emphasizes Beowulf's innocence:

Næs hē goldhwæte gearwor hæfðe
āgendes ēst ǣr gescēawod. (ll. 3074–3075)[89]

(Yet by no means too eagerly had Beowulf
before gazed upon its owner's treasure of
gold with the curse on it.)

Traditionally the curse is related to human weakness and gold-greediness.[90] Andvari puts a curse on the gold because of Loki's insistence on obtaining the last ring. Regin and Fáfnir's quarrel over Andvari's gold leads to the death of the two brothers. That this ethical element must also have been in the mind of the *Beowulf* poet can be seen from the inclusion of the "hoard and gold" motivation in Beowulf's actions and from the admonishment given as Wiglaf gathers the treasures:

Sinc ēaðe mæg,
gold on grund(e) gumcynnes gehwone
oferhīgian, hȳde sē ðe wylle! (ll. 2764–2766)

(Treasure, gold in the earth, may easily
get the better of any man, conceal it who
will.)

One of the tasks of a typical hero is to win magic objects or valuable

[89] I do not accept Klaeber's proposed change in l. 3074 of *Næs hē* to *næfne* (*Beowulf*, p. 227 n.), or his interpretation of *āgendes* as a kenning for God. However, Klaeber, too, would interpret the line generally as a declaration of Beowulf's innocence. As we have seen, Beowulf has by no means been lacking in desire to win gold and the hoard. It is perfectly consonant with the tenor of the poem to have God's favor, the dominance of Fate, the eagerness for fame and gold, and the hero's virtue all present simultaneously, as it were.

[90] See de Vries, *Altnordische Literaturgeschichte*, I, 298.

treasure. Their acquisition is attended by hindrances and peril. The serpent Ladon guards the Golden Apples of the Hesperides; Herakles must slay the serpent to gain the prize. Another prototype, Sigemund, with whom Beowulf is compared, conquered a dragon and carried off the hoard. But Beowulf is more like the other famed dragon hero, Sigurd (Siegfried), whose desire for gold and possession of the hoard wrested from the dragon Fáfnir meant his ultimate downfall because of Andvari's curse.[91]

One might speculate here on the origin of the firmly established connection between dragon, hoard, and curse. As discussed elsewhere, the political enemy was in fact visualized as the archenemy, the dragon. War booty, treasures, and weaponry were the prizes of victory over "the dragon." This wealth, symbol of power, often gave rise to envy, betrayal, and strife. Tragic death through the cunning of relatives ensues for the chieftain; leaderless, his tribe dies out amid internal dissension. The possession of the treasure is felt to be the ultimate cause of disaster and thus as a curse. Höfler tentatively ventures such a hypothesis for the Siegfried legend. Briefly, the historical facts upon which he bases this part of his argument are as follows:[92]

The silver treasure discovered at Hildesheim in 1868 belonged to Varus and was confiscated by Arminius and divided with his father-in-law, Segestes, after the victorious battle in the Teutoburg forest (A.D. 9). Segestes later capitulated to the Romans (A.D. 15), and his share of the treasure found its way back to Rome (Tacitus, *Ann.* I, lvii, 5). As the weight markings on the pieces indicate, precisely one half of the original treasure is represented at Hildesheim. Arminius met his end through the cunning of his relatives (*dolus propinquorum*, Tacitus, *Ann.* II, lxxxviii) in A.D. 21. Within the century, *ca.* A.D. 100, Arminius' tribe, the Cherusci, had lost all political significance (Tacitus, *Germania,* Ch. 36) and had succumbed to civil strife (Tacitus, *Ann.* XI, xvi). The Varus booty was buried at Galgenberg near Hildesheim, a place associated with cult sacrifices. Thus it is surmised that

[91] It has long been a matter of speculation why the *Beowulf* poet drew his comparison with Sigemund as dragon-slayer rather than Sigurd. It would seem that the famous deed of Sigurd was transferred to the father, instead of vice versa, as Schneider assumes (*Germanische Heldensage,* I, 164). The further back in time an event can be placed the more venerable, the more wondrous it becomes. A similar tendency toward contamination and confusion of stories surrounding father and son with alliterating names can be witnessed in the miraculous-boat origin attributed both to Scyld and Scef (see Chambers, *Beowulf: An Introduction,* p. 86).

[92] Höfler, *Siegfried, Arminius,* pp. 118–119 n. 305 and pp. 174 ff.

the treasure was offered to the gods or buried there to annul its curse. It had brought about the downfall of the tribe.

The sinking of the royal treasure of the Burgundians in the Rhine at the approach of the Huns, A.D. 437, perhaps offers another historical parallel. In that case, the hoard motif may have served as one of the links connecting the two cycles of legends in the *Nibelungenlied*.[93]

Since the *Beowulf* poet deliberately creates the hypothetical situation of the Last Survivor of a noble race in possession of a hoard with a curse on it, thereby setting up a parallel with Beowulf's predicament and the downfall of the Geats, it seems reasonable to assume that similar legends from history served as prototype. The Danes fall to the *dolus propinquorum,* and the Geats lose their leader and fall prey to their enemies because of a curse on wealth and power. History had shown the same things time and again, revealing itself as repetitive archetypal instances. And this is what the *Beowulf* poet wished to convey.

In Christianizing his pagan hero, the poet brought Beowulf closer to the Thor type of dragon-slayer (preserver of humanity, champion against the forces of chaos and destruction). But he also felt obliged to include the other side of the *topos.* Desire to win gold also motivates Beowulf's act (Sigurd-type), despite the poet's attempt to exonerate his hero from all blemish of avarice. Here again the poet could not refrain from endowing his hero with all the typical components of his inherited pattern, as variation and elaboration on his one theme.

Thorough investigation of this motif complex is beyond the purposes here, but no matter what its ultimate origin in myth or in history (history experienced, to be sure, as exemplification of archetypes), it

[93] Schröder, "Mythos und Heldensage," pp. 294–295. Saxo Grammaticus (*The First Nine Books of the Danish History,* trans. Oliver Elton [London: David Nutt, 1894], Book II, p. 50) relates a similar incident where the tribal hoard was abandoned: "Handwan, seeing that the fortunes of his country were lost and overthrown, put all his royal wealth on shipboard and drowned it in the sea, so as to enrich the waves rather than his enemy." Höfler (*Siegfried, Arminius,* p. 95) suggests that the associative links in combining the two legends may have been two such analogous happenings as: (1) the fall of the Cherusker through treachery of relatives in the murder of Arminius = Siegfried and the subsequent burial of the tribe's treasure and (2) the fall of the Burgundians caused by strife when a near relative of the king, his Frankish son-in-law, also with a name in *Sig-* (cf. Helmut de Boor, "Hat Siegfried gelebt?" in *Zur germanisch-deutschen Heldensage,* hrsg. von Karl Hauck, pp. 35, 43), was murdered, and thereafter the tribal wealth sunk in the Rhine. It would seem that these recurrent types of events in history became literary *topoi.*

was already a firmly established tradition with which the *Beowulf* poet was acquainted and which he employed in a manner suitable to the peculiar structure of his work.

Grettis saga

The similarity of motifs in *Beowulf* and *Grettis saga* was first noted by Gudbrand Vigfússon in 1878.[94] Later, Friedrich Panzer traced the motifs to the Bear's Son and Strong John fairy tales.[95] Since then, the consensus has been that the two literary works drew on the fairy-tale material independently, but most likely on the same variant because of the coincidence of the words *hæftmēce* and *heptisax* and the occurrence of the identical excuse for the desertion of the comrade(s), namely blood on the water, a component otherwise not attested in the known Märchen variants.[96] One of the most characteristic elements of the fairy tale, however, the freeing of a princess, enters into neither *Beowulf* nor *Grettis saga,* and the motifs in these two *Heldensagen* can be explained only by recourse to several Märchen.

It will be well first to sift out those elements in the *Grettis saga* which parallel the typical *Heldenleben* as defined above and then to determine in what respects Grettir deviates from the pattern and from Beowulf.

Archetypal Characteristics in Grettir

BIRTH AND YOUTH

Grettir's genealogy can be found in the *Landnámabók,* which confirms that he was a historical person, an Icelander who died A.D. 1031. Reference to his ancestor Ófeig grettir suggests that the name *Grettir* was originally an agnomen: "Ófeigr hét maðr ok var kallaðr grettir" (Chap. 3).[97] Etymologically, it goes back to **grantjan* and to derivative

[94] Prolegomena to the *Sturlunga saga, including the Islendinga saga of Lawman Sturla Thordson and other Works*, ed. Gudbrand Vigfússon (Oxford: Clarendon Press, 1878), p. xlix.

[95] Panzer makes use of some 202 variants of these fairy tales to illustrate similarities with the Beowulf elements.

[96] Panzer, *Beowulf,* p. 176.

[97] Quotations from the *Grettis saga* are from Guðni Jónsson (ed.), *Íslenzk fornrit,* Vol. VII (Reykjavík: Hið íslenzka fornritafélag, 1936). For the occurrence of the name *grettir* in the genealogies of Grettir inn sterki (Ásmundarson), see *Landnámabók Íslands* (udgiven efter de gamle håndskrifter af det kongelige nordiske oldskriftselskab

words meaning "to sneer, snarl, make a wry face."[98] The *ævikviða* in the saga use *kennings* for *ormr* (snake), and these in turn signify Grettir.[99] Association of the name with the snake apparently derives from the snake's snarly face when producing its hissing noise.[100] The snake association had not been lost by the time the saga was composed, for not all the *ævikviða* can be attributed to Grettir himself as author.[101] The epithet later became a personal name and as such is not uncommon,[102] no doubt applying to persons with surly and mean temperaments.

Grendel's name, among other tenuous solutions, has been traced to the Old Icelandic *grenja* (to bellow, to gnash the teeth), which is related to **grantjan.* Thus, Grendel and Grettir have certain chthonic connotations in common. Grettir's name may possibly have attracted the author of the saga to the ogre tales which became attached to the historical Grettir. The outlaw-hero suggested a monster-hero at the same time, with the evil and the good combined in one figure.

Hallbjorn Hálftroll counts among Grettir's ancestors; thus he is placed in the company of at least half supernatural beings. Many a hero, like Hygelac, became equated with giants, monsters, or trolls. Beowulf, too, exhibited a marked likeness to Grendel. *Berserkir* and *úlfheðnar* functioned as protectors for the tribe, but also embraced demonic qualities, as noted earlier. On two occasions, Grettir is actually likened to a troll: when, covered with ice from his swim, he comes into the hall to fetch fire (Chap. 38) and when he carries Steinvor of Sandhaugar across the raging river (Chap. 64). Steinvor tells her kinsmen that she cannot say whether it was a man or a troll that helped her. Glám is another such figure, half man, half beast.

From the beginning a dark brooding and restless dissatisfaction possess Grettir. As a boy he develops late, is surly and sullen, speaking in ditties and rhymes or terse proverbs, prone to violent deeds (slothful-youth motif). When set at chores on the farm, he is resentful and takes

til minde om dets hundrede år 1825–1925 [København: H. H. Thiele Bogtrykkeri, 1925]), Sec. 8 of *Sunnlendingarfjórðungr,* pp. 11, 24, and 41.

[98] De Vries, *Altnordisches etymologisches Wörterbuch,* p. 187 (s.v. *gretta*).

[99] *Ævikviða* in *Grettis saga*: verse 26, *þinul fjalla* ("chain of mountains") = *ormr* = Grettir; verse 34, *lautar áll* ("land's eel") = *ormr* = Grettir; verse 42, *þvengr þundar beðju* ("Earth's clamp") = *miðgardsormr* = Grettir.

[100] *Grettis saga,* Chap. 3, p. 7, n. 2.

[101] *Ibid., Formáli,* pp. xxxvii–xxxviii.

[102] *Ibid.,* Chap. 3, p. 7, n. 2.

revenge by killing all the goslings he was to tend, by brutally scraping his father's back with a sharp comb instead of giving him a back rub, by flaying the prized mare so as not to have to watch the herd. His unusual strength first becomes known at a contest of ball when he is fourteen and badly worsts Audun, who is bigger and older. Grettir's phenomenal strength remains that feature throughout his life which distinguishes him above all men. He heaves great stones (Chaps. 16, 30, and 59), bails water as fast as eight men (Chap. 17), carries a huge ox alone (Chap. 50), outwrestles two men, who, it is claimed, have the combined strength of four (Chap. 74), and swims long distances in icy waters (Chaps. 38, 58, and 76). He is willing to face unbelievable odds, on one occasion dauntlessly attempting to ward off no fewer than eighty men single-handed (Chap. 57).

This ne'er-do-well of great brawn also kills a bear at a farm in Halogaland, thereby putting to shame the champion, Bjorn (Chap. 21). It is at once apparent that Grettir's indolent and remarkable youth, his abnormal strength, his theriomorphic and troll-like qualities, and the slaying of a bear belong to the traditional schema of a *Heldenleben.*

ADVENTURES

Five of Grettir's exploits in particular should be considered in their relationship to the episodes in *Beowulf.*

Háramarsey (Chap. 18). Thorfinn's father, Kár the Old, has been ghostwalking on the island. Grettir notices fire burning on a mound and says that fire burning above ground means hidden treasure there. Oblivious to all warnings, he descends into the barrow by means of a rope. He and Kár wrestle and topple over everything in the barrow. Using an ancestral sword, Grettir lays the ghost by striking off its head and placing it at the thigh. He finds great treasures of gold and silver in the barrow and also Kár's choice sword. Upon hearing the great din inside, Grettir's comrade waiting at the rope deserts him. Winning of the hoarded treasure is compared to Fáfnir's gold by a kenning in a poem which Grettir sings in his triumphant success.[103]

Halogaland (Chap. 21). In the winter a ferocious bear begins to ravage the region around Halogaland, sparing neither man nor beast. Thorkel's farm is special object of his preying. People attribute the

[103] Verse 7. The kenning, *Fáfnis mýri* ("Fáfnir's moor"), recalls the archetypal situation: treasure in the earth, whether guarded by *draugr* or dragon.

calamity to the boisterous carousing of Bjorn and his companions, who stay abroad at night. The enraged beast stays in his lair by day, but prowls at night. The cave lair is situated on a sheer cliff by the sea. At Yule, an expedition to the lair is made; Grettir slays the bear single-handed after the others have departed, for he wants to show off his prowess, alone and unaided. He hews off one of the bear's paws; they fall down the cliff and grapple with one another. Grettir strikes him through the heart with his sword. He brings back the paw as a trophy.

Thórhallsstadir (Chap. 35). At Yuletide, Glám, a troll-like creature himself, is killed by monsters inhabiting the rocky glens. Thereafter, Glám haunts the farm and neighborhood. A year later, at the Winter's Nights, Grettir comes to the farm. He lies in wait for the ogre, does not take off his clothes, and a light burns in the farm hall, already badly shattered from all the previous hauntings. Grettir and Glám wrestle mightily, breaking up everything in their path. Grettir is dragged outside. He succeeds in laying the ghost, using Kár's good sword, and places the head at the thigh, but not before Glám has spoken his curse:

> "Þú hefir frægr orðit hér til af verkum þínum, en heðan af munu falla til þín sekðir ok vígaferli, en flest ǫll verk þín snúask þér til ógæfu ok hamingjuleysis. Þú munt verða útlægr gǫrr ok hljóta jafnan úti at búa einn samt. Þá legg ek þat á við þik, at þessi augu sé þér þá erfitt þykkja einum at vera, ok þat mun þér til dauða draga." (Chap. 25, p. 121)
>
> ("You have earned fame up until now from your deeds, but henceforth only penalties and manslayings will fall to your lot, and most all your deeds will turn to your misfortune and ill-hap. You will be made an outlaw, and it will be your fate always to dwell outside alone. Then I place this curse on you, that these eyes of mine make it difficult for you to be alone, and that will drag you to your death.")

Sandhaugar (Chap. 65). During two successive winters, at Yuletide, first the farmer, then a bondman vanish from the farm, taken by the trolls. In the third winter, at Yule, Grettir comes to the farm. He lies in wait for the troll; he keeps his clothes on and a light burns in the hall all night. A troll woman appears with trough and knife. They wrestle and break all before them. Grettir is dragged outside to the brink of a gorge, but succeeds in striking off the troll woman's arm. She falls into the waterfall and disappears into the gulf. (According to the folk version, she turns into a stone image that can be seen at the edge of the cliff.)[104]

The Waterfall (Chaps. 65–66). Grettir is curious to find out if the missing men are in the watery gorge. He lets down a rope, which the priest Stein is to guard. He dives in and struggles against whirlpools until he comes to the bottom and up under the falls into a cave. A fire gleams within, and a hideous giant is sitting there. The giant smites him with a *heptisax* and is about to reach for a sword that hangs on the wall in the cave when Grettir deals him his bane. Blood stains on the water indicate to Stein that the hero is dead, and he deserts the rope. Grettir investigates the cave. He finds the bones of the two men who had disappeared. No mention is made of the troll woman. The saga teller states:

> Ekki er frá því sagt, hversu mikit fé hann fekk í hellinum, en þat ætla menn, at verit hafi nǫkkut. (Chap. 66, p. 216)
>
> (It is not told how much treasure he found in the cave, but people think that it must have been a great deal.)

No gods are invoked to aid the hero, and, on the whole, no supernatural powers give succor to Grettir in his ordeals. But what can be said about Fate as the unalterable force behind his tragic life? The turning point in Grettir's career begins properly with Glám's curse. Yet, throughout the saga, his ill-starred lot is anticipated and re-emphasized: predictions in the beginning all mark him as a trouble-maker and the "bane of many" (Chaps. 16, p. 45; 23, p. 82; 31, pp. 104–105; 40, p. 137). The misgivings expressed about Grettir's temperament and future luck, Glám's curse, his mother's warning prophecy and the sorceress' magic trick could be construed as tangible signs for a fate that predetermined Grettir's end. Although effects of Glám's curse and the witch's magic prove ineluctable, it is not so much destiny which predisposes Grettir for his end, but ill luck. The fatalistic view of life can be expressed in two ways, either as destiny which brings to completion what was foreordained or as good and bad fortune experienced in in-

[104] Such stories were commonly invented by the folk to explain the strange lava and rock formations seen around waterfalls and gorges, as at Goðafoss or the Trollkonuhlaup in the Þjórsá. See *Grettis saga,* Chap. 65, pp. 213–214, n. 2.

dividual lives, the whimsical winds of chance. Grettir's great physical strength may be turned to good or to evil. He is unpredictable, one time deliberately inviting trouble, picking quarrels, delighting in showing off his capabilities and brawn, the next time using his gifts to aid people in distress. The few laudable acts are overridden at first by his meanness and quarrelsome nature. Ultimately, circumstances and his ill temper work against him. The curse tips the balance toward disaster. Chance would have it that the men burn in the house where he fetched fire, that the lawman dies just before his possible acquittal, that Thorbjorn glaum brings in the cursed tree. But even sorcery no longer holds absolute sway. The old woman's craft works its spell but is condemned by others. With the acceptance of Christianity went naturally the diabolization of the heathen ways. But there are scarcely any obviously Christian elements in *Grettis saga* (if one disregards the epilogue). On the other hand, the more tragic conception of Fate is also lacking.

That Grettir's tragedy is not that of destiny can be seen in the lighter touches in the saga. Not all troll-like creatures are malicious. Hallmund and his daughter in the cave on the heath are helpful and friendly (the only time when one could say that Grettir receives the aid of benevolent powers). But most striking is Grettir's manner of speaking in proverbs and ditties. This reflects an attitude that passes off the vicissitudes of life with a kind of shrug that says, "so life goes, such is fortune's way." This almost happy-go-lucky air in face of adversity is particularly well brought out in the relayed exchange of verses between Grettir and Svein, as Grettir goes riding along on the horse stolen from Svein, just after having learned that his father has died, his brother been killed, and a price placed on his own head (Chap. 67).

Beowulf and *Grettis saga* Contrasted

Scholars have unanimously felt that the correspondences in motifs between the *Grettis saga* and *Beowulf* are too close to be merely fortuitous. As has been repeatedly pointed out, the events at Sandhaugar, with the subsequent struggle against the giant under the waterfall, bear an undeniable resemblance to Beowulf's encounters with Grendel at Heorot and to his subterranean combat against Grendel's dam in the fen, although with a reversal of sequence in the role of the troll woman. Yet, the fact that many of the motifs are reused in the ghost-laying in Kár's barrow, in the Halogaland bear episode, and at Thórhallsstadir suggests an interchangeability and availability of a common stock of closely associated motifs. The remarkable sword in the barrow or cave may assume different functions under varying circumstances; the hoard motif comes up in Kár's barrow and in the giant's waterfall cave, as well as in Grendel's cave and in the dragon's lair. It would appear that an established tradition makes it possible to connect the hoard with any class of chthonic beings: dragons, troll-monsters, giants, or *draugar* (ghosts).

No one, to my knowledge, has taken into account the fact that both Grendel and dragon motifs appear in a recombined form in the Halogaland bear episode. This should not seem surprising since even in the *Beowulf* poem there are points of contact between the Grendel episodes and the dragon event. The bear in *Grettis saga* is roused by noise and gaiety, as is Grendel in his attacks on Heorot (*Grettis saga,* Chap. 21, p. 74; *Beowulf,* ll. 86–90). Grendel holds such sway over Heorot and the misty moors that men may not venture forth (*Beowulf*, ll. 161–163); the bear comes forth to stalk man and beast, particularly plaguing Thorkel's farm; the dragon lays waste the whole region with fire (*Beowulf,* ll. 2333–2335). (Similarly, Kár spirits away all the farmers on the island, Glám ravages cattle and men, the troll woman at Sandhaugar causes two men to vanish). The bear, like Grendel, the dragon, and all the other ghosts and trolls, haunts at night. Hand-to-hand grappling takes place when the bear and Grettir topple down over the precipice and when Beowulf struggles with the mere-wife in the cave (*Beowulf*, ll. 1539–1546). (Similarly, Kár falls over on his back, as does Glám with Grettir.) Boastfully, like Beowulf in the fights against Grendel and the dragon—although Beowulf in his eagerness disclaims all boasting (ll. 2527–2528), illustrative of the poet's innovation in handling his theme—Grettir wants to demonstrate his prowess and courage single-handed against the bear (*Beowulf,* ll. 424–426, 431, 436–438, 2532–2535 [note the words *āna, ānes*]; *Grettis saga*, Chap. 21, p. 76: "mun hann vilja hafa frægð af ok drepa einn dýrit"). That the bear wards off all spear thrusts with his teeth and is hard to get at recalls an invulnerability to weapons and the bite of iron continually referred to in respect to Grendel, Grendel's dam and the dragon (*Grettis saga,* Chap. 21, p. 75; *Beowulf,* ll. 433–440, 677–685, 798–805, 1522–1525, 1531–1534, 2575–2580, 2677–2684).

Grettir also follows well-known tradition by striking the bear to the heart (*Grettis saga*, Chap. 21, p. 77).[105] The dragon, too, succumbs only when pierced in his most vulnerable spot:

> Nē hēdde hē þæs heafolan,   ac sīo hand gebarn
> mōdiges mannes,   þær hē his mǣg*es* healp,
> þæt hē þone nīðgæst   nioðor hwēne slōh,
> secg on searwum,   þæt ðæt sweord gedēaf
> fāh ond fǣted,   þæt ðæt fȳr ongon
> sweðrian syððan.   (ll. 2697–2702)
>
> (He cared not about the head: but the brave man's hand [Wiglaf's] was scorched the while he helped his kinsman, so that he, the man in armour, struck the vengeful stranger a little lower down, in such wise that the sword, gleaming and overlaid, plunged in, and the fire began thenceforth to abate.)

That Beowulf does not accomplish the fight alone and the fact that Wiglaf actually deals the decisive blow exhibit the poet's free handling of his theme.

Grettir not only strikes off the troll woman's arm, he also hews off the bear's paw (*Grettis saga*, Chap. 21, p. 76). Thus Grendel, the Sandhaugar ogress, and the bear are all mutilated in a similar manner by their assailant. Grendel's clawlike hand and the bear's paw are shown off in triumph (*Beowulf*, ll. 835–836; *Grettis saga*, Chap. 21, p. 77). The bear's cave lair near the sea, with a narrow path, difficult of access, and with rocky cliffs plunging to the sea (*Grettis saga*, Chap. 21, p. 74), recalls the dragon's lair (*Beowulf*, ll. 2241–2243).

Chambers has summarized the results of comparisons between Saxo's account of Bödvar bjarki (Book II of the *Gesta Danorum*), *Hrólfs saga kraka* (in the *Fornaldarsögur*), and the *Bjarkarímur*, which deal with similar material and motifs. Because the winged beast in *Hrólfs saga kraka* turns out to be a bear in Saxo's narrative, Chambers claims that the resemblances all but disappear and that the comparison between Beowulf and Bödvar bjarki should be limited to the Grendel episode,

[105] See also *Fáfnismál* in the *Poetic Edda*, where Sigurd digs a trench and strikes the dragon from below, and also Saxo, *The First Nine Books*, Book 2, pp. 45–46, concerning Frotho, son of Hadingus, and his slaying of the dragon: "Though the force of his scales spurn thy spears, yet know there is a place under his lowest belly wither thou mayest probe the snake to his centre."

a restriction that excludes consideration of the dragon encounter.[106] In *Hrólfs saga kraka* Bjarki kills the winged beast, which is immune to all weapons, later boasts of slaying the *berserkr* Agnar, and claims a previous battle with King Hjörvardi, who miraculously stayed alive after feigning death when Bjarki had cut off his hand and foot.[107] In Saxo's account Biarco kills an Agnar in a duel, meets with a bear in a thicket and slays it. In the *Bjarkarímur* the foe is a man-eating she-wolf and a grey bear. In the final analysis these are all adversaries of the same genus. If in the cult-practices taming of bears or wild boars (some monstrous beast) makes up part of the initiation rites, it is to be understood as preparation for defeating the tribal enemy, envisioned as a monster or dragon. As noted on the helmets,[108] bearlike beast or dragon may function as a symbol of inimical and destructive forces. Thus, in the later heroic literature in particular, feats against any beast of great ferocity, or against ogres like Grendel, may well be interchanged, for they all demonstrate prowess. Only the *Beowulf* poet has kept a distinction between preliminary and less significant deeds and the final monumental act. Beowulf (his name tells us he is a bear hero) fells giants and fights sea monsters prior to his encounters with the Grendel ogres; these latter are then in turn but preparation for the dragon fight. Grettir kills a bear, subdues *berserkir,* lays ghosts and trolls; Bjarki kills a *berserkr* Agnar, brings to submission a group of other *berserkir*, and slays a winged beast in one account, a bear according to another. In contrast to Beowulf's deeds, these episodes are all on the same level.

Since the beast type is also interchangeable, the bear episode in *Grettis saga* may well exhibit points of similarity with both the Grendel and the dragon motifs in *Beowulf*. Grendel resembles a bear but has in fact a pouch made of dragon skins (*Beowulf*, ll. 2085–2088). These

106 Chambers, *Beowulf: An Introduction,* pp. 57–58. Chadwick ("The Monsters," p. 180) equates Agnar or the bear with Grendel, the winged monster with the dragon.

107 *Hrólfs saga kraka,* in *Fornaldarsögur norðurlanda,* ed. Guðni Jónsson (Reykjavík: Íslendingasagnaútgáfan, 1954), Vol. I, Chap. 35, pp. 66–67, Chap. 50, pp. 100–101, Chap. 51, p. 103.

108 The monster or bear motif appears as a dragon-like creature on the Valsgärde 8 helmet. See Heinrich Beck, *Das Ebersignum im Germanischen: Ein Beitrag zur germanischen Tier-Symbolik,* in the series *Quellen und Forschungen zur Sprach- und Kulturgeschichte der germanischen Völker,* begründet von Bernhard ten Brink und Wilhelm Scherer (N. F., hrsg. von Hermann Kunisch, Vol. 16 [140]; Berlin: Walter de Gruyter & Co., 1965), pp. 26–27, on relatedness of these chthonic images.

similarities and interchanges are common stock in the later *Fornaldarsögur.* The giant Fáfnir transforms himself into a dragon to guard his gold, as does Hárek in the *Valsþáttr*, and also Val, and Gullthórir in the *Þorskfirðinga saga.* Bödvar bjarki himself takes on the form of a bear in the fight against Hjörvardi and Skuld. Hero and adversary are also alike, it will be remembered. In later folk belief a mixing of all these elements was bound to take place. *Berserkir* and *úlfheðnar* in the far distant past had participated in the *Totenheer* procession of ancestors, were one with the dead. They, like Beowulf and Grettir, resembled demons, sharing characteristics with their adversaries and with monsters. They could take on, therefore, a purely demonic role. Agnar is called a *berserkr* in *Hrólfs saga kraka,* and, among the *berserkir* at Thorfinn's farm in the *Grettis saga*, one is named Ogmund (names in *Ag-* and *Og-* frequently designate trolls). In *Grettis saga,* the *draugar*, the trolls, the bear, and the *berserkir* conspicuously make their appearance at the time of the Winter's Nights or Yule. In *Hrólfs saga kraka*, the winged beast and the *berserkir* also make their visit at Yule. This is the same time of year when the *Totenheer,* according to long since forgotten custom, stormed through villages and over the countryside on their periodic ride.[109] Thus, ghostwalkers and all evil creatures came to be associated with that particular time of year.

Traces of other religious beliefs can be discerned in the description of Thórisdal and in the amusement Grettir enjoyed with the daughters of Thórir, the troll ruler of the valley. This forsaken and fertile valley, hedged in by icy glaciers, while strikingly representative of the Icelandic landscape, in all likelihood harks back to the mythical land of the dead, Glæsisvellir, with its ruler Guðmund and his daughters.[110]

The author of *Grettis saga* drew on diverse traditions in order to outfit his hero with adventures and to magnify his historically attestable deeds. The associations with Bjorn hitdœlakappi, Glæsisvellir, and the Halogalanders may suggest familiarity with themes from Bjarmaland and East Scandinavia. N. K. Chadwick has attempted to demonstrate a closer and more precise relationship between *Beowulf-Grettis saga* on the one hand and some of the *Fornaldarsögur* on the other, particularly *Hrólfs saga kraka, Hálfdanar saga Eysteinssonar, Þorsteins*

[109] See de Vries, *Altgermanische Religionsgeschichte,* I, 448–450, 453, 496–499.
[110] See Höfler, *Kultische Geheimbünde,* pp. 172–173; de Vries, "Betrachtungen," pp. 61, 63, 145, and *Altgermanische Religionsgeschichte,* II, 285; Chadwick, "The Monsters," p. 191.

þáttr bæjarmagns, Harðar saga ok Hólmverja, Bósa saga ok Herrauðs konungs, Valsþáttr, and *Gull-Þóris saga*. It appears that descendants of one family from among the Geats and Halogalanders assail a group of related monsters generation after generation. The fact that dragons, barrows, waterfalls, and guarded treasure occur as motifs in the majority of the *Fornaldarsögur*, as well as in *Beowulf* and *Grettis saga*, and the fact that Beowulf, too, is a Geat, constitute the only real points of similarity between them. Except for *Hrólfs saga kraka*, the circumstances and contexts under which the elements occur in the other *Fornaldarsögur* immediately impress one as far too dissimilar, weakened, or contaminated to establish any meaningful connection. Besides, the motifs constitute standard components in such tales. Whether in the remoteness of time all the *membra disjecta* in these tales formed together a unified cycle similar to the complex of motifs in *Beowulf, Hrólfs saga kraka*, Saxo, and *Grettis saga* will have to remain a moot question. For comparison, the elements must present something more distinctive and must form an analogously knit-together complex, as is present in the latter group.[111]

Chadwick's suggestion on the interrelationship between mythological and secular events applies to any and all such ogre feuds:

> The struggles between the hero and the monsters is a hereditary one in the leading families of the north, and the members are the nucleus of a family of evil spirits, whether euhemerized as a political unity, or transformed at some time from actual hostile people into a family of monsters on a traditional pattern.[112]

As a further sidelight on this question, she mentions the identification of Hárek with the historical king Horik and of Raknar in *Bárðar saga* and *Valsþáttr* with the viking Ragnar, who raided the Frankish kingdom, and she states that "if correct, it can hardly be other than a case of transference of names and of adaptation of an old mythological conception to a political situation."[113] (This widespread phenomenon has been discussed earlier.) It would seem, then, that only the most general assumptions can be ventured concerning the common origin for all these tales.

[111] On this point, see de Vries, "Betrachtungen," p. 46; Chambers, *Beowulf: An Introduction*, p. 95.

[112] Chadwick, "The Monsters," p. 200.

[113] *Ibid.*, p. 184 n. 1.

The occurrence of the forms *hæftmēce* and *heptisax* probably should not carry too much weight in establishing a dependency or common source for the motifs in *Beowulf* and *Grettis saga,* since this weapon may merely belong to the paraphernalia of trolls and giants, much as troll women traditionally appear with trough and *skálm*, a stubby knife or sword with which one could both thrust and cut.[114] Beowulf bears the *hæftmēce* Hrunting, an ancient heirloom of Unferth, "patterned by twigs of venom." Its origin would seem therefore to go back to the work of giants, as does so much of the other weaponry mentioned in *Beowulf.* In *Grettis saga,* it is the giant under the waterfall who uses such a weapon. Both Hrunting and the giant's *heptisax* fail in the battle's need. The reason that both authors used the motif of blood stains on the water to indicate the hero's supposed death and thus to exonerate the companion(s) for their desertion may not incontestably be attributed to borrowing from the same Märchen variant. The author of *Grettis saga* has in another place substituted into the same mold a different substance: Grettir's companion at Kárs barrow deserts the rope because he hears a *din* inside. The particular subterranean situation, under water or in a barrow, would seem to be the determining factor in selecting the type of sign for the hero's death, and the underwater cave is not a motif unique to these two works.

Although a certain combination of motifs is paralleled in the *Beowulf* and *Grettis saga,* it is the use to which these motifs are put in the individual works that is decisive in any appraisal or analysis. Despite the similarities in "raw material," how different the presentation and tone! In *Grettis saga*, it is at once obvious that the ogre motifs function aptly as arbitrary, episodic adventures attached to the hero along with all the manslaughters and other ostentatious exhibitions of his daring and strength, whereas in *Beowulf* they form the very nucleus of the poem and are causally motivated. Grettir jumps from one adventure into another without apparent connection:

> Þá þótti Gretti mikit mein, er hann mátti hvergi
> reyna afl sitt, ok fréttisk fyrir, ef nǫkkut væri
> þat, er hann mætti við fásk. (Chap. 31, p. 107)

[114] Johan Fritzner, *Ordbog over det gamle norske sprog* (3 vols.; nytt uforandret opptrykk av 2. utgave, med et bind tillegg og rettelser redigert av D. A. Seip og Trygve Knudsen [Oslo: Tryggve Juul Møller Forlag, 1954]), Vol. III, p. 278 (s.v. *skalm*).

> (It seemed to Grettir a great shame that he could nowhere prove his strength, and he inquired about if there might not be something against which he could contend.)

It is Grettir's curiosity and eagerness for adventure that cause him to pursue the troll woman's lead to the waterfall. There is no revenge, no ethical cause for the continuation of the feud. *Grettis saga* is based on the conception of arbitrariness and chance, *Beowulf* on necessity and destiny—each valid and aptly presented in its own poetic framework.

The ghosts and trolls may be just as seriously believed in as Grendel and the dragon were by the eighth-century English audience, yet these beings that peopled the very land, ravaged cattle and men and caused people to go mad lack the religious and mythical dimension. They are rooted in the Icelandic countryside. The awesomeness of this land with its sheer cliffs, cave lairs, raging waterfalls, and Drangey rising from the sea mirror perfectly the aloneness and utter desolation of the outlaw in his helpless plight. The landscape looms up before us as in no other saga and contributes to the tone of the story. All the conceptions of dark and evil lairs of monsters found here concretion. Caves under torrential gulfs, deep gorges, and eerie hideouts abound in reality. The clarity and realism in the waterfall description leaves room, however, for an explanation other than the visible presence of the Icelandic setting. Grettir's deeds—heaving stones, carrying an ox, flaying a mare, killing goslings—emerge from a folk culture. The fights with ogres take place in ordinary farm houses, not in the most illustrious of all kingly halls. The tragic significance, the loftiness of theme and diction in *Beowulf* accord with its kingliness. Is the tone in *Grettis saga* merely a case of "Icelandicizing" the inherited patterns? I think not.

It has been demonstrated in the foregoing sections of this essay that the ultimate origin for these motifs is to be sought in mythical conceptions and cult practices. The *Beowulf* poet and the author of *Grettis saga* had at their disposal this ancient cultural heritage; the latter author, however, was much further removed from it. Even if one assumes a traditional heroic cycle involving a certain set of motifs and ogres who plagued one of the Nordic royal houses, the tonal quality of this set of motifs has undergone a complete change over against *Beowulf*. In *Grettis saga* those heroic elements—a remarkable youth, the slaying of monsters (the bear and *draugar*)—have lost their original efficacy. The author received his motifs via a different medium, one closer to the level and tone of the *Fornaldarsögur* and *Hrólfs saga kraka*. The bear episode suffers a burlesquing in *Grettis saga,* even more noticeably so in the later *Hrólfs saga kraka,* where the winged beast is propped up dead for the cowardly Hjalti to kill.[115] Grettir chagrins the bear champion Bjorn, who boasts that he will kill the bear because he and the bear are namesakes. Bear heroes are no longer taken quite seriously, for the etymological relationship has become a conscious one about which witticisms can be made. The use of the terms *víkingr, berserkr,* and *úlfheðinn* reveals a similar consciousness implying distance from the original function. The same can be detected in the explanation for fire emanating from barrows and caves: Grettir says in his country fire above ground indicates hidden treasure, apparently a long standing folk superstition that can be reiterated like a slogan without hesitation over its dangerous import. Likewise any hoarded treasure becomes "Fáfnir's gold." The forms are all there in *Grettis saga,* but emptied of their mythical content, filled in with other substance. The pat delineations and repetitions—the threefold ogre feud of *Beowulf* is now fivefold in *Grettis saga*—bring to mind stereotypes rather than archetypes. What remains of any religious connection—hauntings at night and at Yule, conquering bears and monsters, fiendish gleams of fire, Glæsisvellir—is experienced on an entirely different plane, that of magic and superstition, common to folklore. Such is one of the qualitative distinctions between the myth and the Märchen as defined by de Vries.[116] All the high purpose and nobility of the deeds have been

[115] The winged beast corresponds, of course, to the bear in Saxo's account. For another example of burlesquing, see the *Nibelungenlied* (nach der Ausgabe von Karl Bartsch, hrsg. von Helmut de Boor; 14. Auflage [Wiesbaden: F. A. Brockhaus, 1957]), ll. 946–962, where Siegfried tames and slays a bear in a humorous scene that has no hint of its original mythical significance for a *Heldenleben.*

[116] De Vries' proposal ("Betrachtungen," pp. 34, 35, 42–43, 48, 120, 154–155, 171–172, 174, 175) revives to some extent the "broken-down myth" theory. Because of its undeviating and highly abstract form, de Vries reasons, the Märchen would appear to be a conscious achievement, something like a parody of the myth. As soon as the mythical interpretation of the world waned, the Märchen too ceased to flourish in its ironic capacity. It continued to live on among the common folk as a never-never land, its first function and origin long since forgotten. By virtue of the underlying affinity and similarity of motifs in myth and Märchen, nothing would be more natural than attraction from one form to the other. The *Heldensage* could draw on either, but it would most likely come into direct contact with the folk-Märchen at a time when the former was on the verge of losing its vitality (the *Fornaldarsögur* in Iceland and the *Spielmanndichtung* in Germany, for example).

weakened in *Grettis saga*. Beowulf swims with thirty suits of armor, Grettir carries an ox. Beowulf's struggles with Grendel and Grendel's dam in the mere have all the turgid, indefinable, and primordial qualities proper to the poem's religious base. Grettir's fights with ghosts and trolls are completely bereft of a mythical dimension and supraindividual concerns. Just as the kenning containing names and metaphors of the gods became *sinnentleert* (emptied of meaning), so, too, the archetypal motifs lost their vital substance and function.[117]

The flattening of the heroic dimension fits in well with the late date of composition of the saga. The basically historical stories around the figure of Grettir were gleaned from the *Landnámabók* and probably from accounts given by Halldór Oddsson, the last known survivor of Grettir's family († *ca.* 1230). This material was composed into a saga by Sturla Thordarson around 1280.[118] By this time, other influences were making themselves felt in saga writing, folklore, and *stjúpmœðra* stories. The heroic tradition was on the wane; the *Fornaldarsögur* and *lygisögur* gained in popularity. In addition, Southern Romances were becoming known in the North and gained ascendancy. This latter influence accounts for the amalgamation of the epilogue of the saga with the Tristram material. Just how early this material was incorporated is not known, since the saga has come down to us from the fourteenth century already in the expanded version.

Grettir is neither paradigmatic nor a model to be followed by others. Rather it is his individuality, his setting of an inimitable record, his historicalness and humanness that impress us. His pitiful condition, hunted and haunted throughout the land, living in desolate lairs, the contrast between his physical strength and his psychical fear of the dark and being alone, brought on by the curse of Glám's eyes, make him an individual with whom we have compassion. His remarkable stamina and the injustice of his fate ultimately evoke admiration and sympathy, outweighing incensement over his evil deeds. Though an outlaw, almost an ogre feared by all, he captures the minds and hearts of friend and foe in the end. Grettir's disaster is a personal one, not the fate of all warriors, of all life. In his indomitable courage and strength he becomes a national hero, close to the lives of the Icelandic people with their farmsteads and troll-inhabited landscape. In a new milieu and in a new poetic creation that absorbed material from a different

117 De Vries, *Altnordische Literaturgeschichte,* I, 106, 111.
118 See *Grettis saga*, Formáli, pp. xiv–xvi, lv–lvii.

level of experience, the elements of a *Heldenleben* served an entirely altered function. *Grettis saga* borders on the Märchen in respect to the substance and quality of the motifs that have been under discussion, but its historical base holds it within the framework of a tragic heroic legend, removed from the unrealistic fantasy of the *Fornaldarsögur*. History and biography destroy the Märchen form and the saint's legend. Grettir's individuality and record-breaking deeds make him a hero, but not an archetype nor a saintlike figure whose actions should be imitated. No doubt the author saw in Grettir the qualities of a hero type to whom he could attach feats and characteristics of other heroes. These he employed not in order to display Grettir's typicalness, but rather in order to multiply his daring exploits and enhance his uniqueness.

The essential themes associated with the heroic tradition can be traced back to the typical course of a warrior's life formed by cult practices. These forms crystallized into *topoi* and developed independently in the plastic and literary arts (traditional oral patterns no doubt preceding those which appear already firmly established in the early written literature). The *Heldensage* in the Germanic world drew on this material until time, distance, and constant usage emptied the forms of their mythical content, leaving molds that could be filled in with stuff from all levels of experience and from any period. Every *Heldensage* which displays the traditional themes of the heroic pattern must be examined for qualitative differences. The impression of similarity between *Beowulf* and *Grettis saga,* between myth and Märchen, is both real and chimeric. Whereas the *Beowulf* poet retained the religious and mythical connection through amalgamation with Christian themes and the new Christian heroes, the saints, the author of *Grettis saga* borrowed a similar set of motifs from an area of experience and a literary milieu that had lost the essence but retained the forms of the traditional pattern. The one revitalizes archetypes, the other employs them as stereotypes. All these considerations offer good evidence for the progressive secularization of the motifs first discussed from the plates of Torslunda, Vendel, Pliezhausen, Valsgärde, and Sutton Hoo.

A Contribution to the Interpretation of Skaldic Poetry: Tmesis

KONSTANTIN REICHARDT

The first philologist to mention tmesis in skaldic poetry was Óláfr Þórðarson hvítaskáld (*ca.* 1212–1259). As the author of the so-called *Third Grammatical Treatise,* he transferred Latin grammatical and rhetorical terminology into Old Icelandic and illustrated given examples in his native tongue. Donatus says: "Tmesis est unius compositi aut simplicis verbi sectio, una dictione vel pluribus interjectis, ut: 'septem subjecta trioni' pro septemtrioni, et 'saxo cere commituit brum', et 'Massili portabant juvenes ad litera tanas'—hoc est cerebrum et Massilitanas." The Icelandic version of this passus in Óláf's *Treatise* is: *Temesis slítr ísundr eitt orð ok setr annan part ímilli, sem hér*:

ekl vas ógn á Stiklar
óblíð stǫðum síðan.[1]

[1] See *Den 3. og 4. gramm. Avhandling i Snorres Edda,* ed. B. M. Ólsen (København, 1884), pp. 30, 112–113. Óláf's tmesis example was reprinted by Finnur Jónsson as "Anon. (XII), B26" in A 1, 596 and B 1, 597 of *Den norsk-islandske skjaldedigtning* (4 vols.; København and Kristiania: Gyldendalske Boghandel/Nordisk Forlag, 1908–1915). (References to this work will be cited as *A 1* or *A 2* [texts according to the manuscripts] or as *B 1* or *B 2* [emendated text]). See also Ernst Albin Kock, *Den norsk-isländska skaldediktningen,* Vol. I (Lund: C. W. K. Gleerup, 1946), p. 291 (hereafter cited as *I*).

The text is in *Snorra Edda* manuscripts W and 748. W has the negated *vara*, 748 only *var*. If the two lines should be complete and not a fragmentary quotation from a longer text, the translation with W should be "the terrible battle of Stiklastaðir left nothing to be wanted." Important for us is only what Óláfr considered to be a tmesis: *á Stiklar- -stǫðum*.

Comparison of Óláf's example with the three offered by Donatus reveals a noticeable difference. Donatus provides instances of separated compound elements without possibility of a grammatically correct combination: in *septem subjecta trioni* there is a meaningless element, *trioni*, and neither *cere- -brum* nor *Massili- -tanas* have compositional elements with any independent linguistic value. The Icelander, however, offers the splitting of a compound into two natural grammatical parts: *Stiklar* is the genitive singular of *Stikl*, a river, and *stǫðum*, the dative plural of *staðr*, "place."

In many examples in Eddic and skaldic poetry nominal compounds are separated into grammatically correct—or allegedly correct—elements. *Þrymskviða* three times has *men Brísinga* for *Brísingamen*; *Atlamál* 4 mentions the Danish Limfjord as *fjǫrð Lima*; the Norwegian *Ekersund* occurs in Þórarin's loftunga *Tøgdrápa* 4 b as *sund Eikunda*; and Canterbury is mentioned in Merl II 30 as *borg Kantara*. The place name Stiklastaðir, famous in Norwegian-Icelandic history, was utterly unadaptable to the requirements of *dróttkvætt* meter and resulted in frequent separation beyond Óláfr Þórðarson's pedagogical example:

rekin bitu stól á Stiklar stǫðum	Þorm 2, 23. Esk 6, 43.
mikill varð á stað Stiklar stálgustr	Sigv 12, 10.
fyrr gekt á stað Stiklar	BjH 5.

Such separations of grammatically recognizable word elements have occasionally been called "tmesis" in skaldic research, although technically and in accordance with Donatus a tmesis should consist only of a compound separation with a grammatically unnatural result.

In his *lausavísa* 14a (B 1, 65) Eyvindr skáldaspillir speaks of a cloak-pin which the Icelanders had given him as a present. The text is

þanns álhimins útan
oss lendingar sendu.

Þanns - útan - oss - sendu means simply "which they sent to me from Iceland." The subject is *álhimins lendingar*. Old Norse vocabulary has no word *lendingr*(m.). *Āl-himinn*, "sky of the sea," is a kenning for "ice." *Ālhimins lendingar* in this *lausavísa* stand doubtless for *Īs-lendingar*, "Icelanders," and the helming represents a tmesis.

In older Skaldic research tmesis was a natural assumption in methods of interpretation. No attention was paid to the position of alleged tmesis elements in rhythm and text. This study deals with a small and incomplete section of the problem: it examines twenty-four helmings in which tmesis may be represented within one *dróttkvætt* line.

1.

Þjóðólfr ór Hvini, *Haustlǫng* 2a.

B 1, 14

Segjǫndum fló sagna
snótar ulfr at móti
í gemlis ham gǫmlum
glamma ó- fyr -skǫmmu.

I.e., *Snótar ulfr fló glammi* [sic] *fyr ó- -skǫmmu at móti segjǫndum sagna í gǫmlum gemlis ham*—"Kvinderøveren flöj med vingesus (el. skrigende?) for lang tid siden imod skarens anførere i en gammel örneham."

The change *glamma* > *glammi* is unnecessary because the genitive plural is attribute to *gemlir*.

Anne Holtsmark discussed the helming in *Studier i norrøn diktning*.[2] I disagree with her interpretation of *segjǫndum sagna*, but this is of no significance. We are interested in the fourth line.

For F. Jónsson's *ó- fyr* the *Snorra Edda* manuscripts show a variety of forms: *á fyr* R, W 1–2; *á fyrir* U; *o fyr* T1; *ofra* T2; *ófyrs* 748; *æigi firi* 757; *vlfr fyr* 1eβ. See A 1, 16. There is no doubt that a negation is used before the preposition *fyr*. R, W, and U have *a*, whereas 748 and T have *o*. I. Lindquist and Kock suggest a negation *æ* without further comment.[3] The adverb *æ* is well known and means "always." *Vafþrúðnismál* 36 contains a doubtful exception:

[2] Oslo: Gyldendal, 1956 (reprinted from *Arkiv för nordisk filologi*, LXIV [1950]), pp. 103–106.

[3] Lindquist, *Norröna Lovkväden* (Lund: C. W. K. Gleerup, 1929), p. 82; Ernst Albin Kock, *Notationes Norrœnæ* (Lund: C. W. K. Gleerup, 1923–1941) § 1810 (hereafter cited as *NN*).

Segðu þat it níunda, allz þik svinnan kveða
ok þú, Vafþrúðnir, vitir:
hvaðan vindr um kømr, sá er ferr vág yfir?
æ maðr hann siálfan um sér.[4]

The last line combines the texts of R and 748. R has *æ menn hann sjálfan um siá*; 748, *æ maðr um siálfan hann sér*. The adverb, here, must have the meaning "never." The situation is difficult: ON *æ* "always" has its historical parallel in Goth. *aiwa*, as ON *ey* "always" is close to Goth. *aiw*, with *Vafþrúðnismál* 55 providing the negative *ey mann né þat veit*[5] (cf. OHG *nioman* < *ni io man*).[6] The loss of the original negation before or after *æ* "always" being assumed, the meaning should still be "never" and not just "not." The *Vafþrúðnismál* 55 line should be *æ maðr hann siálfan né sér*.

I cannot consider seriously Lindquist's and Kock's translations of the *Haustlǫng* line and share Miss Holtsmark's doubts. The text *glamma ó- fyr -skǫmmu* is an example of tmesis. Both compositional elements carry full metrical stress.

2.

Þjóðólfr ór Hvini, *Haustlǫng* 4b, ll. 1–2.

B 1, 15 ving- rǫgnir lét -vagna
vígfrekr ofan sígask

I.e., *vígfrekr ving- -vagna rǫgnir lét sígask ofan*—"jætternes kampgridiske fyrste lod sig glide ned (fra træet)."

The giant Þjazi, in the shape of an eagle, glides from the tree.

The exact translation is not possible because no agreement has been reached in regard to the meaning of *ving*. F. Jónsson, s.v. *ving-Rǫgnir*, states without assurance that *ving-* may belong to *vengi*, "land, earth," and that *ving- -vagna Rǫgnir* would be the "leader of the whales of the earth," "leader of the giants."[7] If accepted, this interpretation would

[4] Gustav Neckel (ed.), *Edda. Die Lieder des Codex Regius nebst verwandten Denkmälern,* Vol. I: *Text* (2nd ed.; Heidelberg: Carl Winter, 1927), p. 49.

[5] *Ibid.*, p. 53.

[6] Neckel, (ed.), *Edda,* Vol. II: *Kommentierendes Glossar* (2nd ed.; Heidelberg: Carl Winter, 1927), p. 34, and Adolf Noreen, *Altisländische u. altnorwegische Grammatik* (4th ed.; Halle/Saale: Niemeyer, 1923) § 97, par. 3.

[7] Finnur Jónsson, *Lexicon poeticum. Ordbog over det norsk-islandske skjaldesprog.* 2. udgave. [København: S. L. Møllers, 1931], p. 618. Hereafter cited as *Lex.poet.* (*2nd ed.*).

indicate a tmesis with kenning base-word and predicate surrounded by the two members of the kenning key-word.

Kock (*NN* §§ 136, 2505) takes *vingrǫgnir* as a compound and translates *vingrǫgnir vagna* as "winged prince of the giants"; *ving-* should belong to ON *vængr*, Swed. *vinge*, Engl. *wing*. Although the phonological side of the element is not clear, the result reached is good and perhaps superior to F. Jónsson's hesitant interpretation. I believe, however, that Anne Holtsmark has made the thus far most probable suggestion in regard to *ving-Rǫgnir*.[8] Although the meaning of the first element is not known, the closest parallel to the combination is *ving-Þórr, Vingþórr* in two Eddic stanzas and in the *Þulur*. We know *Rǫgnir* as one of the Odin names, and we find in *vingrǫgnir vagna* a witty combination of a first element normally belonging to Thor, a second normally indicating Odin, and a third associated with the giants. "The god of the giants" is Þjazi. Whether in addition to this there may be some subtle wordplay in connection with "wing" cannot be ascertained.

3.

Egill Skallagrímsson, *lausavísa* (7) 6a.

B 1, 43 Upp skulum órum sverðum,
ulfs tannlituðr, glitra,
eigum dǫ́ð at drýgja
í dalmiskunn fiska.

I.e., *Skulum glitra sverðum órum upp, ulfs tannlituðr; eigum at drýgja dǫ́ð í fiska dal* [ɔ: *dalfiska*] *miskunn*—"Vi skal svinge vore lynende sværd, kriger; vi har en dåd at udføre i sommer."

The helming has formidable support because we know it not only from the *Egils saga* manuscripts M, W, ϵ, but also from *Snorra Edda* R, W, T, U, and 757. No significant discrepancies can be found. See A 1, 50.

The text is naively simple but receives some lift at the end. The consensus in regard to the fourth line is unusual. Svb. Egilsson (s.v. *dalmiskunn*),[9] F. Jónsson (see above), Sigurður Nordal,[10] and Kock

[8] Holtsmark, *Studier*, pp. 111–112.

[9] Sveinbjörn Egilsson, *Lexicon poeticum antiquæ linguæ septentrionalis* (København, 1860). Hereafter cited as *Lex. poet.*

[10] *Íslenzk fornrit*, Vol. II: *Egils Saga Skalla-Grímssonar*, ed. Nordal (Reykjavík: Hið Íslenzka Fornritafélag, 1933), p. 119.

(*NN* § 2008 G) all assume an inverted kenning, *í dalmiskunn fiska,* equivalent to *í dalfiska miskunn*, "in the mercy of the valley-fish." Because a valley-fish is a "snake," its detriment is winter, its mercy is summer. Egil's kenning was imitated twice in later centuries.[11]

In Kock's very compressed and in many ways surprising *NN* § 2008 statement, he deals briefly, incompletely, but well with inverted kennings. He saw, of course, that the addition of an inflectional ending, in many cases *-s,* would normalize otherwise difficult skaldic features. As far as I always understood and still understand his statement, Kock—with rather unusual modesty—left the decision to the future. We could, against all the manuscripts, add the *-s*, avoid the problem, and decide on

í dals miskunn fiska.

But we could also claim a tmesis in the line and suggest

í dal- miskunn -fiska.

4.

Goþþormr sindri, *Hákonardrápa* 2b.

B 1, 55 þás ellifu allar
allreiðr Dana skeiðar
valsendir hrauð vandar
víðfrægr at þat síðan.

I.e., *þás vandar valsendir, víðfrægr síðan at þat, hrauð allreiðr allar ellifu skeiðar Dana*—"da krigeren, som siden blev vidt berømt, havde med heftigt mod fuldstændig ryddet 11 danske krigsskibe."

The manuscripts of *Heimskringla* and *Óláfs saga Tryggvasonar* do not permit another text. Kock (*I*, p. 34) follows F. Jónsson.

The subject of the sentence is *valsendir vandar. Valr* has several meanings, but only "the slain," "the corpses," makes sense here. Svb. Egilsson (*Lex. poet.*, s.v. *valsendir*) suggested an inverted kenning: *valsendir vandar* = *valvandar sendir,* "sender of the corpse-wand," "brandisher of the sword," warrior. F. Jónsson (see above) and Kock (*NN* § 2008 G) agree.

Here again the addition of a genitival *-s* would solve difficulties, especially because *vals sendir* could have easily resulted in *valsendir.* Distrusting inverted kennings in old poetry, I suggest tmesis:

[11] Rudolf Meissner, *Die Kenningar der Skalden* (Bonn and Leipzig: K. Schroeder, 1921), pp. 109, 113–114.

val- sendir hrauð -vandar.

The two members of the compound carry full metrical stress.

5.

Goþþormr sindri, *Hákonardrápa* 7b.

B 1, 56 bǫðsœkir helt bríkar
brœðr, sínum, ok flœðu
undan, allar kindir
Eireks, á haf snekkjum.

I.e., *bǫðsœkir bríkar helt snekkjum sínum á haf, ok brœðr, allar kindir Eireks flœðu undan*—"krigeren styrede sine krigsskibe ud på havet, og brødrene, alle Eriks sönner, flygtede for ham."

This is a very difficult helming. The eight manuscripts of *Heims-kindir Eireks flœðu undan*—"krigeren styrede sine krigsskibe ud på and all but J insert *rak* before *flœðu, floþe.* In a previous discussion of the text[12] I rejected F. Jónsson's text, my own suggestion very closely following Svb. Egilsson's reconstruction in *Fornmannasögur.*[13] I have come to doubt the validity of the version then proposed, but I cannot accept either Kock's or Aðalbjarnarson's suggestions.[14]

The first line has *bǫðsækir bríkar.* The great antagonists F. Jónsson and Kock agree again that an inverted kenning is to be assumed: *bǫðbríkar sœkir,* "seeker of the battleplank," "seeker of the shield," warrior.

In my opinion the text shows tmesis:

bǫð- sœkir helt -bríkar,

a full parallel to stanza 2b of the same poem:

val- sendir hrauð -vandar.

Kenning base-word and predicate are surrounded by key-word members. The addition of a genitive ending *bǫð* > *bǫðvar* would destroy the meter.

[12] *Studien zu den Skalden des 9. und 10. Jahrhunderts* (Leipzig: Mayer and Müller, 1928), pp. 173–174 (hereafter cited as *Studien*).

[13] Egilsson (ed.), *Fornmannasögur* (Kaupmannahofn, 1837), XII, 28.

[14] *I,* p. 35, and *Íslenzk fornrit,* Vol. XXVI: Snorri Sturluson, *Heimskingla I,* ed. Bjarni Aðalbjarnarson (Reykjavík: Hið Íslenzka Fornritafélag, 1939), p. 175.

6.

Gísli Súrsson, *lausavísa* 12a.

B 1, 98 Luku (þunglig) á þingi
(þau eru orð komin norðan)
sæ- deilandi -sólar,
sómlaust á mik dómi.

I.e., *Luku sómlaust dómi á mik á þingi, sæ- deilandi -sólar; þau þunglig orð eru komin norðan*—"Uden hæder (for dem selv) har de domfældt mig pa tinget, gavmilde mand; det tunge bud er kommet nordfra."

The text is in the manuscripts 761, 149, 556, 445c. See A 1, 103. The first line in all but 556 is *Luku þungliga a þingi.* In the third line F. Jónsson's *deilandi* is taken from 149 and 556, whereas 761 has *deilandar* and 445 *deilendr.* All manuscripts have *sal* for F. Jónsson's *sæ-*.

The structure of the helming is simple. Line 2 has the parenthesis "this news has come from the north." The surrounding sentence may be *luku þungliga á þingi sómlaust á mik dómi* ("at the thing they passed severely and without honor judgment on me"), perhaps meaning that the judgment passed did not honor the judges. This is Kock's suggestion in *NN* § 351. F. Jónsson considers the sentence overloaded because of its two adverbs and follows 556, the only manuscript which has *þungliga þingi* for *þungliga á þingi.* In *Studien* (p. 95) I followed Kock and listed the helming as an example of sentence structure *a b a.*

The third line, which contains the vocative "man", is the concern here. The participle is either *deilandi* (sing..) or *deilendr* (pl.), but *sal* at the beginning and *sólar* at the end of the line are troublesome. Svb. Egilsson (*Lex. poet.*, s.v. *saldeilandi*) favored a kenning, *deilandi sal (s) sólar* ("largitor clipei, vir": *salr* is "hall" and its "sun" would denote the shields hanging there). Although singular, such a kenning cannot be called impossible.[15]

In his Halle edition of the *Gísla saga*, F. Jónsson remarks that in the *Hauksbók* version of *Vǫluspá* 20 *sal* is miswritten for *sæ,* and he sug-

[15] Cf., however, Björn Þórólfsson, *Íslenzk Fornrit*, Vol VI (Reykjavík: Hið Íslenzka Fornritafélag, 1943), p. 68.

gests the same mistake here.[16] His explanation of the kenning follows Svb. Egilsson's pattern:

saldeilandi sólar = sal(s) sólar deilandi

sædeilandi sólar = sæ(var) sólar deilandi,

the latter being "distributor of the sun of the sea," "distributor of gold."

Kock (*NN* § 351) offered an unacceptable explanation which was unfortunately incorporated in his edition *I*, pp. 56–57: "Tinget hölls i den stora, ej af människohänder uppbygda salen. Jfr. lagens *unz sól kemr á þingvǫll* och uttryck sådana som fe. *hæleð under heofenum*." Therefore, the judges in Gísli's stanza become *saldeilandar sólar*, "men in the hall of the sun." I wonder how Gísli Súrsson or the anonymous Pseudo-Gísli would have reacted to this explanation of their kenning.

Svb. Egilsson suggests a unique kenning. F. Jónsson changes the manuscript text slightly and with good support. The tmesis in Svb. Egilsson's text could be avoided by adding the magic *-s*, whereas F. Jónsson's version would result in a true tmesis:

sal- deilandi -sólar

sæ- deilandi -sólar.

In either case the base word is surrounded by the two members of the key word.

7.

Gísli Súrsson, *lausavísa* 14b.

The *draumavísur* attributed to Gísli belong to the most attractive specimens of skaldic tradition. They are remarkable poetry, showing excellent technique and unusual insight.

The first half of stanza 14 describes Gísli's good *draumkona* showing him fires burning in the hall and asking him to notice their number. In the second helming we learn that the fires equal the remaining years of Gísli's life.

The manuscripts are AM 761, 149, 556, 445c. See A 1, 104.

AM 761 so attu qvaþ bil blæiu
biargs olifat marga
veþrs skiolldunga valldi
vetr nu er skamt til betra

[16] F. Jónsson (ed.), *Gísla saga Súrssonar* (Halle: Niemeyer, 1903), p. 54.

Important variants are: *biargs: biarg* 149, *baurks* 445; *veþrs:veðr* 149, 556, 445c. F. Jónsson follows an older emendation, *veðr(s)* > *veig*, and suggests

B 1, 99 svá átt, kvað Bil blæju,
bjargs, ólifat marga,
veig- Skjǫldunga -valdi,
vetr, nú's skamt til betra.

I.e., *svá átt, kvað Bil blæju, marga vetr ólifat; nú's skamt til betra bjargs Skjǫldunga veig- -valdi*—"så mange år, sagde hun, har du endnu at leve i; nu er der ikke langt til et bedre liv for digteren."

I have stated my disbelief in this interpretation in *Studien* (p. 97 n. 40). Although the tmesis in the third line would not be a matter of surprise, *veig-* is not in the manuscripts, whereas *Skjǫldunga veðr* forms a perfect kenning for "battle." Evidently F. Jónsson chose the emendation because of the preceding *bjargs: bjargs Skjǫldungar*, "giants"; their *veig*, "poetry"; and its *valdi*, "master," a poet.

A glance at the manuscripts seems to ascertain the following:

svá átt, kvað Bil blæju,
. . . ólifat marga
(veðr(s) Skjǫldunga valdi)
vetr. Nú's skamt til betra.

The third line indicates a vocative. Lines 1,2, and 4 contain the sentence *Svá átt, kvað Bil blæju, ólifat marga vetr*, "so many years, said the woman, are left to you." The concluding statement in line 4, *nú's skamt til betra*, may mean "there will be improvement, remedy within a short time."

But the helming has *bjargs* at the beginning of line 2. Svb. Egilsson (*Lex. poet.*, s.v. *bjarg*) connected *Skjǫldunga veðrs bjarg*, "rock of the Skjoldungs' weather," "rock of battle," shield. Meissner followed,[17] listing parallels such as *branda veggberg, baugs bifkleif, ǫgnar sker*, and *Skǫglar elda sker*.[18] In *NN* §2437 D Kock discarded a former statement (*NN* §353) and decided in favor of *skjǫldunga veðrs bjargs valdi*, without mentioning Sveinbjörn Egilsson's name.

The latest statement can be found in Agnete Loth's edition of the

[17] *Die Kenningar*, p. 173.
[18] See *ibid.*, p. 169.

Gísla saga.[19] She takes *veðrs Skjǫldunga valdi* as a vocative and connects *biargs vetr* as "bjærgningsvintre." Björn K. Þórólfsson's position is not clear.[20]

I still believe that the helming would receive more strength and inner validity if *bjargs* in line 2 and *betra* in line 4 were combined. Elsewhere I have suggested *nú's skamt til betra bjargs,* "better care is not far away," "salvation (i.e., Christian salvation) is close."[21]

In this context the third line is of importance. I have no doubt that it contains the vocative

veðr(s) Skjǫldunga valdi.

Only one of the four manuscripts has the genitive *veðrs*; the others have *veðr.* With or without the magic *-s* we again meet two closely connected words surrounding their supplement. In this case the subject, *valdi*, is preceded by the key-word elements *Skjǫldunga veðr(s).*

8. 9. and 10.

Einarr Skálaglamm, *Vellekla* 27a.

B 1, 122

Ok við frost at freista
fémildr konungr vildi
myrk- Hlǫðvinjar -markar
morðalfs, þess's kom norðan.

I.e., *Ok fémildr konungr myrk- -markar Hlǫðvinjar vildi at freista morðalfs, þess es kom norðan við frost*—"Og Jyllands gavmilde konge vilde prøve krigeren, der var kommen nordfra ved vintertide."

Probably, the third line is an attribute of *morðalfs*, not of *konungr,* and the geographic statement refers to Norway, not to Denmark, although this is not our present concern. The adverbial *við frost* in line 1 should not be taken out of its immediate context; adverbial expressions are used in skaldic poetry quite frequently as auxiliaries to denote atmosphere, time, place, and so on, without necessarily close syntactical connection with one or the other part of the complete statement.

Kock (*NN* §406) takes the third line as *myrkhlǫðvinjar markar,* "dark land of the forest," while F. Jónsson (see above) believes in the

19 *Gísla saga Súrssonar* (Copenhagen: Munksgaard, 1956), p. 82.

20 *Íslenzk fornrit,* VI (1943), p. 71.

21 *Aus der Gíslasaga* (*Altnordische Übungstexte,* Vol. 7 [Halle: Niemeyer, 1935]), p. 2.

tmesis *myrk- -markar,* with *Myrkviðr* as the obvious association. Although the two translations seem to differ insignificantly, a preferable choice seems possible.

Hofgarða-Refr Gestsson (1,2), according to F. Jónsson:

B 1, 295 Kná myrkdreki markar
mínn, þars ýtar finnask,
æfr á aldar lófum
eikinn borðs at leika,

I.e., *Mínn æfr myrkdreki markar borðs kná at leika eikinn á aldar lófum, þars ýtar finnask*—"Min rasende spyd spiller fjendsk i mandens (min) hånd, hvor mænd mødes (til kamp)."

This helming is quoted in *Snorra Edda,* I, 428, with the introductory remark *Spjót er ormr kallat, sem Refr kvað.* Therefore *myrkdreki markar* should be taken as a spear kenning (see *NN* §783). In regard to F. Jónsson's text in general, it must be observed that among the *Snorra Edda* manuscripts only 748 has *borz,* whereas W, R, and T show *bezt, bez.* I agree with Kock that the line should be *eikinn bezt at leika,* "my violent, savage spear plays best in my hand when men have an encounter."

Illugi Bryndœlaskáld composed a poem on Haraldr harðráði, four helmings of which are extant. The first is:

B 1, 354 Vargs vas munr, þats margan
(menskerðir stakk sverði
myrkaurriða markar)
mínn dróttinn rak flótta.

I.e., *Vas munr vargs þats mínn dróttinn rak margan flótta; menskerðir stakk markar myrkaurriða sverði*—"Det var fest for ulven, at min konge så ofte drev mænd på flugt; den gavmilde mand (Sigurd) gennemborede ormen (Fafne) med sværdet." All four Illugi helmings have insertions referring to the Nibelungen legend in their second and third lines.

There is no comment on this helming in Kock's *Notationes Norrœnæ.*

The three passages mentioned above contain the following closely related lines:

myrkhlǫðvinjar markar, "dark land of forest"

myrkdreki markar, "dark dragon of forest"

myrkaurriði markar, "dark trout (fish) of forest"

Kock was consistent in regarding the two first-word elements each time as a compound. F. Jónsson assumed tmesis in the first case, but normal compounds otherwise.

I believe that the three lines should be interpreted alike. The adjective *myrkr* in Old Norse poetry denotes darkness but does not refer to color. The *myrkviðr* in Old Norse tradition is an impenetrable forest, darkened by the trees. The dragon in Illugi's stanza is certainly not a "dark trout of the forest," but a "trout of the dark forest." The three helmings discussed here have tmesis, with the base word surrounded by two key word elements:

Einarr skálaglamm:	*myrk- Hlǫðvinjar -markar*
Illugi:	*myrk- aurriða -markar*
Hofgarða-Refr:	*kná myrk- dreki -markar*

The tmesis elements have metrical stress in every instance.

11.

Eilífr Goðrúnarson, *Þórsdrápa* 7a.

Eilífs poem is the most challenging and difficult text of the older skaldic period. Its wit and individuality surpass *Haustlǫng*, and it is remarkable how the *Snorra Edda* manuscripts, several centuries after the original composition, were able to retain the unique spirit of the poet. F. Jónsson wrote a complete account of the text in 1900;[22] I published my own interpretation in 1948.[23]

Although the helming is difficult, the immediate problem is obvious. The fourth line raises the question of tmesis. Eilífr is describing Thor's wading through the Vimur River and his vexations. The *Snorra Edda* manuscripts R, W, and T offer the text.[24]

To avoid renewed discussion of the particulars I have treated else-

22 *Þórsdrápa Eilífs Goðrúnarsonar,* Oversigt over det Kgl. Vid. Selsk. Forhandlinger, No. 5 (København, 1900).

23 "Die *Thórsdrápa* des Eilífr Goðrúnarson," *PMLA,* LXIII (June, 1948), 329–391.

24 Cf. *Studien*, pp. 207–208, *NN* § 449, and "*Thórsdrápa*," pp. 351–352.

where, I simply state that the helming consists of two sentences with only one, obvious subject, Thor. The first two lines are

> Harðvaxnar lét herðar
> hall-lands of sik falla

"(He) let the hard-grown shoulders of the rock-land (the stones) fall on himself."

The second half offers

> gatat maðr njótr inn neytri
> njarð rǫ̇ð fyr sér gjarðar.

The metrically ugly *maðr* of the manuscripts supplies unnecessary explanation. Without it the text appears to be clear enough:

> harðvaxnar lét herðar
> hall-lands of sik falla
> (gatat) njótr inn neytri
> njarð rǫ̇ð fyr sér gjarðar.

I.e., *Njarð- -gjarðar njótr inn neytri lét hall-lands harðvaxnar herðar of sik falla. Gatat rǫ̇ð fyr sér.* "The clever user of the power-belt let the hard-grown shoulders of the rock-land fall on himself. He could not find a way out."

If *maðr* of the manuscripts is inserted in line 3, as I suggested in *PMLA*,[25] the parenthesis would receive its grammatical subject, but Eilífr otherwise shows such a mastery of rhythm that I prefer to make later Icelandic scribes responsible for the addition. The god is known as the owner of a "power-belt," *megingjǫrð*. There can be little doubt that *njarð- -gjarðar* in Eilífs text stands for *megin- -gjarðar*. Since transformation into a grammatically correct genitive (*njarðar*) seems to be out of the question, a true example of tmesis must be considered here.

12.

Eilífr Goðrúnarson, *Þórsdrápa* 12a.

> B 1, 142
>
> Dreif fyr dróttar kneyfi
> dolg- Svíþjóðar kolgu
> (sótti) -ferð (á flótta
> flesdrótt í vǫ́) nesja.

[25] "*Thórsdrápa*," pp. 351–352.

I.e., *Dolg- -ferð kolgu-Svíþjóðar dreif fyr kneyfi nesja dróttar; flesdrótt sótti á flótta í vǫ́*—"Det kolde Sverrigs fjendeskare flygtede for jætternes undertrykker; i faren greb de flugten."

See A 1, 150.

F. Jónsson's text is most intricate in introducing a tmesis *dolg- -ferð*, at the beginning of the second and in the middle of the third line and in translating *kolga*, "wave," *ad hoc* as "cold, frost."

Kock, also *ad hoc,* suggested a kenning, *dolg-Svíþjóðar kolgu,* "people of the wave of hostile Sweden" (*NN* §458). I am not able to understand the meaning of this, and I maintain my earlier interpretation:[26]

Dreif fyr dróttar kneyfi
dolg- Svíþjóðar -kolgu
(sótti ferð á flótta)
flesdrótt (í vǫ́ nesja).

I.e., *Flesdrótt dreif fyr kneyfi dolg- -kolgu Svíþjóðar dróttar. Nesja ferð sótti á flótta í vǫ́.*

Flesdrótt and *nesja ferð,* "rock-people," are giants. *Dolg- -kolgu Svíþjóðar drótt,* "people of the land of the hostile wave," are also giants, who, as inhabitants of the River Vimur region, cause the difficulties for Thor and his companion. Their *kneyfir* is Thor.[27]

The result is a tmesis:

dolg- Svíþjóðar -kolgu.

13 and 14.

Hallfreðr vandræðaskáld, *Erfidrápa* (3) 11a.

B 1, 152

Firðisk vætr, sás varði
víð lǫnd, Breta stríðir
bleyði firðr við bráðan
bekkdóm Heðins rekka.

I.e., *Breta stríðir, sás varði víð lǫnd, firðisk bleyði firðr vætr við bráðan bekkdóm Heðins rekka*—"Britternes fjende, som forsvarede sine vide lande, undgik, tapper, ingen fare in krigens hidsige gang."

[26] *Studien*, p. 210, and "*Thórsdrápa*," pp. 367–368.

[27] F. Jónsson ("*Skjaldekvad*," *Arkiv för nordisk filologi*," XLV [1929], 148) misunderstood my explanation in *Studien*, p. 210.

See A 1, 161.

F. Jónsson (*Lex. poet.* [2nd ed.], s.v. *bekkdómr*) explains the battle-kenning *Heðins rekka bekkdómr* as follows: "bænkedom, vel egl. en dom, der er fældet af de i deres sæder siddende domere, altså en retmæssig, inappellabel dom, kun i kenningen *b. Heðins rekka . . .*" This is pure hypothesis, but the text was repeated by Kock (*I*, p. 83). In *PMLA*[28] I suggested tmesis:

bekk- dóm Heðins -rekka.

Heðins bekk- -rekkar, "Heðin's bench-fellows," are the Hjaðningar and their *dómr* is "battle." Compare *bekksǫgn, bekkjunautr*.

Eilífr Goðrúnarson, *Þórsdrápa* 19b.

B 1, 143
komat tvíviðar tívi
tollur karms, sás harmi,
brautar liðs, of beitti
bekk-, fall, jǫtuns -rekka.

I.e., *fall brautar liðs komat tvíviðar tollur, karms tívi, sás of beitti bekk- -rekka jǫtuns harmi*—"heller ikke manglede han, vognens gud, som voldte jætterne sorg, bistand af sin rejsefælle."

Although it is conceded that *tvíviðar tívi tollur karms* denotes Thor, no satisfactory explanation of the kenning has been found. I differ from F. Jónsson only in the translation of *fall,* which I prefer to take in its normal meaning of "fall, death."[29] The helming says that Thor—who caused harm to the giants—did not suffer the loss of his companion Thjalfi.

Line 4 contains tmesis of its first and last word elements:

bekk-, fall, jǫtuns -rekka.

This is exactly the same tmesis as in the previously discussed helming.

15.

Hávarðr halti ísfirðingr, *lausavísa* 8b.

This example is included only because of its interesting manuscript environment. AM 160, 157b, 552b, 502, and 486 of the *Hávarðar saga*

[28] "*Thórsdrápa,*" p. 388 f.
[29] *Ibid.*, pp. 387–388.

record the helming without understanding. (See A1, 190 and Björn K. Þórólfsson's edition).[30]

AM 160	vera kuada ham enn hogguid hier saklausa baurna Isfirdinga angre

Line 1: *kueda,* 157, 552b; for *vera kuada ham,* 502 and 486 have *vara hara.*

Line 2: *hiǫr,* 552b; *saklausan bera,* 502, 486; *borva,* 552b.

Line 3: *Isfirdingum urdu,* 502, 486.

Line 4: *eirlaust skartit trausta,* 502, 486.

On this uncertain ground F. Jónsson suggests the following reconstruction:

B 1, 180	vesa kveða, hǫgg en hǫggvin hjǫr- saklaussa -bǫrva, Ísfirðinga, urðu eirlaust, farit trausti.

I.e., *kveða vesa farit trausti Ísfirðinga, en hǫgg saklaussa hjǫr- -bǫrva urðu hǫggvin eirlaust*—"man siger, at Isfjordingernes tillid er borte; de sagesløse krigeres hug blev rettede uden skånsel."

Kock (*NN* §1101) accepts this text in general but eliminates the tmesis *hjǫr- -bǫrva* by adding the genitive *-s* to the first element and simplifies the helming by using *Ísfirðingum* of manuscripts 502 and 486. The result is the short sentence *vesa kveða færit trausti* and a long uninterrupted parenthesis (see Kock *I*, p. 96).

In spite of the very bad tradition, the second line appears clear. Unless the magic *-s* is introduced, it contains tmesis:

hjǫr- saklaussa -bǫrva.

16.

Halldórr ókristni, *Eiríksflokkr* 2b.

B 1, 193	þás hún- lagar -hreina hafði jarl of krafða (sætt gekk seggja ættar sundr) Skǫ́nunga fundar.

[30] B. K. Þórólfsson (ed.), *Hávarðar saga Ísfirðings* (København, 1923), p. 38.

I.e., *þás jarl Skǫ́nunga hafði of krafða lagar hún- -hreina fundar; sætt seggja ættar gekk sundr*—"da Skåningernes jarl havde samlet skibene til møde. Freden brødes mellem mændene."

The numerous manuscripts permit no better text (see A 1, 202). F. Jónsson explains the kenning *húnlagar hreinn* as *lagar hún- -hreinn,* "mast-reindeer of the sea," ship.[31] The kenning is somewhat surprising because the base word *hreinn* would technically not require more than either *lagar* or *hún* for a kenning result, but a better interpretation seems not to be possible.[32]

Kock (*NN* § 556), before his adventure with inverted kennings, took *húnlagar hreina* as "mast-water reindeer," "sea-reindeer," "ships," but he later added in the note to *NN* § 2008 H that *hún* is a superfluous addition. His kenning is not possible: whenever a part of a ship is used as a key word in a kenning for "sea," the base word can only be "land," not "water."

Line 1 may be considered an example of tmesis:

þás hún- lagar -hreina.

17.

Halldórr ókristni, *Eiríksflokkr* 5a.

B 1, 194 Hykkat vægð at vígi,
vann drótt jǫfur sóttan,
(fjǫrð- komt) jarl (at -jǫrðu)
ógnharðan, sik spǫrðu.

I.e., *Hykkat jarl spǫrðu sik vægð at vígi; drótt vann sóttan ógnharðan jǫfur; komt at fjǫrð- -jǫrðu.*"—"Jeg tror ikke jarlen sparede sig ved eftergivenhed under kampen; hæren overvandt den kampraske konge —du fik fjordenes land (Norge) i besiddelse -."

The text is in *Fagrskinna* A and in various *Óláfs saga Tryggvasonar* manuscripts (see A 1, 203–204). In the third line *komt* has the competition of *kom* and *komz, komzst.*

F. Jónsson's arrangement is complicated and exemplifies one of the

[31] See F. Jónsson (ed.), *Heimskringla* (4 vols.; København: 1893–1901), IV, 96; *Lex. poet.* (2nd. ed.), s.v. *húnlǫgr;* and F. Jónsson, "Kenningers led-omstilling og tmesis," *Arkiv för nordisk filologi,* XLIX (1933), 5.

[32] See Meissner, *Die Kenningar,* p. 219.

many skaldic stanzas where our printed texts cannot quite revive spoken poetry.

The helming praises Jarl Eiríkr for his military success against Óláfr Tryggvason. The word *jarl* has a central position in the text: it should be recited with a high pitch. Analyzing the helming, we find three rudimentary statements: (1) *hykkat vægð at vígi sik spǫrðu,* (2) *vann drótt jǫfur sóttan*, and (3) *fjǫrð komt (kom, komsk) at jǫrðu.* Neither *1* nor *3* have a subject, but *jarl* is available for either purpose. Finally, *ógnharðan* may refer to *jǫfur* or to *jarl*, if the latter is taken as an accusative. A decision is not easy, especially because *fjǫrð* and *jǫrðu* cause some concern. Kock (*NN* § 557) suggested the following text:

Hykkat vægð at vígi
—vann drótt jǫfur sóttan;
fjǫrð komsk jarl at jǫrðu—
ógnharðan sik spǫrðu.

Kock's own poetry is: "Ej jag tror på någon hänsyn / under kampen, ej att jälten / sparat sig: man angrep kungen; / jarlen fick sig fjord till land." Kock believes that *hykkat* may govern both the accusative *vægð* and the accusative with infinitive *ógnharðan sik spǫrðu.* Such constructions are impossible in Old Norse poetry. Furthermore, "jarlen fick sig fjord till land," where "fjord" is supposed to mean Norway, is out of the question.

There is no doubt in my mind that *fjǫrð-* (or *fjarð-*) *-jǫrðu* in line 3 is a tmesis. Norway is the fjordland. The attribute *ógnharðan* should belong to *jǫfur*, praising the defeated enemy. The word *jarl*, however, seems to have an *apò koinoũ* part: it belongs to the third line as well as to the surrounding statement in lines 1 and 4. F. Jónsson, with his great experience, came very close to the truth, as did Svb. Egilsson (*Lex. poet.*, s.v. *fjörðjörð*). I must confess, however, that I am not certain how the helming should be arranged in an optically satisfactory manner.

Hykkat vægð at vígi
- vann drótt jǫfur sóttan -
(fjǫrð- komsk) JARL (at -jǫrðu)
- ógnharðan - sik spǫrðu.

JARL is the important word, and whoever listened to this helming knew it. In regard to tmesis, however, we notice the separation of

fjǫrð- -jǫrðu.

18.

Óttarr svarti, *Hǫfuðlausn* (2) 13b.

B 1, 270

næði straumr, ef stœði,
strangr kaupskipum angra,
innan borðs of unnir
erringar- lið -verra.

I.e., *strangr straumr næði angra kaupskipum of unnir, ef erringar- -verra lið stœði innan borðs*—"den stride ström vilde have kundet fortrædige handelsskibene på bølgen, hvis en mindre kraftig skare havde været der ombord."

See A 1, 294. *Heimskringla* K and many *Óláfs saga helga* manuscripts have *a unnum* for *of unnir*. In *Heimskringla* II, 36, F. Jónsson followed K.

Svb. Egilsson (*Lex. poet.*, s.v. *erring*) combined *erringar lið* as "copiae strenuae," but *verra* makes this improbable. In regard to the connection of *illr* with an object genitive, compare *matarillr, tillagaillr, illr viðreignar, illr heimsóknar, illr aptrhvarfs,* and so on. The fourth line

erringar lið verra

does not necessarily contain a tmesis, because *erringar* and *verra* have their independent grammatical values. The position of the two elements, however, exemplifies the general skaldic tendency discussed in this context.

19.

Anon. (XI), *lausavísa* 6.

B 1, 395

Skǫ́ru jast- ór -osti
(eybaugs) Dana meyjar
(þau of ǫngruðu þengil
þing) akkeris-hringa.

I.e., *Dana meyjar skǫ́ru akkeris-hringa ór jast- -osti; þau eybaugs þing of ǫngruðu þengil*—"Danerness møer snittede ankerringe af myseost; de søredskaber ærgrede kongen."

This little piece of "poetry" has amused and bothered me for a very long time. Although I believe that it contains tmesis, I am more certain that it proves the already medieval popularity of Danish cheese.

Snorri, in *Heimskringla* III, 120, relates that the daughters of the

Dane Þorkell geysa made anchors out of cheese, ridiculing Harald harðráði's announcement that he would attack Denmark. After the Norwegians had burned Þorkel's estate and captured his daughters, this anonymous helming is said to have been recited. The second half of it adds: "but this morning many a maiden sees a few hooks of iron hold the ships of the powerful king—they do not laugh about it any more."

A 1, 425 lists ten manuscripts of *Heimskringla, Fagrskinna,* and *Haralds saga harðráða.*

Line 1. *jast: oss,* Fsk. B, A.; *or: af,* Fsk. A.

Line 3. *þau of ǫngruðu,* only in Hkr 47; *þat angraði,* Hkr K, J 2, F, 39, Fsk. B, A, Har Fl.; *þat vm angraði,* Har Mk; *þat of angraði,* Har 66, Hr.

In order to find a shelter for *eybaugs*, F. Jónsson in the third line follows *Heimskringla* 47 against all other manuscripts. *Þau eybaugs þing* ("these things of the island-ring," "these sea-things") are supposedly anchors. In Old Norse poetic vocabulary "anchor" is not a kenning-making word. Meissner does not refer to the clumsy combination just mentioned, and *kaldnefr* in ÞjóðA 4,11 belongs in a different category.

If the majority of the manuscripts are followed, the parenthesis should be *þat þing (of) angraði þengil,* "this (thing) made the prince angry" (see *NN* §909). The first line *skǫ́ru jast- ór -osti* = *skǫ́ru ór jastosti* was recognized as a tmesis example by Svb. Egilsson (*Lex. poet.*, s.v. *jastr*). In *Heimskringla* IV, 218, F. Jónsson comments on the cheese sort: "snarest myseost, hvis fasthed er endnu ringere end andre ostearter." The *Fagrskinna* manuscripts avoid the *lectio difficilior* and offer *skǫ́ru oss ór osti,* "they cut for us out of cheese."

The type of tmesis with the first member of a compound separated from the second by a preposition is reminiscent of *Haustlǫng*'s *ó- fyr -skǫmmu* (no. 1 *supra*). Kock (*NN* § 1953 A) tried to avoid tmesis by changing to *skǫ́ru jastar osti*; he overlooked that the second helming has *krók ór jarni.* In *I*, p. 196, he decided on *skǫ́ru ór jastar ósti*, a version contemplated in one of his earlier paragraphs (*NN* § 909).

The helming should be edited to read:

Skǫ́ru jast- ór -osti
eybaugs Dana meyjar

(þat of angraði þengil
þing) akkeris-hringa.

Eybaugs was connected with *Danir* long ago (see *Lex. poet.,* s.v. *eybaugr*), and "Sea Danes" brings to mind OE *Sæ-Dene*. Egilsson, following Vidalin, took *ey baugs* to be a vocative "ring island," "woman." This interpretation is possible,[33] but we do not know to whom the anonymous stanza was addressed.

20.

Einarr Skúlason, *Geisli* (6) 19b.

B 1, 432 fyr vas hitt, es harra
hauðrtjalda brá dauða
happ- (nýtask mér) -mætu
(máltól) skini sólar.

I.e., *hitt vas fyrr, es skini sólar happ- -mætu brá dauða herra hauðrtjalda; máltól nýtask mér*—"det skete för (fordum), at solens lykkebringende skin sluktes ved guds (Kristi) død; mine taleredskaber nyttes."

See A 1, 461. The *Bergsbók* and *Flateyjarbók* manuscripts differ considerably.

Line 1. *es: at,* Fl.
Line 2. *brá dauða: bra alldre*, Bb; *bar dauða*, Fl.
Line 3. *happ: hept*, Bb; *mætu: mættu*, Fl.
Line 4. *skini: skinu*, Fl.

In the first half of the stanza Einarr Skúlason mentions the solar eclipse of 1030, the year of King Óláf's death. According to F. Jónsson's interpretation, the second helming refers to the eclipse at the time of Christ's death. Kock (*NN* § 933) follows *Bergsbók* and suggests, with Cederschiöld,[34]

Fyr vas hitt, es harri
hauðrtjalda brá aldri
- hept nýtask mér - mætu
- máltól - skini sólar.

[33] *Ibid.*, p. 409, and *Lex. poet.* (2nd ed.), s.v. *ey*.
[34] G. Cederschiöld, *Geisli eða Óláfs drápa ens helga, efter "Bergsboken" uutgifven, Lunds Universitets Årsskrift*, X (1873).

I.e., "Förut var det så, at herren / över himlavalvet aldrig / - tungans band jag nu kan lossa - / släckte solens klara sken."

In such a text, Einarr Skúlason would have stated that the eclipse of 1030 had been the first in history. He also would have shown a deplorable lack of knowledge concerning one of the most significant events in the history of Christian tradition: the circumstances of Christ's death according to the New Testament. Yet Einarr recited his poem in 1153 in the Church of Christ at Trondheim before Cardinal Nikulás and the Kings. Therefore, there should be no *aldri,* "never," in his text.

The parenthesis in Kock's helming makes no sense. *Hept nýtask mér máltól,* "my impeded speech-organs are useful to me," is neither "tungans band jag nu kan lossa" nor "although I am inhibited, my speech organs are in good shape." F. Jónsson dryly remarked: "Bergsb. har v.l. *hept* 'forhindrede, stansede'; formelt måtte det henføres til *máltól*, men *nýtask* viser det modsatte, nemlig at digterens taleredskaber fungerer godt; *hept* er således en forvanskning."[35]

In F. Jónsson's text, the parenthesis *nýtask mér máltól* is beyond criticism. The tmesis *happ- mætu* has the now familiar position in one line, and the resulting compound is most probable (cf. *happmildr* [Christ] in *Plácitúsdrápa happkunnigr* [Mary] and *happvinnandi* [Christ] in *Harmsól*). *Happmætt sólar skin,* "blessed light of the sun," is most appropriate. The dative *skini* is governed by *brá* (impers.), "it changed." Therefore, *Brá skini sólar,* "the sun grew dim."[36] *Harra hauðrtjalda dauða* is "because of the death (or at the time of the death) of the lord of the earth-tent, the sky."

What the gifted skald said to the Kings and the Cardinal and all the others in the church of Trondheim was: "It happened before that the blessed light of the sun grew dim—on the day of the death of our Heavenly Lord."

21.

Einarr Skúlason, *Øxarflokkr* (11) 5a.

B 1, 450 Gaf, sás erring ofrar,
ógnprúðr Vanabrúðar
þing-Váfaðar þrøngvir
þróttǫflga mér dóttur.

[35] "Kenningars led-omstilling," p. 20.

[36] R. Cleasby and G. Vígfusson, *An Icelandic-English Dictionary* (Oxford, 1874), s.v. *bregða.*

I.e., *Ógnprúðr Váfaðar þing-þrøngvir, sás ofrar erring, gaf mér þróttǫflga dóttur Vanabrúðar*—"Den kampmodige kriger, som viser udholdenhed, gav mig en stærk kostbarhed."

The *Snorra Edda* R, W, T, and U manuscripts have only one important variant: U begins the third line with the meaningless *þings vaforlaga* (see A 1, 478).

The helming contains an interesting kenning: *Vanabrúðar dóttir*, "daughter of the bride of the Vanir," "daughter of Freyja," whose name was *Hnoss*, i.e., "jewel."

F. Jónsson (*Lex. poet.* [2nd ed.], s.v. *þing-Vǫ́fuðr* and *þrøngvir*) and Kock (*NN* § 2008 N and *I*, p. 221) assume inverted kenning, although *þings Váfaðar þrøngvir* would result in a line without special style characteristics. The U manuscript happens to have *þings*.

The magic *-s*, to be sure, solves the difficulty, but the form of line 3 in this helming belongs in the group under discussion:

þing- Váfaðar -þrøngvir.

22.

Haukr Valdísarson, *Íslendingadrápa* 12b.

B 1, 542

hvardyggva lét hǫggva
hann armviðu fannar
(sverðs frák él at yrði
allhǫrð) í gras bǫrðum.

I.e., *hann lét hvardyggva armfannar viðu hǫggva bǫrðum í gras; frák at yrði allhǫrð sverðs él*—"han lod meget dygtige mænd bide i græsset; jeg har hørt, at der blev holdt meget kraftige kampe."

The poem is only in AM 748. There the first line is *huardogguar læt hogga* (see A 1, 558).

The kenning *armviðu fannar* is taken as one of the inverted type by Svb. Egilsson (*Lex. poet.*, p. 20), F. Jónsson (*Lex. poet.* [2nd ed.], p. 16) and Kock (*NN* § 2008 G). The Index to *NN* does not refer to the paragraph mentioned.

The line in question can be understood as

hann arm- viðu -fannar,

"arm-snow trees," "gold trees," men.

23.

Haukr Valdísarson, *Íslendingadrápa* 14b.

B 1, 542 ok háraddar hræddir
hrings ófáir gingu
fyr þrymsvelli þollar
þeim sárjǫkuls geima.

I.e., *ok ófáir hrings háraddar þollar gingu hræddir fyr þeim sárgeima jǫkuls þrymsvelli*—"og mange krigere frygtede den helt."

Eleven Danish syllables are in F. Jónsson's translation of the twenty-four in the Icelandic text. *Hrings háraddar þollar* ("trees of the loud voice of the sword," "trees of battle") is a normal kenning for "men." It has two attributes: *ófáir*, "many," and *hræddir* "fearful." Fearfully they went before *þeim sárgeima jǫkuls þrymsvelli,* obviously before the - hero. In the preceding helming Finnbogi enn rammi is mentioned as the fear-inspiring man.

F. Jónsson's text follows the manuscripts (see A 1, 558).

F. Jónsson (*Lex. poet.* [2nd ed.], s.v. *sárjokull*) and Kock (*NN* § 2008 G) take *sárjǫkuls geima* as *sárgeima jǫkuls,* "wound-sea ice," "blood-ice," sword.[37]

Arranging the line in accordance with the previous discussion, we arrive at

þeim sár- jǫkuls -geima.

24.

Krákumál 12, ll. 2–4.

B 1, 651 hrunði -dǫgg af sverðum
brún í Barðafirði
bleika ná- fyr hauka.

I.e., "Det brune blød fllød af sværdene i Bardefjord for de grå høge."

Ná- -dǫgg, "corpse-dew," is understood as a blood-kenning with tmesis, the two members of which are distributed in reverse position in the second and fourth line of the helming.

Kock (*NN* § 1276) took *dǫgg*, "dew," as an incomplete kenning for "blood" (key word missing) and changed *ná* > *nás* to ascertain the kenning *nás haukr*, "corpse-hawk," raven.

[37] See Meissner, *Die Kenningar*, p. 152.

Elsewhere I showed that *dǫgg* is not incomplete.[38] Gísli Súrsson used *bláfold*, "blue earth," for "sea," therefore *brún dǫgg*, "brown dew," is "blood." F. Jónsson accepted this explanation (*Lex. poet.* [2nd ed.], s.v. *dǫgg*).

Kock was right in assuming a raven-kenning in the last line. For the general question of tmesis with its two members in the same line the text here is of little significance, but the manuscripts certainly suggest

bleika ná- fyr -hauka.

In conclusion, a look at the twenty-four examples discussed shows that two should be omitted from statistic consideration: No. 2, *vingrǫgnir lét vagna,* because *vingrǫgnir* appears to be a true compound; and No. 18, *erringar lið verra*, because the two members are separated according to the common method resulting in *Stikla staðir* or *men Brísinga.*

Of the remaining twenty-two instances, twelve could be "mended" by addition of a genitive *-s.* (Occasionally, as was pointed out, a manuscript offers the ending).

4. val- sendir hrauð -vandar
7. veðr- Skjǫldunga -valdi
12. dolg- Svíþjóðar -kolgu
15. hjǫr- saklaussa -bǫrva
21. þing- Váfaðar -þrøngvir

3. í dal- miskunn -fiska
16. þás hún- lagar -hreina
22. hann arm- viðu -fannar
23. þeim sár- jǫkuls -geima
24. bleika ná- fyr -hauka.

13. bekk- dóm Heðins -rekka
14. bekk- fall, jǫtuns -rekka.

Number 6, *sal- deilandi -sólar*, could have been included in this list, but the kenning is doubtful, and emendation to *sæ- deilandi -sólar*

[38] "Beiträge zur Skaldenforschung II. Die unvollkommene Kenning," *Arkiv för nordisk filologi*, XLVI (1930), 212–213.

would put the line into the next group, where tmesis seems to be indicated. In my opinion, there are nine clear examples:

1. glamma ó- fyr -skǫmmu
19. skǫ́ru jast- ór -ósti

5. bǫð- sœkir helt -bríkar
20. happ- nýtask mér -mætu
11. njarð- rǫ́ð fyr sér -gjarðar
17. fjarð- komsk jarl at -jǫrðu

8. myrk- Hlǫðvinjar -markar
10. myrk- aurriða -markar
9. kná myrk- dreki -markar.

I am honored to dedicate this article to the only American scholar who, in many decades of fruitful work, never lost interest in the intricacies of skaldic poetry.

On Reflections of Germanic Legal Terminology and Situations in the *Edda*

WINFRED P. LEHMANN

In dealing with literature of the past, we meet some of our greatest difficulties when we try to understand its position in its own culture. The words which have come down to us often seem little more than a string of entries from the lexical stock of a vanished language, arranged in accordance with metrical principles that are equally obsolete. Among the examples that might be cited are the genealogical lists, which have little appeal for readers who find small comfort in their putative ancestry. But although obscurities of terminology, of poetic devices, and of cultural practices may baffle us, the most troublesome problems are those for which we give easy answers. Skaldic verse, for example, has seemed for more than a century to be a formalistic, degenerate continuation of Eddic verse. Recently however, in a notable essay, Professor Hollander has demonstrated that some of its components and their design are equivalent to the greatly admired epigrams of Martial.[1] Surface difficulties of skaldic verse had claimed the entire attention of readers. A bold glance below these disclosed its position in its ancient context. In my homage to Professor Hollander I will not

[1] "Observations on the Nature and Function of the Parenthetic Sentence in Skaldic Poetry," *The Journal of English and Germanic Philology,* LXIV, No. 4 (1965), 635–644.

discuss such a general topic, but will restrict myself to a few comments on the use of legal situations and of legal terms in the imagery of ancient Germanic literature, chiefly Eddic verse. I refer to other Germanic literature to take account of common features of heroic poetry, in which, according to W. P. Ker,[2] the poets of England and Iceland shared.

The importance of legal concerns, and of legal language, in early Germanic culture was recognized more than a century ago. Jacob Grimm studied Germanic legal customs as well as the Germanic languages and produced an account not yet superseded; and the study of Germanic law in its relation to Germanic literature has been carried on, among others, by Amira and Heusler.[3] Yet the use of legal language for the poetic imagery of Germanic verse is highly complex, as Donahue has demonstrated in a recent essay on *Beowulf*.[4] In interpreting Germanic verse, the poet's conception of the culture he is describing must be understood, as well as the culture in which the poetry was maintained and the earlier situation itself. The problem, then, is threefold: determining the meaning of words, and of poetic devices at the time the poems were composed; determining their earlier meanings; and determining the poet's conceptions of these earlier meanings.

A theme which retained its interest throughout Germanic verse was the concern with the role of the individual in his social group. And the achievement of a proper relationship continued as a dominant theme in the medieval Germanic epic, though the society itself had changed. In Wolfram the individual must maintain himself in a culture with principles modified from those of Germanic times by importations from Christianity. For Hartman, as for Gottfried, the modifications come largely from the courtly world. But the heroes—Parzival, Erec, Iwein, and Tristan—are all faced with a set of cultural conventions into which they must fit. In the course of learning the conventions of his culture the hero may break them, as did the young Parzival; he may

[2] *The Dark Ages* (reprinted [London: Nelson, 1955]).

[3] Grimm (ed.), *Deutsche Rechtsaltertümer* (reprinted after the 4th ed., prepared by Andreas Heusler and Rudolf Hübner, 1889 [Berlin: Akademie Verlag, 1956]). The works of Amira and Heusler, central to my theme, are: Karl von Amira, *Germanisches Recht* I Rechtsdenkmäler, Fourth edition prepared by Karl August Eckhardt (Berlin: Walter de Gruyter and Co., 1960); Andreas Heusler, *Das Strafrecht der Isländersagas* (Leipzig: Duncker and Humblot, 1911).

[4] Charles Donahue, "*Beowulf* and Christian Tradition: A Reconsideration from a Celtic Stance," *Traditio*, XXI (1965), 55–116.

wander for a time outside his society, as do Parzival, Erec, and Iwein; or, like Tristan, he may even become an outlaw. For all of these heroes, except Tristan, the offenses against a culture tempered by Christian optimism are forgiven, and the hero finally achieves his proper role. To the early Germanic audience, however, reconciliation between the individual and his society was not the favored solution. Moreover, in early Germanic literature there was little interest in the process of learning that role. Even in the Icelandic sagas a stable society, which participants adhere to, is assumed. Rather than the mastery of social conventions, the problems an individual may have in maintaining his position provide the chief epic interest.

Possibly the most difficult role, at any rate the one which seems most appealing in early Germanic literature, is that of the individual who leaves his social group, whether to find favor and fortune, like Auðun with his bear, or to remain a permanent outcast, like Grettir. The dramatic encounters between such an individual and his own society, or between him and his host away from home, usually a king but also a freeman, are among the favorite incidents in Germanic literature. These encounters may have various outcomes.

The wanderer Hildebrand encounters irremediable tragedy when he meets his own people again. Even less easily than the exile can the declared outlaw find reconciliation with society; he lives out his life on the wastes, whether field, forest, or rocky caves, and eventually comes to an evil end. Though modified by Irish and Oriental conceptions of monsters, Grendel may be the best-known Germanic outlaw. He is a less realistic approximation to actual outcasts from society than are the Icelanders Grettir and Gísli, but below the poetic trappings of the monster Grendel we find the terminology used for the Germanic outlaw. For, to a Christian audience, descent from the confused outcast Cam[5]—an ancestor with the characteristics of the fratricide Cain and the irreverent Ham—accounts for the characteristics of the typical outlaw from Germanic society: an outcast *heoro-wearh,* outside the household, asocial *unhīore,* lives away from settled country as a *hæðen.* Of the roles an individual may play in Germanic society, Grendel's, like Grettir's, is most severe.

An individual may fill one of several roles in his social group: he

[5] See my review of A. J. Bliss, *The Metre of Beowulf* (Oxford: Blackwell, 1958), in *The Journal of English and Germanic Philology,* LIX, No. 1 (1960), 137–142, esp. pp. 140–141.

may be completely rejected, put outside the protection of the law; or, like Flosi in *Njáls saga,* he may leave his society temporarily and live outside it, accepted by a different social group; or, like Gunnar, he may occupy a favorable position in spite of conflicts with its code of behavior. The conflicts may occur at any time in life and to the most eminent men. An honored Njáll dies like an outlaw because he supported sons who were vulnerable to the fate of an outlaw. His friend Gunnar had earlier exposed himself to the danger of an outlaw's death by rejecting the mild imposition of three years of exile from his home. On the other hand, Gunnar's brother, Kolskegg, and Flosi, the leader of the group that burned Njáll, find positions of esteem because they obey the sanctions imposed on them. With such possible shifts in fortune well-known among his audience, the Germanic poet had a stock of roles to which he could allude, whether to suggest a position approximating that of an outlaw or a wanderer or to label a figure with terms suggesting outlawry, using them literally or ironically.

Although these roles varied as the patterns of society changed, the sagas of the thirteenth century report a consistent, if possibly romanticized, structure of the social conventions of several centuries earlier.[6] For, as Snorri relates in *Heimskringla,*[7] when Iceland was being settled the immigrants were objecting to being incorporated in social units larger than the family. Even though Harald Fairhair's control was scarcely greater than that of the earlier chieftains of "kins," the threat of greater domination was oppressive to the westlanders, who carried to Iceland a society based on family structure. The legal arrangements within this structure—the position of a hero like Grettir, who lives the life of an outlaw, of a hero like Gunnar, who is declared an outlaw but refuses to accept the verdict of the expanding government in his country, and of an Egil, who keeps his legal balance in spite of various desperate activities—make up the story of the sagas. Yet, although the social arrangements described were in large part superseded by the time the sagas were composed,[8] the contrast between the society of the

[6] See Heusler, *Das Strafrecht,* pp. 6–7 and *passim.*

[7] See Professor Hollander's superb translation of Snorri Sturlason's *Heimskringla* (Austin: University of Texas Press, 1964), p. 76: "During the times of warfare when Harald brought Norway under his domination, foreign lands such as the Faroes and Iceland were settled [by Norwegians]. There was a great exodus to the Shetlands, and many of the nobility fled King Harald as outlaws . . ."

[8] The differing arrangements may be determined from contrasts with their accounts in the subsequent legal codes; see Heusler, *Das Strafrecht,* p. 223.

thirteenth century and that depicted in the sagas was not as great as the contrast between the society of the *Beowulf* author and the culture he describes or between that of the sagas and the Eddic poems. The position of a Germanic outlaw is so remote from the *Beowulf* author's Christian conception that he must be refashioned as a monster, the *wearh* Grendel; his mother, the *wyrgen,* in contrast with the *sekr* of the family sagas, belongs not to the society of Heorot but to a totally different race. The northern *vargr* may regain his role in society; for the *weorh* there is no solution but death and *werhðo,* 'punishment in hell.' In contrast with the society of *Beowulf,* the society of the *Edda* consists of families of smaller scope, the head of the household surrounded by his wife and children, plus a few servants. We are reminded of the "homesteads with a simple large circular house . . . of England in the sixth and fifth centuries B.C." more than of the "villages of rectangular houses" excavated in Scandinavia.[9] The *Edda* accounts lack the many retainers depicted in the hall of Heorot or even on the farm of Njáll. Yet whatever the size of the social unit, offenses against its codes brought various sanctions, of which the most serious was banishment. Heusler[10] admirably points out how the accuser changed in time, from the wronged individual himself to the wronged individual in cooperation with the "state," and finally to the state alone. Yet his questioning of Amira's assumption that outlawry could be imposed by the state only, rather than by a group as small as the family, is not valid. If the family sagas reflect an earlier stage of society, in which the family formed a legal unit, we can assume, supported by Tacitus' *Germania,* that the "large family" which we posit for the Proto-Germanic period followed legal conventions in which the individual was even more on his own, in which he maintained a certain status with regard to his family. It is this society which is reflected in the *Edda* and is accordingly of importance for its interpretation.

The society was composed of those with ties to the family, *frǽndr,* and those outside it, *fiandr.* Of prime importance was maintenance of one's honor, distinction, and reputation (*virðing, sómi, sæmð*). If someone encroached on these, recompense, *bót,* was required. If the recompense was not granted, the guilty member was formally expelled

[9] For an excellent survey of the early culture, see Stuart Piggott, *Ancient Europe* (Edinburgh: University Press, 1965). The passages quoted are from p. 199 and p. 236.

[10] *Das Strafrecht,* p. 234.

from the group, for a period varying with the seriousness of his offense. When totally outlawed, he was like a wolf (*vargr*), outside the family (*á hyrr*), forced to live on the wastes (*heiþinge*), free to be hunted (*sekr*). These varying roles, and the uncertain status of every individual, form the chief dramatic interest of the *Edda* stories. It is the way a hero meets his fate, rather than love, or even warfare and death, which is the prime concern of the heroic poems. Even in the late "Greenlandish Lay of Atli" it is the king, Gunnar, who decides to accept Atli's invitation and who is the last member of the Gjúkungs to die, unlike the south German *Nibelungenlied,* which gives the leading role to the courageous Hagen. In the Germanic society the individual has certain responsibilities, and his fame depends on how he meets these.

Dramatic ambiguity was especially possible when the individual was away from home, for the stranger, including the unattractive one who might be an outcast from his own society, had to be accorded due honor, in death as well as in life. Because of the ambiguous character of a stranger and the potentially ambiguous position of any Germanic freeman, the wanderer, even the voluntary visitor like the brothers of Guðrún in "The Greenlandish Lay of Atli," created situations which were of greatest poetic interest to Germanic audiences. The Eddic poems cannot be expected to read like sociological or legal treatises, but those which have come down to us reflect this interest, although some of their legal references are veiled or obscure, and probably were so even to contemporary audiences.

Possibly the most straightforward story in the *Edda* of the man outside a social group, and mistreated by it, is that of Volund.[11] As the poem has come down to us, it is a ballad of revenge.[12] But ancient details on supernatural actions, which we will not discuss here, and on social relationships can be found in it. Volund is a Finn, outside

[11] My citations of the Old Norse text are taken from Gustav Neckel, *Edda,* ed. Hans Kuhn (3rd ed.; Heidelberg: Carl Winter, 1962). Unless otherwise specified, the translations are taken from Lee M. Hollander (trans.), *The Poetic Edda* (2nd ed.; Austin: University of Texas Press, 1962). I have also observed his transliterations of proper names and used his titles for the individual poems. Listing the other essential aids for a study of the *Edda* would yield an extensive bibliography, but any attempts at interpretation are greatly facilitated by Hugo Gering's *Vollständiges Wörterbuch zu den Liedern der Edda* (Halle: Buchhandlung des Waisenhauses, 1903).

[12] See my "Composition of Eddic Verse," in Eric Hofacker and Liselotte Dieckmann (eds.), *Studies in Germanic Languages and Literature* (St. Louis: Washington University Press, 1963), pp. 6–14.

Nithoth's social group. He marries an *alvitr,* in *Beowulf* an *æl-wiht,* 'alien.' And when his wife leaves the happy marriage (*heil hiú*), he takes up habitation in Wolfdales. Though the terse poem does not specifically depict him as an outlaw with regard to Nithoth's social group, the terminology used for him is that applied to someone outside the law. It is scarcely too subtle to assume that an inhabitant of Wolfdales would be a *vargr,* 'wolf,' that is, an outlaw. Another name reflecting punishment of an outlaw is Nithoth—*Níþ-hoþr,* 'the warrior of vengeance.' Although the poem is filled with such vocabulary, in the typical Eddic manner it underplays the outlawed state of Volund.

Yet when Volund comes into Nithoth's hall, Nithoth's wife feels that he is a man foreign to her social group, not *hýrr,* like the *unhīore* dragons in *Beowulf.*[13] Moreover, like the *weard unhīore* in *Beowulf,* (l. 2413), Volund possesses gold treasures; and like Beowulf, Nithoth has no scruples about robbing these, as though Volund is a proscribed outlaw.

We may interpret the interplay between the king and the outlaw by comparing *Beowulf,* notably a comment on the last battle concerning the effect of gold (l. 2764 ff.):

	Sinc ēaðe mæg,
gold on grund(e)	gumcynnes gehwone
oferhīgian,	hȳde sē ðe wylle!

In his usual fashion, the *Beowulf* poet here includes a moral generalization, which Klaeber in one of his less capable comments calls "an apparently uncalled for ethical reflection on the pernicious influence of gold."[14] Because the gold in this passage had caused many problems and was to cause Beowulf's death, it is in keeping with the poem that an ethical reflection be made. The view of the destructive effect of gold is of special interest for an interpretation of "The Lay of Volund." The best-known instance in Germanic story is the Niebelungen hoard, to which the Volund poet refers (st.14, ll. 1–4). But also in the Volund story it is the desire for gold which brings grief to Volund and to Nithoth's family.

The terminology links the two poems together. We have already noted the use of ON *hýrr,* OE (*un-*)*hīore,* for the accepted member of

[13] See Donahue, "Beowulf and Christian Tradition," *Traditio,* p. 75.

[14] Friedrich Klaeber, *Beowulf and the Fight at Finnsburg* (3rd ed., with 1st and 2nd supplements; Boston: D. C. Heath, 1950), p. 220 n.

the social group in contrast with the outlaw. I suggest that it may also settle the dispute concerning the much discussed *ofer-hīgian* in line 2766 of *Beowulf*. With Sedgefield[15] I equate the base with *hīwian*. Sedgefield translates *oferhīwian* by 'deceive.' I suggest that the word may be even more pointedly related to social interrelationships, being derived from Gmc. *hīwa-/hiwa-*, 'peace' > 'the peaceful one, Angehöriger, Hausgenosse, Gatte.'[16] A further derivative would be *hīore, hýrr,* 'one who is socially acceptable.' With *ofer-* the verb has a deprecatory meaning—not merely 'deceive' but 'lead to a conflict with society, make someone an outcast.' The poet's aside therefore cautions that "treasure, buried gold, may well lead anyone to a position of an outlaw—heed it who will."

Like the story of Volund and Nithoth, *Beowulf* suggests an interplay between gold and disaster, between the possessor of gold and the outcast. After the departure of his wife, Volund established his home in Wolfdales, working his red gold. Whatever the circumstances that took him there, that let him be regarded as an outlaw and open to plunder, Volund recalls after his capture the time when the family was undivided. The contrast of his *heil hiú* (st. 14, l. 7) with the queen's statement that he is not *hýrr* can scarcely be accidental. Formerly Volund, with his brothers, was not an outlaw. But now Nithoth treats Volund as one, imprisoning him and forcing him to produce *gørsimar*. These were indeed treasures, as is clear from stanza 21, line 8. But it may also be noted that in Old Danish law *gørsum* means 'recompense.' Volund is sentenced to produce the treasures in the only severe punishment which Nithoth is able to inflict on him. After Volund's subsequent revenge, Nithoth would like to punish him even worse (*verr um níta*), but Volund, using supernatural means, escapes.

Accordingly it is Volund who obtains *bót,* 'recompense.' In the complex of outrage and counter-outrage, Nithoth first took matters into his own hands but was unable to contain Volund from achieving the final *bót*. In its execution the exchange of violence does not differ greatly from the legal action and counter-action in the sagas. Gunnar in

[15] W. J. Sedgefield, *Beowulf,* (3rd ed.; Manchester: University Press, 1935). See also his "Notes on 'Beowulf'," *The Modern Language Review*, V (1911), 286–288.

[16] See Sigmund Feist, *Vergleichendes Wörterbuch der Gotischen Sprache* (Leiden: E. J. Brill, 1939), pp. 253–254.

Njáls saga repeatedly provided *bót* for his victims, as in Chapter 66.[17] Yet the *bót* in the "Lay of Volund" is far more personal, with no hint of the formal recompense based on a codified legal system that had been developed by the tenth century. Similarly, throughout the poem the "legal situations" are simple: Volund against Nithoth, with no formal social group to enforce sanctions, as in the sagas or even in *Beowulf*.

The other heroic poems of the *Edda,* those dealing with the Volsungs and Niflungs, also reflect legal situations paralleling those of the sagas, without involving formal social groups. The basic stories concern actions that conflict with the social code and require recompense. Guthrún's mother expects her sons to get recompense for the killing of Sigurth (*Guðrúnarkviða* II, st. 17, ll. 9–12):

hverr vildi son systor bœta,
eða ver veginn vildi gialda.

(if amends to me they meant to make
for Sigurth slain and his young son.)

Gunnar is ready to grant recompense for the crime, *sacar at bœta* (*Guðrúnarkviða* II, st. 18, l. 3); as for Brynhild, the recompense is to be with gold (*Oddrúnargrátr,* st. 21, ll. 1–4):

"Buðo þeir Atla bauga rauða
oc brœðr mínom bœtr ósmár:"

("to Atli they offered untold riches
of bright gold rings, to my brother dear.")

Yet, like many of the antagonists in the sagas and like Brynhild (*Grípisspá,* st. 46, ll. 1–2):

"Hvat mun at bótom brúðr sú taca,"
("What will I give, the grief to allay
of the woman, . . .")

Guthrún will not accept the recompense to make peace (*Guðrúnarkviða* II, st. 20, ll. 7–8):

[17] References to *Njáls Saga* are taken from the edition of Guðni Jónsson (Reykjavík: Bókaverzlun Sigurðar Kristjánssonar, 1945).

trygðir vinna, né ec trúa gerðac.

(win me a truce; but I trusted them not.)

In *Guðrúnarhvǫt* also Guthrún refuses to come to terms, taking instead of recompense the lives of her sons (st. 12, ll. 3–6):

"máttigac bǫlva bœtr um vinna,
áðr ec hnóf hǫfuð af Hniflungom."

("to wreak my wrath I wrought it thus:
I hewed off the heads of the Hniflung heirs.")

Similarly in the most prosaic of the heroic poems, "The Greenlandish Lay of Atli," the role of the actors is of central interest. Atli can never provide for Guthrún recompense for the death of her brothers ("Atlamál hin grœnlenzku," st. 72, ll. 7–8):

"bana mundo mér brœðra bœta aldregi"

("no amends canst make e'er for my murdered brothers,")

And Guthrún accuses him of never having been able to settle suits in the thing (*Atlamál hin grœnlenzku,* st. 101, ll. 3–4):

"at þú sǫc sóttir né slecþir aðra;"

("having pleaded pluckily or o'erpowered thy foeman;")

We may then look on the heroic poems dealing with the Volsungs and Niflungs as cases (*sǫk*) in which the heroes are involved. Like most of the legal cases in *Njáls saga,* they do not find solution in recompense (*bót*) or in reconciliation (*sǫtt*).

Nor is there acceptable *bót* in the remaining heroic poems, those dealing with Helgi. In these we find the most poetic description of the outlaw, a role Sigrún would like for her brother Dag after he killed her husband Helgi (*Helgakviða Hundingsbana* II, st. 33, ll. 5–12):

"Þá væri þér hefnt Helga dauða,
ef þú værir vargr á viðom úti,
auðs andvani oc allz gamans,
hefðir eigi mat, nema á hræom spryngir."

("Then had I vengeance for Helgi's death,
if a wolf thou wert in the wilderness,
wretchedly roving, and ravenous,
and feed to bursting on foul carrion.")

Yet Dag does not become an outlaw; he offers *bauga rauða* in recompense, a *bót* which Sigrún does not accept any more than would the Helgi of *Helgakviða Hundingsbana* I (st. 12, ll. 1–4):

> Létað buðlungr bótir uppi,
> né niðia in heldr nefgiǫld fá;
>
> (But Helgi would hear not of haggling gifts
> nor weregild award them, though they wanted it;)

In the supernatural situation of "The Lay of Helgi Hjorvarthsson," Helgi's *bót* to the witch Hrímgerth becomes further vengeance: he keeps her until daylight when she turns to stone. The Helgi poems, like the other heroic poems, tell of offenses against the social code and of retribution.

But in a society composed of small groups the retribution was only local. Even in the codified culture of Iceland an outlaw who left the group which banished him might be thoroughly respectable elsewhere —a situation not untypical of other frontiers, from the days of Lot to recent times. Hence the poetic interest in the wanderer. For whatever his background, he would relieve the monotony for his host. The receptivity to even unattractive strangers is well-indicated in the story of Hrapp, who was taken from Iceland to Norway by Kolbein, though Kolbein thinks that the one who takes him abroad will not profit by it (*Njáls saga,* sec. 87 at *sá hafi verr, er þik flytr*). With similar foreboding, Hrapp is accepted in the house of Gudbrand and by the outlaw Tofi; eventually he was even given a homestead in Iceland. The audience of the *Edda* could then not have been unaware of the dramatic situations and problems which a wanderer might bring. These are reflected in some of the mythological poems, not the least in the confrontation of Thór with the ferryman Hárbarth. Conversation between a wandering guest and his host must often have led to similar tension, as we may assume from the sagas. Hrapp and the woodman Tofi sparred with each other until Hrapp, concluding the dialogue (*vit förum kynliga með okkr um málin* [*Njáls saga,* sec. 87]), told the truth about himself; Odin never did in "The Lay of Hárbarth."

Much of the sparring in "The Lay of Hárbarth" hinges on double entendres, but their meaning is no longer obvious, as Professor Hollander points out in the preface to his translation: "the meanings of a number of the insulting flings which so incense Thór completely elude us."[18] I would like to suggest that one of these may revolve around a double meaning based on legal language used for defining the position of an individual.

When Odin had told Thór of his harrying ("Lay of Hárbarth," st. 40), Thór suggests that he is also planning warfare now (st. 41): "Þess viltu nú geta, er þú fórt oss ólubann at bióða." In contrast with proposed emendations, Professor Hollander translates: " 'To my mind thou callest that thou camest to war on us'." The key word is *ólubann.* I agree with Professor Hollander that we should interpret it as the negative of *luba,* 'love.' Used only here in the *Edda,* its adjectival cognate *unlēof* in Old English poetry refers to the cowardly followers of Beowulf (l. 2863), and it is twice used in *Genesis,* in line 2452, in reference to the Sodomites who were *unlēofe* to God. Besides its central meaning 'unloved, unloving,' it therefore apparently had erotic overtones. It is these which Odin takes up (st. 42), using a legal reference to heighten the humor:

"Bœta scal þér þat þá munda baugi,
sam iafnendr unno, þeir er ocr vilia sætta."

The terms *iafnendr* ('arbiter') and *sætta* ('settle a suit') are clearly from legal language, as Professor Hollander indicates in his translation:

"I shall make up for that with a mickle ring,
as daysmen may deem in dooming between us."

He offers further explanation in his footnote to the passage: " 'Hárbarth has done harm to Thór by disturbing the work of the farmers' (Gering)." Now Hárbarth offers a ring in atonement. Or, as has been suggested, the word for 'ring' in the original may also be understood *in malam partem,* which may account for Thór's indignation in St. 43." But by neither interpretation could the words be called 'hateful' (*hnœfiligo*), as does Thór in his response (st. 43):

"Hvar namtu þessi in hnœfiligo orð,
er ec heyrða aldregi hnœfiligri?"

("Whence hast thou these hateful words,
for more hateful ones heard I never.")

[18] *The Poetic Edda,* p. 74.

I propose accordingly that Odin twists Thór's sentence to an expectation of perversion when he replies in legal language that he will "recompense" such action with the payment of the sum which a bridegroom pays for the bride. For *baug* is a legal term referring to the payment of weregild, as in *lǫg-baugr,* and *mundr* is the sum of money which any groom had to pay to his bride to make the marriage legal. Odin then "mishears" Thór's suggestion and blandly replies that he can readily recompense him for any love. By the reply he issues the worst insult—*hnœfiligri*—a Germanic warrior could receive, that Thór was *argr.* It is Skarpheðinn's similar comment about Flosi (*Njáls saga,* st. 123) which causes Flosi to reject the recompense for Höskuld and to continue the feud that led to the death of Njáll; and the term apparently played a similar role in the Old High German *Hildebrandslied.* As in "The Flyting of Loki," sts. 23 and 24, and in "The Lay of Thrym," st. 17, the Eddic audience must have been amused to see the burly Thór accused of such a role, even more than to hear in a later exchange that Thór's wife reputedly is entertaining another man (*Hárbarzljóð,* st. 48, l. 1):

"Sif á hó heima, hans mundo fund vilia,"
("With Sif someone sleeps in her bower;")

In spite of its light approach, rather because of this very approach, we can reconstruct the attitude of the Eddic audience to the conventions of the past. Though the figures in the poem are gods, and in this way contribute heightened irony, the confrontation of two strangers, one of whom might be an outlaw (*sekr*), on opposite sides of a stream must have seemed as alluringly obsolete as the unperturbable heroes of westerns are today or as the wanderings of Odysseus must have seemed to the merchants and fishermen of Athens. But in addition to the attitude of the contemporary audience, we would also like to recapture the sentiments of the society to whom the conventions were real. Unfortunately we have only scanty resources, but among them the runic inscriptions give the strongest evidence.

Of the scant glimpses they have maintained of earlier relationships between individuals,[19] those provided by the Eggjum inscription are

[19] For such references in a different sphere see my "Lín and Laukr in the Edda," *Germanic Review,* XXX, No. 3 (1955), 163–171.

most intriguing. Though obscure in many details, the inscription is fortunately being clarified by capable insights. The latest of these is Professor Springer's convincing reading of the worn section in the second line.[20] Moreover, he interprets this reading *sakr* in the context of the inscription, and a later Swedish inscription, as meaning "open to pursuit—der Verfolgung ausgesetzt." For Professor Springer, as we too have noted above, the *sakr maðr* of the time was not outlawed by the state, but rather is one who is exposed to the revenge of the person harmed and of his relationship.

With this interpretation, the reluctance of the runemaster of the Eggjum inscription to give the name of the dead man may be clarified by Thór's remark in "The Lay of Hárbarth" (st. 11 [translation mine]):

> "Hvat scaltu of nafn hylia, nema þú sacar eigir?"
>
> ("Why should you hide your name unless you are an outcast?")

This naive question gives Hárbarth another chance for an insult (st. 12 [Hollander's translation]):

> "Enn þótt ec sacar eiga, fyr slícom, sem þú ert,
> þá mun ec forða fiǫrvi míno, nema ec feigr sé."
>
> ("Even though sought I were: from such as thee
> I would fend my life but I were fey and doomed.")

The implication that a *sakr maðr* should not reveal his name agrees well with the puzzling circumlocution for the dead man's name in the Eggjum inscription.

If we follow this interpretation, the entire second line of the inscription might well be reinterpreted. The verb *lAgi* might be taken as the

[20] Otto Springer, "Zur Eggjum-Inschrift. Ein rechtsgeschichtlicher Beitrag," *Zeitschrift für deutsche Philologie,* LXXXV, No. 1 (1965), 22–48. In a paper, "Inscriptional Evidence of Early North Germanic Legal Terminology" given at the Third Indo-European Conference, Philadelphia, April 21–23, 1966, Professor Springer discussed *sakr* from a more general point of view, and dealt among other problems with the status of Germanic legal or prelegal terms. For a similar discussion, see Karl Bader, "Deutsches Recht" *Deutsche Philologie im Aufriss,* ed. Wolfgang Stammler (2nd ed.; Berlin: Erich Schmidt Verlag, 1962), III, 1971–2024. Bader points to the difficulty of distinguishing between "law" and "custom," especially in early periods. In spite of this problem and the greater similarity of early codes of behavior to regulation by "custom" than by "law," I have used the term "legal" for the sanctions imposed even by the simplest Germanic social groups.

preterite optative of the intransitive *liggja,* and the line would then read, following Professor Springer's translation:

ni sakr maR nAkda ni snAr(þi)R ni wiltiR manR lAgi.
(Neither a pursued man should lie bare nor distressed nor stray men.)

With this interpretation *nAkda* would be a weak nominative masculine, with the same ending as *farawisa* in the Seeland bracteate; in contrast with the descriptive adjectives with their strong endings, *nAkda* would specify that the individual described should not be allowed to remain uncovered and unburied. Accordingly the magical burial was carried out, with rites that have been widely discussed but are not a concern here.

Yet, for further understanding of the Eggjum inscription, we may obtain some insights from "The Sayings of Hár," stanza 49, which has not yet received its definitive reading. This stanza follows one which praises the *mildir,* 'generous man'—an adjective also used as the final epithet for Beowulf and often woefully translated. Stanza 49 goes on to say:

Váðir mínar gaf ec velli at
tveim trémǫnnom;
reccar þat þóttuz, er þeir rift hǫfðo,
neiss er nøcqviðr halr.

Ostensibly the stanza says: "My clothes I gave in the fields to two tree-men; they seemed to be respectable men when they had the clothing; despised is the naked man." Without going into detail, I should like to recall that the hapax *neiss* has legal overtones in its meaning 'despised, dishonored.' The last line of the stanza may then be taken as a proverb, referring to the status of the outlaw. I do not wish to speculate further here on the meaning of *trémaðr,* but it too leads us to the area of northern magic concerning the individual who might bring disgrace by a *tréníð,* as did Egil so elegantly.[21] Whatever the terms may have meant to the preserver of the stanza in the *Edda,* I suggest that

[21] See *Egils saga Skalla-Grímssonar,* ed. Guðni Jónsson (Reykjavík: Bókaverzlun Sigurðar Kristjánssonar, 1945), Chap. 57, p. 185: "Hér set ek upp níðstöng, ok sný ek þessu níði á hönd Eiríki konungi ok Gunnhildi dróttningu" (Here I'm setting up a staff of disgrace and I'm directing this disgrace against King Eirik and Queen Gunnhild).

the stanza indicates the most exemplary kind of "generosity"—the clothing of an outcast.

Whether or not these suggestions are followed, they may remind us how obscure many of the earlier customs had become by the time the *Edda* was written down and how groping we must be in our reconstructions of the lines in their ancient context. But if the ancient practices are only obscurely reflected in Icelandic texts, they have almost vanished in the South. One of the areas of frequent comment is the loss of meaning of the old terms for the outcast, particularly in the South, but even in Scandinavia.[22] This linguistic situation is related to the changing cultural situation. The Germanic outcast was simply evicted from his social group; there was no universal judgment, not even a judgment through a wider society. When, however, a wider society was instituted and, further, when Christianity brought a universal judgment of good and evil, the *sekr* and the *vargr* had to be total outcasts from human society, criminals. Hence they were no longer temporary, or local, outlaws. Instead they belonged to a criminal race, like the monsters in *Beowulf*.

Even some of the Eddic poems have been influenced by the southern view that the outlaw must be a monster. In the poems with a southern background, the outcasts have taken on some of the traits of monsters like Grendel and his mother. The patricide Fafnir "lay on the Gnita Heath" and was *í orms líki* (*Reginsmál,* st. 14, prose). Although he maintained human form, Volund seemed to Nithoth's wife to have eyes like a dragon (*Volundarkviða,* st. 17, l. 5):

"ámun ero augo ormi þeim inom frána;"
("are his eyes awful, like the adder's glittering.").

We recall Grendel's "horrible light flashing from his eyes much like fire" (*Beowulf*, l. 726):

him of ēagum stōd
ligge gelīcost lēoht unfǣger.

To a culture adopting universal standards of law, the Germanic outlaw could not be conceived of as a temporary outcast from a small social group; he had special stigmata and was of a different race.

22 For a recent discussion of the problems, and a fine study of legal terms and conventions, see Klaus von See, *Altnordische Rechtswörter* (Hermaea, No. 16 [Tübingen: Max Niemeyer Verlag, 1964]).

Although still the object of interest, stories of him could no longer be directed at levity, as in "The Lay of Hárbarth." Nor could he be rehabilitated. As this change in the outlaw was imposed by the later culture, the wanderer, gradually disassociated from the outlaw, became a separate literary type. He might be a bard, like the Wanderer in Old English poetry, but was more likely to be a knight-errant. This type in turn underwent further development, to become the honored *recke* in the South but the wretched wanderer in England. These developments extend beyond my comments, however, and they are well-known. It is the earlier concept of the wanderer which is only vaguely reflected in the northern writings, as a substratum of the Germanic period. Just as the legal conventions of the sagas must be drawn from the texts of the sagas themselves rather than from the legal practices in force when the sagas were written down, so the simpler legal situations of the early period must be recaptured from the few materials that have survived. Interpretations of these will differ among the audience of the *Edda* today, as they did between the audience of the thirteenth century and of the earlier centuries. But our interpretations may become more certain as runic texts and other early materials are better understood and as new data are associated with them. In the hope of encouraging further insights to the many provided by Professor Hollander, I should like to suggest that comparison with the legal status of the individual in early Germanic society may lead to a fuller understanding of some difficult passages in the early texts, particularly the *Edda*.

Fertility of Beast and Soil in Old Norse Literature

E. O. G. TURVILLE-PETRE

Those who go into the Bronze Age room in the National Museum in Copenhagen must be struck by the so-called Trundholm chariot, found buried in a peat bog in north Zealand, which is widely believed to be a votive offering. It consists of a model vehicle on six wheels and a model horse of bronze. The load carried is a disc, about a foot in diameter. This is elaborately worked and decorated and on one side brilliantly gilded. It has been dated variously from 1600 to 1000 B.C., or perhaps somewhat later.[1] It is not an isolated find, for remains of other models of this kind have been found. One, discovered at Tågaborg in Hälsingborg in 1895 and now largely destroyed, evidently consisted of a bronze disc in a little chariot, apparently drawn by two horses.[2]

The rock-carvings of the Bronze Age, many of them found in southern Sweden, have a large number of wheels or discs depicted on them. Some of these stand on movable objects, such as a pair of wheels;

1 See H. Shetelig and Hj. Falk, *Scandinavian Archaeology* (Oxford: Clarendon Press, 1937), pp. 156 ff.

2 On the Tågaborg wagon see M. Stenberger, *Sweden* (London: Thames and Hudson, 1963), p. 89.

others are carried by men.[3] It is now generally agreed that those who executed these carvings, often in places where few would see them, had an object which was other than artistic. It is not difficult to believe that the disc represented the sun, but why are discs placed in chariots or on ships or carried by men?

Since no documents from this early period are available, we can only speculate. We may suspect that, when placed on wheels—or even drawn by a horse or a pair of horses—the disc is seen as the sun, drawn daily across the sky. Other interpretations may be possible, but this supposition is supported in two early Norwegian or Icelandic poems. The first is the "Words of Vafþrúðnir" (*Vafþrúðnismál,* st. 12):

> Skinfaxi heitir, er inn skíra dregr
> dag um dróttmǫgu;
> hesta beztr þykkir hann með *H*reiðgotum
> ey lýsir mǫn af mari

In Professor Hollander's translation:[4]

> He is Skinfaxi hight which skyward brings
> every day at dawn to mankind;
> of horses best he to heroes seems
> his mane glisters like gold.

According to another poem, the "Words of Grímnir" (*Grímnismál,* st. 37, ll. 1–2), the sun is drawn by two horses, as he appears to be on the wagon of Tågaborg. These horses are called Árvakr (Early Awake) and Alsviðr (Very Strong or Swift):

> Árvakr ok Alsviðr, þeir skolu upp heðan,
> svangir, sól draga

> Árvakr and Alsvith they up shall draw
> the sun's wain wearily;[5]

These lines may well express a belief similar to that expressed by the Trundholm chariot and the Tågaborg wagon, but if they do, what a

[3] On the rock-carvings of this period, see *ibid*., pp. 98 ff.; J. de Vries, *Altgermanische Religionsgeschichte.* (2nd ed.; Berlin: Walter de Gruyter, 1956), I, 101 ff.; and O. Almgren, *Hällristningar och Kultbruk* (Stockholm, 1926).

[4] Lee M. Hollander (trans.), *The Poetic Edda* (Austin: University of Texas Press, 1962), p. 44.

[5] *Ibid*., p. 61. This is stanza 38 in Hollander's translation.

long tradition to allow! The Trundholm chariot is said to have been made about 1000 B.C.; at the earliest, the Norse poems quoted were composed in the tenth century A.D.,[6] and they were not written down before the thirteenth century. The tradition seems to be unbroken for some twenty centuries.

If this is true, it implies that certain elements in the religion of Scandinavia survived all social and political upheavals and remained virtually unchanged from the Bronze Age until the conquest of Christianity in the tenth and eleventh centuries. This is not impossible. Many tribes, Goths and others, emigrated from Scandinavia, the factory of nations (*officina gentium*),[7] but there has been no major immigration, some say, since that of the Battle (or Boat) Axe People about 2000 B.C.[8]

This may provide some foundation for the use of late literary sources to explain symbols of prehistory, although the dangers are obvious, for it does not follow that when two peoples do or depict the same thing they mean the same thing by it. However, religious tradition and ritual have long lives, and literary sources may shed some light on prehistoric monuments.

But here another problem is involved. The poetry quoted above I believe to be the work of pagans of the tenth century, but these pagan poems which survive are little more than scraps. Apart from them, the only literary sources describing the pagan religion of the Northmen were written by nonbelievers. Some were outsiders, missionaries like St. Anskar or chroniclers like Adam of Bremen, whose writings were often inspired by fear or by contempt for the barbarism they witnessed. The most prolific authors were Icelanders, writing between the twelfth and fourteenth centuries. These men had an antiquarian, and sometimes romantic, interest in the religion their pagan ancestors supposedly followed two or three centuries before.

But to return to the artifacts of the Bronze Age, we may find that the literary authorities, writing many centuries later, are able to suggest

[6] On the ages and provenance of *Vafþrúðnismál* and *Grímnismál*, see Einar Ól. Sveinsson, *Íslenzkar Bókmenntir í Fornöld* (Reykjavík: Almenna Bókafélagið, 1962), I, 269 ff.

[7] Jordanes, *Getica* IV.

[8] See Shetelig and Falk, *Scandinavian Archaeology*, pp. 68 ff.; Stenberger, *Sweden*, pp. 51 ff.; Ólafur Briem, *Vanir og Æsir* (*Studia Islandica*, Vol. 21 [Reykjavík: Leiftur, 1963]), pp. 8–9.

ideas which may help to clarify the meaning of both the chariots and the discs carried within.

Most scholars would agree that the chariots and discs had a religious meaning and purpose. If so, the disc depicted honorifically in a ship or chariot or on the shoulders of a man is a sacred object. If, as seems most probable, it represents the sun, we may suspect that the people of the Bronze Age worshipped the sun. This has led to the conclusion that the people of the Bronze Age worshipped natural objects but knew no personal gods; that they worshipped the sun but did not know the sun-god. This brings to mind Caesar's description of the religious beliefs and practices of Germans at his time: they had no druids and counted as gods only objects which they could see—the sun, Vulcan, and the moon.[9]

Such a conclusion would not be justified on the evidence available. Literary sources show that the worship of inanimate objects is not incompatible with the worship of personal gods. In fact pagan Norsemen who brought sacrifice to rocks, waterfalls, trees, and groves did not worship these objects for themselves, but for the deities who dwelt in them. Sometimes these were protective spirits (*ármenn* or *landvættir*), said to dwell in rocks, mounds, and waterfalls.[10]

Returning to the six-wheeled chariot on which the Trundholm disc rests, we may ask: if the disc is a sacral object, is the same true of the chariot that bears it? For the answer, we shall have to pursue the chariot through many lands and centuries.

It might well be argued that a chariot, a normal means of conveyance, need have no religious significance. In Iceland and many northern regions, however, where roads were few and rough, chariots were evidently less usual than *vagar* (*vǫgur*) and various kinds of sledges,[11] to say nothing of the mounted horse, and plainly many chariots were built for ceremonial purposes. To quote Shetelig and Falk: "It must be regarded as practically certain that the wagons from Dejbjærg (early Iron Age) were intended for use in religious ceremonies . . ."[12]

[9] *De Bello Gallico*, VI, 21.

[10] I have discussed this problem in some detail in *Myth and Religion of the North* (London: George Weidenfeld and Nicolson, 1964), esp. pp. 230 and 236 ff.

[11] See Einar Ól. Sveinsson (ed.), *Brennu-Njáls Saga* (Reykjavík: Hið Íslenzka Fornritafélag, 1954), p. 251 n.

[12] *Scandinavian Archaeology*, p. 187.

If this is true of the Dejbjærg chariots, what can be said of the elaborately worked Oseberg chariot, a splendid object but hardly an efficient means of conveyance? Nor should we forget the Oseberg tapestries, so ably described by Bjørn Hougen and reconstructed by Mary Storm.[13] Three chariots, drawn by stately, high-stepping horses, are there depicted. Swastikas and other mystic signs surmount and underlie them, and they are accompanied by men in procession. Two of the chariots are covered (as, we suppose, was that of the goddess Nerthus, to be mentioned later). In the third chariot sit two figures, probably a man and a woman.

Tacitus' story[14] about the seven tribes of north Germany in the first century A.D. is well known. Together these tribes worshipped a goddess Nerthus, said to be none other than Terra Mater. Upon an island, probably in the Baltic, was a sacred forest (*castum nemus*), and in it a veiled chariot (*vehiculum veste contectum*), to be touched only by the priest. The tribesmen believed that the goddess would come among them and that the priest would know when she was in her chariot, which was then drawn around by cows (*bubus feminis*). This was a time of rejoicing and of peace, and all weapons had to be laid aside. In the end, when Nerthus tired of the company of men, she was washed by slaves with all her trappings in a secret lake. Only the slaves were allowed to see her, and immediately afterwards they were drowned in the same lake.

We may be satisfied that the slaves were drowned as a sacrifice to the goddess, for drowning was a recognized form of sacrifice among northern peoples. Beneath the evergreen tree of unknown kind, standing beside the temple of Uppsala, was a well, in which pagans would drown a man. If his body were not found, the wishes of the people would be fulfilled.[15] In one Icelandic saga we read of *blótgrafar* (sacrificial pits), in which men and beasts were said to be sacrificed.[16] Another saga[17] mentions a *blótkelda,* evidently a marsh in which men were immersed. Admittedly, however, the two sources last quoted are

[13] *Viking* (Oslo: Norsk Arkeologisk Selskap, 1940), pp. 85 ff.

[14] *Germania,* Chap. 40.

[15] Adam Bremensis, *Gesta Hammaburgensis Ecclesiae Pontificum,* ed. B. Schmeidler (Hannover and Leipzig: Hahnsche Buchhandlung, 1917), pp. 257–258., Schol. 138.

[16] *Vatnsdœla saga,* Chap. 30.

[17] *Kjalnesinga saga,* Chap. 2.

late, and little is known of the traditions upon which they were based.[18]

The story told in the *Hrafnkels saga*[19] about the end of the sacred, or accursed, horse, Freyfaxi, reads like a parody of pagan sacrifice. The Þjóstarssynir, who destroyed Freyfaxi, said that it was proper that the horse's owner (i.e, Freyr) should now take him. They put a bag over the horse's head, as if to protect themselves from his evil eye, tied a stone round his neck, and pushed him over a cliff into a deep pool below. There is evidence that other horses were done to death in this way.[20]

Tacitus does not explain the purpose of the feast of Nerthus, nor the significance of the goddess, except to say that she was Mother Earth, but if we follow the chariot further we may begin to see what the ceremony meant.

Some ten, perhaps twelve, centuries can be skipped before the chariot is encountered once again. This time it is in Sweden, probably in Uppsala. In a story written in Iceland in the Middle Ages,[21] a Norwegian Christian, Gunnarr, fled his country in the days of Ólafr Tryggvason, late in the tenth century. When Gunnarr reached Sweden, he found that great sacrifices were held there. The god whom the Swedes chiefly worshipped was Freyr.

The idol of Freyr was not one of those lifeless objects of which we so often read; rather it was so bewitched that it talked, or more properly, as the author says, the devil talked out of it. This is characteristic of highly revered idols. In another text[22] an idol of Þórr, to which so much sacrifice was given that the devil talked out of it, walked with its owner round the island. In the Christian view, this idol was "possessed," but heathens might say that it incorporated the god.

The animate idol of Freyr would naturally need a wife (*kona*), and a beautiful girl was appointed to serve him. Whatever may be said of

[18] Cf. Ólafur Briem, *Heiðinn Siður á Íslandi* (Reykjavík: Menningarsjóður Íslands, 1945), pp. 148 ff.

[19] *Hrafnkels Saga Freysgoða*, ed. Jón Jóhannesson, in *Austfirðinga Sǫgur* (*Íslenzk fornrit*, Vol. XI [Reykjavík: Hið Íslenzka Fornritafélag, 1950]), Chap. 6, pp. 123–124.

[20] See K. Liestøl, "Tradisjonen i Hrafnkels saga Freysgoða, *Arv*, II, (1946), pp. 99–100.

[21] *Ǫgmundar Þáttr Dytts*, ed. Jónas Kristjánsson, in *Eyfirðinga Sǫgur* (*Íslenzk fornrit*, Vol. IX [Reykjavík: Hið Íslenzka Fornritafélag, 1956]), pp. 101–115.

[22] *Þáttr Rǫgnvalds*, in *Flateyjarbók*, ed. G. Vigfússon and C. R. Unger (Christiania: P. T. Malling, 1860), I, 288 ff.

the relations between Nerthus and her priest, this can only be a kind of sacral marriage.

The Norwegian fugitive could think of nothing better to do than to take refuge in the temple (*hofstaðr*) and throw himself on the mercy of Freyr's wife. The god eyed Gunnarr with suspicion, but Gunnarr stayed the winter, until the time came for Freyr to set out on his travels so that he might be entertained by the householders and, in return, bring fertility to their crops (*árbót*). The god and his wife were to ride in the chariot, while their attendants walked ahead in procession, the Norwegian leading the horse.

The road was long and the going rough, and when Gunnarr felt tired he jumped into the chariot to take his place beside Freyr and his wife. The jealous idol became enraged, and he and Gunnarr wrestled until, evidently through divine intervention, the idol fell, and nothing was to be seen but a block of wood. Gunnarr then put on the gorgeous raiment of the god, rode in the chariot, and pretended to be Freyr.

When Gunnarr, as Freyr, visited the farmers, they were delighted at the change which had come over the god. Now, more like one of themselves, he sat chatting and had an excellent appetite for food and drink. He no longer wanted animals slaughtered as sacrifice, though he was ready to accept gold, silver, and such fine clothes as they would give him. The farmers thought that the change boded well for the crops, especially when they saw that Freyr's wife was with child. The Swedes knew then that they could expect a better harvest than ever before.

This story is preserved in many manuscripts. A part of it, although not the part quoted, is in the damaged *Vatnshyrna*[23] of the late fourteenth century. It is also in the *Flateyjarbók*[24] of the end of the fourteenth century and in all texts of the Greater Saga of Ólafr Tryggvason. Since this saga was apparently compiled from older works early in the fourteenth century, the story of Gunnarr must be older than that. It was suggested long ago that it was the work of Gunnlaugr Leifsson, the Benedictine of Þingeyrar, who died in 1218.[25] The famous story of

[23] The text is in *Víga-Glúms Saga*, ed. G. Turville-Petre (Oxford: Clarendon Press, 1960), pp. 96 ff.

[24] Eds. Vigfússon and Unger, I, 332 ff.

[25] P. A. Munch, *Kong Ólaf Tryggvesöns Saga* (Christiania, 1853), p. xii; See also *Ǫgmundar Þáttr*, ed. Kristjánsson, in *Eyfirðinga Sǫgur*, p. lxiii, and references there given. Bjarni Aðalbjarnarson, *Om de norske kongers sagaer* (Skrifter utgitt av det Norske videnskapsakademi i Oslo II, Hist.-filos Klasse 1936, No. 4 [Oslo: Dybwad,

Þiðrandi, who was killed by the *dísir*, is also said by some to be Gunnlaugr's work,[26] although probably based upon older tradition. In any case, both stories are clerical pieces; they are Christian propaganda.

Some say that, in his allusions to Víga-Glúmr and his family, the author of our story shows that he knew *Víga-Glúms saga*,[27] which was probably written about 1220–1240. This argument is not convincing because the allusions are only to the genealogies of Glúmr's family, which the author of the story could have known from a source other than the saga. But the age of the story of Gunnarr is of less interest at the moment than the traditions upon which it is based.

Several scholars have drawn attention to southern European analogues and concluded that the Icelandic story is based on one of these. According to one scholar, Nectanebos (Neptanabus), king of Egypt, led the queen of Macedonia to believe that the god Ammon desired her. The King pretended to be the god, and thus became the father of Alexander the Great.[28]

The only reason for alluding to this story is the fact that, although not commonly realized by the critics, it was known in Iceland in the thirteenth century, albeit in a very different form. It is told in the Saga of Alexander (*Alexanders Saga*),[29] which was based upon the poem of Philippe Gautier. The Saga was written by Abbott Brandr, who died in 1264. However, I do not think the story of Nectanebos has had anything to do with that of Gunnarr.

A. H. Krappe has drawn attention to a much closer parallel. This was written by Valerius Flaccus towards the end of the first century A.D. The women of Lemnos had murdered all their men. Only one, Hypsipele, saved her father. She took him into the temple of Bacchus, disguised him as the god, dressed herself as a "bacchinite," and led the supposed god in a chariot to the seashore, saying that she must wash him. There he boarded a raft, and so escaped from the murderous women.[30]

1937]), p. 117, rejects the ascription of the tale to Gunnlaugr largely on grounds of style. The style could well have changed during scribal transmission.

[26] On this question see D. Strömbäck, *Tidrande och Diserna* (Lund: C. Bloms boktryckeri, 1949), pp. 12 ff.

[27] See Kristjánsson (ed.), *Ǫgmundar Þáttr* in *Eyfirðinga Sǫgur*, p. lvi.

[28] See H. Reuschel, "Der Göttertrug im Gunnars þáttr Helmings," *Zeitschrift für deutsches Altertum*, LXXI (1934), 155 ff.

[29] *Alexanders Saga*, ed. C. R. Unger (Christiania: Feilberg, 1848), p. 1.

[30] A. H. Krappe, "Le légende de Gunnar Half," *Acta Philologica Scandinavica*, III (1928), 226 ff.

In this story a man masquerades as the god. In some of the parallel stories quoted, the pretender is motivated by the desire to gain possession of a woman, though in the Norse story the woman is not deceived. But, in any form of the ritual drama, the god must be represented by a man, and perhaps the goddess by a woman, as were the May King and May Queen.

Both the Norse story and that of Bacchus may preserve memories of similar ritual procession or drama in which a man impersonates the god and a woman the goddess. But so great are the differences between these two stories that it would be hard to believe the story of Valerius Flaccus could serve as a model for that of Gunnarr.

The Icelandic story contains several interesting points which cannot be fantasy alone. The first of these is the chariot and the ceremonial procession. Evidence indicates that in the Bronze Age the image of the sun ceremoniously conveyed in a chariot, as in the account of Tacitus, was the hidden image of the goddess Nerthus. The purpose of these processions is not clear, but the purpose of Freyr's journey was to bring fertility to the crops (*árbót*).

It may help to consider a little more closely the character of the god Freyr. As Snorri tells us,[31] he rules rain and sunshine, and thus the fertility of the soil and the prosperity of men. In other words, Freyr may be seen as a sun- or sky-god. Since sunshine has greater significance for farmers of western Scandinavia than has rain, it is not surprising that the brilliance of Freyr is emphasized in our sources. He is *skírr*, or "brilliant,"[32] and the name of his servant is Skírnir (the brilliant). He was invoked, not only for fruitful harvests, but also for peace,[33] standing in sharp contrast to the warlike Þórr and to Óðinn, the wily promoter of battle. He is the son of Nerthus (Njǫrðr), and when the feast of Nerthus was held all weapons were laid aside, for this was a time of peace and tranquility.

Adam of Bremen describes the idol of Freyr (or Fricco, as he calls him),[34] kept in the famous temple of Uppsala. Adam saw Fricco much

[31] *Edda Snorra Sturlusonar*, ed. Finnur Jónsson (Copenhagen: Gyldendal, 1931), *Gylfaginning, Chap.* 13, p. 31.

[32] *Grímnismál*, st. 43.

[33] *Heimskringla*, ed. Bjarni Aðalbjarnarson (*Íslenzk fornrit*, Vol. XXVI [Reykjavík: Hið Íslenzka Fornritafélag, 1941]), Vol. I, *Hákonar Saga Góða*, Chap. XIV.

[34] *Gesta Hammaburgensis*, pp. 258–259.

as the Norse writers saw Freyr, as god of peace, as well as of voluptuary and marriage. Adam remarked that the idol was furnished *cum ingente priapo*. It was like a bronze statuette of *ca.* A.D. 1000 found at Rällinge (Sweden), also *cum ingente priapo*.[35]

Much can be learned about Freyr from the *Skírnismál*. This poem in dramatic, dialogue form cannot be of great age.[36] It is, first of all, a love story, but it appears to contain some very ancient elements.

The theme of the *Skírnismál* is the love of Freyr for Gerðr, daughter of the giant Gymir. The god sent his servant, Skírnir, into the world of giants to court the maiden. He sought to do so first with promises of precious gifts and, when these were of no avail, with threats. He would cut off her head and would lay terrible curses upon her. The maiden then gave way and agreed to meet the god after nine nights in the grove called Barri.

In 1909 M. Olsen gave an explanation of the story underlying the *Skírnismál*.[37] Most subsequent scholars[38] have accepted Olsen's explanation in outline, although it has been challenged.[39] Olsen saw Freyr as god of sunshine and fertility. His servant, Skírnir, was hardly more than a form of Freyr himself.

Olsen related the name of the maiden, Gerðr, to *garðr* (field). Gerðr was held fast in the clutches of frost-giants, winter demons, among whom was *Hrímgrímnir* (Frost-masked). She was taken from them by the god, or his agent. Barri, the name of the place where the god and his bride were to meet, was related by Olsen to *barr* (barley). The meeting place was, in this case, the cornfield, and the underlying myth was something of a season myth. If this explanation of the myth underlying the *Skírnismál* is accepted, Gerðr appears to have some affinities with Nerthus and to be a Terra Mater.

Much more could be said of Freyr. Sources show him primarily as a god of fertility and peace, but, as J. Sahlgren emphasized, he is not only that. Several suggestions have been made about the origin of the name Freyr, but it is unlikely that it means other than "Lord," being

[35] Illustrated in my *Myth and Religion of the North*, Plate 13.

[36] See Einar Ól. Sveinsson, *Íslenzkar Bókmenntir*, I, pp. 276 ff.; also J. Sahlgren, *Eddica et Scaldica* (Lund: C. W. K. Gleerup, 1928), pp. 211 ff.

[37] "Fra gammelnorsk myte og kultus," *Maal og Minne*, I (1909), 17–36.

[38] See especially U. Dronke in *English and Medieval Studies Presented to J. R. R. Tolkien* (London: Allen and Unwin, 1962), pp. 250 ff.

[39] Most strongly by J. Sahlgren, *Eddica*.

thus related to OE. *frēa* and Goth. *frauja*.[40] As the Lord, Freyr was something of a warrior, as several allusions in early poetry suggest. He is *ása jaðarr* (protector of gods);[41] he rules the armies (*folkum stýrir*),[42] and war is called "the sport of Freyr" (*Freys leikr*).[43]

Freyr is particularly the god of the Swedes (*svíagoð*)[44] and *blótguð svía* (sacrificial god of Swedes).[45] The Swedes called him *veraldargoð* (god of the world),[46] and sources make it plain that the cult of Freyr was most prevalent in Sweden, probably in the glorious temple of Uppsala, where the idol already described was kept at the end of the pagan period. This might be expected of a god who chiefly represents peace and fertility. The people of central Sweden, far more than the Norwegians or Icelanders, depended on the fertility of their crops.

Similarities have been noticed between the god Freyr and the goddess Nerthus. It might, therefore, be tempting to think of Nerthus as the mistress or perhaps the mother of the god, Freyr. But, surprisingly, in the Norse sources Nerthus, far from being Freyr's mistress or mother, was his father.

In Norse this deity is called *Njǫrðr*, and the name is declined as a normal *u*-stem, like *fjǫrðr*. In form, it corresponds exactly with *Nerthus*. An explanation of the difference of sex between the Nerthus of Tacitus and the Njǫrðr of the old Norse sources will not be attempted here. However, some have suggested that Nerthus was originally hermaphrodite; others say that the name Nerthus could be applied to a god as well as to a goddess. In this case, Nerthus was perhaps originally the name of a pair of deities, who were husband and wife or brother and sister. Njǫrðr at one time had his sister to wife; Freyr and Freyja, children of Njǫrðr, were brother and sister and yet they were said to have sexual relations.[47]

40 See A. Jóhannesson, *Isländisches Etymologisches Wörterbuch* (Bern: Francke Verlag, 1956), p. 548.

41 *Lokasenna*, st. 35.

42 Ulfr Uggason, *Húsdrápa*, in *Den norsk-islandske Skjaldedigtning*, ed. Finnur Jónsson (Copenhagen: Gyldendal, 1912), B, Vol. I, p. 129, st. 7.

43 Bjarni Aðalbjarnarson, in *Heimskringla*, I, 112 n. alternatively suggests that this kenning might refer to some religious sacrifice to promote fertility.

44 *Flateyjarbók*, eds. Vigfússon and Unger, III, 246.

45 *Ibid.*, I, 339.

46 *Heimskringla*, ed. Aðalbjarnarson, I, p. 25.

47 *Lokasenna*, st. 32.

That Nerthus was originally a goddess is no less probable, but since feminine *u*-stems nearly died out in the Norse language, the Scandinavians changed the sex of the deity.[48] The evidence of Swedish place-names suggests that there was, in Sweden, a goddess Njǫrðr (*Njarð-*), but in the west there seems to have been only a god.

Like the Swedes, the Danes depended greatly on the fertility of their crops and they might be expected to worship the chief fertility god also. But very little is heard about the cult of Freyr in Denmark, although it has been said that the Danes worshipped the same god, calling him Fróði instead of Freyr. On the other hand, Professor W. Baetke has recently said that all attempts to identify Fróði with Freyr or to show that there ever was a god Fróði have failed.[49]

Which of these views is correct? The Danish regnal lists include no less than five kings who bore the name Fróði. Whatever the basis of the tradition, it is plain that the regnal lists have confused it. But, in any case, one of the Kings Fróði bore the nickname *friðgothæ* (generous of peace) or *frið-Fróði* (peace-Fróði). According to the Danish records, this was the third king with the name Fróði, but the Icelanders, Snorri, Arngrímur Jónsson, and the *Sǫgubrot af Fornkonungum*, say that it was the first. This discrepancy need worry us little, for the Fróði of concern here ruled about the time of Christ, or of Augustus Caesar, an age of peace and plenty, which was called the "Peace of Fróði" (*Fróðafriðr*).

Allusion is made to Fróði's age of peace and plenty by skaldic poets, and it is the subject of the *Grottasǫngr* ("Song of Grotti"), in which the poet describes the peace and its disastrous end. Such peace was there that no man would even strike his brother's slayer if he found him bound:

Hér skyli engi ǫðrum granda,
til bǫls búa né til bana orka,

[48] I have discussed this question briefly in *Proceedings of the Leeds Philosophical and Literary Society, Literary and Historical Section*, III, No. 6 (Leeds: Chorley and Pickersgill, 1935), pp. 330 ff., and in *Myth and Religion of the North*, pp. 171 ff. The name Nerthus is thoroughly discussed by E. Polomé, "Nerthus-Njord," *Handelingen van de Zuidnederlandse Maatschappij voor Taal- en Letterkunde en Geschiedenis*, V (1951), 99 ff., and "À propos de la déesse Nerthus," in *Latomus*, XIII, 2 (1954), 167 ff. See also E. Elgqvist, *Studier rörande Njordkultens spridning bland de nordiska folken* (Lund: Olins Antikvariat, 1952), esp. pp. 26 ff.

[49] *Yngvi und die Ynglinger* (Berlin: Akademie-Verlag, 1964), pp. 85 ff.

né hǫggvagi	hvǫssu sverði
þóat bana bróður	bundinn finni

which may be rendered:

Here shall no one	harm another
plot his injury	nor seek his life,
though his brother's slayer	he finds in chains.

Now, according to a statement ascribed to Ólafr Tryggvason in the conflated Saga, the Danes ascribed the peace to their King Fróði, but the Swedes said that it was Freyr who had brought it.[50] For Freyr was king of Swedes and at the same time Fróði was king of Denmark.

If Freyr and Fróði were both gods, they were turned into earthly kings, euhemerized. If they were both earthly rulers, they were turned into gods; i.e., they were divine kings. The distinction between a god and a king does not seem very great, in spite of Baetke's arguments to the contrary.[51]

Gods, and especially those conceived as earthly kings, must die. Saxo's Fróði III was gored to death by a mythical monster, a sea-cow (*maritima bos*),[52] but the chieftains refused to publish the news, fearing tumult and despair among the people. They embalmed the corpse, dressed it in regal attire, and carried it ceremonially in a chariot. In the same way, when Freyr died in Sweden, his death was concealed, and he was placed in a great mound, where he still received his tribute while peace and prosperity persisted.

The name Fróði might mean "the wise," but it is no less likely that it means "the fruitful," and may thus be compared with the Swedish and Norwegian *frodig* (luxuriant, fruitful). It is worth noting that in one text Freyr has the title *inn fróði*, which may well mean "the fruitful."

As already mentioned, the name Freyr probably means only "lord." Therefore, it is not surprising that the Swedes knew their god or king under another name as well; they called him Yngvi, and his supposed descendants, the rulers of Sweden, were called Ynglingar.

[50] *Flateyjarbók*, eds. Vigfússon and Unger, I, 404.

[51] *Yngvi*, pp. 39 ff.

[52] Saxo Grammaticus, *Gesta Danorum*, ed. A. Holder (Strassburg: Karl Trübner, 1886), Chap. 5, pp. 170 ff.

The name Yngvi inevitably makes us think of the Old English "Runic Poem," with the following cryptic sentences:

> Ing wæs ærest
> mid East-Denum
> gesewen secgun,
> oþ he siððan est
> ofer wæg gewat;
> wæn æfter ran;
> ðus Heardingas
> ðone hæle nemdun.

These lines have been rendered:

> Ing was first
> among the East-Danes
> seen by men,
> until afterwards eastward
> over the wave he departed;
> his chariot ran after him;
> thus the Heardingas
> called this hero.[53]

This is not the place to discuss these lines, for they would carry us too far. But who is Ing?[54] Since Freyr was called Yngvi and Freyr too had a chariot, we may suppose that Ing is Freyr, although he may be someone else as well.

The people of Germany in the time of Tacitus fell broadly into three great tribes, whose names alliterated. Those to the southeast were called Erminiones; to the west were the Istræones (?), and to the north the Ingvæones.

The form of the name Istræones is uncertain. Some have supposed that there was a god *Istraz, whose name would derive from the tribe while he himself might be seen as their divine ancestor. But if there

[53] See *Runic and Heroic Poems*, ed. Bruce Dickins (Cambridge: University Press, 1915), p. 20.

[54] The origin of the name has been widely discussed. See especially F. R. Schröder, *Ingunar-Freyr* (Tübingen: J. C. B. Mohr, 1941). E. Polomé, "À propos de la déesse Nerthus," *Latomus*, p. 176 ff., draws attention to the suggestion of W. Krause and others that the name Ing is related to Tocharian B *eṅkwe*, 'man.' The suggestions offered are too speculative and insecurely based to throw light on the problems of Old Norse mythology.

ever was a god *Istraz, nothing is known about him. The Erminiones, if this line of reasoning is followed, might be said to descend from a god *Erminaz.

We have rather more evidence of a god *Erminaz. The chief idol of the Saxons was Irminsul, or Erminsul. This was destroyed by Charles the Great and is described variously as a temple, a famous grove, and as a tree trunk. In Latin it was said to be a universal column, seeming to uphold the universe.[55]

The supposed god *Ingvaz is the chief concern here. Since both he and Freyr had chariots and Freyr was called Yngvi, we may suppose that Freyr is Ing. In this case, Freyr was the ancestor god not only of the Ynglingar but also of the Ingvæones. At the risk of being daring, a symbolic meaning may perhaps be discovered in the words of the "Runic Poem." Ing was seen first among the eastern Danes; afterwards he went east and the chariot followed. The cult of Ing was carried with all its trappings over the sea to Sweden, and it found its center in Uppsala.

It was the Heardingas who gave the name to Ing. Who are they?[56] As has frequently been observed, their name corresponds closely with that of the (H)asdingi, who were the ruling house of the Vandals, as well as with that of the Haddingjar, a name given to certain obscure figures in Norse tradition. Scholars do not agree about the meaning of this name, but the suggestion that it is related to the word *haddr*, meaning a "woman's hair-style," is hard to reject. This implies, perhaps, that the Haddingjar wore their hair like women. They might be like the German priest of Nahanarvali, who was said by Tacitus to be *muliebri ornatu*. The gods whom these priests served were twin gods, conceived as young men. Now, a cryptic passage in a Norse text says that there were two Haddingjar; they were twins and together could only do the work of one man.[57]

55 See J. de Vries, "La valeur religieuse du mot germanique *irmin*," in *Cahiers du Sud* (Marseilles, 1952), pp. 18 ff.; G. Turville-Petre, "Thurstable," in *English and Medieval Studies presented to J. R. R. Tolkien* (London: Allen and Unwin, 1962), pp. 241 ff.

56 See especially G. Dumézil, *La Saga de Hadingus* (Paris: Presses Universitaires de France, 1953). I have discussed the Haddingjar in *Myth and Religion of the North*, pp. 213 ff.

57 *Heiðreks Saga*, ed. Jón Helgason (Copenhagen: Samfund til Udgivelse af gammel Nordisk Litteratur, 1924), p. 4.

Thus the Haddingjar, or Heardingas might be thought of as priests of Ing and thus of Freyr. The scorn and charges of effeminacy which Christian writers lavish on the cult of the god Freyr supports this suggestion. Saxo is shocked by the effeminate gestures and the unmanly clapping of bells; in other words, by the *ergi*, or baseness, of the cult.

But if the Haddingjar were originally priests of Freyr and his tribe, one of them seems to grow up in Norse tradition and to become a fertility god, one of the Vanir, as this tribe of gods was called. The Hadingus, whom Saxo describes, was said to have founded the cult of Freyr in Sweden, and Hadingus himself acquired the characteristics and performed some of the feats of Freyr's father, Njǫrðr. Both Hadingus and Njǫrðr took their brides from the giant world, and in neither case was the marriage a success.

There are sharp differences between the two tribes of gods, Æsir and Vanir. The Æsir, Þórr, Týr and even Óðinn, represent a high and even noble aspect of religion, but Christians often write of the Vanir as if they were low. The differences were such that those who worshipped them wondered how the two tribes came to be combined. The explanation was provided in a story outlined in the *Vǫluspá* (st. 21–24) and in rather closer detail in the prose of Snorri.[58] This story tells of the first war in the world.

According to the poem, if the difficult lines are correctly interpreted, the war began in this way: the Æsir had lived peacefully until the arrival in their citadel, first, of three giant-maidens, and then of a wicked sorceress. The gods ran her through with spears and burned her three times, but yet she went on living, casting spells and especially corrupting women. Though the course of the war is not made clear in the poem, at one stage the Vanir pierced the walls of the stronghold of the Æsir and held the field by the force of their "battle-magic" (*vígspá*).

The name of the sorceress, who seems to have provoked the war, is of some interest. She is Gullveig. The name, found nowhere else, seems to mean something like "the power of gold," "the corrupting passion." or even "the drunkenness of gold." This may imply that Gullveig came from the world of the Vanir. As gods of fertility they were also gods of riches. No one is richer than Njǫrðr;[59] Freyr possessed the boar Gull-

[58] *Ynglinga saga*, Chap. 4.
[59] Cf. *Vatnsdœla saga*, Chap. 47.

inbursti (Golden Bristled); and Freyja, as the early poets knew, wept tears of gold, and hence gold may be called *Freyju tár* (tears of Freyja).

The account given by Snorri in the *Ynglinga saga* (Chap. 4), written in the third decade of the thirteenth century, follows the course of the war between the Æsir and the Vanir. First one side held the field and then the other, until both tired of the war and made peace. Under the pact which followed, hostages were exchanged, and Njǫrðr and his son Freyr came to the Æsir and dwelt among them permanently, although Njǫrðr was eventually to return to his own tribe in the Ragnarǫk.[60]

Snorri, as well as Saxo and other writers and poets, gives some insight into the meaning of the Vanir. They are not necessarily evil, but rather are base, at least if regarded through Christian eyes. Before Njǫrðr came to live with the Æsir, he had his sister to wife, a myth which might help to explain the difference of sex between Nerthus and Njǫrðr. It is also said that Freyja had consorted with her brother Freyr, and Snorri explains that such unions were forbidden among the Æsir. Emphasis is often laid on the base sexual morality of the Vanir, and in one passage Snorri mentions the practice of *seiðr,* which was said to be common among the Vanir. It is not altogether clear what *seiðr* was, but it was a kind of magic, generally despised.[61] The Goddess Freyja was mistress of *seiðr*, and she taught it to the Æsir. Óðinn became a master of it, and by such means he could see into the future and could cause sickness and death. Accompanied by *ergi* and such reprehensible practices, *seiðr* was considered unfit for men and was commonly left for the priestesses.

It was noted that the Vanir, Njǫrðr and his son Freyr, came as hostages to live among the Æsir. How Freyja came to be among them is not clear. She is a sorceress, she is immoral, and she weeps tears of gold. If we dare to equate Freyja with Gullveig, we may understand her better.[62] Gullveig had entered the citadel of the Æsir; she cast spells and was the joy of evil women. They called her Heiðr, a name probably meaning "the bright one." The Æsir tried to destroy Gullveig with spears and fire, but she still lived. If Gullveig is Freyja, this may help

[60] *Vafþrúðnismál*, st. 39.

[61] The most thorough study of *seiðr* is by D. Strömbäck, *Sejd. Textstudier i nordisk religionshistoria* (Stockholm: Hugo Gebers Förlag, 1935).

[62] Particularly useful remarks on Gullveig and her relations with the Vanir were made by S. Nordal, *Völuspá* (2nd ed.; Reykjavík: Helgafell, 1952), p. 89., and by G. Dumézil, *Tarpeia* (Paris: Gallimard, 1947), pp. 259 ff.

to explain why the war between the two tribes of gods began and how Freyja came to live among the Æsir.

Since the Vanir are the chief, although not the only gods who promote fertility of the soil, it comes as no surprise to find that farms, cornfields, and meadows, were frequently dedicated to them and that their memory is preserved in numerous place-names.[63] Typical are Freysakr (Freyr's Cornfield), Njarðarvin (Njǫrðr's Meadow), and Njarðartún (Njǫrðr's Field). Names like these are not evenly distributed throughout Scandinavia, but clustered in certain districts. Most of them are to be found in central and eastern Sweden, centering upon Uppsala. Another, though smaller, cluster is found in south-eastern Norway. Among the names which commemorate the Vanir, those compounded with *Frey(r)* predominate in these regions, suggesting that there, at any rate, Freyr was the foremost of his tribe. But on the western sea-board of Norway, the picture changes. There names commemorating Njǫrðr heavily outnumber those in which Freyr is remembered. They are also of a different kind; they are not so much names of fields and pastures as of harbors, islands, and landing places (e.g., Njarðarey, Njarðvík). This difference can be explained. In earlier times Njǫrðr was worshipped beside Freyr as patron of the crops, but later their functions became distinct. Freyr remained patron of the crops, but Njǫrðr came to be regarded as patron of another kind of fertility, the fertility of the sea and its riches. His dwelling was Nóatún (the Home of Ships), and he was to be invoked by fishermen. He was regarded as the richest of the gods, and thus, while Freyr remained the chief fertility god for the farmers of the east, Njǫrðr assumed this role for the fishermen of the west.

Further west, in Iceland, these fertility gods played a comparatively small part, but yet they retained some of their original characteristics. Freyr still presided over the ever-fertile cornfield, Vitazgjafi (the Certain Giver), taking vengeance when its sanctity was violated by bloodshed.[64] We read also of a family called Freysgyðlingar (priestlings of

[63] Most thoroughly studied by M. Olsen, *Hedenske kultminder i norske Stedsavne*, Vol. I (Oslo: Dybwad, 1915), and *Njarðarlǫg*, republished in *Norrøne Studier* (Oslo, 1938), pp. 63 ff.; see also E. Wessén, "Schwedische Ortsnamen und altnordische Mythologie," in *Acta Philologica Scandinavica*, IV (1929), pp. 97 ff.; E. Elgqvist, *Studier rörande Njordkultens*, esp. pp. 50 ff. Interesting maps showing the distribution of these names are in J. de Vries, *Altgermanische Religionsgeschichte*, II, pp. 194–195 and 309.

[64] *Víga-Glúms Saga*, passim.

Freyr) in the southeast of Iceland[65] and of a Freysgoði (priest of Freyr) in the northwest,[66] who would hold a feast at the beginning of winter and offer sacrifices to Freyr. So much did Freyr love this man that after he was dead he would never allow the snow to lie on his cairn. The Icelandic place-names in which Freyr is commemorated are, however, few and probably of little significance.

Even less is remembered in Iceland of the cult of Njǫrðr, although together with his son, Freyr, he had to be invoked when the oath on the temple-ring, the most sacred oath, was sworn.[67] Only two place-names containing Njǫrðr's name are recorded in Iceland, too few to provide evidence of his cult since they might well have been transferred from Norway.

I suggested earlier that the worship of inanimate objects was concurrent with the worship of personal gods. Such revered objects as trees, rocks, and rapids might come to be associated with one god or another. The god might be thought to live in them, to guard them jealously. If this is true of inanimate objects, how much more likely it is to be true of animals. Some animals might be worshipped in their own right, others because they were sacred to the gods. Many stories illustrate this. One of the first explorers of Iceland was the Norwegian Flóki.[68] Before he set sail, he offered sacrifice to three ravens which were to guide him on his voyage. The raven was sacred to Óðinn.

Among the beasts particularly closely associated with Freyr and the Vanir were pigs, perhaps because of their productivity. (They may, of course, have been sacred in their own right and need not always be regarded as evidence for the cult of Vanir.) And, one of the settlers of Iceland, Helgi the Lean, in accordance with the custom that new settlers throw overboard some sacred object as they neared land, put ashore a boar and a sow. When he found them three years later, they were a herd of seventy.[69] It is known that there was a strong tradition of Freyr-worship in the family to which Helgi belonged, and perhaps he regarded his pigs as sacred to Freyr, who, after all, owned the splendid boar Gullinbursti. (When this boar galloped through the sky, all the

[65] *Landnámabók*, ed. F. Jónsson (Copenhagen: Thiele, 1900), p. 125; cf. Einar Ól. Sveinsson, *Landnám í Skaftafellsþingi* (Reykjavík: Skaftfellingafélagið, 1948), pp. 139 ff., and Turville-Petre, *Myth and Religion of the North*, pp. 166 ff.

[66] *Gísla Saga Súrssonar*, ed. B. Sveinsson (Reykjavík: Kristjánsson, 1922), pp. 137, 144.

[67] *Landnámabók*, ed. Jónsson, p. 96.

[68] *Ibid.*, pp. 5, 130.

[69] *Ibid.*, pp. 72, 193.

heavens shone). Another name for Freyr's sister, Freyja, was Sýr, a name which probably means "Sow."[70]

Beasts considered sacred to the gods are particularly acceptable to them as sacrifice. Some texts mention a *sonargǫltr*, probably the chief boar of the herd, upon whose bristles men would place their hands as they took vows and swore oaths. According to one text, a mighty boar, the size of an ox, was given to Freyr at Yuletide, so that the harvest might be fruitful.[71]

Horses were revered among many Germanic peoples, and their cult can be followed from the time of Tacitus to the Conversion. The future could be divined from their neighing, for they were the mouthpiece of the gods. One text (*Vǫlsa þáttr*) explains in somewhat drastic terms how the generative organ of a horse was worshipped as a god, as if it embodied the god Freyr *cum ingente priapo.*[72]

Some of the horses were dedicated to Freyr, and not a few texts emphasize this. Best known is the story of Hrafnkell, priest of Freyr, who shared his favourite horse with the god and killed the man who rode him without his leave. The horse was slain by being pushed over a cliff and drowned in a pool below.[73] The story of Hrafnkell has often been judged fictitious, although some are beginning to question this.[74] It probably is fictitious, but the author did not make up this story out of his head. Again and again we read that horses were dedicated to Freyr, and Norwegian traditions suggest that one way of sacrificing horses was to push them over a cliff, drowning them in a pool below, just as the slaves of Nerthus and the sacrificial victims at Uppsala were drowned.

It is also plain from many sources, not all of them Icelandic or even Scandinavian, that it was sacrilege for any but the priest or other authorized persons to mount a horse which had been dedicated to Freyr. Once, when the great Christian king, Ólafr Tryggvason, landed in

[70] Cf. Turville-Petre, *Myth and Religion of the North,* pp. 176 and 308 nn.

[71] *Helgakviða Hjǫrvarðssonar,* st. 30, prose; cf. *The Saga of King Heidrek the Wise,* ed. C. Tolkien (Edinburgh: Thomas Nelson and Sons, 1960), Chap. 8.

[72] I have discussed the significance of this tale in *Myth and Religion of the North,* pp. 256 ff.

[73] *Hrafnkels Saga Freysgoða,* ed. Jóhannesson, Chap. 6.

[74] See S. Nordal, *Hrafnkatla* (*Studia Islandica,* Vol. VII [Reykjavík: Leiftur, 1940]); K. Liestøl "Tradisjonen i Hrafnkels Saga Freysgoða," *Arv,* 1946, pp. 94 ff.; A. Liestøl, "Freyfaxi," *Maal og Minne,* 1945, pp. 59 ff.; M. Scovazzi, *La Saga di Hrafnkel* (Milan: Paideia, 1960); P. Halleux, *Aspects Littéraires de la Saga de Hrafnkel* (Paris: Société d'Édition "Les Belles Lettres," 1963).

Þrándheimr near a temple, he noticed a stud of horses and was told that they belonged to Freyr. The King mounted the stallion, his men mounted the mares, and together they rode off to destroy the temple and its idols.[75]

Cattle were also among animals which might be dedicated to Freyr and the Vanir. In other words, the beasts sacred to Freyr were those useful to the farmer—the pig, the horse, the cow—not the raven, eagle, wolf, or bear, all of which had some religious significance.

The Vanir expressed the ambitions of the peasant: they were fruitful and rich.

[75] *Flateyjarbók*, ed. Vigfússon and Unger, I, 401.

Some Comments on *Vǫluspá*, Stanzas 17–18

EDGAR C. POLOMÉ

Among the controversial problems of Eddic cosmology, the identification of the Scandinavian trinity that presides over the creation of man is certainly one of the most disputed. This creation episode is related in two stanzas of the *Vǫluspá* ("The Seeress' Prophecy"), whose wording reads as follows in Dr. Hollander's rhythmical translation:[1]

To the coast then came, kind and mighty,
from the gathered gods three great Æsir;
on the land they found, of little strength,
Ask and Embla, unfated yet.

Sense they possessed not, soul they had not,
being nor bearing, nor blooming hue,
soul gave Óthin, sense gave Hœnir,
being, Lóthur, and blooming hue.

In like manner, Snorri Sturluson[2] gives this account in the *Gyl-*

[1] Lee M. Hollander (trans.), *The Poetic Edda* (2nd ed.; Austin: University of Texas Press, 1962), p. 3.

[2] Anne Holtsmark and Jón Helgason (eds.), *Snorri Sturluson Edda, Gylfaginning og Prosafortellingene av Skáldskaparmál* (Copenhagen: Ejnar Munksgaard, 1950), p. 10: *þá er þeir Bors synir gengu með sævarstrǫndu, fundu þeir tré tvau ok tóku upp tréin ok skǫpuðu af menn, gaf hinn frysti ǫnd ok lif, annarr vit ok hrœring, .iii. ásiónu, málit ok heyrn ok sión . . .*

faginning ("Beguiling of Gylfi"): "While the sons of Borr[3] were walking along the shore, they discovered two tree trunks, took them up, and made men out of them; the first gave them breath and life, the second wit and movement, and the third appearance, speech, hearing and vision." Here, the gods are not explicitly mentioned by name, but the structural similarity of the two versions of the creation myth is obvious.

Several attempts have been made to find parallels to this myth, without great success, however. Thus, it is quite striking to notice that Hesiod, in his *Works and Days*, reports that "Zeus created a . . . race of men . . . from the ash-trees"[4] since the Eddic name of the first man, *Askr*, is precisely the Germanic word for 'ash-tree,' although the parallelism of the two traditions does not go any further. Friedrich von der Leyen[5] compared the Eddic account to an Indian tale in which a sculp-

[3] Name of the father of Othin as well as of *Vili* (lit., 'strong will' [if its first *i* is originally short]) and of *Vé* (lit., 'religious feeling'). The name appears as *burr* in the manuscripts and is undoubtedly identical with ON *burr*, 'son' (Sveinbjörn Egilsson, *Lexicon Poeticum Antiquae Linguae Septentrionalis*, ed. Finnur Jónsson [2nd ed.; Copenhagen: S.L. Møller, 1931], p. 57).

[4] Lines 143–145: *Ζεὺς δὲ πατὴρ . . . γένος μερόπων ἀνθρώπων ποίησ᾽ . . . ἐκ μελιᾶν* (A. Rzach [ed.], *Hesiodi Carmina* [Stuttgart: B.G. Teubner, 1958],p. 62). The meaning of *μερόπος* remains obscure ('articulate'? 'mortal'? see Hjalmar Frisk, *Griechisches etymologisches Wörterbuch,* [Heidelberg: Carl Winter, 1963], II, 211–212). Ancient *scholia* already identified *μελιᾶν* with the Μελίαι Nymphs mentioned in line 187 of the *Theogony* (see Agostino Pertusi, *Scholia Vetera in Hesiodi Opera et Dies* [Milano: Vita e Pensiero, s.a.], p. 59), but this presumably reflects a cosmogonic tale in which Ash-nymphs were the mothers of the human race (Paul Mazon, *Hésiode* [Paris: Les Belles Lettres, 1947], p. 37 n. 1). The translation '(ashen) spears' (Hugh G. Evelyn-White, *Hesiod: The Homeric Hymns and Homerica* [London: W. Heinemann, 1936], p. 13; Richmond Lattimore, *Hesiod* [Ann Arbor: University of Michigan Press, 1959], p. 35) has little to commend itself in this context (cf. *μελιηγενής* [Apollonius Rhodius], 'ashborn'). On Hesiod's myth of the generations of men, cf. the collection of articles by F. Bamberger, R. Roth, E. Meyer, R. Reitzenstein, A. Heubeck, A. Lesky, and Th. G. Rosenmeyer in Ernst Heitsch (ed.), *Hesiod* (Darmstadt: Wissenschaftliche Buchgesellschaft, 1966), pp. 439–648.

[5] Quoted by Jan de Vries, *The Problem of Loki* (Helsinki: Suomalainen Tiedeakatemia, 1933), pp. 34–35; for a complete translation of the tale, see Johannes Hertel, *Indische Märchen* (Düsseldorf: Diederichs, s.a.), pp. 182–183: "Die belebte Puppe." Von der Leyen's comparison appears in *Das Märchen in den Göttersagen der Edda* (Berlin: Reimer, 1889), p. 12:

Derselbe glaube findet sich auch in dem folgenden indischen belebungsmärchen (vgl. meine 'Indische Märchen,' s. 145 f.): Ein jüngling schnitzt ein mädchen aus h o l z , ein zweiter bemalt sie, ein dritter verbessert sie und macht sie einen frauenzimmer ähnlich, ein vierter beseelt sie und sie wird ein schönes weib. Alle vier streiten sich um sie: wem soll sie gehören? — Von diesem punkt an ist der verlauf der geschichte ein

tor, a goldsmith, a weaver, and a priest are seen traveling together. After cutting a piece of sandalwood into the effigy of a pretty woman, the sculptor successively hands it over to the weaver, who dresses it, and to the goldsmith, who adorns it with jewels. Then, the priest succeeds through his incantations in breathing life into it, after which the problem arises as to who will get the pretty creature as his wife.

If the point of departure is apparently the same—a human being fashioned out of a piece of wood—the elaboration upon the theme is obviously totally different. The Hindu tale is a curious apologue intended to throw light upon a problem of casuistry; it describes step by step the shaping of a human being who is endowed with life only in the final stage, as the crowning act of a long process. In the Scandinavian tradition, on the contrary, there is no trace of a similar process: the triad of gods creates the primordial *couple* straight away. We witness a *creative act*, performed through *direct divine intervention*; through it, the pieces of wood immediately acquire the fullness of life.[6] In other words, the characteristic feature of the Eddic account is the *unity* of the creative act in spite of the *distribution of the human attributes by three different gods*. This has evidently been the understanding of the exegetes of the *Vǫluspá* stanzas who have also tried to reduce the triad of gods to one by considering Lóðurr and Hœnir

---

doppelter; in ihrer türkischen fassung, die wie ich glaube, auf der älteren indischen beruht, wird schliesslich ein gottesurteil angerufen, da tut sich ein baum auf, an dem das mädchen gelehnt und nimmt es wieder zu sich (Rosen, *Tuti Nameh* I, 151).

To this he adds the following comments:

In diesen beiden berichten also, dem nordischen und dem indischen, wird die schöpfung, hier eines menschenpaares, dort eines menschen, von verschiedenen wesen vollzogen. Im nordischen werden die lebenskräfte verteilt, während sich im indischen die beseelung in einem akt vollzieht, die herrichtung des baumes dagegen, bis er einem menschen äusserlich ähnlich wird, den erzähler hauptsächlich beschäftigt. Demgemäss ist es den mythologen bis auf den heutigen tag unklar, wie man sich Ask und Embla vor ihrer belebung zu denken habe: ob als baumhölzer (Mogk, s. 378) oder ob als menschen in baumgestalt (Golther, s. 526). Vgl. auch Mannhardt, W[ald- und] F[eld]k[ulte], s. 8.

Man darf hier auch auf Hygin, fabula CCXX verweisen: Cura, cum quendam fluvium transiret, vidit cretosum lutum, sustulit cogitabunda et cœpit fingere hominem. Dum deliberat secum, quidnam fecisset, intervenit Jovis. Rogat eum Cura, ut ei daret spiritum; quod facile ab Jovē impetravit. Cui cum vellet Cura nomen suum imponere, Jovis prohibuit, suumque nomen ei dandum esse dixit. Dum de nomine Cura et Jovis disceptarent, surrexit et Tellus, suumque nomen ei imponi debere dicebat, quandoquidem corpus praebuisset. Sumpserunt Saturnum judicem, quibus Saturnus secus videtur judicasse: "Tu Jovis quoniam spiritum dedisti, corpus recipito. Cura, quoniam prima eum finxit, quamdiu vixerit, Cura eum possideat. Sed quoniam de nomine ejus controversia est, h o m o vocetur, quoniam ex h u m o videtur esse factus."

[6] Friedrich von der Leyen, *Die Welt des Märchen*, (Düsseldorf: Diederichs, 1953), I, 205–206.

merely as poetic creations due to Christian influence[7] or as hypostases of Othin.[8] Without drawing such far-reaching conclusions, we cannot fail to notice with surprise that, whereas the attribution of vital breath to the human being normally falls within Othin's province, this is not also the case with the inspired cerebral activity which Hœnir's gift implies.

Let us reexamine the facts, text in hand.[9] From Othin, man receives *ǫnd*, in which everyone agrees to recognize the 'breath of life' (it would, indeed be rather imprudent to translate it as 'soul,' considering the Christian implications of this term, which the Old Norse substantive acquired only at a later date; literally, *ǫnd* means 'breath'). Such a gift is quite in keeping with the very nature of Othin as the sovereign god meting out *life-giving* power. Besides, it should be remembered that his name in Proto-Germanic, **Wōðanaz*, is ultimately derived from an Indo-European theme **awē-*, meaning 'to blow,' whose participial form, **wē-nt-*, supplied the Indo-European word for 'wind.' Further analysis of this theme led George van Langenhove to posit a root *H_2*éw-*, which would designate the 'life-giving power.'[10] But the name of Othin, **Wōðanaz*, is more directly connected with the Western Indo-European stem **wāt-*, which appears in Lat. *vātes*, 'soothsayer,' OIr. *fáith*, 'seer, prophet,' and Ger. *Wut*, 'rage'; Adam of Bremen himself considered the name of Othin as synonymous with *furor*. Actually, Othin is the inspired god, the prince of poets, the magician *par excellence*, the master of divinatory runes—attributes which agree perfectly with the meaning of his name, of which the stem

[7] Elard Hugo Meyer, *Mythologie der Germanen* (Strasbourg: K. Trübner, 1903), pp. 411, 449–450.

[8] Friedrich von der Leyen, *Die Götter der Germanen* (Münich: C. H. Beck, 1938), p. 268.

[9] The edition used here is Gustav Neckel, *Edda. Lieder des Codex Regius nebst verwandten Denkmälern*, ed. H. Kuhn (3rd ed.; Heidelberg: Carl Winter, 1962), I, 4–5:

(17)	Unz þrír qvómo	ór þrí liði,
	ǫflgir oc ástgir,	æsir, at húsi;
	fundo á landi,	lítt megandi,
	Asc oc Emblo,	ørlǫglausa.
(18)	Ǫnd þau né átto,	óð þau né hǫfðo,
	lá né læti	né lito góða;
	ǫnd gaf Óðinn,	óð gaf Hœnir,
	lá gaf Lóðurr	oc lito góða.

[10] *Linguistische Studiën*. II: *Essais de linguisıique indoeuropéenne* (Antwerp: De Sikkel, 1939). p. 46–47.

denotes inspired cerebral activity and the suffix possession and mastery.[11]

The same meaning, 'inspired cerebral activity,' should also be ascribed to ON *óðr*, which is usually translated 'mind,' 'reason (understanding),' or 'sense' in the context of the *Vǫluspá* stanza, where it appears as Hœnir's gift to man. The noun *óðr* can indeed hardly be dissociated from the adjective *óðr*, which means 'mad, frantic' or 'furious, vehement' or 'eager, impatient,' meanings which point either to strong emotional stress or to lack of control of the power of reasoning. This is in keeping with the fact that the inspired mental activity expressed by Germanic **wōð-* can verge on ecstasy, as shown by the name of the poetic mead stimulating inspiration: *óðrærir*, literally 'rousing to the point of ecstasy.'[12] That ON *óðr* denotes an 'inspired mental activity,' and not merely 'intelligence,' conceived as the faculty of reasoning, is further confirmed by its second meaning, 'poetry,' especially in the skaldic phrase designating the poet as *óðar smiðr*, 'smith of inspired thought.'[13] Actually, the only context in which the meaning 'intelligence, mind, reason' is assumed for *óðr* is in stanza 18 of the *Vǫluspá*, and in modern Norwegian the noun continued to exist as a neuter under the form *od*, besides a feminine *oda*, with the meaning 'strong desire' (*sterk lyst*).[14] The current interpretation of *óðr* as 'mind, intelligence, reason' in the Eddic passage under reference is ascribable to the parallel text of Snorri, where the second god participating in the creation of man endows him with *vit ok hrœring*, usually translated 'wit and movement,' with special focus on *vit,* because the association of 'movement' with 'intelligence' sounds rather awkward. However, *hrœring* does not necessarily apply to a physical movement: in the compound *hugarhrœring*, as well as in numerous contexts and phrases like *geðs hrœringar*, it indicates emotion and may therefore, better than *vit*, reflect the connotations of the Eddic noun *óðr*, which Leiv Heggstad glosses more adequately *hugrørsla* (movements of the mind).[15] It is consequently legitimate to question Georges Dumézil's statement:

[11] See my "L'étymologie du terme germanique **ansuz* 'dieu souverain'," *Études Germaniques*, VIII (1953), 39.

[12] Jan de Vries, "Über das Verhältnis von Óðr und Óðinn," *Zeitschrift für deutsche Philologie*, LXXIII (1954), 344.

[13] In a line in *Egils saga* (cf. Rudolf Meissner, *Die Kenningar der Skalden* [Bonn and Leipzig: Kurt Schroeder, 1921], p. 364).

[14] Leiv Heggstad, *Gamalnorsk Ordbok* (Oslo: Det Norske Samlaget, 1930), p. 501.

[15] *Ibid.* See also de Vries, "Über das Verhältnis von Óðr und Óðinn," *Zeitschrift*

la répartition des tâches est claire: le premier dieu fait le grand miracle, il anime, donne aux deux planches cette force vitale qui est commune à l'homme, aux animaux et aux plantes; le second leur donne ce qui est le propre de l'homme, l'esprit, l'intelligence ou la raison; le troisième leur donne les moyens de s'exprimer, la parole et l'apparence ou les "belles couleurs,"

because it implies that:

sous le grand dieu *Odh*inn, qui fait le don primordial et la plus général (la vie), H*œ*nir patronne donc la partie profonde, invisible de l'intelligence, "l'intelligence en soi", tandis que Lô*dh*urr patronne l'intelligence incarnée dans le "système de relation", dans les organes, accrochée aux sens, au gosier, à la peau, comme une araignée à sa toile.[16]

Dumézil's assumption that Hœnir is the god of careful thought is the basis of this interpretation, which would confirm the ingenious etymology of the name *Hœnir* proposed by George van Langenhove, namely its derivation from a Germanic prototype **hōnija-*, reflecting Indo-European **kōniyo-*, derived from the root **kō-*, 'make keen, sharpen,' Hœnir being the 'sharpener'[17]—the god who sharpens the wit.

This view is based mainly on the interpretation of Hœnir's attitude on two occasions: (a) when Þjazi, in the shape of an eagle, requests of him a full share of the gods' meal, Hœnir does not answer, but cannot help breathing heavily with anger;[18] (b) whenever he attends the þing

für deutsche Philologie, p. 345. In this article (pp. 340–343), de Vries also discusses Dr. Hollander's interpretation of the god Óðr in his relationship with Freyja as a Scandinavian reflex of the myth of Cupid and Psyche ("The Old Norse God *Óðr*," *Journal of English and Germanic Philology*, XLIX [1950], 307–308.) In view of the semantic content of ON *óðr*, it is undoubtedly disputable that "*Óðr* . . . as closely as possible translates ψυχή 'animus, spirit'."

[16] Dumézil, *Loki* (Paris: G.P. Maisonneuve, 1948), p. 283; German edition (Darmstadt: Wissenschaftliche Buchgesellschaft, 1959), p. 232–233.

[17] *Linguistische Studiën*, II, p. 70–72.

[18] *Haustlǫng*, st. 4: *hlaut . . . hrafnásar vinr blása.* On the interpretation of this line, cf. Ernst A. Koch, *Notationes Norrœnæ* (Lund: C.W.K. Gleerup, 1926), Part 7, sec. 1016, p. 18–19). Anne Holtsmark ("Myten om Idun og Tjatse i Tjodolvs Haustlong," *Arkiv för nordisk Filologi*, LXIV [1950], 17), however, thinks that Loki is meant, to continue the comic effect of the preceding stanza, but Dumézil (*Loki* [1948], p. 275 n.7, 276; [1959], p. 226 n. 94) is presumably right in claiming that the described reaction would hardly fit with the subsequent readiness of Loki to parcel out the meat to Þiazi. In the parallel tale in the *Snorra Edda* (*Skáldskaparmál*, Chap. 1), Hœnir is not even mentioned in this connection.

as chief of the Vanir and fails to get Mímir's advice, he does not take a stand but merely says: *ráði aðrir* (Let others decide).[19] Dumézil considers Hœnir's refusal as the only wise attitude under the circumstances and contrasts it with Loki's rash decision, which turns to disaster for him when he tries to beat Þjazi with a stick after snatching four pieces of beef away from the sacred table to feed him. Hœnir knows the giant is not supposed to receive any of the food of the gods, but since he can do nothing about it, he remains passive, though not without emotion.

In the case of his refusal to make decisions in the absence of Mímir, Dumézil offers an ingenious explanation:

Le binôme Hœnir-Mîmir . . ., réuni, fait un chef parfait et . . ., séparé, ne vaut plus rien. . . . [It constitutes] une juste image du mécanisme de nos meilleures pensées: devant une question, une difficulté, nous suspendons d'abord notre réaction et notre jugement, nous savons d'abord ne pas agir et nous taire, ce qui est déjà une grande chose; et puis nous écoutons la voix de l'inspiration, le verdict qui nous vient de notre savoir et de notre expérience antérieurs ou de l'expérience héréditaire de l'espèce humaine ou de plus loin encore, cette parole intérieure qui, comme la Raison des philosophes ou la "conscience collective" des durkheimiens, est à la fois en nous et plus que nous, autre que nous. Mîmir, près de Hœnir . . . représente cette partie mystérieuse, intime et objective, de la sagesse, dont Hœnir représente la partie extérieure, individuelle, l'attitude conditionnante. Hœnir a l'air d'un sot? Il pourvoit seulement au vide, à l'attente que remplira Mîmir.[20]

For all the brilliant style of the French scholar, one cannot help wondering whether he has not begged the question. All the texts show is that Hœnir is incapable of acting on his own. If this does not make him weak in wits, as has often been assumed,[21] it hardly points him out

[19] *Heimskringla*: *Ynglinga saga*, Chap. 4. This is the only context in which a specific description of Hœnir is given: "*kǫlloðu hann allvel til hǫfðingja fallinn; hann var mikill maðr ok inn vænsti*" (they [i.e. the Æsir] said he was very worthy, indeed, to be a chief; he was a big man, and a very beautiful one). The only additional information is from kennings, which characterize him as 'the rapid Ás' or as 'long-legged'—a feature which may also account for his designation as 'pace-Meili' (*fet-Meili*) in the fourth stanza of *Haustlǫng* (cf. A. Holtsmark, "Myten om Idun og Tjatse," *Arkiv*, p. 46). No further clue can be derived from the kenning for Loki: *Hœnis hugreynandi* (*Haustlǫng*, st. 12), literally 'Hœnir's mind-assayer.'

[20] Dumézil, *Loki* (1948), p. 278; (1959), pp. 228–229.

[21] See, e.g., Wolfgang Golther, *Handbuch der germanischen Mythologie* (Leipzig: S. Hirzel, 1895), p. 398–399: "Hönir [ist] zwar schön und stattlich, aber s c h w a c h

as the "dieu de la pensée réfléchie"; he is much rather the instrument of godly inspiration, the one who utters the message conveyed by outside wisdom. Therefore, he remains mute in the discussions of the þing of the Vanir when this inspiration, embodied by Mímir, fails him; therefore, he is described as the most fearful of the Æsir in the *Sǫgubrot*,[22] since he cannot act without being advised; therefore, also, he appears in a sacerdotal function after Ragnarǫk, when he will *hlautvið kjósa,* that is, consult the oracles according to the age-old practice of picking up sticks marked with divinatory symbols.[23] Here, again, interpreting the signs given by an outside Power, he is the vehicle of divine inspiration. It is also in this capacity that he is instrumental in endowing man with 'inspired mental activity' (*óðr*).[24]

---

i m G e i s t e und unselbständig im Urteil. Er braucht stets Mimirs Beirat, sonst weiss er sich nicht zu helfen." That Hœnir should grant *óðr* to man "is surprising when we remember how w i t l e s s Hœnir appeared to be when Snorri described him in the *Ynglinga Saga*" (E.O.G. Turville-Petre, *Myth and Religion of the North* [London: Weidenfeld and Nicolson, 1964], p. 142). Following R. M. Meyer (*Altgermanische Religionsgeschichte* [Leipzig: Quelle and Meyer, 1910], p. 370), where the exchange of Kvasir against Mímir and Hœnir is considered as "später Mythologenwitz," Jan de Vries wrote in the first edition of his *Altgermanische Religionsgeschichte* ([Berlin and Leipzig: W. de Gruyter, 1937], II, 309–310): "Die Geschichte ist sehr sonderbar; wenn sie nicht ganz für den Roman des Skaldenmetes, den Snorri in seiner Edda aufgenommen hat, erdichtet worden ist, so ist sie doch wohl bei der Einarbeitung so start umgemodelt worden, dass wir die ursprüngliche Form and Bedeutung nicht mehr herausfinden können." In the second edition ([1957], II, 270), however, he no longer questions the authenticity of the tale and follows Dumézil in stating: "eine schweigende Rolle . . . braucht aber . . . dennoch nicht die Rolle des Unverstandes zu sein."

22 *Sǫgubrot af fornkonungum*, Chap. 3: *er hræddastr var ása.*

23 *Vǫluspá*, st. 63. This practice of divination is described by Tacitus (*Germania*, Chap. 10; see the comment of Rudolf Much, *Die Germania des Tacitus* [Heidelberg: Carl Winter, 1937], pp. 130–132). On its relation with the Scandinavian sacrifice, see de Vries, *Altgermanische Religionsgeschichte*, (2nd ed.; 1956), I, 417, 432–433.

24 This does not, by far, solve the problem of Hœnir. His interpretation as a vehicle of divine inspiration has recently been illustrated from a different angle: reexamining Elof Hellquist's derivation of the name *Hœnir* from Gmc. **hōnya-,* 'belonging to the rooster,' "a *vṛddhi*-formation from *hani,*" Anne Holtsmark ("Mythen om Idun og Tjatse," *Arkiv*, pp. 48–53) considers Hœnir as an emanation of Othin in the shape of a rooster, whose part is played by a priestly performer imitating the rooster's step in a cultual drama. Folke Ström (*Loki. Ein mythologisches Problem* [Göteborgs Universitets Årsskrift, LXII, No. 8 (1956)], pp. 56–58; "Une divinité-oiseau dans la mythologie scandinave," *Ethnos*, XXI, [1956], 73–84; "Guden Hœnir och odensvalan," *Arv*, XII, [1956], 41–68), while dismissing the poorly documented hypothesis of the cultural drama, confirms the view that Hœnir must be a hypostasis of Othin in bird-shape: names like *aurkonungr*, translated 'king of the silt,' or phrases like *inn langi fótr*, 'the long-legged,' currently designating Hœnir in skaldic poetry, seem to point to a stilt, and Ström ultimately identifies Hœnir with the black stork, also

But, to return to the third component of the divine triad, what do we actually know about Lóðurr? Very little indeed. Aside from the reference to him in the stanza under consideration, he appears only in a poetic paraphrase designating Othin by the name of 'friend of Lóðurr,'[25] a phrase which tells us nothing new, since the association of this divine personage with the majestic sovereign god of the *Edda* is already known. Besides, in a considerable number of parallel kennings Othin is associated with the most diverse gods.[26] In short, Lóðurr is practically unknown to us except by the role he plays in the creation of man according to Scandinavian mythology.

This has not prevented exegetes from indulging in numerous conjectures concerning Lóðurr. Numerous are those who, relying upon the parallel association between Othin, Hœnir, and Loki in Snorri's prose *Edda*, wish to compare Lóðurr with Loki, but one would seek in vain for any cogent argument backing up this hypothesis. Proceeding from the idea that Loki was a god of fire, these authors merely resort to etymology in endeavoring to associate the two names more closely. Because the nature assigned to Loki is most debatable[27] and because, on the other hand, Lóðurr has apparently not the least connection with fire, it is superfluous to analyze the multiple etymological reconstructions advanced in order to justify this parallel.[28] In an important study

---

called *odensvala,* 'Othin's swallow.' E.O.G. Turville-Petre, however, argues that, if Hœnir's name is derived from a bird-name, he must be Othin's bird, i.e., a raven: "When divorced from their master, Óðinn's ravens could have little wit, for it was his wit which they incorporated. When separated from Mímir, Hœnir had no wits, and was no better than a barnyard cock" (*Myth and Religion of the North*, p. 142).

[25] *Lóðurs vinr* (Eyvindr skáldaspillir, *Háleygjatal,* 10.7: *vinar Lóðurs*; Haukr Valdísarson, *Íslendingadrápa*, 1.2: *Lóðurs vinar*; cf. Ernst A. Kock [ed.], *Den norsk-isländska Skaldediktningen* [Lund: C.W.K. Gleerup, 1946], I, 38, 261); cf. Rudolf Meissner, *Die Kenningar der Skalden*, p. 252.

[26] Meissner, *Die Kenningar der Skalden*, p. 252; Jan de Vries, *De Skaldenkenningen met mythologischen inhoud* (Haarlem: H.D. Tjeenk Willink, 1934), p. 19; the parallel kenning *Lopts vinr*, 'friend of Loptr (i.e., Loki)' in Einarr skálaglamm, *Vellekla,* 12.2 (tenth century), is assumed to have served as a model for the twelfth century *Lóðurs vinr*.

[27] On the challenging study of Dumézil, *Loki*, see mainly the comments of de Vries, *Altgermanische Religionsgeschichte* (1957), II, 265–267, and Turville-Petre, *Myth and Religion of the North*, pp. 144–146. Recent efforts to interpret Loki, including Folke Ström, *Loki*, and Anna Birgitta Rooth, *Loki in Scandinavian Mythology* (Skrifter utgivna av Kungl. Humanistiska Vetenskapssamfundet i Lund, Vol. LXI [Lund: C.W.K. Gleerup, 1961]), are discussed by Anne Holtsmark in "Loki—en omstridt skikkelse i nordisk Mytologi," in *Maal og Minne*, 1962, pp. 81–89.

[28] They are briefly analyzed by Jan de Vries, *The Problem of Loki*, pp. 50–51.

devoted to Loki, E.J. Gras[29] has, however, attempted to bring new elements into the debate by comparing the name *Lóðurr* with the name *logaþore*, which appears beside *wigiþonar* and *wodan* in the runic inscription of the Nordenhof brooch, and with the name of the Brabantine demon *Lodder.*

This hypothesis is based on three postulates, which Jan de Vries[30] has seriously questioned:

1. the identification between Loki, Lóðurr, and the demon Lodder, also known by the name *Loeke;*
2. the interpretation of runic *logaþore* as a divine name, related to ON *logi* 'fire';
3. the survival in the Lodder-Loeke of Brabant of an ancient Germanic divinity.

The idea that Loki, Lóðurr, and Lodder belong to the same religious sphere had already been expressed by H. Grüner-Nielsen and Axel Olrik in 1912.[31] By describing Lodder as a definite, facetious, nocturnal creature, most frequently a kind of will-o'-the-wisp ("et eller andet natligt gækkende væsen, snarest af lygtemandsartig art"), they manage to associate the Brabantine demon rather plausibly with the Lokke of Scandinavian folklore, which appears especially in connection with certain natural phenomena such as the vibration of the air as a result of heat or the sulfurous odor following a flash of lightning, with certain sacrificial ceremonies on the family hearth, with certain weeds and vermin (particularly spiders), as well as in phrases referring to lying and deceit.[32] However, this association remains superficial, because the Brabantine Lodder is somewhere halfway between a werewolf and a fiery ghost,[33] and he definitely appears to be very remote from the Scandinavian conception of the demon of the hearth, to say nothing of the possibility of comparing him to the Eddic god Loki. Several years

29 *De Noordse Loki-Mythen in hun onderling verband* (Haarlem: H.D. Tjeenk Willink, 1931), pp. 9–11.

30 *The Problem of Loki*, pp. 53–55.

31 "Efterslæt til Loke-myterne. I. Loeke, Lodder i flamsk folktro," in *Danske Studier*, 1912, pp. 87–90.

32 De Vries, *The Problem of Loki*, pp. 225–227 (summarizing the extensive collection of popular traditions by Axel Olrik); Dumézil, *Loki* (1948), pp. 71–79, (1959), pp. 45–52; Rooth, *Loki in Scandinavian Mythology*, pp. 196–202.

33 Jos. Schrijnen, *Nederlandsche Volkskunde*, (2nd ed.; Zutphen: W.J. Thieme, 1930), I, 97–98.

ago, I suggested[34] considering him as a 'wanderer'—a sort of *terrā vagans*—a hypothesis which is confirmed by the use of the term *lodder* to designate a vagrant in Middle Dutch and by the clear etymological parallel of Russ. *lytát,* 'to wander,' and I see no reason to reconsider this opinion. Nothing, indeed, justifies the assertion that the Lodder of Brabant is a distant reminiscence of any Germanic god. On these grounds the third postulate of Miss Gras's hypothesis can be safely dismissed. Indeed, if Lodder is only a local variant of the *kludde*, a demonic horse which hurls into the water the drunken peasant who thinks to be dealing with one of his own animals that has not been taken back to the stable,[35] one can hardly see what such an equine and aquatic demon would have in common with the god Loki. To be sure, it could be objected that Othin's horse, Sleipnir, was born to Loki, transformed into a mare, after intercourse with Svaðilfœri, stallion of the giant builder of the stronghold of the gods, as is told in Chapter 42 of *Gylfaginning*. But, enlarging upon a suggestion of Jan de Vries, Georges Dumézil[36] has clearly shown that the bringing forth of Sleipnir is a merely episodic event in the life of the Scandinavian god: "si Loki se transforme ici en jument, c'est que, seul des dieux scandinaves, il a une faculté illimitée de métamorphoses animales." This is not the only case in which Loki has functioned as a female in order to give birth to some monstrous creature. The short *Vǫluspá,* inserted in the *Hyndluljóð*, gives another example of it in stanza 43: "with child he grew from the guileful woman. Thence are on earth all ogres sprung."[37] His association with the horse is accordingly rather fortuitous: it just happened to be necessary to deprive the master-builder of the stronghold of the Æsir of the aid of his horse Svaðilfœri in order to provide

[34] Marcel Renard, "Les figurines d'Asse-Elewijt et le culte d'Epona," in *Latomus,* X (1951), 182 n. 2.

[35] Cf. Schrijnen, *Nederlandsche Volkskunde*, I, 97–98. On the alleged relationship of this *kludde* with the Celtic goddess Epona, see Renard, "Les figurines," *Latomus,* pp. 181–187.

[36] *Loki* (1948), pp. 116–120; (1959), pp. 80–83 (see also de Vries, *The Problem of Loki*, pp. 74–78).

[37] Hollander, *The Poetic Edda,* p. 139 ("The Short Seeress' Prophecy," st. 14). Loki, called *Loptr* in this context, had eaten a woman's heart which he found half-roasted. Hollander's translation of ON *flagð* by 'ogre' is presumably too specific; as Turville-Petre points out (*Myth and Religion of the North,* p. 129), "the poet probably expresses an ancient tradition, when he says that every female monster (*flagð hvert*) on earth comes from Loki's brood."

the gods with an excuse for not meeting their obligations to him; hence, the *ad hoc* metamorphosis of Loki to distract the stallion from his duty. Furthermore, the superficiality of possible resemblances disregarded, there is a matter of principle involved. Lodder is a strictly localized demon of little importance. Nowhere in the region where Lodder appears do we find any trace of Loki. The latter does not appear anywhere in pagan tradition as an aquatic and equine demon; if the Lokke of Scandinavian folklore is actually a distant survival of Loki,[38] there is a gap between these traditions and those to which the Brabantine Lodder was supposed to go back. How can one, in this case, reasonably conclude in favor of the identity of Lodder, Lokke, and Loki?

What about Lóðurr? It is hard to see what would make his association with Lodder possible, except for a vague etymological possibility of considering the Dutch term as derived from a Germanic stem **lōðr-*.[39] It would then be necessary to show that this god, associated with Othin in the work of creation, could have degenerated into an aquatic spirit—or should it be assumed that the role assigned to Lóðurr results from a promotion of a secondary demonic being, similar to the modern Lodder or Lokke? All of this is, indeed, too hypothetical.[40]

As for Miss Gras's second point, if *logaþore* is assumed to be identifiable with Lóðurr—which would entail the identification of Hœnir with Donar, the triads Oðinn-Lóðurr-Hœnir and Wodan-Logaþore-Wigiþonar being interchangeable[41]—the same problems as with Lóðurr

[38] On the basis of the meaning 'spider' of the appellative *locke* and on the basis of the spider's role as a trickster in other cultures, Rooth has tried in her study on *Loki in Scandinavian Mythology* (1961) to correlate some constitutive elements of the Old Norse myths, like Loki's invention of the net, with modern folklore material, but her argumentation fails to convince. See, e.g., Willy Krogmann, "Neue Untersuchungen zur germanischen und keltischen Mythologie. I. Loki in der germanischen Mythologie," in *Zeitschrift für Religions- und Geistesgeschichte,* XV (1963), 361–363.

[39] E. J. Gras, *De Noordse Loki-Mythen,* p. 10, follows H. Grüner-Nielsen and A. Olrik in considering Brabantine *Loeke* (which appears sporadically instead of *Lodder*) as hypocoristic to *Lóðurr.* This implies a prototype with long **ō*. Consequently, in *Lodder,* the voiced dental must have been "geminated" before *r* with shortening of the preceding vowel. It is, however, more plausible to derive the Dutch dialectal word from Germanic **luðar-* (= OHG [Gl.] *lotara* vana, inania), with "expressive gemination" as in OE *loddere,* 'beggar' (cf. André Martinet, *La gémination consonantique d'origine expressive dans les langues germaniques* [Copenhagen: Levin and Munksgaard, 1937], p. 179).

[40] Cf. de Vries, *The Problem of Loki,* pp. 54–55.

[41] *Ibid.,* p. 55 n. 1. But one can hardly conceive of Donar bestowing man with "inspired mental activity" (*óðr*)!

arise: how to explain his importance with regard to the ghostlike nature of the Brabantine Lodder in view of his association with such gods as Donar and Wodan in Old High German in the seventh century?

But is it really justifiable to associate Logaþore with Lóðurr? While admitting that the term _logaþore_ is rather difficult to interpret, Wolfgang Krause, in the first edition of his _Runeninschriften im älteren Futhark,_[42] subscribed to the hypothesis of Friedrich von der Leyen and W. von Unwerth, who consider _logaþore_ an alternate form, under the conditions of Verner's Law, of Gmc. *_lohaþoraz,_ from which _Lóðurr_ would have developed. It would originally mean 'der mit Feuer Andringende,' the second element being related to the Old Norse verb _þora,_ 'have the courage to do something'. But the only argument which Krause presented in favor of this interpretation was the fact that one of the two gifts Lóðurr grants to man in the eighteenth stanza of _Vǫluspá_ is _lá,_ that is, 'vital warmth,' as the Old Norse term is usually translated.[43] Upon closer examination, the grounds on which the translation of ON _lá_ by 'vital warmth' was based, however, appear to be most questionable. First of all, this meaning is not confirmed by any parallel passage; it merely results from a rather disputable etymological comparison of a conjectural Germanic prototype *_wlahō_ with Lat. *_volca,_ contained in _Volcanus,_ and with Skt. _ulkā,_ 'heat of the fire.'[44]

[42] Halle/Saale: Max Niemeyer, 1937, p. 204–205 (Schriften der Königsberger Gelehrten Gesellschaft, XIII, 626–627).

[43] This interpretation is based on Hugo Gering, _Kommentar zu den Liedern der Edda,_ Vol. I: _Götterlieder_ (Halle/Saale: Buchhandlung des Waisenhauses, 1927), p. 21. Cf., e.g., Jan de Vries, _Edda_ (Amsterdam: Elsevier, 1944), p. 25 ('warmte'); C. A. Mastrelli, _L'Edda. Carmi Norreni_ (Firenze: Sansoni, 1951), p. 3 ('calore'); E. A. Philippson, _Die Genealogie der Götter in germanischer Religion, Mythologie und Theologie_ (Urbana: University of Illinois Press, 1953), p. 42 ('Lebenswärme'). F. Genzmer, _Die Edda,_ Vol. II: _Götterdichtung und Spruchdichtung_ (Iena: Eugen Diederichs, 1934), p. 76, translates it first by 'Lebenswärme' and, then, simply by 'Leben,' and Hollander, _The Poetic Edda,_ p. 3, merely uses the rather vague term 'being.'

[44] Adolf Noreen, _Tidskrift for philologi og pædagogik,_ N.R., IV, 31 ff. (quoted from H. Gering, _Kommentar zu den Liedern der Edda,_ cf. also Sigurður Nordal, _Völuspá. Vølvens spådom_ [Copenhagen: H. Aschehoug, 1927], p. 46). Karl Schneider, _Die germanischen Runennamen_ (Meisenheim am Glan: Anton Hain, 1956), pp. 318–321, goes a step further. He derives both ON _Lóðurr_ and Runic _logaþore_ from Germanic alternating forms *_wlōhaþuraz_ ~ *_wlōγaþuraz,_ reflecting IE *_wlōkāturos,_ assuming a lengthened grade *_wlōk-_ to *_wlok-_ in *_wlokā,_ 'brightness,' > Gmc. *_wlahō_ > ON _lá, lǫ́,_ 'blooming hue,' reconstructing an alliterative line: *_vlá gaf_ *_Vlóðurr ok_ *_vlito góða._ He does not pay enough attention to the implied chronological problem: the loss of initial _w-_ before _-l-_ is assumed to have taken place between

However, the name *Volcanus* is presumably a borrowing from the pre-Italic Mediterranean culture, like the fire-god who bears it,[45] whereas the Old-Indic term *ulkā* means in fact 'meteor, fiery appearance in the sky' and is related to Gk. ἀϝλαξ. λαμπρῶς (Hesychios), ἠλέκτωρ, 'bright sun.'[46] Accordingly, the interpretation of ON *lá* as 'vital warmth' re-

---

650–850, whereas *Vǫluspá* is usually considered to have been composed after 950. Furthermore, the assimilation of Lóðurr with the 'sky-god' Tyr on the basis of this etymology is unwarranted.

[45] In his *Griechische Götter im alten Rom* (Giessen: Alfred Töpelmann, 1930), pp. 172–208, Franz Altheim made a strong case for the Etruscan origin of *Volcanus*, pointing out Etruscan names to which it bears resemblance. His argumentation on such premises has, however, been strongly criticized (cf., e.g., J. L. M. de Lepper, *De Godsdienst der Romeinen* [Roermond and Maaseik: J. J. Romen and Zonen, 1950], pp. 27–28). Furthermore, Rætic *velχanu* (on the Caslir situla; *Prae-Italic Dialects of Italy,* Vol. 2, ed. J. Whatmough [Cambridge, Massachusetts: Harvard University Press], No. 215, pp. 26–29) and Cretan ϝελχανος have also been connected with Lat. *Volcanus*. Leaving aside the obscure Rætic form, the Cretan ϝελχανος, who appears on coins from Phaistos as a young man sitting in a tree with a rooster in his lap, can hardly be closely identified with the fire-god Volcanus, though the latter's association with Zeus may be a rather late phenomenon (Margherita Guarducci, "Velchanos-Volcanus," in *Scritti in onore di B. Nogara* [1937], p. 183 ff., quoted by Martin P. Nilsson, *Geschichte der griechischen Religion,* Vol. I [Münich: C. H. Beck, 1941], p. 300 n. 2; 2nd ed. [1955], p. 323 n. 2). It remains preferable to keep them apart, in spite of the efforts to correlate the widely divergent functions of ϝελχανος and Volcanus (Guarducci, "Velchanos-Volcanus"; Paul Kretschmer, in *Glotta,* XXVIII (1939), 109–110; Albert Grenier, *Les Religions étrusque et romaine* [Paris: Presses Universitaires de France, 1948], pp. 44–45). Nevertheless, Volcanus' name is "certainly not Latin" (H. J. Rose, "Volcanus," in *The Oxford Classical Dictionary* [Oxford: The Clarendon Press, 1949], p. 953), and ϝελχανος is "offenbar vorgriechisch" (Hjalmar Frisk, *Griechisches etymologisches Wörterbuch,* I, 503–504). Perhaps Kurt Latte (*Römische Religionsgeschichte* [Münich: C. H. Beck, 1960], p. 130 n. 3) is right when he suggests: "Es könnte sich nur um einen Gott der Mittelmeerkultur handeln, dem die italischen Einwanderer eine andere Bedeutung unterlegten"—presumably by divinizing the 'third aspect of fire,' the 'hungry' fire on the lurk for evil spirits, corresponding to the *dakṣināgni* of Old Indic liturgy (cf. Georges Dumézil, *La religion romaine archaïque* [Paris: Payot, 1966], p. 315). If, however, this should be the original function of Volcanus, as Dumézil claims ("Quaestiunculae Indo-Italicae. 2. Les *pisciculi* des Volcanalia," in *Revue des Etudes Latines* XXXVI (1958), 121–130), his suggestion that Lat. **Volco-* would be related to Skt. *várcas-*, Avest. *varəčah-*, 'brilliance' (*ibid.*, p. 123 n. 4) would deserve further consideration. Further relation with Hittite ᵈGUL-*aššeš* (read *Valḫannaššeš* by E. Forrer) is improbable (see Alois Walde and J. B. Hofmann, *Lateinisches etymologisches Wörterbuch,* [3rd ed.; Heidelberg: Carl Winter, 1954], II, 825–826; on the nature of the ᵈGUL-*aššeš* deities, whose Hittite name remains unknown, see Emmanuel Laroche, *Recherches sur les noms des dieux hittites* [Paris: C. P. Maisonneuve, 1947], p. 99).

[46] Although approved without reservation by Manfred Mayrhofer, (*A Concise Etymological Sanskrit Dictionary,* [Heidelberg: Carl Winter, 1954], I, 112) and by

mains unfounded, and this line of argument for relating Logaþore to Lóðurr has to be abandoned. One would then be tempted to subscribe to de Vries's stern judgment about Logaþore: "Die oft versuchte Gleichsetzung mit dem altnordischen Gott Lóðurr ist nur eine etymologische Spielerei und ist auch sachlich unbedingt abzulehnen."[47] But historians of Germanic religion find it difficult to give up the tempting identification Lóðurr = Logaþore = Loki, and if Karl Helm considers the identification Logaþore = Lóðurr only as "quite possible,"[48] interpreting Logaþore as a "Feuerdämon," his disciple Ernst A. Philippson endeavors to save the whole set of correlations of divinities through the expedient of an ingenious etymology. Pointing out that Loki is handsome and attractive in appearance, but evil in conscience,[49] Philippson asserts that Loki's beauty evokes the gift of a 'beautiful complexion' (*lito góða*), attributed to Lóðurr, while Lóðurr's name suggests the wiliness of Loki. According to him, *Lóðurr* and *logaþore* are, indeed, closely related with OE *logðor, logeðer,* which Joseph Bosworth and T. Northcole Toller[50] translate 'plotting mischief, wily, crafty'—epithets perfectly fitting the essential trait of Loki's personality.[51] Furthermore, his name could be merely a hypocoristic of the appellative contained in *logaþore.*

J. B. Hofmann (*Etymologisches Wörterbuch des Griechischen* [Münich: R. Oldenbourg, 1950], p. 106), this etymology is considered as unacceptable, without further comment, by Hjalmar Frisk (*Griechisches etymologisches Wörterbuch,* I, 629), who considers Gk. ἠλέκτωρ unexplained.

47 *Germanische Religionsgeschichte,* (Berlin and Leipzig: Walter de Gruyter, 1935), I, 234; see also Vol. II (2nd ed., 1957), pp. 271–272.

48 *Altgermanische Religionsgeschichte,* Vol. II: *Die nachrömische Zeit.* 2. *Die Westgermanen* (Heidelberg: Carl Winter, 1954), pp. 276–277.

49 *Gylfaginning,* Chap. 33: *Loki er fríðr ok fagr sýnum, illr í skaplyndi.*

50 *An Anglo-Saxon Dictionary* (London: Oxford University Press, 1898), p. 646. The Old English adjective is glossed *cacomicanus* (from Gk. κακομήχανος, 'mischief-plotting') or *marsius* (Middle Latin derivation from the name of the Marsi, who were celebrated as magicians and snake-charmers).

51 According to Ernst Alfred Philippson, *Die Genealogie der Götter in Germanischer Religion,* pp. 45–48, this etymology "betont das Dämonisch-Böse in Loki," but he does not succeed in establishing that this "Arglist" is indeed Loki's fundamental feature, as he fails to take fully into account the complexity of the dossier assembled by Dumézil. This was briefly attempted by Friedrich von der Leyen in his study "Zur grösseren Nordendorfer Spange" (*Beiträge zur Geschichte der deutschen Sprache und Literatur,* LXXX [Western ed.; 1958], 210–213). Pointing out that Loki appears as a god of all shapes ("Keiner beherrscht wie er die Künste der Verwandlung"), von der Leyen suggests that, in a later, Christian context, the evil side of his complex personality was strongly emphasized, whereas, in Logaþora and Lóðurr, his creative-

Without endeavoring to discuss in detail the cogency of this etymology, first proposed by Willy Krogmann[52] and now adopted by various runologists,[53] it must be recognized that the argument set forth in order to connect *Lóðurr* to these terms is hardly convincing. The mere possibility of an etymological explanation of the name *Lóðurr* by comparison with *logaþore* and an Old English term meaning 'cunning', and the rather vague statement that the attribution of a beautiful complexion to man by *Lóðurr* evokes the purely external beauty of Loki,[54] is not enough to legitimately justify the conclusion that *Lóðurr* is just another name for *Loki* in the divine triad involved in the creation of man in Scandinavian cosmogony.

But who, then, is Lóðurr? Attempts have also been made to identify him with Lotherus, the son of Dan, the eponymous hero of the Danes, and of a Teutonic noblewoman, Grytha. According to the account of Saxo Grammaticus,[55] Lotherus dethroned his brother Humblus and was then killed by the people. But this identification is erroneous because this tale is related to the epic tradition of the struggle between the Huns and the Goths, and Saxo's Lotherus is to be identified with Hlǫðr, appearing in the *Hervarar saga*. The Danish chronicler has obviously related this name to the Norse poetic epithet *hløðir,* 'destroyer, vanquisher,' when, in fact, it came by metathesis from *Hrøþil*, the Old Norse form of the Old English personal name *Hrēþel* of the king of the Geats in *Beowulf*.[56] Thus, no more than Humblus ulti-

ness prevailed ("das Schöpferische blieb das Überwiegende"). In those two cases, the ethical approach is different: for the pagan, there is no such strong moral censure for his "kluge Überlistungen" and "frechen und übermütigen Betrug." However, von der Leyen concedes that his suggestions are purely tentative and rejects Krogmann's etymology as "sprachgeschichtlich zu künstlich und inhaltlich ein Fehlgriff."

[52] "Loki," *Acta Philologica Scandinavica,* XII (1938), 67–69. The etymology was suggested independently by Siegfried Gutenbrunner to Helmut Arntz and Hans Zeiss in *Die einheimischen Runendenkmäler des Festlandes* (Leipzig: Otto Harrassowitz, 1939), p. 297.

[53] E.g., Lucien Musset, *Introduction à la Runologie* (Paris: Aubier, 1965), p. 371; Wolfgang Krause and Herbert Jankuhn, *Die Runeninschriften im älteren Futhark,* Vol. I: *Text* (Göttingen: Vandenhoeck and Ruprecht, 1966), p. 293. Cf., however, the negative comment of de Vries, *Altgermanische Religionsgeschichte* (1956), I, 310–311.

[54] Obviously, in this context, the *deceitful* outward appearance is meant to contrast with the evil disposition of Loki.

[55] *Gesta Danorum,* ed. J. Olrik and H. Ræder (Copenhagen: Levin and Munksgaard, 1931), I, 10–11; see de Vries, *Altgermanische Religionsgeschichte* (1957), II, 271.

[56] Cf. Kemp Malone, "Humblus and Lotherus," *Acta Philologica Scandinavica,* XIII (1939), 200–214, esp. 213–214.

mately goes back to the same origin as Gaulish (Mars) Camulus[57] is Lotherus identifiable with Lóðurr.

It would be rather futile to enumerate all the attempts to explain this term through etymology. Those who wanted at all costs to compare Lóðurr with Loki sought by ingenious parallels to attribute to his name an original meaning in keeping with the assumed essential traits of Loki's personality. Thus, Lóðurr is the 'seducer' (*der Verführer*) for Hugo Gering,[58] who compares MHG *luoder*, 'bait.' F. Holthausen[59] is thinking of Loki's perfidy when he relates *Lóðurr* to ON *lómr*, 'treachery,' mainly preserved in compounds. Such constructions, which usually neglect to analyze in detail the formation of the Scandinavian divine name, can hardly be taken very seriously—no more, actually, than the hypothesis of George van Langenhove[60] which derives *Lóðurr* from IE **lāturo-*, from the root **lā(t)-*, 'to be concealed,' attested by Gk. λήθω, Lat. *lateo*, and so on, with the primary meaning 'he who conceals, makes invisible,' or 'he who is concealed, the invisible one.' None of these interpretations, indeed, shows any direct relation with the text of the only Eddic stanza in which the name they pretend to explain occurs. In the absence of any other positive element related to Lóðurr, would it not seem obvious to look first for the basis of a plausible explanation in the context in which he appears? And rather than overemphasize his association with Othin and Hœnir in the creational work by taking *Lóðurr* for a hypothetical surname of Loki merely because Loki forms, in other circumstances, a triad with the two aforementioned gods, isn't it preferable to examine more closely the attributes with which he endows man?

Before Lóðurr's intervention, man was without that which the Norse text calls *lá, læti*, and *lito góða.* What is to be understood by these terms?

The last of these attributes—in the Old Norse nominative plural *litir góðir*, literally 'good colors'—is the indication of good health. The Old Norse term *litr*, 'complexion,' corresponds to OE *wlite*, which designates physical beauty, a sign of noble ancestry with the Anglo-

[57]Against this identification, see my remarks in "Notes critiques sur les concordances germano-celtiques," *Ogam*, VI (1954), 157–158.

[58] *Kommentar zu den Liedern der Edda*, I: *Götterlieder*, p. 23.

[59] *Vergleichendes und etymologisches Wörterbuch des Altwestnordischen* (Göttingen: Vandenhoeck and Ruprecht, 1948), p. 184–185; on the meaning of ON *lómr*, see Stefán Einarsson, *Acta Philologica Scandinavica*, IX (1934), 94–5.

[60] *Linguistische Studiën*, II, 67–70.

Saxons as with the Germanic peoples in general. It will be remembered that Beowulf differs from his companions by his handsome appearance, which the poet describes with the term *wlite* and *ǣnlic ansȳn*, 'peerless appearance.'[61] In this connection it is worth noticing that in the *Gylfaginning* Snorri uses precisely the Old Norse term *ásjóna* 'appearance,' corresponding with OE *ansȳn*, in order to designate the attribute indicated by the phrase *lito góða* in *Vǫluspá.*

The second trait characterizing Lóðurr's intervention in the creation of man is *læti*, but the text of the Eddic stanza hardly insists on it, since it is only cited among the things man is deprived of and is not repeated, like the other two, among the attributes the various gods confer upon him. Its interpretation does not present much of a problem: ON *læti* is a well-attested term, with the meanings 'noise, voice,' 'gestures, attitude.' It corresponds to MHG *gelǣze*, 'behavior, conduct,' and is closely related to ON *lát*, 'manners.'[62] This is probably also the meaning that should be ascribed to it in the Eddic stanza, as Gering does,[63] in view of the parallelism with the first line of stanza 39 of *Grípisspá —lit hefir þú Gunnars ok læti hans* ("thou hast the appearance and the manners of Gunnar")—where *læti* is contrasted with *mælska*, 'way of speaking,' in the following line. Nevertheless, it should also be pointed out that Snorri mentions speech (*malit*) specifically among the gifts of the third divinity creating man, but in association with sight (*sjón*) and hearing (*heyrn*). In addition to external appearance (*ásjóna*), Snorri actually attributes to the divinity the principal sensory perceptions, which is apparently not the case in the corresponding Eddic stanza.

But the third attribute is presumably the key to the whole problem.

[61] Cf. *Beowulf*, ll. 247–251, where the Danish coast guard immediately recognizes Beowulf as a nobleman because of his impressive stature and fine presence: "Never did I see a bigger man among the warriors on earth . . .; he is no mere retainer . . . unless his countenance [*wlite*], his peerless appearance [*ǣnlīc ansȳn*] deceives . . ." (see Willi Gramm, *Die Körperpflege der Angelsachsen* [Heidelberg: Carl Winter, 1938], p. 8).

[62] Swedish *later* (plural to the obsolete *laat* [Stiernhielm]) and Danish *lader* (plural to *lade*, O. Dan. *ladh(œ)*) are late loan words from Middle Low German (*lāt(e)*, 'Benehmen,' Gebärde,' *gelāt*, 'Aussehen, Gebärde, äusseres Benehmen'). See Elof Hellqvist, *Svensk etymologisk ordbok* (3rd ed.; Lund: C. W. K. Gleerup, 1948), I, 563; Niels Åge Nielsen, *Dansk etymologisk Ordbog* (Copenhagen: Gyldendal, 1966), p. 221.

[63] *Kommentar zu den Liedern der Edda*, I: *Götterlieder*, p. 22.

What does *lá* designate? It has been pointed out that the meaning 'vital warmth,' most often ascribed to it, is hardly plausible, What of other interpretations?

The translation 'blood' has also been proposed[64] by a rather audacious interpretation of the Old Norse substantive *lá*, 'sea, wave, shoal water along the shore.'[65] It has been attempted to make the implied shift more plausible by referring to the kenning for 'blood': *oddlǫ́*, appearing in the fifth line of the eighth stanza of the *Hákonarmál* of Eyvindr skáldaspillir.[66] However, the verb *ymia*, 'resound,' of which this term is the subject in this context, only applies to sounds, and the compound *oddlǫ́* is strictly parallel to the Old Norse kenning for 'combat': *oddregn*, literally 'rain of shafts.' This is why Jöran Sahlgren is justified in ruling out the translation of *oddlǫ́* as 'blood.' The simile indicates that the tips of the shafts (*oddar*) resound upon the shields, weapons, and breastplates as the waves (*láar*) driven by the storm boom upon the shore.[67]

Quite different, however, must be the meaning of *lá* in a stanza of the skald Kormákr Ǫgmundarson,[68] in which the term appears associated with the adjective *sǫlr*. This is the only attestation of *sǫlr* in Old Norse poetry, although the term survives in dialectal Norwegian in the

[64] Cf., e.g., Johan Palmér, "Till Vǫluspá," *Studier tillägnade Axel Kock* (Lund: C. W. K. Gleerup, 1929), p. 100; Egilsson, *Lexicon poeticum*, ed. Jónsson, p. 390; Heggstad, *Gamalnorsk Ordbok*, p. 397; Johan Fritzner, *Ordbog over Det gamle norske Sprog* (reprint of 1891 ed.; Oslo: Tryggve Juul Møller, 1954), II, 391.

[65] Cf., e.g., Richard Cleasby and Gudbrand Vigfusson, *An Icelandic English Dictionary*, ed. William A. Craigie (2nd ed.; Oxford: The Clarendon Press, 1957), p. 376. In this meaning, it corresponds to MLG *lā*, 'boggy water, spring,' and reflects a Gmc. prototype **lahō*, akin to Lat. *lacus*, 'lake'; it survives in Norw. *laa*, 'boggy water (esp. reddish with iron ore).' See, e.g., Jan de Vries, *Altnordisches etymologisches Wörterbuch* (Leiden: E. J. Brill, 1961), p. 343.

[66] *Umðu oddláar í Óðins veðri* (Kock, *Den norsk-isländska Skaldediktningen*, I, 36). "the . . . resounded in the fight (literally: 'Othin's weather')." On the translation of the kenning by 'blood,' see, e.g., Meissner, *Die Kenningar der Skalden*, p. 205; Egilsson, *Lexicon poeticum*, ed. Jónsson, p. 434; Heggstad, *Gamalnorsk Ordbok*, p. 501.

[67] *Eddica et Scaldica. Fornvästnordiska Studier*, Vol. I (Lund: C. W. K. Gleerup, 1927), pp. 69–71, 122.

[68] 'Visor,' st. 6 (Kock, *Den norsk-isländska Skaldediktningen*, p. 43):

Svǫrt augu berk sveiga
snyrti-Grund til fundar
-þykkik erma Ilmi
allfǫlr - ok lǫ́ sǫlva.

form *sal* in Røldal.[69] Old Norse *sǫlr* means 'pale' and is related to OE *salu*, 'dusky, dark' (surviving in Modern English *sallow*, applying to the complexion), to OHG *salo*, 'turbid, dull' (from which the French word *sale* 'dirty' is derived), and to MDu. *salu(w)*, 'yellowish, dirty.' Obviously, the association of such an adjective with a noun meaning 'blood' would be rather unexpected; therefore, the phrase *lǿ sǫlva* in line 4 of the stanza under reference is usually translated 'sallow-complexioned.'[70] Why, then, could not *lǿ* simply mean 'look, mien, face'?

In this case, a plausible etymology would be available for the Old Norse term. There is, indeed, in the Tocharian texts, a noun *lek*, meaning 'appearance, mien,'[71] for which, to the best of my knowledge, no satisfactory etymology has as yet been supplied.[72] This word can reflect an Indo-European prototype **lēk-*, whose reduced grade would yield Gmc. **lah-*; the *-ō* theme derived from this root[73] would, indeed, nor-

[69] Heggstad, *Gamalnorsk Ordbok,* p. 487; see also Egilsson, *Lexicon poeticum,* ed. Jónsson, p. 561.

[70] Cf. e.g., Egilsson, *Lexicon poeticum*, ed. Jónsson, p. 390, where it appears in association with the translation of *lá* in *Vǫluspá* by 'blood,' but as reflecting a particular semantic development: the phrase *sǫl lǫ* means 'pallor' ('blegt udseende, lød'), as is confirmed by its relation with *allfǫlr* in the context of the stanza ("With black eyes and a pallid countenance, I betake myself to a meeting with the elegant lady with the snoods—very pale do I seem to be to the lady" [literally: 'the *Ilmr* of the sleeves']).

[71] Wilhelm Schulze, Emil Sieg, and Wilhelm Siegling, *Tocharische Grammatik* (Göttingen: Vandenhoeck and Ruprecht, 1931), p. 49 (etwa 'Aussehen, Geste'); Pavel Poucha, *Institutiones Linguae Tocharicae*, Vol. I: *Thesaurus Linguae Tocharicae Dialecti A* (Prague: Státní Pedagogické Nakladatelství, 1955), p. 271 ('aspectus, gestus'). It appears frequently in a phrase with *pikār* in the meaning 'appearance and gestures,' e.g., *k̥leñci waṅke lek pikār* (55b4) 'weibliches Geschwätz, Miene und Gebärde.'

[72] A. J. van Windekens, *Lexique étymologique des dialectes tokhariens* (Louvain: Muséon, 1941), p. 56, derives it from IE **wlek-*, 'shine,' and compares Skt. *ulkā*, 'meteor'; since this is semantically rather unconvincing, Vittore Pisani (*Glottica Parerga. 5. Etimologie tocariche* [Milan: Ulrico Hoepli, 1942–1943], p. 26) prefers to compare OCS *lice.* πρόσωπον, Russ. *lic,* 'face' (about which, see Max Vasmer, *Russisches etymologisches Wörterbuch*, [Heidelberg: Carl Winter, 1953], II, 41), but he must admit that Toch. B *e*, instead of **ai*, hardly agrees with the Indo-European prototype **leyk-* implied by the Slavonic terms. In genuine Tocharian words, A B *e* is, indeed, deemed to reflect IE **ē* (cf. Walter Couvreur, *Hoofdzaken van de Tochaarse Klank- en Vormleer* [Louvain: Philologische Studiën, 1947], p. 10; Wolfgang Krause and Werner Thomas, *Tocharisches Elementarbuch* [Heidelberg: Carl Winter, 1960], p. 56).

[73] With initial stress like Gmc. **lahō*, 'water,' in ON *lá, lǿ* (see Charles Clyde Barber, *Die vorgeschichtliche Betonung der germanischen Substantiva und Adjektiva* [Heidelberg: Carl Winter, 1932], p. 44).

mally be reflected by *lá* in Old Norse. This interpretation, furthermore, fits perfectly into the context of the Eddic stanza: "Lóðurr has given man his mien and fair complexion." *Lá* and *lito góða* would then be associated into a kind of hendiadys to designate the physical aspect of the newly created human being, both indications of his external appearance being summarized by Snorri's *ásjóna*, which means altogether 'face,' 'mien,' 'countenance,' and 'look.'

But this interpretation remains dependent upon the correctness of an always disputable etymology.[74] One can, accordingly, wonder whether the poetic meaning of 'hair,' which *lá* also shows,[75] cannot, after all, supply an acceptable interpretation for the term in the text of *Vǫluspá.* Adolph Noreen[76] once suggested it, but Hugo Gering[77] utterly rejected such an interpretation. Nevertheless, it rests upon an etymologically flawless explanation: *lá, lǫ́* reflect a Germanic prototype **lawō*, meaning literally 'cutting,' derived from a root **lu-*, attested in another connection by OHG *lō*, 'tan,' ON *lǫgg*, 'croze,' and by Lith. *lóva*, 'bedstead,' Russ. *láva*, 'bench, board.' The transition from the idea of 'cutting' to that of 'hair' (i.e., 'that which one cuts') is also illustrated by OInd. *lava-*, 'cutting, wool, hair,' and Alb. *lēš*, 'wool, hair,' derived from the same Indo-European root. As for the importance of the hair in the creation of man, one could refer to the numerous passages in the sagas where it appears as the most significant element of human appearance. The hair was sacred for the ancient German; freely growing hair hanging on the shoulders was characteristic of priests, kings, and women; hair was the vehicle of the *hamingja*, of the soul, of happiness.[78] In support of this, it might be relevant to cite paragraph

[74] "Wörter mit *-e-* im Ost- und Westtoch. sind selten und sämtlich etymologisch dunkel, soweit es sich nicht um Lehnwörter handelt" (Wolfgang Krause, in a personal communication). Though Krause considers *lek* as "echt tocharisch" (*Tocharisches Elementarbuch*, p. 55), one may therefore wonder whether the term is not borrowed from a common source in the two dialects? Because of the *-e-* vocalism, the possibility of a Bactrian origin might be taken into consideration (see Werner Winter's paper "Bactrian Loanwords in Tocharian," read before the American Oriental Society meeting at New Haven, Connecticut, on March 22, 1967).

[75] *Skáldskaparmál* Chap. 69: *Hár heitir lá.*

[76] *Tidskrift for philologi og pædagogik*, N.R., IV, 31 ff.

[77] *Kommentar zu den Liedern der Edda*, I: *Götterlieder*, p. 21.

[78] F. de Tollenaere, *De schildering van den mensch in de Oudijslandsche familiesaga* (Louvain: De Vlaamsche Drukkerij, 1942), p. 67; with reference to Vilhelm Grønbech, *Vor Folkeœt*, III, 157 ff. (= *The Culture of the Teutons,* [London: Oxford University Press/Copenhagen: Jespersen and Pios, 1931], II, 123–125, with further bibliographical data, III, p. 100–101) and to Åke Ohlmarks, *Heimdalls Horn und*

35 of Salic law, in which the act of cutting the hair of a young girl without the permission of her parents is taxed forty-five shillings, whereas one pays only thirty for having seduced a female servant of the king.[79] Important also are Tacitus' notes[80] on Germanic manners of wearing the hair, in which he describes the Suevian chiefs and deals with the Chatti warriors' custom of cutting their beards and hair only after killing an enemy. The cutting of the hair is also a rite of passage, which marks the accession of the adolescent to manhood.[81] Furthermore, descriptions in the sagas closely associate complexion and hair to suggest the fine presence of their heroes, and a particular shade of hair color is never dissociated from a definite hue of the face.[82] Would it be surprising, then, that features so essential to the noble bearing of the Norsemen be put directly under the patronage of Lóðurr in the Eddic line "Lóðurr gave hair and fair complexion to man"?

Thus, a choice between two interpretations of *lá* is offered. Without trying to settle the question of which is the more plausible, it should be pointed out that both emphasize, like *litir góðir*, the physical aspect of man, whereas the qualities bestowed upon him by Hœnir and Othin are essentially spiritual. Accordingly, it is likely that the divinity responsible for these purely external features of man is a god governing the physical aspect of living beings, a god closer to nature than the

---

Odins Auge (Lund: C.W.K. Gleerup/Copenhagen: Levin and Munksgaard, 1937), p. 362 (in Saxo's narrative the priest of Svantovit has long hair and a long beard, in contrast with current fashion). See also Wolfgang Krause, *Die Frau in der Sprache der Altisländischen Familiengeschichten* (Göttingen: Vandenhoeck and Ruprecht, 1926), p. 82; Willi Gramm, *Die Körperpflege der Angelsachsen,* pp. 9, 13–16, 70–79 (to which should be added the remarks of Valtýr Guðmundsson on "Haarpflege" and "Haartracht" in Johannes Hoops, *Reallexikon der Germanischen Altertumskunde,* [Strasbourg: Karl J. Trübner, 1914], II, 345–347). On the concept of *hamingja,* see, e.g., de Vries, *Altgermanische Religionsgeschichte,* (1937), II, 348–351; (1956), I, pp. 222–224.

[79] Karl August Eckhardt (ed.), *Lex Salica: 100 Titel-Text* (Weimar: Hermann Böhlau, 1953), pp. 148–149 (XXXV.2, XXXVI.2).

[80] *Germanica*, Chap. 38 (*Suebi*); see Much, *Die Germania des Tacitus* pp. 332–337. Whether the description *muliebri ornatu* of the Naharvalian priests (Chap. 43) also implies long hair is more doubtful; if the Vandalic (H)astingi are to be closely associated with the Naharvali, as Karl Müllenhoff claims, their name (Gmc. **Hazdingōz,* derived from **hazdaz,* 'woman's hair' [ON *haddr,* OE *heord*], would point in that direction (see Much, *Die Germania des Tacitus,* p. 380; Georges Dumézil, *La Saga de Hadingus* [Paris: Presses Universitaires de France, 1953], pp. 126–127).

[81] Tacitus, *Germania,* Chap. 31; cf. V. Grønbech, *The Culture of the Teutons,* II, 123; Much, *Die Germania des Tacitus,* pp. 291–298.

[82] Cf. de Tollenaere, *De schildering van den mensch*, pp. 100–101.

Æsir—the majestic sovereigns—were. In a word, a god of the Vanic group of the ancient Germanic fertility cult.

These are the kind of considerations that led F. Detter and R. Heinzel[83] to identify Lóðurr with Freyr, without, however, being able to give any more support to such an identification than the derivation of the name *Lóðurr* from the stem contained in ON *lóð*, 'produce of the land.' Since such an etymology can hardly be considered as a sufficient argument to interpret *Lóðurr* as a mere surname of Freyr, the god *par excellence* of agricultural production, this hypothesis has been abandoned. In my opinion, the principle of interpretation which motivated it was, however, correct. This is why, in his *Altgermanische Religionsgeschichte*,[84] Jan de Vries gave preference to the explanation of Jöran Sahlgren,[85] which proceeds from the same principle. Having recognized the zero grade of the Indo-European root **leudh-* 'grow,' in the first component, *lud-* of a series of Swedish toponyms,[86] Sahlgren identifies the deity *Ludhgodha,* attested by place-names, as one of the Germanic hypostases of the Great Goddess of fertility. Because, in the parish-name *Locknevi* (1378: *Lodkonuvi*), this deity also appears under the name *Loþkona,* whose second component is ON *kona,* 'woman,' corresponding to Goth. *qino* and OE *cwene,* Sahlgren interprets Lóðurr as her male counterpart, deriving the name from an original **Loþverr,* whose second component would be ON *verr,* 'man, husband,' akin to Goth. *wair,* Lat. *vir,* and so on. The long *-ō-* of *Lóðurr,* required by Eddic metrics, would then be of secondary origin, since it would replace the short *-o-* of **Loþverr*—long by position in the line *lá gaf *loþverr* —when this term became *Lóðurr* by reduction of the unstressed syllable of the second component. The *Edda* manuscript merely shows *loðvR* without indication of quantity, but the length of *-ō-,* implied by the meter, is confirmed by the skaldic kenning *Lóðurs vinr,* 'Lóðurr's friend,' for Othin.[87] On the other hand, parallels like *Ǫnundr* from

[83] *Beiträge zur Geschichte der deutschen Sprache und Literatur* XVIII (1894), 560.

[84] (1937), II, 312; (1957), II, 272.

[85] "Förbjudna namn. V. Luggude, Ludgo och Luggavi," *Namn och Bygd,* VI (1918), 28–40.

[86] E.g., *Luggude* (Skåne, thirteenth century: *Lyuthgudhœret*; on the secondary insertion of *-j-*, see Sahlgren, "Förbjudna namn," *Namn och Bygd,* pp. 36–37. *Ludgo* (1293: *Liuthguthuwi*); *Luggavi* (1310: *Ludhgudwi*; the second component is OSwed. *gudha,* 'goddess,' [see Sahlgren, "Förbjudna namn," p. 32]).

[87] Hugo Gering (*Kommentar zu den Liedern der Edda,* I: *Götterlieder,* p. 23) considers that the "völlig gesicherte länge des wurzelvokals (*Lóþors* steht in der

Ǫnvǫndr, adduced by Sahlgren, show that the loss of the vowel of the second component does not necessarily entail compensatory lengthening of the vowel of the first component. Unless lengthening for metrical purposes may be admitted, there remains, accordingly, an unsolved phonological difficulty connected with Sahlgren's interpretation.[88]

Should it, therefore, be abandoned? I think not, for various reasons. First of all, the interpretation of Lóðurr as a male counterpart of the goddess of agrarian fertility fits in neatly with the purely physiological qualities he grants man—the more so since the root to which **Loþverr* is linked is that of Goth. *liudan*, 'grow,' whose Old Norse correspondent occurs only in the past participle *loðinn*, meaning 'hairy, shaggy, woolly, covered with thick grass'[89]; in Old Swedish *ludhin* means 'hairy, shaggy' (as *luden* still does in Modern Swedish), and in the Swedish dialects, a word *lå* occurs, meaning 'hair of animal, spring

---

Ísl[endinga] dr[ápa] in aðalhending mit *glóþa*)" excludes Sahlgren's hypothesis; to this, de Vries (*The Problem of Loki*, p. 53) comments: "The objection of Gering . . . is of no value, for Haukr Valdísarson, who lived in the 12th century has borrowed the kenning *Lóþurs vinr* for Othin from Eyvindr's Háleygjatal, where the vowel may be short as well as long. In fact, the Vǫluspá proves the length of the vowel, as in the line of st. 18 *lǫ gaf Lóðurr* no other quantity is possible." Willy Krogmann ("Loki," *Acta Philologica Scandinavica*, p. 61) however, objects: "Wir haben gar keinen Grund anzunehmen, dass *Lóðurr* sein *ō* erst dem Verfasser der Íslendinga drápa verdanke, ganz abgesehen davon, dass schon wegen des Unterschiedes zwischen *líð Lóðurs vinar* und *gnýr vinar Lóðurs* nicht an eine unmittelbare Uebernahme aus Eyvindrs Háleygjatal zu denken ist." Actually, de Vries does not assume that the length of *ō* only developed in the twelfth century, since he states: "Sahlgren has aptly suggested that the long *ó* may be the consequence of the fact that in course of time the name Lǫðverr (where the first syllable is by position long) was changed into Lǫðurr and then the syllable *Lǫð-*, used in the same line, had to lengthen its vowel." However, as Krogmann pointed out ("Loki," p. 61), Sahlgren merely said: "Det metriska skemat fordrar hos *loðv*R lång första stavelse. Man har därfor i normaliserade texter insatt *Lóðurr*. Detta är enligt min mening fullständigt oriktigt. Sättes i stället in *Loþverr* blir stavelsen fortfarande lång och ett begripligt fonem erhålles."

[88] The basic difference between personal names like *Ǫnundr* and *Lóðurr* is that the former reflect the loss of *-v-* with a change of *ǫ* to *u* (see Adolf Noreen, *Altnordische Grammatik. I. Altisländische Grammatik* [4th ed.; Halle/Saale: Max Niemeyer, 1923], pp. 127–128, sec. 148), whereas a syncope of *-e-* in the second syllable seems to be involved in **Loþverr*. At any rate, at the time of the reduction of **Loþverr* to **Loðurr* (which must be posterior to the composition of *Vǫluspá*, i.e., after 950), the use of the term was confined to verse reflecting mythological tradition, in which the metrical length of *o* in **Loþverr* had to be preserved.

[89] See, e.g., Alexander Jóhannesson, *Isländisches etymologisches Wörterbuch* (Bern: A. Francke, 1954), p. 746; Jan de Vries, *Altnordisches etymologisches Wörterbuch*, p. 363.

fleece.'[90] The meaning of these terms obviously brings to mind the interpretation of ON *lá* as 'hair,' whereas the meanings of related Germanic terms—Goth. *ludja.* *πρόσωπον* (Matt. 6:17), *laudi* (marginal gloss for *μορφή*); OS *lud*, 'figure' (*Heliand*, vs. 154);[91] OHG *antlutti,* 'face'[92]—correspond to those of *ásjóna,* which replaces *lá* and *litir góðir* in Snorri. Furthermore, it should be remembered that the root whose zero grade occurs in **Loþverr* is the same as appears in the Germanic term for 'people' (ON *ljóðr*, OE *lēode*, OHG *liuti*) in the meaning of 'full-fledged members of the ethnic community,' which points to its close semantic link with Lat. *līber* and Gk. *ἐλεύθερος*. Also derived from the same root is the name of the Italic god *Liber,* the deity of Eddic *loðvR,* applying to a divinity of generation and growth, as, cluded the protection of the popular community.[93] Sahlgren's hypothesis accordingly shows far-reaching implications, not even surmised by its author, and the minor objection concerning the vocalism of *Lóðurr* can easily be dismissed if one takes into consideration the semantic field to which he belongs. Indeed, two West Norse terms, at least, could promote the lengthening, required by the meter, of the short *-o-* of Eddic *loðvR,* applying to a divinity of generation and growth, as, for example, ON *lóð*, 'produce of the land' (which belongs etymologically with Gk. *λάτρον*, 'pay, hire,'[94] and Icelandic *lóða,* 'in heat' (applying to a bitch), which Evald Lidén has compared with MIr. *lāth,* 'rut' (of a sow).[95] If these arguments are cogent, *Lóðurr*, bestower of

[90] J. Sahlgren, "Förbjudna namn," *Namn och Bygd,* pp. 34–35.

[91] *is unca lud giliðen, lîk gidrusnod* (Otto Behaghel, *Heliand und Genesis* [4th ed.; Halle/Saale: Max Niemeyer, 1933], p. 9. OS *lud* is translated by German 'Gestalt' by Edward H. Sehrt (*Vollständiges Wörterbuch zum Heliand und zur altsächsischen Genesis* [Göttingen: Vandenhoeck and Ruprecht, 1925], p. 352) and by Ferdinand Holthausen (*Altsächsisches Wörterbuch* [Münster and Köln: Böhlau, 1954], p. 48). Heinrich Wagner, however, translates 'Lebenskraft' and compares MIr. *lúth,* 'Kraft' (*Zeitschrift für celtische Philologie,* XXIV [1953], 92).

[92] Sigmund Feist, *Vergleichendes Wörterbuch der gotischen Sprache* (Leiden: E. J. Brill, 1939), p. 323, 337; Jóhannesson, *Isländisches etymologisches Wörterbuch,* p. 146.

[93] Cf. my comments on Adrien Bruhl's *Liber Pater* (Paris: E. de Boccard, 1953), in *Latomus,* XIII (1954), 295–296.

[94] Jóhannesson, *Isländisches etymologisches Wörterbuch,* p. 732; de Vries, *Altnordisches etymologisches Wörterbuch* (1959), p. 343; see also Frisk, *Griechisches etymologisches Wörterbuch,* pp. 89–90.

[95] "Wortgeschichtliches. 3," in *Mélanges linguistiques offerts à M. Holger Pedersen* (Aarhus: Universitetsforlaget, 1937), pp. 41–42. Ferdinand Holthausen (*Verglei-*

beautiful complexion and hair, appears in the Germanic North as the counterpart of the Italic Liber, just as the Scandinavian Viðarr corresponds to the Illyrian Vidasus[96]—a new element in the rich set of common features between Germanic and Italic culture and religion.[97]

---

chendes und etymologisches Wörterbuch des Altwestnordischen-Altnorwegisch-isländischen [Göttingen: Vandenhoeck and Ruprecht, 1948], p. 365) considers *Lóðurr* as possibly derived from this etymon.

96 "Die illyrischen Götter *Vidasus* und *Thana*," in *Glotta*, XXXI (1951), 238–243. For a different interpretation of *Viðarr*, see Dumézil, "Le dieu scandinave Viðarr," *Revue d'Histoire des Religions*, CLXVIII (1965), 1–13, and *La religion romaine archaïque*, p. 331.

97 A brief oral presentation of some of the ideas discussed in this paper was given at the March 1955 meeting of the *Société pour le Progrès des Etudes philologiques et historiques* (Brussels, Belgium); see *Revue Belge de Philologie et d'Histoire*, XXXIII (1955), 493–494. Further research for this paper was made possible through a University of Texas Research Council grant (no. R O 45). Not all the problems connected with the Eddic myth of the creation of man have been tackled here; further research would have to focus, for example, on the etymology of the name *Embla* (see Sigurður Nordal, *Völuspá*, p. 44–45; de Vries, *Altgermanische Religionsgeschichte* (1957) II, pp. 371–372.

APPENDIX A

Lee M. Hollander: A Biographical Sketch

Born on November 8, 1880, in Baltimore, Maryland, the son of Samuel Hollander and Amelia Herstein, both of Baltimore, Lee Milton Hollander belonged to a family that had preserved strong links with its former homeland, Germany, from where his grandfather had emigrated to the States in 1848. Young Hollander spent the happy years of his prime in Baltimore, until the death of his father, who was running a furniture factory as a family business. Sorrowfully deprived of her husband, his mother decided to take her two sons, Lee and his older brother, back to Germany to live with relatives in Frankfurt-am-Main. There he went to primary and secondary school from 1886 to 1897, when he left the Obersekunda of the Realgymnasium at the age of seventeen to return to the States. Back in Baltimore, he attended the College at Johns Hopkins University, where he obtained his B.A. in 1901, with a major in Germanic Philology and a minor in English and Comparative Philology. He then went on to the Ph.D., working under Henry Wood on a dissertation on prefixal *s*- in Germanic, which was published at Hermann Collitz' personal encouragement. After graduation, he financed a trip to Norway and also visited Sweden and Denmark, learning the Scandinavian languages and reading their literature during these *Wanderjahre*. He developed a great admiration for Peter Dass, the author of *Nordlands Trompet*, and he still feels extremely proud that his article in the *Aftenposten* in 1906 was instrumental in the decision to restore the poet's home, beyond the Arctic Circle. While in Scandinavia, he also visited many classes in the universities, listening to Carl Marstrander, Magnus Olsen, Otto Jespersen, Moltke Moe, and attending Sophus Bugge's seminar on the *Edda* in Oslo. But he mainly availed himself of the opportunity to read and study at the King's Library in Stockholm, as well as in the rich libraries of the University of Oslo and of Copenhagen, where he devoted special time and attention to the Arnamagnæan Collection.

After two years abroad, he returned to the States in 1907 and became an instructor in German at the University of Michigan in Ann Arbor. While teaching the beginners' course in German, as well as some Norwegian, he published the first of an impressive series of translations in *Poet Lore.* After three years, he transferred to The University of Wisconsin, where he also taught German and Norwegian at the beginner's level and where he began more substantial research which led to various articles, mainly on Scandinavian literature, in *Modern Language Notes, Scandinavian Studies, Arkiv för Nordisk Filologi*, and other publications.

The First World War, with the violent and irrational anti-German reaction it entailed, deprived him of his job, like all the other instructors in German, and for quite a while he devoted the best of his time to compiling large files of clippings about the war from the chief newspapers in England, Germany, and the United States. He thoroughly hated the job, but was, nevertheless, very grateful to Librarian Smith of The University of Wisconsin, for having created it for him so that he would not simply be dismissed like most of his colleagues, who were often considered to have a double allegiance because of their bilingualism.

In 1920, events finally took a turn for the better, and he came to The University of Texas as an assistant professor. By that time, the study of foreign languages began to boom again, and the chairman of the Department, Dr. Boysen, who had had to switch to teaching French while German was in bad odor, now had more students than he could handle. Therefore, the addition of Lee Hollander to the staff was heartily welcomed, and this was the beginning of an uninterrupted career of forty-seven years at The University of Texas for the brilliant young scholar.

Those were fruitful and happy years. The University gradually grew, and, being a very successful instructor, Lee Hollander was soon promoted to associate professor and professor, before taking over the chairmanship of the Department of Germanic Languages in 1929.

Under his leadership, the Department became nationally known as one of the most active centers of Germanic studies, and several prominent scholars joined the staff. But apart from unselfish devotion to the task of building up the quality and reputation of his Department, Lee Hollander continued to work strenuously in his chosen field of research: excellent scholarly studies and translations followed each other in quick succession. Numerous articles show how much time and effort went into the preparation of the major works—*The Poetic Edda* (1928), *Old Norse Poems* (1936), *The Skalds* (1945)—in which he tried to re-create the tone of the original in his very personal style and diction.

Reaching the age limit in 1946, he had to relinquish the chairmanship of the Department, but while less strong and devoted souls would have indulged in the fallacious peace of a serene retirement, Lee Hollander became more active than ever, continuing enthusiastically both his teaching and his research until the present day. He went on guiding students on the thorny paths of Germanic studies, publishing more valuable articles on problems of Old Norse and excellent translations of sagas. Meanwhile, having become the Nestor of Scandinavian Studies, he was made Knight of the Order of the Icelandic Falcon, Member of the Norsk Videnskaps Akademi, President of the Society for the Advancement of Scandinavian Studies, and Honorary Life Member of the Viking Society for Northern Research. But perhaps no man in the world is less concerned about such honors than Lee Hollander: he simply remains faithful to his *grande passion*—Old Norse literature and mythology—and his unwavering devotion to it leaves no room for smaller ambitions. Perhaps the sponsoring function he enjoys most is directing the Department of Germanic Languages Journal Club. The best scholars in the country and from abroad come to speak informally about their work and research, and Lee Hollander masterfully leads the open discussion.

APPENDIX B

LEE M. HOLLANDER: A CHRONOLOGICAL BIBLIOGRAPHY

1905

Thesis:
Prefixal S in Germanic. Baltimore: The Johns Hopkins University.

1906

Articles:
"Danske Indtryk," *Tidens Tegn* (Copenhagen), November.
"Kleine Beiträge," *Zeitschrift für Deutsche Wortforschung,* VII (1906), 296–307.
"Peder Dass Hjem," *Aftenposten* (Kristiania), August 20.

Review:
Laurvik, J. N., and M. Morison, *Ibsen's Letters* (New York: Duffield and Co., 1905). *The Nation,* LXXXII (1906), 243–244.

1907

Article:
"Nogle Ture paa Moskenesö." *Den Norske Turistforenings Aarbog,* 1907, 105–111.

1908

Translations:
Nielsen, H., "Robert Herrick": in *Poet Lore,* XIX (1908), 337–363.
Drachmann, H., "Renaissance": in *Poet Lore,* XIX (1908), 369–419.

1909

Review:
Olsen, J., *Ibsen's Brand* (Chicago: John Anderson Co., 1908): in *Modern Language Notes,* XXII (1909), 140–142.

1910

Book:

(with Arne Kildal). *Ibsen's Speeches and New Letters.* Boston: Badger, 1910, pp. 222.

Reviews:

Flom, G. T., "*The Lay of Thrym* (*Journal of American Folklore,* XX [1907]): in *Journal of English and Germanic Philology,* IX (1910), 120–121.

Grønbech, V., *Lykkemand og Niding: Vor Folkeæt i Oldtiden, Förste Bog* (Copenhagen: V. Pio, 1909): in *Journal of English and Germanic Philology,* IX (1910), 269–278.

Hermann, P., *Island in Vergangenheit und Gegenwart* (Leipzig: Engelmann, 1907): in *Modern Language Notes,* XXV (1910), 27–28.

1911

Translation:

Bjørnson, B., "When the New Wine Blooms." *Poet Lore,* XXII (1911), 1–69.

Articles:

"Bjørnstjerne Bjørnson's Last Drama, 'When the New Wine Blooms'," *Poet Lore,* XXII (1911), 70–78.

"The Drama in Iceland," *Scandinavian Studies and Notes,* I, 99–106.

"A Revival of Learning of Iceland," *The Dial,* LI (1911), 246–247.

"Zu einigen Stellen in Goethe's Egmont," *Modern Language Notes,* XXVI (1911), 174–176.

Reviews:

Andrews, L. (ed.), *Hálfs Saga ok Hálfsrekka* (Altnordische Saga-Bibliothek, Vol. XIV [Halle: M. Niemeyer]): in *Modern Language Notes,* XXVI (1911), 58–60.

Fraser, H., and H. van der Smissen, *A German Grammar for Schools and Colleges* (Boston: D. C. Heath and Co.): in *Monatshefte für Deutsche Sprache und Pädagogik,* XII (1911), 286.

Maal og Minne (Norske Studier) (Kristiania: H. Aschehoug and Co., 1909): in *Modern Language Notes,* XXVI (1911), 29–30.

1912

Translation:

Einarsson, Indrithi, "Sword and Crozier." *Poet Lore,* XXIII (1912), 225–283.

Articles:

"The Faithless Wife Motif in Old Norse Literature," *Modern Language Notes,* XXVII (1912), 71–73.

"The Gautland Cycle of Sagas," *Journal of English and Germanic Philology,* XI (1912), 61–81; 207–217.

"Hagbards Billede (*Kormákssaga,* Chap. 3)," *Danske Studier,* 1912, 189–192.

"Indrithi Einarsson: Icelandic Dramatist and His Saga Drama," *Poet Lore,* XXIII (1912), 284–289.

1913

Article:

"The Relative Age of the Gautrekssaga and the Hrólfssaga," *Arkiv för nordisk filologi,* XXV (1913), 120–134.

Reviews:

Björkman, E. (trans.), *Plays by Bjørnstjerne Bjørnson* (New York: Charles Scribner and Sons, 1913): in *American-Scandinavian Review,* I, No. 5 (September, 1913), 26.

Garret, F. E., *Lyrics and Poems from Ibsen* (London: J. M. Dent and Sons, 1913): in *American-Scandinavian Review,* I, No. 4 (July, 1913), 26.

Hartmann, J. W., *The Gǫngu-Hrólfs Saga* (dissertation, Columbia University, 1912): in *Modern Language Notes,* XXVIII (1913), 254.

Heller, C., *Henrik Ibsen* (Boston and New York: Houghton Mifflin and Co., 1912): in *Monatshefte für Deutsche Sprache und Pädagogik,* XIV (1913), 184–185.

Hermannsson, H., *Icelandic Authors of Today* (Ithaca, New York: Cornell University Press): in *American-Scandinavian Review,* I, No. 6 (November, 1913), 26.

Zoëga, G. T., *A Concise Dictionary of Old Icelandic* (Oxford: Clarendon Press): in *Modern Language Notes,* XXVIII (1913), 153–154.

1914

Article:

"Bjørnson's 'Beyond Human Power'," *The Drama,* IV (1914), 110–117.

" 'Hagbards Hoved' endnu en gang (D. St. 12, 189)," *Danske Studier,* 1914, pp. 195–196.

Reviews:

Björkman, E. (trans.), *Karen Borneman. Lynggaard and Co. Two Plays by Hjalmar Bergström* (*Modern Drama Series,* Vol. 1 [New York: Mitchell Kennerley]): in *American-Scandinavian Review,* II, No. 4 (July, 1914), 41.

Gosse, E., *Two Visits to Denmark* (London: Smith Elder and Co.): in *American-Scandinavian Review,* II, No. 2 (March, 1914), 51.

Roberts, R. E. (trans.), *Peer Gynt: A Dramatic Poem by Henrik Ibsen* (*The Modern Drama Series,* Vol. 3 [New York: Mitchell Kennerley, 1913]): in *American-Scandinavian Review,* II, No. 4 (July, 1914), 41.

von Unwerth, W., *Untersuchungen über Totenkult und Oðinverehrung bei Nordgermanen und Lappen* (Germanistische Abhandlungen, Vol. 37 [Breslau: M. and H. Marcus]: in *Scandinavian Studies and Notes,* II (1914), 53–56.

1915

Translations:

Bjørnson, B., *Beyond Human Power*: in T. H. Dickinson (ed.), *Chief Contemporary Dramatists.* Vol. I, pp. 573–597. Boston and New York: Houghton Mifflin and Co., 1915.

Stephansson, S. G., "However Far Thou Mayest Travel": in *American-Scandinavian Review,* III (1915), 69.

Stifter, Adalbert, *Bergkristall,* in *The German Classics,* Vol. VIII, pp. 356–403. New York: Putnam, 1914.

Reviews:

Craigie, W. A., *The Icelandic Sagas,* and A. Mawer, *The Vikings* (The Cambridge Manuals of Science and Literature [Cambridge: University Press; New York: Putnam, 1913): in *American-Scandinavian Review,* III (1915), 249–250.

Grønbech, V., *Vor Folkeæt i Oldtiden* ("Our Race in Antiquity") (Copenhagen: V. Pio, 1909–1912): in *Journal of English and Germanic Philology,* XIV (1915), 124–125.

Hermannsson, H., *Catalogue of the Fiske Icelandic Collection* (Ithaca, New York: Cornell University Press, 1913): in *Modern Language Notes,* XXX (1915), 23–24.

1916

Articles:

"In Old Telemarken," *American-Scandinavian Review,* IV (1916), 98–103.

"Notes on the Nornagests þattr," *Scandinavian Studies and Notes,* III (1916), 105–111.

Reviews:

Krijn, S. A., *De Jómsvíkingasaga* (dissertation, Amsterdam University [Leiden: E. IJdo, 1914]): in *Modern Language Notes,* XXXI (1916), 52–53.

Six Scandinavian textbooks, in *The Nation,* CII (1916), 494.

1917

Articles:

"*Beowulf* 33," *Modern Language Notes*, XXXII (1917), 246–247.

"Friedrich Förster, German Pacifist," *The Nation*, CVI (1917), 155–157.

"Roskilde," *American-Scandinavian Review*, V (1917), 93–99.

"Realpolitik at Stake," *The Nation*, CVI (1917), 155–157.

"Studies in the Jómsvíkingasaga," *Arkiv för nordisk filologi*, XXIX (1917), 193–222.

Reviews:

Flom, G. T., *The Phonology of the Dialect of Aurland, Norway* (Urbana: University of Illinois Press, 1915): in *Journal of English and Germanic Philology*, XVI (1917), 614–617.

Hewlett, M., *Thorgils of Treadholt* (New York: Dodd, Mead and Co., 1917): in *American-Scandinavian Review*, V (1917), 375.

Olsen, O. L., *The Relation of the Hrólfssaga Kraka and Bjarkarímur to Beowulf* (dissertation, University of Chicago, 1916; *Publications of the Society for the Advancement of Scandinavian Studies*, Vol. 3, No. 1 [Urbana, Illinois]): in *Journal of English and Germanic Philology*, XVI (1917), 147–148.

1918

Reviews:

Larsen, L. M., "The King's Mirror (Speculum Regale-Konungs Skuggsjá)" (New York: Oxford University Press, 1917): in *Modern Language Notes*, XXXIII (1918), 421–424.

Larsen, L. M., and G. T. Flom, *The Main Manuscript of Konungs Skuggsjá* (Urbana: University of Illinois Press, 1915): *The Nation*, CVII (1918), 20.

1919

Translation:

(with Axel Olrik). Axel Olrik. *The Heroic Legends of Denmark*. New York: American-Scandinavian Foundation; Oxford: University Press, 1919. Pp. xvii + 530.

Articles:

"Gjenmæle," *Arkiv för nordisk filologi*, XXXI (1919), 207–208.

"Language Bills in State Legislatures," *American-Scandinavian Review*, VII (1919), 273–277.

1920

Translation:

"Hávamál Stanzas," *American-Scandinavian Review*, VIII (1920), 45.

Article:

"Concerning a Proposed Translation of the Edda," *Scandinavian Studies and Notes,* V (1920), 197–201.

Review:

Franc, M., *Ibsen in England* (Boston: The Four Seas Co., 1919): in *Journal of English and Germanic Philology,* XIX (1920), 300–302.

1921

Review:

Phillpotts, E., *The Elder Edda and Ancient Scandinavian Drama* (Cambridge: University Press, 1920): in *Scandinavian Studies and Notes,* VII (1921), 108.

1922

Articles:

"Eddic Notes," *Scandinavian Studies and Notes,* VII (1922), 113–121.

"Hávamál Strofe 81," *Maal og Minne,* XX (1922), 113–121.

1923

Book:

Selections from the Writings of Søren Kierkegaard. Austin: University of Texas Bulletin No. 2326, pp. 239.

Reviews:

Flom, G. T., *The Language of the Konungs Skuggsjá, I.* (Urbana: University of Illinois Studies in Language and Literature, Vol. VII, No. 3): in *Scandinavian Studies and Notes,* VII (1923), 175–177.

Flom, G. T., *The Arnamagnæan MS 243B Folio* (Urbana: University of Illinois Press, 1916): in *Journal of English and Germanic Philology,* XXII (1923), 145–147.

1924

Articles:

"Gustaf Frenssen and Germany," *The American Review,* II (1924), 543–545.

"Recent Studies in the Helgi Poems," *Scandinavian Studies and Notes,* VIII (1924), 108–125.

Reviews:

Bellows, H. A., *The Poetic Edda* (New York: American-Scandinavian Foundation, 1923): in *Journal of English and Germanic Philology,* XXIII (1924), 450–456.

de Boor, H., *Schwedische Literatur* (Breslau: Hirt, 1924): in *Monatshefte für deutsche Sprache und Pädogogik,* XVI (1924), 110.

1925

Reviews:

Olsen, M., *Norrøne Gude- og Heltesagn* (Kristiania: P. F. Steensballes Boghandel, 1922): in *Scandinavian Studies and Notes,* VIII (1925), 34–36.

Veblen, T., *Laxdæla Saga* (New York: B. W. Huebsch, 1925): in *Scandinavian Studies and Notes,* VIII (1925), 258–259.

Vogt, W. H., *Vatnsdœla Saga* (Altnordische Saga-Bibliothek, Vol. XVI [Halle: M. Niemeyer, 1921]): in *Modern Language Notes,* XL (1925), 243–245.

1926

Article:

"The Didactic Purpose of Some Eddic Lays," *The Germanic Review,* I (1926), 72–85.

Reviews:

Festschrift für Eugen Mogk (Halle: M. Niemeyer, 1924): in *The Germanic Review,* I (1926), 273–276.

Flom, G. T., *The Language of the Konungs Skuggsjá II, Pronouns, Numerals and Particles, the Verbs and Their Conjugations* (Urbana: University of Illinois Studies in Language and Literature, Vol. VIII, No. 4): in *Journal of English and Germanic Philology,* XXV (1926), 125–130.

1927

Book:

(ed.). E. von Wildenbruch. *Das edle Blut* (with Introduction, Notes, and Vocabulary). New York: A. Knopf, 1927, pp. xi + 98.

Article:

"Were the Mythological Poems of the Edda Composed in the Pre-Christian Era?" *Journal of English and Germanic Philology,* XXVI (1927), 96–105.

Reviews:

Gosse, E., and W. Craigie, *The Oxford Book of Scandinavian Verse* (Oxford: University Press, 1925): in *The Germanic Review,* II (1927), 176–178.

Hardy, G., *Norway* (New York: Charles Scribner and Sons, 1925): in *Scandinavian Studies and Notes,* IX (1927), 232–234.

Robertson, J. G., *Goethe* (New York: E. P. Dutton and Co.): in *The Nation,* CXXVI (1927), 491.

Zoëga, G., *Íslenzk-Ensk Orðabók* (Reykjavík: S. Kristjánsson, 1922): in *Journal of English and Germanic Philology*, XXVI (1927), 438–440.

1928

Translation:

The Poetic Edda. Austin: University of Texas Press, 1928. Pp. xxi + 396.

Articles:

"Notes on the Sverris Saga," *The Germanic Review*, III (1928), 262–276.
"Queen Thýra Danmarkarbót," *Scandinavian Studies and Notes*, X (1928–1929), 111–114.

Reviews:

Berendsohn, W. A., *Selma Lagerlöf* (München: Albert Langen, 1927): in *Monatshefte für deutschen Unterricht*, XX (1928), 195.
Clark, D. E. Martin (ed. and trans.), *The Hávamál, With Selections from Other Poems of the Edda* (Cambridge: University Press, 1923): in *The Germanic Review*, III (1928), 284–285.
Festskrift til Hjalmar Falk (Oslo: H. Aschehoug and Co., 1927): in *Scandinavian Studies and Notes*, X (1928–1929), 206–208.
Hermannsson, H., *Jón Guðmundsson and His Natural History of Iceland*; E. Ólafsson, *Two Cartographers* (*Islandica*, Vols. XV, XVI, and XVII [Ithaca, New York: Cornell University Press, 1924, 1925, and 1926]): in *Journal of English and Germanic Philology*, XXVII (1928), 111–114.
Hermannsson, H., *Supplementary Catalogue of the Fiske Icelandic Collection* (Ithaca, New York: Cornell University Press, 1927): in *Modern Language Notes*, XLIII (1928), 350–352.
Jensen, H., *Neudänische Syntax* (Heidelberg: Carl Winter, 1923): in *Journal of English and Germanic Philology*, XXVII (1928), 128–130.
Krause, W., *Die Frau in der Sprache der altisländischen Familiengeschichten* (Göttingen: Vandenhoeck and Ruprecht, 1926): in *Journal of English and Germanic Philology*, XXVII (1928), 252–255.
O'Shea, —, *The Reading of Modern Languages* (U.S. Bureau of Education Bulletin No. 16, 1927): in *Scandinavian Studies and Notes*, X (1928–1929), 64–65.
Vowles, G. R., *Bjørnson's "En Glad Gut"* (Minneapolis: The Lutheran Free Church Publishing Co., 1927): in *Scandinavian Studies and Notes*, X (1928–1929), 62–64.

1929

Reviews:

Eicke, H., *Nordlandhelden* (Leipzig and Berlin: B. Teubner, 1927): in *Monatshefte für deutschen Unterricht*, XXI (1929), 83.

Hermannsson, H., *Sir John Banks and Iceland* (*Islandica*, Vol. XVIII [Ithaca, New York: Cornell University Press, 1928]): in *Modern Language Notes*, XLVI (1929), 277.

Vogt, W. H., *Stilgeschichte der Eddischen Wissensdichtung.* (Schriften der Baltischen Kommission zu Kiel, Vol. IV, No. 1 [Breslau: F. Hirt, 1927]): in *Journal of English and Germanic Philology*, XXVIII (1929), 414–415.

1930

Reviews:

Buckhurst, H. M., *An Elementary Grammar of Old Icelandic* (London: Methuen and Co., 1925): in *Scandinavian Studies and Notes*, XI (1930–1931), 185–186.

Olsen, M., *Farms and Fanes of Ancient Norway.* (Instituttet för Sammenlignende Kulturforskning, Series A, Vol. IX [Oslo: H. Aschehoug, 1928]): in *Scandinavian Studies and Notes*, XI (1930–1931), 139–145.

Wagner, F., *Les poèmes héroïques de l'Edda et la saga des Volsungs* (Paris: Librarie Leroux, 1929): in *The Germanic Review*, V (1930), 403–404.

Zucker, F., *Ibsen the Masterbuilder* (New York: Henry Holt and Co., 1929): in *The Nation*, CXXX (1930), 248–249.

1931

Articles:

"Hat die Vollzeile des Ljóðaháttr zwei oder drei Hebungen?" *Journal of English and Germanic Philology*, XXX (1931), 475–493.

"Methods of Exercise Correction," *Monatshefte für deutschen Unterricht*, XXIII (1931), 184–186.

"Notes on the Structure of the Ljóðaháttr," *Acta Philologica Scandinavica*, VI (1931), 39–54.

Reviews:

Hermannsson, H. (ed. and trans.), *The Book of the Icelanders* (*Íslendingabók*) by Ari Thórgilsson (*Islandica*, Vol. XX [Ithaca, New York: Cornell University Press, 1930]): in *Journal of English and Germanic Philology*, XXX (1931), 261–262.

Magon, L., *Ein Jahrhundert geistiger und literarischer Beziehungen zwischen Deutschland und Skandinavien, 1780–1850* (Dortmund: Johannes Ewald, 1926): in *The Germanic Review*, VI (1931), 398–400.

Niedner, F., *Grönländer und Färinger Geschichten* (Jena: Diederichs, 1929): in *Monatshefte für deutschen Unterricht*, XXIII (1931), 90.

Steche, T., *Die Deutsche Rechtschreibung* (Breslau: F. Hirt, 1931): in *Monatshefte für deutschen Unterricht*, XXIII (1931), 165–166.

1932

Articles:

"Deutsche oder lateinische Schrift," *Monatshefte für deutschen Unterricht,* XXIV (1932), 184–187. (German translation reprinted in *Die deutsche Schrift,* 1933, 6–9.)

"Is the Lay of Eric a Fragment?" *Acta Philologica Scandinavica,* VII (1932), 249–257.

"Two Eddic Cruxes," *The Germanic Review,* VII (1932), 280–287.

1933

Article:

"The Battle on the Vín-Heath and the Battle of the Huns," *Journal of English and Germanic Philology,* XXXII (1933), 33–43.

Translation:

"The Oath of Truth (Tryggthamól)," *American-Scandinavian Review,* XXI (1933), 91–94.

Reviews:

Dal, I., *Ursprung und Verwendung der altnordischen "Expletivpartikel" of -um* (Oslo: Dybwad, 1930); H. Kuhn, *Das Füllwort of-um in Altwestnordischen* (Göttingen: Vandenhoeck and Ruprecht, 1929): in *Journal of English and Germanic Philology,* XXXII (1933), 399–402.

Engel, E., *Deutsche Stilkunst* (Leipzig and Berlin: G. Freytag, 1931); *Deutsche Meister-Prosa* (Hamburg: Westermann, 1931): in *Monatshefte für deutschen Unterricht,* XXV (1933), 216.

Hermannsson, H., *Icelandic Manuscripts* (*Islandica,* Vol. XIX [Ithaca, New York: Cornell University Press, 1929]): in *Journal of English and Germanic Philology,* XXXII (1933), 89–90.

Hübner, A., *Die Mittelhochdeutsche Ironie oder die Litotes im Altdeutschen* (*Palæstra,* Vol. 70 [Leipzig: Mayer und Müller, 1930]): in *Journal of English and Germanic Philology,* XXXII (1933), 86–88.

Koht, H., *The Old Norse Sagas* (New York: W. W. Norton and Co., 1931): in *Scandinavian Studies and Notes,* XII (1933), 60–61.

1934

Article:

"Observations on Bernard Kummer's 'Midgards Untergang'," *Journal of English and Germanic Philology,* XXXIII (1934), 255–269.

Reviews:

Cawley, F. S. (ed.), *Hrafnkels Saga Freysgoða* (Cambridge, Massachusetts: Harvard University Press, 1932): in *The Germanic Review,* IX (1934), 143–144.

de Vries, J., *De Skaldenkenningen met mythologischen Inhoud* (Haarlem: Tjeenk Willink, 1934): in *Scandinavian Studies and Notes,* XIII (1934), 88–90.

Hermannsson, H., *Sæmund Sigfússon and the Oddaverjar* (*Islandica,* Vol. XXII [Ithaca, New York: Cornell University Press, 1932]): *Old Icelandic Literature* (*Islandica,* Vol. XXIII [Ithaca, New York: Cornell University Press, 1933]): in *The Germanic Review,* IX (1934), 282–283.

Monsen, E. (ed.), *Heimskringla, or the Lives of the Norse Kings* (Cambridge: W. H. Heffer and Sons, Ltd., 1932): in *The Germanic Review,* IX (1934), 210.

1935

Article:

"The Poet Egil Skallagrímsson and His Poem 'On the Irreparable Loss of his Sons' (Sonartorrek)," *Scandinavian Studies and Notes,* XIV (1935), 1–12.

Reviews:

Buchanan, D., *Substantivized Adjectives in Old Norse* (Language Dissertations No. 15 [Philadelphia: Linguistic Society of America, 1933]): in *Journal of English and Germanic Philology,* XXXIV (1935), 432–433.

de Vries, J., *The Problem of Loki* (F. F. Communications No. 110 [Helsinki: Suomalainen Tiedeakatemia, 1933]): in *Journal of English and Germanic Philology,* XXIV (1935), 245–246.

Ludwig, W., *Untersuchungen über den Entwicklungsgang und die Funktion des Dialogs in der isländischen Saga* (Rheinische Beiträge und Hilfsbücher zur germanischen Philologie und Volkskunde, Vol. XXIII [Halle: M. Niemeyer, 1934]): in *Journal of English and Germanic Philology,* XXXIV (1935), 584–585.

Mills, S. M., *The Saga of Hrolf Kraki* (Oxford: Basil Blackwell, 1933): in *The Germanic Review,* X (1935), 214.

1936

Book:

Old Norse Poems: The Most Important Non-Skaldic Verse Not Included in the Poetic Edda. New York: Columbia University Press, 1936. Pp. xv + 115.

Article:

"The Flyting of Qrvar Odd *(Manniofnuthr Qrvar-Odds),*" *Scandinavian Studies and Notes,* XIV (1936), 51–55.

Reviews:

Birkeli, E., *Høgsætet: Det gamle ondvege i religionshistorisk belysning*

(Stavanger: Dreyer, 1932): in *Journal of English and Germanic Philology,* XXXV (1936), 600–602.

Nordal, S., *Egils Saga Skallagrímssonar,* 1933; E. Ó. Sveinsson, *Laxdœla Saga,* 1934 (Reykjavík: Hið Íslenzka Fornritafélag): in *The Germanic Review,* XI (1936), 66–69.

1937

Article:

"A Neglected Chapter in Our German Text-Books," *Monatshefte für deutschen Unterricht,* XXIX (1937), 69–73.

Reviews:

Reuschel, H., *Untersuchungen über Stoff und Stil der Fornaldarsaga* (Bausteine zur Volkskunde und Religionswissenschaft, Vol. 7, 1933): in *The Germanic Review,* XII (1937), 138–139.

Will, G., *Die Darstellung der Gemütsbewegungen in den Liedern der Edda* (Nordische Brücke No. 2 [Hamburg: Friederichsen, de Gruyter & Co., 1934]): in *Journal of English and Germanic Philology,* XXXVI (1937), 106–107.

1938

Articles:

"Egil Skallagrímsson's Head-Ransom (*Hǫfuðlausn*)," *Scandinavian Studies and Notes,* XV (1938), 42–57.

"The Lay of Arinbiorn (Arinbarnarkviþa)," *Scandinavian Studies and Notes,* XV (1938), 110–121.

"Litotes in Old Norse," *Publications of the Modern Language Association,* LIII (1938), 1–33.

"Some Observations on the Head-Ransom Episode of the Egilssaga," *Acta Philologica Scandinavica,* XII (1938), 307–314.

"Verbal Periphrasis and Litotes in Old Norse," *Monatshefte für deutschen Unterricht,* XXX (1938), 182–189.

Reviews:

Hermannsson, H., *The Sagas of the Kings (Konunga Sögur)* and *The Mythical-Heroic Sagas (Fornaldar Sögur)* (*Islandica,* Vol. XXVI [Ithaca, New York: Cornell University Press, 1937]): in *The Germanic Review,* XIII (1938), 306–307.

Kvaran, E. S., *Sippengefühl und Sippenflege im alten Island im Lichte der biologischen Betrachtungsweise* (Greifswald: Archiv für Rassen- und Gesellschaftsbiologie, 1936): in *Scandivanian Studies and Notes,* XV (1938), 69–70.

1939

Reviews:

Dru, A., *The Journals of Søren Kierkegaard* (New York: Oxford University Press, 1938): in *Boston Transcript,* May 7, 1939.

Jaffé, G., *Geschichte der Runenforschung* (Berlin and Leipzig: B. Behr, 1939): in *Scandinavian Studies and Notes,* XV (1939), 169–170.

Olsen, M., *Norrøne Studier* (Oslo: H. Aschehoug and Co., 1939): in *Scandinavian Studies and Notes,* XV (1939), 279–281.

1940

Book:

(ed.). E. von Wildenbruch. *Das edle Blut* (with Introduction, Notes and Vocabulary). New York: F. Crofts, 1940. Pp. xi + 98.

Articles:

"Sigvat Thordson and His Poetry," *Scandinavian Studies and Notes,* XVI (1940), 43–67.

"Some Reflections on Language Training," *German Quarterly,* XIII (1940), 72–76.

Reviews:

Graf, H. J., *Untersuchungen zur Gebärde in der Íslendinga saga.* (dissertation [Bonn, 1938]): in *Journal of English and Germanic Philology,* XXXIX (1940), 389–391.

Haeckel, M., *Die Darstellung und Funktion des Traumes in der isländischen Familiensaga.* (dissertation [Hamburg: H. Proctor, 1934]): in *The Germanic Review.* XV (1940), 232–233.

Hermannsson, H., *The Icelandic Physiologus* (Islandica, Vol. XXVII [Ithaca, New York: Cornell University Press, 1938]): in *The Germanic Review,* XV (1940), 151–152.

Hermannsson, H., *Illuminated Manuscripts of the Jónsbók* (*Islandica,* Vol. XXVIII [Ithaca, New York: Cornell University Press, 1940]): in *The Germanic Review,* XV (1940), 156–157.

Kelchner, G. D., *Dreams in Old Norse Literature and Their Affinities in Folklore* (Cambridge: University Press, 1939): in *The Germanic Review,* XV (1940), 151–152.

Smith-Dampier, E. M., *A Book of Danish Ballads* (Princeton: University Press, 1939): in *Modern Language Journal,* XXV (1940), 157–158.

1941

Article:

"Observations on Taylor's Edition of the Orkneyinga Saga," *Scandinavian Studies and Notes,* XVI (1941), 226–233.

Reviews:

Lehmann, W., *Das Präsens historicum in den Íslendingasǫgur* (Würzburg: Triltsch, 1939): in *Language,* XVII (1941), 74–76.

Schirokauer, Arno, and Wolfgang Poulson (eds.), *"Corona": Studies in Celebration of the Eightieth Birthday of Samuel Singer* (Durham: Duke University Press, 1941): in *Bulletin of the South-Central Branch of the Modern Language Association,* II (1941), 5.

1942

Article:

"Arnórr Thórðarson Jarlaskáld and His Poem 'Hrynhent'," *Scandinavian Studies and Notes,* XVII (1942), 99–109.

Reviews:

Sveinsson, E. O. (ed.), *Vatnsdœla saga, Hallfreðar saga, Kormáks saga* (Reykjavík: Hið Íslenzka Fornritafélag, 1939): in *Journal of English and Germanic Philology,* XLI (1942), 539–542.

Wood, F. T., *Eddic Lays* (Baltimore: Waverly Press, 1940): in *The Germanic Review,* XVII (1942), 132–133.

1943

Translation:

Bjørnson, Bjørnstjerne, *Beyond Human Power*: in T. H. Dickinson (ed.). *Chief Contemporary Dramatists.* Boston: Houghton Mifflin, 1943, 573–597.

Article:

"The Case of the Skald Kormák," *Monatshefte für deutschen Unterricht,* XXXV (1943), 107–115.

Reviews:

Haugen, E., *Norwegian Word Studies,* Vols. I–II (Madison: University of Wisconsin Press, 1942): in *Scandinavian Studies and Notes,* XVII (1943), 265–266.

Larsen, Henning, and C. A. Williams (eds.), *Scandinavian Studies Presented to George Flom by Colleagues and Friends* (Urbana: University of Illinois Press, 1942): in *Scandinavian Studies and Notes,* XVII (1943), 179–182.

1944

Article:

"Erlkönig und Sommernachtstraum," *Monatshefte für deutschen Unterricht,* XXXVI (1944), 145–146.

Reviews:

Hermannsson, H., *Bibliographical Notes* (*Islandica,* Vol. XXIX [Ithaca, New York: Cornell University Press, 1942]): in *Modern Language Notes,* LIX (1944), 430–431.

Hermannsson, H., *Supplementary Catalogue of the Icelandic Collection Bequeathed by Willard Fiske* (Ithaca, New York: Cornell University Press, 1943): in *The Germanic Review,* XIX (1944), 312–313.

Jørgenson, T., *Norwegian-English School Dictionary* (Northfield, Minnesota: St. Olaf College Press, 1943): in *Scandinavian Studies and Notes,* XVIII (1944), 120–124.

Williams, C. O., *Thraldom in Ancient Iceland* (Chicago: University of Chicago Press, 1937): in *Modern Language Notes,* LIX (1944), 507–508.

1945

Book:

The Skalds: A Selection of Their Poems with Introduction and Notes. Princeton: Princeton University Press, 1945. Pp. viii + 216.

Articles:

"The Translation of Skaldic Poetry," *Scandinavian Studies and Notes,* XVIII (1945), 233–240.

Letter to the Editor. "News and Notes," *Monatshefte für deutschen Unterricht,* XXXVII (1945), 62.

Reviews:

Jones, G., *The Vatnsdalers' Saga* (Princeton: Princeton University Press, 1944): in *Modern Language Quarterly,* VI (1945), 365–366.

Müller, Maria, *Die Verhüllende Metaphorik in der Saga* (Bonner Beiträge zur deutschen Philologie, Vol. 8 [Würzburg-Aumühle: Triltsch, 1939]): in *The Germanic Review,* XX (1945), 232–234.

Sherwin, R., *The Vikings and the Red Man* (3 vols.; Bronxville, New York: Funk and Wagnells, 1940–1944): in *Journal of English and Germanic Philology,* XL (1945), 425.

Stork, C. H. (trans.), *Anthology of Norwegian Lyrics* (Princeton: Princeton University Press, 1942): in *The Germanic Review,* XX (1945), 156–157.

1946

Translation:

von Scholz, W., " 'Souls Exchanged': The Comedy of Resurrections": *Poet Lore,* LVII (1946), 202–256, 291–352.

Articles:

"Introduction to 'Souls Exchanged'," *Poet Lore,* LVII (1946), 195–201.

"Observations on Skaldic Rime Usage, With Special Reference to the *dunhent* and *liðhent* Varieties of *dróttkvætt,*" *Publications of the Modern Language Association of America,* LXI (1946), 891–909.

Reviews:

Einarsson, Stefán, *Icelandic Grammar* (Baltimore: The Johns Hopkins Press, 1945): in *Journal of English and Germanic Philology,* XLV (1946), 221–224.

Ellis, H. R., *The Road to Hel* (Cambridge: University Press, 1943): in *Scandinavian Studies and Notes,* XIX (1946), 37–39.

Hermannsson, H., *The Saga of Thorgils and Hafliði* (*Islandica,* Vol. XXXI [Ithaca, New York: Cornell University Press, 1945]): in *The Germanic Review,* XXI (1946), 230–232.

Turville-Petre, G. (ed.), *Víga-Glúms Saga* (Oxford: University Press, 1940): in *The Germanic Review,* XXI (1946), 230–231.

1947

Articles:

"Commentary on Three Eddic Passages: Lokasenna 5, 3; 24, 2; and Skírnismál 27, 3," *Scandinavian Studies and Notes,* XIX (1947), 298–305.

"Is the Skaldic Stanza a Unit? *The Germanic Review,* XXII (1947), 298–319.

"Middle High German *sch,*" *Journal of English and Germanic Philology,* XLVI (1947), 82–91.

Reviews:

Birkeli, E., *Huskult og Hinsidighetstro* (Skrifter utgitt av det Norske Videnskaps-Akademi i Oslo, Hist.-filos. Klasse, 1943, No. 1 [Oslo: Dybwad]): in *Journal of English and Germanic Philology,* XLVI (1947), 211–213.

1948

Translation:

Hölderlin, Friedrich, "An die Parzen": in *Monatshefte für deutschen Unterricht,* XL (1948), 254.

Reviews:

Sagabook of the Viking Society for Northern Research, 1945. Vol. XII, No. 5 (London: University College, 1945): in *The Germanic Review,* XXIII (1948), 319.

Genzmer, F. (ed.), *Eddische Heldenlieder* (Heidelberg: Carl Winter,

1947): in *Journal of English and Germanic Philology,* XLVII (1948), 288–289.

Kock, E. A., *Den norsk-isländska skaldediktningen.* Vol. I. (Lund: Gleerup, 1948): in *Scandinavian Studies and Notes,* XX (1948), 243–245.

Undén, O., *Nordisk samhørighet en realitet* (Stockholm: Svenska Foreningen Norden, 1945): in *Scandinavian Studies and Notes,* XX (1948), 61–62.

1949

Translation:

The Sagas of Kormák and the Sworn Brothers. Princeton: Princeton University Press, 1949. Pp. xiii + 217.

Article:

"The Rôle of the Verb in Skaldic Poetry," *Acta Philologica Scandinavica,* XX (1949), 267–276.

Review:

Berulfsen, B., *Kulturtradisjon fra en storhetstid* (Oslo: Gyldendal, 1948): in *Scandinavian Studies and Notes,* XXI (1949), 184–185.

1950

Articles:

(with F. Genzmer), "The Lay of Albwin and the Lay of Iring," *Monatshefte für deutschen Unterricht,* XLII (1950), 253–264.

"Notes on Two Eddic Passages: 'Helreið Brynhildar,' Stanza 14 and 'Baldrs Draumar,' Stanza 12," *Scandinavian Studies and Notes*, XXII (1950), 166–175.

"The Old Norse God Óðr," *Journal of English and Germanic Philology,* XLIX (1950), 304–308.

Reviews:

Janzén, A. (ed.), *Nordisk Kultur. Vol. VII. Personnavne* (Stockholm: Albert Bonniers; Copenhagen: J. H. Schultz; Oslo: H. Aschehoug and Co., 1947): in *Language,* XXVI (1950), 432–435.

Rubow, P. W., *Henrik Ibsen* (Copenhagen: Gyldendal, 1949): in *Scandinavian Studies and Notes,* XXII (1950), 80–81.

1951

Article:

"Egil Skallagrímsson, lausavísa VII, 45; Thormóðr Bersason, lausavísa II, 5," *Arkiv för nordisk filologi,* LXV (1951), 100–108.

Reviews:

Baldus, A., *Nordische Dichtung der Gegenwart* (Nürnberg: Die Egge, 1948): in *Books Abroad,* XXV (1951), 47.

Beck, R., *A History of Icelandic Poetry: 1800–1940* (Ithaca, New York: Cornell University Press, 1950): in *Books Abroad,* XXV (1951), 386.

Krause, W., *Abriss der altwestnordischen Grammatik* (Halle: M. Niemeyer, 1948): in *Journal of English and Germanic Philology,* L (1951), 533–534.

Schneider, H., *Eine Uredda. Untersuchungen und Texte zur Frühgeschichte der eddischen Götterdichtung* (Halle: M. Niemeyer, 1948): in *The Germanic Review,* XXVI (1951), 139–140.

Tjomsland, A., *The Saga of Hrafn Sveinbjarnarson* (*Islandica,* Vol. XXXV [Ithaca, New York: Cornell University Press, 1951]): in *American-Scandinavian Review,* XXXIX (1951), 346–348.

1952

Articles:

"The Eddas," *Encyclopedia Americana,* IX (1952), 575–576.

"The Skalds," *Encyclopedia Americana,* XXV (1952), 66a.

"Snorri Sturluson," *Encyclopedia Americana,* XVI (1952), 148.

"Some Syntactic Analogies Between German and English," *The German Quarterly,* XXV (1952), 88–92.

"Two Unrecognized Celtic Names, *Vagn Åkason* and *Thorvald Tintein,*" *Studies in Honor of A. M. Sturtevant,* pp. 71–75. Lawrence: University of Kansas Press, 1952.

1953

Article:

"Some Observations on the *dróttkvætt* Meter of Skaldic Poetry," *Journal of English and Germanic Philology,* LII (1953), 189–197.

Reviews:

Bredhoff, E., B. Mortensen, and R. Popperwill, *Introduction to Scandinavian Literature* (Cambridge: University Press, 1951): in *Books Abroad,* XXVII (1953), 303.

Olsen, M., *Fra norrøn filologi* (Oslo: H. Aschehoug and Co., 1949): in *The Germanic Review,* XXVIII (1953), 313–315.

Schneider, H. (ed.), *Edda, Skalden, Saga. Festschrift zum 70. Geburstag von Felix Genzmer* (Heidelberg: Carl Winter, 1952): in *Journal of English and Germanic Philology,* LII (1953), 381–384.

1954

Articles:

"The Problem of the Proper Translation of Old Norse Names," *Scandinavian Studies and Notes,* XXVI (1954), 125–129.

"Wilhelm von Scholz, 80 Years," *Monatshefte für deutschen Unterricht,* XLVI (1954), 282.

Review:

Sprenger, U., *Praesens historicum und Praeteritum in der altisländischen Saga. Ein Beitrag zur Frage Freiprosa-Buchprosa* (Basler Studien zur deutschen Sprache und Literatur, Vol. II [Basel: Schwabe, 1950]): in *Scandinavian Studies and Notes,* XXVI (1954), 33–35.

1955

Translations:

(with C. F. Bayerschmidt). *Njál's Saga.* New York: New York University Press, 1955. Pp. xv + 390.

Sveinbjörnsson, Tryggvi, "Bishop Jón Arason": in *Modern Scandinavian Plays,* pp. 173–242. New York: Liveright, 1955.

Review:

Brown, U. (ed.), *Þorgils saga ok Hafliða* (Oxford: University Press, 1952): in *Journal of English and Germanic Philology,* LIV (1955), 404–405.

1956

Translation:

The Saga of the Jómsvíkings (with Introduction and Notes). Austin: University of Texas Press, 1956. Pp. 116.

Reviews:

Bjarnason, P., *Odes and Echoes* (Vancouver: The People's Cooperative Bookstore, 1954): in *Scandinavian Studies and Notes,* XXVIII (1956), 93–94.

Hannesson, J. S., *Bibliography of the Eddas* (*Islandica,* Vol. XXXVII [Ithaca, New York: Cornell University Press, 1955]): in *Journal of English and Germanic Philology,* LV (1956), 662–663.

Rodnick, D., *The Norwegians* (Washington, D.C.: Public Affairs Press, 1955): in *The Southwestern Social Science Quarterly,* XXXIV (1956), 76–77.

1957

Article:

"Icelandic Literature," *Encyclopedia Americana,* XIV (1957), 638–651.

Reviews:

Holtsmark, A., *Ordforrådet i de eldste Norske Håndskrifter til ca. 1250* (Oslo: Dybwad, 1955): in *Journal of English and Germanic Philology,* LVI (1957), 464–465.

van den Toorn, M. C., *Ethics and Morals in Icelandic Saga Literature* (Assen: Van Gorcum and Co., 1955): in *Scandinavian Studies and Notes,* XXIX (1957), 137–138.

1958

Book:

A Bibliography of Skaldic Studies. Copenhagen: E. Munksgaard, 1958. Pp. 117.

Reviews:

Gordon, E., *An Introduction to Old Norse,* ed. A. R. Taylor (rev. ed; Oxford: Clarendon Press, 1957): in *The Germanic Review,* XXXIII (1958), 314–317.

Hannesson, J. S., *The Sagas of the Icelanders* (*Islandica,* Vol. XXXVIII [Ithaca, New York: Cornell University Press, 1957]): in *Scandinavian Studies and Notes,* XXX (1958), 102–103.

Neuman, E., *Das Schicksal in der Edda* (Beiträge zur deutschen Philologie, Vol. 7 [Giessen: W. Schmitz, 1955]): in *Journal of English and Germanic Philology,* LVII (1958), 762–764.

1959

Translation:

(with Paul Schach). *Eyrbyggja saga* (translation from the Old Icelandic by Paul Schach; Introduction and verse translations by Lee M. Hollander). Lincoln: University of Nebraska Press, 1959. Pp. xx + 140.

Articles:

"The Eddas," *Collier's Encyclopedia,* VIII (1963), 548–549.

"The Structure of the Eyrbyggja saga," *Journal of English and Germanic Philology,* LVIII (1959), 222–227.

Reviews:

Foote, P. G. (ed.), *The Saga of Gunnlaug Serpent-Tongue* (London: Thomas Nelson and Sons, 1957): in *Journal of English and Germanic Philology,* LVIII (1959), 115–116.

Lie, Hallvard, *'Natur og Unatur' i Skaldekunsten* (Avhandlinger utgitt av Det Norske Videnskaps-Akademi i Oslo II, Hist.-filos. Klasse 1957 No. 1 [Oslo: H. Aschehoug and Co., 1957]): in *Journal of English and Germanic Philology,* LVIII (1959), 112–115.

von Hofsten, N., *Eddadikternas djur och växter.* (Skrifter utgivna av Kungl. Gustav Adolphs Akademien, Vol. 30 [Uppsala: Lundequist; Copenhagen: Munksgaard, 1957]): in *Scandinavian Studies and Notes,* (1959), 182–183.

1960

Book:

Selections from the Writings of Søren Kierkegaard. Rev. ed. New York: Doubleday Anchor Books, 1960. Pp. 239.

Article:
"Dictionary," *Scandinavian Studies and Notes*, XXXII (1960), 183–184.

Review:
Benediktsson, J. (ed.), *Sturlunga saga* (Mss. No. 122a Fol. in The Arnamagnæan Collection [Copenhagen: Rosenkilde and Bagger, 1958]): in *Scandinavian Studies and Notes*, XXXII (1960), 38.

1961

Reviews:
Baetke, W. (ed.), *Saga. Untersuchungen zur nordischen Literatur- und Sprachgeschichte*: Heft I: E. Walter, *Studien zur Vápnfirðinga saga;* Heft II: R. Heller, *Die literarische Darstellung der Frau in den Isländersagas*; Heft III: R. Heller, *Literarisches Schaffen in Laxdœla Saga* (Halle: M. Niemeyer, 1956, 1958, and 1960): in *The Germanic Review*, XXXVI (1961), 154–157.
Jones, G., *The Egil's Saga* (Syracuse, New York: Syracuse University Press, 1960): in *Speculum*, XXXVI (1961), 333–335.
Sveinsson, E. Ól., *Handritamálið* (Reykjavík: Hið Íslenzka Bókmentafélag, 1959): in *Scandinavian Studies and Notes*, XLIII (1961), 249–250.
Tolkien, C., *The Saga of King Heithrek the Wise* (London: Thomas Nelson and Sons, 1961): in *Journal of English and Germanic Philology*, LX (1961), 540–541.

1962

Translation:
The Poetic Edda. 2nd. rev. ed. Austin: University of Texas Press, 1962. Pp. 343.
von Scholz, W., "The Jew of Constance": in *Poet Lore*, LVII, (1962), 387 472.

Article:
"The Legendary Form of *Hamðismál*," *Arkiv för nordisk filologi*, LXXVII (1962), 56–62.

Review:
Baetke, W. (ed.), *Bandamanna saga und Ǫlkofra Þáttr* (Halle: M. Niemeyer, 1960): in *Journal of English and Germanic Philology* (LXI (1962), 364–365.

1963

Translations:
von Scholz, W., "The Horse Inoue": in *Poet Lore*, LVIII (1963), 150–158.
von Scholz, W., "Inscription on a Spring": in *Poet Lore*, LVIII (1963), 84.

Articles:

"For Whom Were the Eddic Poems Composed?" *Journal of English and Germanic Philology*, LXII (1963), 136–142.

"Recent Work and Views on the Poetic Edda," *Scandinavian Studies and Notes*, XXXV (1963), 101–109.

Reviews:

Blake, N. J., (ed. and trans.), *The Saga of the Jómsvíkings* (London: Thomas Nelson and Sons, 1962): in *Speculum*, XXXVIII (1963), 327–328.

Corpus Codicum Norvegicorum Medii Ævi (Utgitt ved Didrik Arup Seip. Folio Series, Vol. II. *Norske Diplomer til og med år 1300.* Redigeret av Finn Hødnebø [Oslo: Selskapet til Utgivelse av gamle Norske Håndskrifter, 1960]): in *Scandinavian Studies and Notes*, XXXV (1963), 68–69.

Holm-Olsen, L. (ed.), *Early Icelandic Manuscripts in Facsimile.* Vol. III: *The Sagas of King Sverrir and King Hakón the Old* (Copenhagen: Rosenkilde and Bagger, 1961): in *Scandinavian Studies and Notes*, XXXV (1963), 159–160.

Kummer, Bernhard, *Die Lieder des* Codex Regius (Edda) *und vorwandte Denkmäler.* I. Mythische Dichtung. 1. Die Schau der Scherin (*Vǫluspá*). II. Heldendichtung. 1. Die Dichtung von Helgi und die Walküre (Bremen, 1959, 1961): in *The Germanic Review*, XXXVIII (1963), 313–315.

Smith, L. F., *Modern Norwegian Historiography* (Oslo: Norwegian University Press, 1962): in *Southwestern Social Science Quarterly*, XLIII (1963), 384.

1964

Translations:

Jensen, Johs. V., "The Thundercalf": in *Poet Lore*, LIX (1964), 341–347.

Snorri Sturluson, *Heimskringla: History of the Kings of Norway.* Austin: University of Texas Press, 1964. Pp. xxvi + 854.

Book:

Seven Eddic Lays, with Variants and Vocabulary. Austin: University of Texas Press, 1964. Pp. 154.

Article:

"Three Skaldic Passages: Sigvatr Þorðarson, *Bersǫglivísur* 18; Þjóðólfr Arnórsson IV, 1, and III, 18," *Taylor Starck Festschrift*, eds. Werner Betz, Evelyn S. Coleman, and Kenneth Northcott, pp. 257–262. The Hague: Mouton, 1964.

1965

Articles:

"Observations on the Nature and Function of the Parenthetic Sentence in Skaldic Poetry," *Journal of English and Germanic Philology*, LXIV (1965), 635–644.

"The Quantity of the *o* in *Thor* Names," *Scandinavian Studies Presented to H. G. Leach on the Occasion of His Eighty-fifth Birthday*, eds. Carl F. Bayerschmidt and Erik J. Friis, pp. 97–100. Seattle: University of Washington Press, 1965.

"Two Old Norse Syntactic-Stylistic Peculiarities," *Acta Philologica Scandinavica*, XXVII (1965), 1–7.

Reviews:

Briem, O., *Vanir og Æsir* (*Studia Islandica*, Vol. XXI [Reykjavík: Bókaútgáfa Menningarsjóðs, 1963]): in *Scandinavian Studies and Notes*, XXXVII (1965), 195–196.

de Vries, J., *Altnordische Literaturgeschichte*. Band 1: Grundriss der germanischen Philologie, Vol. 15 (Zweite völlig neubearbeitete Auflage; Berlin: Walter de Gruyter, 1964): in *Journal of English and Germanic Philology*, LXIV (1965), 527–529.

Neckel, G. (ed.), *Edda: Die Lieder Des Codex Regius nebst verwandten Denkmälern. I: Text* (Dritte, umgearbeitete Auflage von Hans Kuhn; Heidelberg: Carl Winter, 1962): in *Journal of English and Germanic Philology*, LXIV (1965), 138–141.

1966

Article:

"*Sigurðarkviða in skamma,* Stanzas 62–63," *Arkiv för nordisk filologi*, LXXXI (1966), 35–38.

Review:

Magnusson, Magnús and Hermann Pálsson, *The Vinland Sagas* (New York: New York University Press, 1966): in *Speculum*, LXI (1966), 758.

1967

Translations:

Barði Guðmundsson, *The Origin of the Icelanders* (with Introduction and Notes). Lincoln: University of Nebraska Press, 1967. Pp. xix + 173.

von Scholz, Wilhelm, "The Emigrant": in *Poet Lore*, LXII (1967), 135–140.

Articles:

"An Unrecognized *vísufjórðungr* of Eyvind Skaldaspillir," *Scandinavian Studies*, XXXIX (1967), 153–154.

"Skírnismál 29.4, Grípisspá 40.1–4, Fáfnismál 38.3, Sigrdrífumál 16.3, Hamþismál 7.3" *Arkiv för nordisk filologi*, LXXXII (1967), 243–249,

Reviews:

Baetke, W., *Yngvi und die Ynglingar: Eine quellenkritische Untersuchung über das nordische "Sakralkönigtum"* (Sitzungsberichte der sächsischen Akademie der Wissenschaften zu Leipzig. Philologisch-historische Klasse, Vol. 109, No. 3 [Berlin: Akademie Verlag, 1964]) : in *Speculum*, XLII (1967), 311–313.

Einarsson, Bjarni, *Skáldasögur. Um uppruna ok eðli ástaskáldasagnanna fornu* (Reykjavík: Menningarsjóðs, 1961): in *Scandinavian Studies*, XXXIX (1967), 375–378.

1968

Book:

The Skalds: A Selection of Their Poems, with Introduction and Notes. 2nd rev. ed.; Ann Arbor: University of Michigan Press, Ann Arbor Paperbacks, 1968.

Reviews:

de Vries, J., *Altnordische Literaturgeschichte.* Band II: *Die Spätzeit von etwa 1150 bis 1300,* Grundriss der germanischen Philologie, Vol. 16 (Zweite völling neubearbeitete Auflage; Berlin: Walter de Gruyter, 1967): in *Journal of English and Germanic Philology,* LXVII (1968), 369–370.

Guðmundsson, Finnbogi (ed.), *Orkneyinga saga* (Reykjavík: Hið Íslenzka Fornrítafélag, 1965) : in *Speculum*, XLIII (1968), 153–154.

NOTES ON THE CONTRIBUTORS

Einar Haugen is Victor S. Thomas professor of Scandinavian and linguistics at Harvard University. From 1931 to 1964 he taught at The University of Wisconsin, where he was Thompson professor of Scandinavian and research professor of Scandinavian and linguistics. During these years he also visited as guest lecturer or professor numerous American and Scandinavian universities, among them the University of Oslo, which awarded him an honorary Ph.D. degree. Dr. Haugen has been president of the Linguistics Society of America (1950) and of the Ninth International Congress of Linguistics (1962); he is currently president of the Permanent International Committee of Linguists. Chief among his published works are *The Norwegian Language in America, Bilingualism in the Americas, First Grammatical Treatise: The Earliest Germanic Phonology, Norwegian-English Dictionary,* and *Language Conflict and Language Planning: The Case of Modern Norwegian.*

Erik Wahlgren, professor of Scandinavian languages at the University of California, Los Angeles, has been visiting professor at Augustana College, the University of British Columbia, the University of Uppsala, the Stockholm School of Economics, and the University of California at Berkeley. A past fellow of both the American-Scandinavian Foundation and the Guggenheim Foundation, he has twice served as chairman of the Scandinavian Group of the Modern Language Association of America and since 1957 as associate managing editor of *Scandinavian Studies.* In 1960 he became a knight of the Swedish Order of the Polar Star. In addition to numerous scholarly articles and reviews, he has written *The Kensington Stone, a Mystery Solved* and *The Maiden King in Iceland* and has translated Halvdan Koht's *Education of an Historian.*

Paul Schach began his teaching career at Albright College in 1938. In the years since he has taught at the University of Pennsylvania, North Central College (Naperville, Illinois), the University of Colorado, and the University of Nebraska, where he is Charles Mach professor of Germanic languages. He has conducted research in Iceland, Germany, Denmark, and Sweden and has lectured in Belgium and West Germany. Dr. Schach has translated *Eyrbyggja Saga*, with Dr. Hollander, and *The Icelandic Saga* by Peter Hallberg. His recent publications include *A Guide to the Study of Old Norse Literature* and articles in many journals, among them *Medieval Literature of Western Europe, American Speech, Modern Language Quarterly, Monatshefte, Rheinische Vierteljahrblätter, Scandinavian Studies,* and *Zeitschrift für Mundartforschung.* Currently he is preparing a critical edition of *Tristrams Saga,* a history of Old Icelandic prose, and American editions of *Á Njálsbúð,* by Einar Ól. Sveinsson, and of *Den fornisländska poesien,* by Peter Hallberg.

A. Margaret Arent, whose translation of *The Laxdœla Saga* was published in 1964, received her Ph.D. degree from the University of Chicago in 1961. Previously she had studied at Carleton College, at the University of Zürich (Germanistic Society of America Fellowship), at the University of Oslo (City of Oslo Award), and at the University of Iceland (Fulbright grant). From 1960 to 1964 she was assistant professor of Germanic languages at The University of Texas at Austin.

Konstantin Reichardt, born in St. Petersburg, Russia, received his Ph.D. degree from the University of Berlin in 1928. In the course of his distinguished forty-year career as a scholar, he has been associate professor and director of the North Germanic Department at Leipzig University; lecturer of German and Old Norse at the University of Gothenburg, Sweden; and professorial lecturer and then professor of German and Scandinavian at the University of Minnesota, where he later became professor and head of the Department of Linguistics and Comparative Philology. Since 1947 Dr. Reichardt has been professor of Germanic philology at Yale University. He is the author of *Studien zu den Skalden des 9. und 10. Jahrhunderts; Beiträge zur*

Skaldenforschung, which appeared in *Arkiv för nordisk filologi;* and *Die Thórsdrápa des Eilífr Góðrúnarson,* published in *PMLA.*

Winfred P. Lehmann began his teaching career in 1946 at Washington University. In 1949 he joined the faculty of The University of Texas at Austin, where he is now Ashbel Smith professor of Germanic languages and of linguistics and chairman of the Department of Linguistics. From 1953 to 1965 he served as chairman of the Department of Germanic Languages. Dr. Lehmann spent a year in Norway as a Fulbright research fellow and was Georgetown English-language program director in Ankara, Turkey, from 1955 to 1956. He is the author of *A Grammar of Formal Written Japanese, Proto-Indo-European Phonology, The Alliteration of Old Saxon Poetry, The Development of Germanic Verse Form,* and *Historical Linguistics: An Introduction.*

E. O. G. Turville-Petre received his B. Litt. and M.A. degree from Christ Church of Oxford University. In 1941, appointed Vigfússon Reader in Ancient Icelandic, he returned to Oxford, where he is now a professor and Student of Christ Church. Previously he had been a lecturer in English at the University of Iceland, which conferred upon him an honorary Ph.D. In 1965 Dr. Turville-Petre was visiting professor at the University of Melbourne. He became a knight and subsequently commander of the Order of Falcon (Iceland) and is a member of the Royal Gustav Adolf Academy of Sweden. His *Víga-Glúms Saga* was reissued in an enlarged edition in 1960. Among his other published works are *The Heroic Age of Scandinavia, Origins of Icelandic Literature,* and *Myth and Religion of the North.*

Edgar C. Polomé, born and educated in Belgium, is professor of Germanic languages and linguistics at The University of Texas at Austin. Beginning his academic career at the Athénée A. Max in Brussels, he has also been professor of Dutch for the Belgian Broadcasting Corporation, professor of linguistics and Germanic languages at the Université Officielle du Congo et du Ruanda-Urundi, where he served as secretary of the Academic Board, and a

Fulbright professor in Kiel, West Germany. Dr. Polomé is team director of the Tanzania Sociolinguistic Survey, 1969–1970, and has recently published the *Swahili Language Handbook*, as well as various articles on the position of Germanic among the Indo-European languages and on problems of comparative Germanic religion and philology.

INDEX

The spelling of names reflects the authors' preferences. In cases where spelling varies between articles, the more normalized form of the name is entered in the Index.